POLITICAL PRISONER

POLITICAL PRISONER

Persecuted, Prosecuted, but Not Silenced

PAUL MANAFORT

Skyhorse Publishing

Copyright © 2022 by Paul Manafort

All Rights Reserved. No part of this book may be reproduced in any manner without the express written consent of the publisher, except in the case of brief excerpts in critical reviews or articles. All inquiries should be addressed to Skyhorse Publishing, 307 West 36th Street, 11th Floor, New York, NY 10018.

Skyhorse Publishing books may be purchased in bulk at special discounts for sales promotion, corporate gifts, fund-raising, or educational purposes. Special editions can also be created to specifications. For details, contact the Special Sales Department, Skyhorse Publishing, 307 West 36th Street, 11th Floor, New York, NY 10018 or info@skyhorsepublishing.com.

Skyhorse® and Skyhorse Publishing® are registered trademarks of Skyhorse Publishing, Inc.®, a Delaware corporation.

Visit our website at www.skyhorsepublishing.com.

10 9 8 7 6 5 4 3 2 1

Library of Congress Cataloging-in-Publication Data is available on file.

ISBN: 978-1-5107-7242-7
eBook ISBN: 978-1-5107-7243-4

Cover design by Brian Peterson

Printed in the United States of America

To my incredible wife, Kathy—the love of my life and my rock, who never wavered in her belief in me and gave me the courage and strength to endure—"You are so Beautiful."

Table of Contents

Introduction

It took almost two hundred years from the election of Andrew Jackson for another outsider as dedicated to the destruction and reconstruction of the Washington establishment to be elected president of the United States. The election of Donald J. Trump—sent to DC with the mission of draining the swamp—was a day of celebration for the silent majority, the "basket of deplorables," the working class, the non-elites. Finally, they had a champion who they were convinced would not forget them after the election.

To Washington, however, and the power establishment of Government, Big Media, Big Tech, and Wall Street, it was the most threatening development in the history of modern America. They never saw it coming and were at a loss for why it happened. The very reason that Trump was successful was the blind spot that kept the establishment from understanding his appeal. The elites on the two coasts believed they knew what was best for the country. They also believed a populist loud-mouth could be ignored. But when Donald Trump won the election on November 8, 2016, neither he nor the people who elected him could be ignored any longer.

It was not just losing control of their power that scared the "swamp." Scariest of all to them was the fact that they knew that the secret of their all-encompassing violations of Americans' constitutional rights was about to be exposed in all of its ugliness and illegalities.

The system did what it has always done when challenged—it doubled down on everything: On illegal surveillance on our private lives. On abuse of our first amendment freedom of speech. On violations of our freedom of assembly. On our right to a fair trial. On the weaponization of the law enforcement and national security apparatus to target Americans and create crimes that they knew did not exist.

In the course of figuring out how to destroy the intruder, the cabal threw truth out of their vocabulary. Living in the US became a political version of the Alice in Wonderland view of reality. The "truth" became whatever lies would promote their narrative. And the Twitter universe and fake social media platforms threatened to destroy the mainstream media (MSM) if it did not come along. It was the perfect storm because the elites had taken over the mainstream news outlets. Journalistic ethics were turned upside down. Social media, identity media, and MSM reporting became one.

I saw this early in the 2016 campaign when the *New York Times* published a front-page story on August 7, 2016, by one of its reporters, Jim Rutenburg.[1] I had to reread the story because I could not believe the *New York Times* could countenance such an approach to journalism. Rutenberg, citing his elite status and his egomaniacal view that he knew what was best for our country, announced that because (in his view) "Trump is a demagogue playing to the nations' worst racist and nationalistic tendencies," Rutenberg and all reputable journalists must "throw out the textbook American journalism has been using for the better part of the past half century." It was the duty of American journalists to become partisans, to forget objectivity, and to "exposing the evil of Trump and his supporters."

While this was a complete dismissal of journalism's ethics, it was late to the game because the social media wannabe journalists had already made that leap. To the social media reporters, who cared more about using identity media to drive their audiences, exploitation of narratives based on partisanship was the "coin of the realm." Facts gave way to diatribe. Twitter revolved around hate, abuse, and fake news. Retweets were the goal, not honest reporting. And if the MSM did not follow the lead of these Potemkin social media reporters, this vitriol would be turned against them. The threat was unnecessary. The MSM reporters, editors, and publishers fell right into line.

Emotion drove the news. The more outrageous the better:

Paul Manafort is a traitor. Paul Manafort is dealing directly with Putin and the Kremlin. Paul Manafort is evil.

These were accusations thrown out not by trashy tabloids, but mainstream staples such as CNN and MSNBC.

The headlines attracted viewers. Truth be damned. It was entertaining and great chatter for the elites at cocktail parties. Plus, it made them feel good about themselves.

And worse, when a truth somehow got through the morass of lies and hate, it was ignored. Journalists no longer knew the meaning of "I was wrong" or "I made a mistake." Hillary Clinton's collusion with Russians and Ukrainians to take down Trump was ignored. It continues to be ignored today even after Special Counsel John Durham has filed the facts exposing these crimes and hypocrisies. They go unreported.

Not one of the many Pulitzer Prizes awarded for incorrect reporting on the collusion between the Trump campaign and Russia was ever returned. I am certain that if he were alive today, Joseph Pulitzer would have revoked the use of his name for these wrongly given acknowledgements.

The journalists were bad, but politicians like Adam Schiff were even more deceptive in their lies. Citing information that he said he had seen as Chairman of the House Intelligence Committee, but really never existed, Schiff boldly lied to the American people and got away with it.

The Senate Intelligence Committee wrote a 1,300-page report in which they repeated unconfirmed stories about me and Russian collusion based on inference and innuendo. The Committee, throughout the section of the report on me, even admits they have either little or no information on any of their conclusions about me. This did not keep them from leaping to such outrageous findings that I attended meetings that never occurred, passed polling data that they have no evidence of, supported a peace plan for Ukraine that they had evidence I rejected, and so on.

In this book, I will get into the details of these matters, but the tragedy is that I even have to do so.

No one—not the OSC (Office of Special Council), the Senate or House Intelligence Committees, the hundreds if not thousands of journalists who investigated me looking for links—found even one smoking gun, never mind a bullet. Yet, in today's Court of Public Opinion I am guilty, guilty, guilty of being pro-Russian.

To reach this conclusion, the body of work I did over thirty-five years must be totally ignored. My work for various governments and political parties that opposed the Soviet Union and later Russia were either ignored or misrepresented, despite the public news stories of my work at the time. Again, I was caught in the twilight of the perfect storm of media and the Washington swamp motivated by the "Anti-Trump jihad."

This is why I am writing this book. I want to get the truth into the public domain. I don't expect to persuade those who don't care about facts or the truth or a lifetime of work. I do believe that any serious student of history can analyze my work and see that the hysteria of Russian collusion blinded the public from the truth.

I want people to understand who I really am. I want to tell the truth. I want to tell the real story. And I want people to understand some of the fears I have about the excesses that are destroying our way of life in America. That is of paramount importance to me.

As I started to emerge in the last year—to go to events and to get involved again—people would come up to me and say, "You need to write a book." I realized that what they needed was not just about me— it's about something bigger than me. They understood the system was broken and feared for their country. They were asking for hope. My story is one filled with danger, but I do believe that in exposing the real truth, there can be hope if we don't give up our quest to "drain the swamp." I was persuaded—I needed to tell my story.

Our government is broken. The guardians at our gates protecting our freedom, privacy, and humanity have disappeared. The last four years have opened my eyes. If these cracks are not fixed, they will bring our country into such a decline that we will no longer be what Ronald Reagan so lovingly called "that shining city on the hill."

I also believe it is important to raise some of the serious issues that are encompassed in the history of the last six years—illegal government surveillance; the weaponization of our law enforcement, legal, and national security departments and agencies; the deliberate targeting of Americans based on their political affiliations in the US; a prosecution system that cares more about getting a conviction than getting the truth; a prison system that does not work or even care to work; and a media that only cares about identity media and promoting themselves at the expense of the truth.

These are issues that need to be understood. My journey touches on all of them. What I found time and time again was people using their power in abusive ways to settle their own scores or to acquire more power. Rogue prosecutors and power-drunk Judges used their platforms to trample on our rights, not protect them. Prison officials used their authority to ensure that inmates felt bad about themselves and learned little that could help them re-enter society. And politicians were so hypocritical that they would change their position on every important fundamental right that our Constitution protects, just to keep power.

My case, by the intentional design of the prosecutors and the Office of Special Counsel, was very complicated—overly complicated. They had me on charges of everything from bank fraud and failure to file under the Foreign Agents Registration Act to tax evasion, money laundering, and obstruction of justice. None of it was true. Of note is that every charge brought by the Special Counsel had been reviewed by the US Government in the past. And in each situation, without the glare of media neon lights flashing, assessed the evidence as not worthy of pursuing. In other words, not guilty of criminal behavior.

The reason the Special Counsel made it so complicated was because of one very simple fact: there was no Russian collusion. Instead of admitting that, they determined to make my life miserable for as long as they could. They used all sorts of unethical tactics to make it happen and they came close to destroying me. At the end of the day, all of it was created in an effort to break me, to get me to give them what they wanted on Trump. I never did. I could not have.

There was no collusion between the Trump campaign and the Russians. There was, however, collusion between the Clinton campaign and foreign governments. I will lay out the hypocrisy of the MSM and the establishment in ignoring the real collusion because they only cared about bringing down Donald Trump and protecting their control over the levers of power. The truth did not matter, especially the inconvenient truths. Their self-defined ends justified any means they chose to use, regardless of legality or ethics.

My story is not unique, but my public image is uniquely centered in these issues. Ordinary Americans are suffering similar abuses—you just don't read about them. I hope this book will cause some reflection and introspection. I don't expect this reaction in Washington. They are locked into their now-discredited narrative. But I do hope that ordinary Americans, the people who sent Donald Trump to drain the swamp, will reflect and think about where they are at risk.

I do not have solutions for all these problems. Everything is rationalized by the moment. But I believe that you can change things and change events. Awareness is very important, and resolve is vital. Unfortunately, the fascist Left/Woke crowd is willing to use even violence on their political enemies, including threats to the family members of active conservative leaders. There is no longer a Sherriff in the Democratic Party. Hypocrisy rules and seeking power justifies any means to get to a desired end.

Barbarians at the Gate could have been the title of this book, but it was already taken. *Political Prisoner* works too. Yes, I was a political prisoner, but so is every American citizen if we don't reform our system and get back to protecting the rights of all Americans no matter who we are.

CHAPTER 1

"The Defendant Will Be Detained"

U p until the very last moment, I still didn't believe it could happen—not to me and not like this. Not in a court of law in the United States of America.

The hearing that day, June 15, 2018, was initially scheduled to deal with my bail package, which had languished since my indictment on October 30, 2017. However, just prior to this court date, the Office of Special Counsel announced that it was filing superseding charges claiming that I had obstructed justice and attempted to tamper with potential trial witnesses. This was a ploy to keep the pressure on me. Realizing that their strategy of keeping me in home confinement was nearing an end, they had changed their tactics and come up with an obstruction charge. Now, preposterously, because of this trumped-up charge, the prosecutors were demanding that I be incarcerated—immediately.

Despite the assumed unlikelihood of a bad outcome, I had a bad feeling that morning, an intuition that things might not go my way. When the arguments finished, and the liberal, Obama-appointed presiding judge, Amy Berman Jackson, said that she wanted to recess to her chambers before rendering her decision, that feeling only intensified. As she departed, I looked to my wife Kathy who was sitting in the first row of the gallery. For the first time, I could see the fear in her face. She knew it, too. She sensed the same thing I did. And it made me want to cry. I could handle my fear, but my heart broke for my wife. She had been by my side, stalwart from the beginning. She knew who I was and had never once doubted me. What she worried about was the kangaroo court that was unfolding before our eyes.

The charade became more apparent when Judge Jackson returned to the court after only a very brief recess. When she placed what looked like a several-page document in front of her, I knew I was going to jail.

Jackson began to read without looking at me. Her words could have been written by the Mueller legal team. She simply repeated their arguments.

In disbelief, I leaned over to my attorney, Kevin Downing, and whispered, "She is sending me to jail." Kevin told me to be quiet and listen, but I didn't need to hear any more. My eyes wandered away from the bench toward the prosecution sitting across from me. Andrew Weissman, the lead prosecutor, and his team sat at their table, fawning over Jackson's embrace of their exact thoughts and words. Staring at them in the courtroom, I thought to myself, *You know these accusations are not true. How could you find satisfaction in destroying a man's life, in harming his family?*

At this point, the judge was summing up her prepared opinion. Finally, she looked at me with a smug, false remorse and dropped her axe.

"And so all of this, at bottom, affects my judgment about whether you can be trusted to comply with the Court's directives," she said. "And that is the finding that the statute also requires me to make if I release you, and I can't make it. You have abused the trust placed in you six months ago. And, therefore, the government's motion will be granted. And the defendant will be detained pending trial as of today."

"... *And the defendant will be detained pending trial as of today.*"

Hearing those words, I felt my face turn white. And just like that, the session was over. It was surreal—a nightmare. Jackson made some perfunctory remarks on scheduling. The two legal teams made some administrative comments. To them it was all business as usual. But not to me. To me, it was my life. My world had stopped. I was no longer in control of anything. I could no longer hold my wife and kids. Despite my intuition that things would not go well that day, this was a new reality for which I was not really prepared.

Suddenly, my mind was racing. I felt fear. I felt numb. It was nearly impossible to wrap my head around what was happening. I worried for my family. I didn't know where I would be sent. The DC jail was notorious for its violence, but I didn't think there were any federal prisons in the area. So, the DC jail was the most likely place. But so much—everything—felt out of my hands. Fear gripped me, but even then, I knew I could not show it. I knew my fear would scare my wife. Plus, I did not want to give Weissman and his team the satisfaction.

The marshal came to me at my table and said I had to go with him. I looked at Kevin, who was clearly in shock and possibly even more confused than I was. Not knowing what was behind the door, I told Kevin to follow me into the next room.

As I was leaving the courtroom, I knew I had to make eye contact with Kathy. I turned to the audience and saw her looking at me. I could see the concern on her face, and I knew that I needed to look brave, to let her know—even without the ability to say anything—that I could handle this situation. But inside I was a mess. I felt like vomiting. With as much strength as I could, I smiled at her from across the room and she threw me a kiss. That kiss stayed with me. I felt it on my lips, and it gave me strength in the moment and in the days to come.

The marshal took me to a cell block off the side of the court where I was instructed to give him all of my valuables, my belt, and my tie, which I did. (I also gave them my suit jacket, which was returned to me. I don't know why I gave it up, but it just seemed like the right thing to do.) The reality of my situation—of all the unknowns so suddenly piling on top of me—started to sink in.

A few minutes later, Kevin came through the door. I gathered that he was not allowed into the area but somehow, he had managed.

"You've got to get me put in a safe environment. I can't be put into the DC prison system," I said. Truthfully, I didn't know anything about DC prisons beyond their terrible reputation. I had all of these preconceived ideas of what jail was and, in that moment, all of the worst things I could think of were running through my head.

Kevin told me that they were going back to the office to deal with this crisis. He assured me that I would be safe. With so little else to hold on to at that point, I took comfort in his words even if I had no reason to believe them. I tried to calm down. I thought, *I've got to pull myself together. I can't lose it. I've got to figure things out. And I can't show fear. I cannot let them think that this tactic they're using—one of intimidation, pressure, and bullying—is working.* I saw myself sitting on this small bench in this cavernous cell. I resolved to appear indifferent to what was happening to me. It didn't matter that I had a thousand thoughts in my head or that my stomach was in turmoil. I wouldn't let them break me.

After forty-five minutes, I was taken to the jail area in the basement of the DC courthouse where I was put into a large cell that could hold groups of prisoners. I was alone. There was just one long bench across the back with a metal toilet. After another half hour a guard came over and asked if I had eaten anything. It was the first time I had even thought about food. It was also the first of many lunches I'd eat from a paper bag filled with a baloney and cheese sandwich on white bread, an apple, and a juice box.

Once I was locked in the cell, no one spoke to me. In handcuffs and leg-cuffs, I realized I was in the same area during the arraignment back in October. Recognizing the cell—a "familiar" environment—brought me some morbid comfort. There was one key difference: in October, I knew that I would be out of the jail as soon as the arraignment was over in an hour. This time I had no idea how long I was in for—or if I'd ever get out.

There were no clocks (there are no clocks anywhere in jail), so I didn't know what time it was, how long I'd be there, what was happening on the outside, where I would be going, or if Kevin or my family even knew where I was anymore. I started to hyperventilate. Once again, I attempted to regain control of my anxiety, now spiraling dangerously out of control. I had to focus myself. I tried practicing a number of mindfulness exercises that I had learned over the past year of my ordeal. I sat on the edge of the metal bench and focused on the only object in the cell—the toilet. I tried to lose myself in the moment and, with some effort, I succeeded.

Finally, after what felt like many hours, three prison guards ushered me from the cell into a large van. It was only when I walked outside that I realized it was dark. No one told me where the van was going. I had to shuffle because I had handcuffs on my wrists and shackles on my legs. As the door was opened to the van, I saw three rows of seats behind a metal screen divider. I sat in the first row, closest to the door. In the van with me were five other prisoners, all dressed in prison garb. I was still in my suit jacket and white shirt.

As we pulled away from the underground area, I closed my eyes, prayed for strength, and felt a surge of adrenaline. I still had no idea where I was going, but I had to remain strong. The adrenaline evaporated as I looked beyond the wired windows at the darkness outside. I almost passed out—from nerves, exhaustion, stress—but caught myself. Again I told myself to pull it together. I needed to be in control. I knew that I had never solved anything by panicking.

A prisoner from the far back corner of the van introduced himself as B. B. He called me "Professor." Why, I don't know. Maybe it was the suit jacket I was still wearing. Either way, I took it as a sign of respect.

After welcoming me, he told me that he was arrested for selling drugs and having an illegal gun. The situation felt so absurd, I couldn't help but smile to myself. The other prisoners ignored him, but I took the opportunity to ask him where we were going.

"Northern Neck Regional Jail," he said. Northern Neck was somewhere in the Chesapeake area, about a hundred miles from DC. I didn't know why I was being taken so far away. But at least I knew I wouldn't be in a DC jail, which brought some small measure of relief.

B. B. told me Northern Neck was a "cool" jail. He said there was good stuff to do there if you are in general population, or "GP." In GP, he said, you could hang out, watch TV, do some exercising. This was all good "cuz ya don' wanna be in your cell all day." I asked him how many beds were in a cell and he told me two to four. When I asked him if he was in a two- or four-bed cell, he said he was not going to be in either. He was going to "the hole"—solitary confinement. I shuddered at the image but dismissed it without thinking. The "hole," I thought, was for hardened criminals, dangerous inmates, prisoners of special distinction. In the hole, B. B. told me, you are alone, with no access to people or any of the "activities" of the jail. Prisoners in this type of confinement are allowed one hour of recreation time a week. He assured me I wouldn't be in solitary because it was only for those who could not be trusted to exist in the general population.

Eventually, after giving me a virtual tour of the jail I was going to, B. B. asked me what I'd been arrested for. He had no idea who I was. No one knew who I was. I was just another prisoner on his way to Northern Neck.

"For something I didn't do," I told him. "I was set up. 'Business crimes.'"

"We *all* set up by the man!" he said.

He was 100 percent right. I had been set up by "the man"—the Office of Special Counsel, Weissman, Mueller, Hillary, Obama, the MSM. The list went on.

After about an hour of talking, B. B. went quiet. We didn't speak for the rest of the trip. I didn't want to push him, even though there was so much I still didn't know. And I didn't want to upset the other prisoners. There were protocols in this system that I needed to learn. That much was clear. But the conversation gave me comfort. For the first time on that terrible day, I had some sense of what to expect. In the quiet darkness of the van, my mind still raced with unanswered questions. Would I be in a two- or four-bed cell? Who were my cellmates? How would I get along with the other inmates in "GP"? How would I contact my family to let them know I was okay? Do they have any idea where I am?

Eventually, these thoughts dissolved into prayer. I prayed for strength. I prayed for my family, and I prayed for a quick resolution of this nightmare that had become my life.

The van drove south on I-95 toward Richmond. It was Friday night. Eventually, we got off of I-95 and on to some side roads. As we crossed a long bridge, I thought I knew where we were, but I was wrong. I could recognize from the signs that we were heading toward the Chesapeake area. I just didn't know where.

We pulled into a jail courtyard after three or four hours of driving. Seeing the sign—Northern Neck Regional Center (NNRC)—triggered a fresh wave of anxiety. I was met by a short security woman who immediately whisked me away from the other prisoners—an unsettling sign of how I was to spend the next twelve months. But the woman was soft-spoken, very caring, and she put me at ease.

She introduced herself as Sergeant Kelly and told me that the warden had called her at home and asked her to meet me upon arrival to process me. Sensing my fear, she told me to try to stay calm.

"Prison is tough," she assured me, "but we will make it a little better for you."

Her compassion in those early moments was as unexpected as it was appreciated. She brought me directly to my cell—a windowless concrete box ten feet long by eight feet wide. It had a ten-inch TV, one bunk bed, a metal shower, a sink, a toilet, and a phone that did not work. With a noticeable hint of pride in her voice, Sergeant Kelly told me I would be in the "VIP cell."

Looking around the room, I examined the door and the horror hit me again. It was solid metal, with a small slot for food trays and a small window that was covered by a hinged metal cover on the outside. Unless the window was opened, the door was solid with no view of the other side. I've suffered from claustrophobia throughout my life and the cell seemed to be designed to break me.

According to Kelly, I would be treated a little differently from the rest of the prisoners. I would not be "booked," so there would be no mug shot that could leak out. I would wear "regular clothes," not a prison jumpsuit. The catch, however, was that I would be in solitary confinement—the VIP cell, or hole, as B. B. had put it. This, she explained, was to keep me from having any contact with any of the prisoners "for my safety." I laughed.

For my "safety," I could not be moved anywhere in the prison without a team of deputies clearing the hallways first. For my "safety," I could not speak to any of the other inmates. For my "safety," I could not have access to the gym or to any of the common facilities like the rec room or the cafeteria. I could not look outside of my cell without the metal window being opened from the outside by a prison guard.

"For my safety" would become the Bureau of Prison's go-to explanation of my situation as I languished in solitary confinement for the next year. Weissman was not interested in my safety. He was only interested in making my life so miserable that I would gladly offer to cooperate to get out of that hellhole.

I sensed immediately—and correctly—that my solitary confinement had less to do with my protection and more to do with the Special Counsel's high-pressure tactics, but on this first day in captivity it was too disorienting for me to assess clearly.

Acutely aware of how I was feeling, Sgt. Kelly asked me if I wanted to call my family. Because I had arrived on Friday night, she said, they had not yet activated the phone in my room. She told me to follow her to her office and she'd let me call from her phone. Not the way the "regs" said it should be done, but she was putting me ahead of the rules.

The first call I made was to Kathy. I needed to let her and my daughter know that I was okay. I knew they would be worried. They were completely in the dark. I wanted to tell Kathy that I was scared but as soon as the call connected, I realized I had to tell her I was better than I really was. Any sense of panic on my end would be unbearable to her. So, for the second time this day, I put on a brave face for her. It was beyond emotional to hear the voices of Kathy and my daughter, but I did what I could to hold myself together, to reassure them of my safety, and to let them know that I was in control of the situation. I know I gave both her and my daughter Andrea comfort, but I ached inside. I explained where I was and gave them the name of the prison. At this time, no one, including my attorneys, knew where I had been taken.

While I was speaking to Kathy, my daughter went online to the NNRC website and looked up all of the information on the facility, including how to set up an account for me to access the commissary, have a phone account to place calls (no money is allowed in the jail), and register me for an iPad/cell phone that allowed me to have phone access in my cell for most of the day and night.

By the time I was finished speaking with Kathy, Andrea had everything set up. She was incredible! It gave me comfort knowing that I would be connected to my family while at NNRC, but I needed to be patient. Nothing was going to be activated until Monday.

Saying goodbye was very difficult. But the truth is that the call had a calming effect on me. I was nowhere near as calm as I pretended to be, but I was clearly in a better frame of mind.

Next, I called my lawyer, Kevin Downing, to set up a meeting to figure things out. To my dismay, he told me he was leaving for Tel Aviv the next day for a trip that had already been postponed when the government filed the witness tampering charges. The timing upset me, but he promised to send another attorney down on Monday to start building our plan. We had to figure out how we would work together to prepare my case. I was very concerned about how we would work now that I was four hours away, in prison, and without access to any of my files. The case was complex, and we needed to collaborate in real time. I had no idea how this could happen and needed to confer with my legal team. Kevin's trip to Israel now made things even more confusing.

While the call to my family steadied my heart and calmed my nerves, the conversation with Kevin focused my mind. For the first time since the judge sent me back to that cell in the courthouse, I could feel myself building a plan, something I've always done, and done well—something I needed to do to hold myself together. Over the course of my life, no matter what environment I have found myself in, I have always used my skills and my instincts to get the job done. It was second nature and it felt good, despite everything, to attempt to assert some degree of control over my situation.

Still, my "situation" was serious, and any feelings of tranquility or clarity were short lived that night. I was in jail—in the hole—for something I didn't do, and the Special Counsel's abuses of power were just beginning. The unthinkable was happening.

I recalled how when I'd left my condo for court that morning, there were two thoughts running through my head. One was of the liberation I'd feel if my bail was finally approved. My lawyer was sure of this outcome. I was confident, too, to some degree, but still apprehensive. And the other was the possibility—horrifying as it was—of home confinement for the duration of the trial, still five months away. Being sent to prison was, of course, a possibility, but it was considered extremely unlikely. I was neither a flight risk nor a threat to the community. I had no criminal past, and I wasn't some dangerous villain like John Gotti, Bernie Madoff, or Bill Cosby.

But to understand what happened—and I was only beginning to see the full picture, myself—it is important to understand that the bail package issue was never just about a negotiation between me and the Special Counsel. It was the opening salvo in the fight to define the stakes of this case. Beyond the narrow legal issues, the Special Counsel had built up the importance of my case to exposing the conspiracy between the Trump presidential campaign and President Vladimir Putin of Russia. I was the key, and they would twist the hell out of me to get what they wanted.

From the moment Andrew Weissman was hand-picked by Robert Mueller to lead the investigation into Russian collusion and the Trump campaign, the ends were always going to justify *his means*. Eight and a half months prior to my incarceration, at my initial arraignment, Weissman had effectively established the magnitude of my indictment and my case's central role in establishing the Russia-Trump conspiracy. The fact that the conspiracy was a politically motivated fabrication and that I was being indicted on statutory violations that were never before cited in criminal indictments was totally irrelevant. In other words, the fact that I was innocent didn't matter.

To that end, on the day I was arrested, October 30, 2017, the DC Magistrate Judge Deborah Robinson imposed an unheard of $10 million bail package on me, effectively making my case the most important legal case in the country. My legal team assured me not to worry. This was an absurd bail amount, they said, and when I appeared before the US

District Court judge, who would manage my case, this amount would be reduced to a more normal bond, somewhere between $500,000 and $1 million.

But, as I knew from my own career, in politics it's crucial to frame the narrative at the earliest possible time. Just as Weissman knew it would, the $10 million bail number reverberated throughout the political and legal system. The mainstream media decided—before a single fact was ever established—that the $10 million bail meant that I was a major criminal who *must* have done some very bad things. Why else would the bail be set so high? Between the bail package and the initial charges filed against me centering on my consulting for a foreign government (Ukraine) that was once a part of the Soviet Union, in the minds of the media, the dots connected themselves: Russia. Manafort. Trump. Collusion. The conspiracy narrative exploded—just as Weissman and the Magistrate Judge knew it would—and I was at the center of it, my "guilt" a foregone conclusion from the moment of my arrest.

Contrary to what my lawyers believed, when the time came, the District Court Judge, Amy Berman Jackson, did not reduce the $10 million bail amount. Jackson was a liberal Democrat who had ambitions to seek higher appointment in the judicial system. As the presiding judge in the trial of President Donald Trump's Campaign Chairman, she now had the perfect platform to audition for future consideration by a Democrat president. Jackson embraced the Special Prosecutor's theory that I was such a flight risk and that the court needed to impose this unprecedented bail amount on me. She acceded to the $10 million amount and remanded me to my home to figure out how to come up with $10 million of unencumbered assets to be allowed to leave my condo.

While I do not know what she knew about my financial situation, I do know that Weissman and the prosecutors knew that this would be a very difficult task for me to accomplish. Any ideas I might have had about receiving fair treatment were swiftly and strongly trampled. I would be used by the Special Counsel and the judicial system to bring down my old boss, President Donald Trump, by any means necessary.

In the months between my initial arraignment on October 31 and the June 15 bail hearing, my legal team presented Judge Jackson with three different bail packages, all of which were rejected. But the fourth package, cobbled together from various approved portions of the three previous proposals, would have to be approved, and Weissman knew it.

So in the week before my Friday bail hearing, a story was leaked to the press that I had attempted to obstruct justice by tampering with potential witnesses for my upcoming trial. Based on this obstruction, Weissman would argue that the Special Counsel could no longer support me being given bail. They were demanding that I be immediately incarcerated because I was now a threat to the community.

The tactics Weissman used—of feeding the allegations to the MSM, Judge Jackson, and the Grand Jury—were characteristic of the way he worked. The approach would center around an "unnamed government official" leaking damning information asserting that I had done something nefarious, then using those stories to go to the Grand Jury.

The intended effect of these stories was to poison the mind of Judge Jackson regarding my violating her rules. Weissman wanted her to feel that I had disrespected her personally and the court administratively. In doing so, he was confident that he could successfully argue that I did not deserve to be "on the street" and could not be trusted to obey any future admonishments of the Judge.

Ironically, Jackson had never issued any order limiting me from communicating with potential witnesses. In fact, despite our repeated requests for several months, Weissman had refused to even provide us with a list of possible witnesses. So, even if I had done what Weissman was alleging, I would not have violated her instructions to me. But this was immaterial to Weissman's strategy. He wanted to influence the emotional atmosphere of the court.

The obstruction accusations were preposterous. They centered on an *attempted* call by me on February 23, 2018, to one of my consultant team members, who had worked with me for several years in Ukraine. Downing was confident going into the June 15 hearing because he did not believe that the Special Counsel could make a serious enough case. "Even in a Russian court," Downing joked to me in the car that morning, "the Judge wouldn't dare to throw you in jail on these facts." He didn't believe I would have my bail denied on the flimsy evidence presented by the Special Counsel, never mind be incarcerated.

I wanted to believe him. But in the back of my mind, I was nervous. Something wasn't sitting right. Over the course of a career in politics, I've developed a certain instinct and I did not trust Jackson. Plus, my confidence in historical legal precedent was flagging. I had grown weary of having trial lawyers tell me they "can't believe this is happening. It never happens."

I have been a success in my political and business career because I never take any outcome for granted. I have always factored a worst-case and best-case scenario. In preparation for this hearing that is exactly what I did.

Fearing the worst outcome, I organized my personal affairs in a way that my wife and family could manage the priorities of my life. Even in undertaking this course, however, I never believed that I would remain in prison for any length of time. Unfortunately, my family did not want to even imagine this possibility, so their attention was not very focused. Nonetheless, I comforted myself in the knowledge that I had organized my affairs and informed my family on what they needed to replace me.

As Jackson opened up the hearing with her summary of the business of the day, she never looked at me. I did not view this as a positive sign.

Next the Special Counsel presented the opening arguments on the issue of why I should be denied bail. They ignored the package that I had submitted. Instead, they focused on my character, on my alleged violations of the court's instructions and expectations, and they finished with the obstruction allegation. Facts were absent, but that didn't matter. I listened in weary disbelief as Weissman quoted news headlines and summarized conclusions as if there was no other interpretation. I tried to stay positive but inside I was a mess. I did not recognize the person Weissman was describing.

Jackson let the Special Counsel ramble on unchallenged. Rarely would she ask for a clarification unless it would serve to further emphasize the prosecutor's point. I grew more and more and more uneasy. I did not like the way Jackson was responding to the prosecutor's arguments. It was like they were sitting at the same table.

Downing kept telling me to relax but I couldn't. I have made my living off of my instincts. I was an expert at assessing how people's body language and verbal language telegraphed their thinking. And the thinking in the room clearly smacked of "I was guilty and needed to be locked up."

I sighed in relief as the Special Counsel summed up their arguments. Now it was my legal team's turn to present. I was hoping to hear a refutation of the absurd claims that I had intimidated a witness. I felt that since there were no real facts that this should be a simple thing to do. But my team decided that it would be better to concentrate on the bail package I had cobbled together. I knew already that Jackson didn't care about the bail package. She listened but didn't engage. Jackson wanted some assurance that we had a plan that would prevent this behavior from happening again. We did not give her any plan. We argued that the obstruction allegations were absurd and that it would be inappropriate punishment for me to be detained on these "facts." The judge wasn't interested. She was looking for a reason to put me in jail and the Special Counsel had given her one. *Paul Manafort is a danger to the community*, Weissman had communicated. *He cannot be trusted to be free. He should be placed in prison for the duration of the trial.* That was all she needed.

It occurred to me that, with the first trial still at least several months off and the trial in Jackson's court not even scheduled yet, I could be in prison for eight to twelve months before my legal cases were finished. I couldn't believe it—couldn't believe I was even in this position. I became more anxious as the reality of the *possibility* of going to prison set in. Downing was telling me that everything was going to be alright. He was trying to cheer me up, but he was failing. I finally realized my fear didn't matter. I—the real Paul Manafort, not the conspiracy mastermind Weissman had created for public consumption—had no power over what was about to happen.

When the decision finally came down, I felt the floor drop out from under me. In a brief moment of clarity, I saw the trial for the charade it was. They were not going to let go of me until I gave them something on Trump. Weissman would continue to put the pressure on me one way or another. For this phase, the pressure was to be incarceration and solitary confinement.

As I walked back into the cell after calling my wife and Kevin, I took another look around, picking up more details. The bed had no blanket or pillow, just a sheet. The television looked like something from the 1960s. Once again, my eyes hung on that metal window. I was so tired. I had no idea what time it was, but I knew I needed to sleep if only to calm myself down and to stop the thoughts racing in my head.

They would be shutting the lights off any minute. I laid down on the bottom bunk. I thought I would pass out, but I was so anxious I could barely keep my heart from beating out of my chest. I couldn't bear the thought of the dark cell that night. Somehow, I managed to get the guard to keep the lights on in my cell.

Exhausted and jittery, I revisited the events of the day. It was like I was remembering a bad movie I had watched years ago. I could picture the car ride to the courthouse that morning. How everyone said there was nothing to worry about. "They would *have* to approve my bail request." "The obstruction charges were a joke." I could see Jackson's smirk as she said she "had to incarcerate me to protect the public." And I could see my wife throwing a kiss as I was led away from the room and into the first of many prison cells.

At that moment, I didn't know what the future would hold, but I knew I wasn't guilty, and I knew that there was no Russian collusion. Weissman knew this too, but the truth didn't matter to him. Never mind that a man's freedom, family, reputation, and livelihood were at stake. I resolved for the last time that day not to let the Mueller team, the MSM, or even my family know how I ached. I would figure out how to manage this phase of my life. It was a crisis, but I had always risen to the occasion. I would do so this time, too.

CHAPTER 2

How It All Started

If my situation at that moment—sitting in solitary, the pawn in a politically-motivated witch hunt—seemed a distinctly *un*-American kind of nightmare, my life up to that point had largely been the product of the American Dream.

Both sets of my grandparents came over to the United States from Italy in the waves of migration around the turn of the century. People have joked over the years that Manafort—"strong hand" in Italian—might be some reference to the family's Sicilian roots, but the Sicilians were on my mother's side. My paternal grandfather was from Naples. At the age of ten, his parents put him on a boat by himself and sent him off for a better life in America. There he was met by a distant relative on Ellis Island and eventually brought to Connecticut.

He was just a kid, my grandfather, without a word of English, and no close family. But he was a hard worker and a smart guy. Within a decade he had started what would eventually become Manafort Brothers—the family business, now in its fifth generation. Back then it was called New Britain House Wrecking. My grandfather started it with a pickaxe, a shovel, and one friend to work for him. They would take down tenement buildings by hand and sell the wiring, the toilets, and whatever other salvage for extra money. He was good at it.

Ours was a typical Italian family, very close and very large. People married young and started families quickly. My grandparents were no exception. While my grandfather was out working, my maternal grandmother took care of the children and operated a still in the basement to keep the tenement supplied with wine and moonshine. My father and mother were both the babies of their families, and I was their firstborn. I grew up in a warm, loving environment. Family was everything. Holidays would see seventy or eighty people sitting around the long tables we'd set up in the unfinished basement of our two-story home. The festivities would last for ten hours.

While we never wanted for anything, we lived a simple life. At the time, New Britain was the home of The Stanley Works and other major hardware manufacturers. In the 1950s, it was a blue-collar town (the city motto: "Industry fills the hive and enjoys the honey"), and growing up there, my outlook was decidedly provincial. A drive to Hartford—twenty minutes away—was a major trip. Going to New York was like going to Europe.

After my father had gone into the family business and things were going well, one of the first things he did, with his brothers, was buy a piece of property in a place called Miami Beach. On weekends, using salvage timber and construction materials, he and his brothers would build the "family" cottage. He wanted to build a family home for the summer. Every summer my mother, my aunt, my cousins, and I would spend from the fourth of July to Labor Day down at the shore. I would tell my school friends I was going to Miami Beach for the summer, and it wasn't until high school that I realized they thought I meant Florida. I had never even heard of Miami, Florida. To me, Miami Beach meant Connecticut.

Our first family home was on the third floor of a tenement building, right across the street from a ball-bearing factory. Next, we moved to a two-family home with my cousins on the first floor, and, finally, to a single-family home in a middle-class neighborhood. This was where the Manafort family would gather. My friends and I would play basketball in the yard and my mother, in typical Italian fashion, would always have good food and snacks ready for us. Food was love to her, and that's how we grew up.

It was a religious community in the sense that the town was organized around the churches. My grandmother lived across the street from St. Ann's, the main Italian church, and that church was her project. She always made sure her sons were doing everything that was necessary to help the church. That was how we practiced our religion. I said my prayers in the morning, of course, but we lived our religion largely by doing things for the community.

My father became active in politics after the war. Of surprise to his family and friends, when my father returned from the European theater of the Second World War, he registered as a Republican—the only Republican in the family. He did so for a principled reason. He had seen friends and comrades die in battle to ensure Europe's freedom. He viewed the Yalta Conference of 1945 between Franklin Delano Roosevelt, Winston Churchill, and Josef Stalin as a selling out of the freedom of the people of Central Europe. He never forgave FDR for this incomprehensible travesty.

There were very few Italian Republicans in New Britain in those days. The Republican party of New Britain was dominated by the college educated and my entire family was blue-collar high school graduates. All politics was local back then and my father began by doing the things that were the bread and butter of political organizing: setting up the precinct operations and mobilizing the votes. In 1962, Tom Meskill, a Republican, was elected mayor of New Britain and he made my father Head of Public Works because my father understood machinery and was a good manager. My father was successful in that role. The winters in the Northeast were brutal and keeping the streets plowed and potholes fixed was essential to Meskill's next political ambition, being elected to Congress.

After Meskill, there was a Democrat mayor, James Dawson, who did a terrible job. My father decided to run against Dawson when he was up for reelection in 1965. The odds were against my father, but he managed to mobilize the blue-collar vote and he won. Fifty percent of the workers at Manafort Bros. were Black, and my father was able to deliver a fair number of their votes to the Republican Party. He was a popular mayor, a mixture of William Buckley and Rockefeller Republicans who believed deeply in equality, fair treatment, and in making life in New Britain better for everyone. He was at every Black event, Polish event, Italian event. It didn't matter to him. He wanted to govern in everyone's interest. He went on to serve three terms and it was from watching my father that I got my first window into politics—and my first lesson in political consequences.

From the very beginning, I was drawn to the contest of politics. When I was in high school at St. Thomas Aquinas, my father was trying to get young people involved in local government, to get kids interested in how government worked. He created a youth program where high schools could participate. There were four major high schools at the time and each school could elect four representatives to a city council. The sixteen representatives would then elect a mayor and that student would get to be Mayor of New Britain for a day. I was elected to the group of representatives from my school and, with nine of the sixteen votes committed to me, I believed I was on track to win the election for mayor. My first lesson halted that expectation when a distant relative of mine cut a deal behind my back. I lost. While at the time I definitely wanted to win—I was competitive even back then—losing was an important life lesson in two ways. The first was that having the votes isn't enough until people have voted. More importantly, it got me thinking about the organizational and management aspects of politics, not just the service.

I also knew from a young age that I didn't want to go into the family business. It just wasn't for me. I remember how, as a punishment, my father would sometimes send me and my brothers down to the salvage yard to pull nails from demolished lumber so they could turn around and sell the wood. One Saturday we were down there in the freezing cold. I can still recall my emotions pulling nails and stacking lumber, pulling nails, stacking lumber—working *hard*—angry as hell at having to be there on a Saturday morning. My brother was just sitting there, barely doing anything.

Finally he looked at me and said, "Paul, why are you working so hard?"

I said, "We have to pull the nails out."

"Why? What's going to happen if we don't?"

He was right. Nothing would happen. But I couldn't just coast like that. What was the point of working if you weren't going to work hard? And why work hard if it wasn't going to pay off?

I got good grades in school, and when the time came, I applied to Georgetown in Washington, DC. My school principal, an Irish priest, told me I wouldn't do well there and encouraged me to apply to schools closer to home. When I got into Georgetown, I became the first person in my family to go to college and I made sure to send that principal my honor roll grades every semester, which he never acknowledged. My father and mother were proud. This is what they had worked for. (My cousins were supportive, if not impressed.)

I went to Georgetown as a business major, but my real interest was in public service and politics. So I quickly became involved with the College Republicans. I had read Barry Goldwater's *The Conscience of a Conservative,* which had a significant impact on me. From an early age, I was oriented more toward the conservative wing of the Republican Party. Which isn't to say the counterculture of the late 1960s passed me by completely: I was at Woodstock; I participated in the first Earth Day. But politically, I was a conservative and more importantly, I had a sense for the organization of political structures, a feel for elections and campaigns. I remember thinking that Goldwater had made dumb mistakes. I don't know how I knew that at the time. But I didn't understand why he was saying some of the things he was saying, even though I agreed with the concepts that he was trying to push. It was an instinct I would develop throughout my career. It was also a challenge I would have when I joined on to help Donald Trump.

In New Britain, they did not have a Young Republicans organization that I was aware of. But within the Republican Party at the time, College Republicans and Young Republicans were a big deal. The College Republicans and Young Republicans were instrumental in Goldwater's insurgent campaign in 1964. And a lot of the people who were part of that were now in their twenties and thirties, managing and influencing Republican politics in all fifty states.

When I joined the College Republicans, I quickly saw the value of the organization because they were reporting to the Young Republicans in the District of Columbia. In most states, you could have twenty chapters of College Republicans. But in DC, it was just based on the colleges in the District. So there were far fewer, and it was much easier to manage.

I decided that with the 1968 presidential race coming up, I would become active and emerge at a senior level within the DC College Republicans organization. Georgetown became the driver, but the girls' schools were the keys in the equation. They were more social members than political, and they all wanted to be part of the Georgetown environment. So I could throw parties and count on their votes. By 1968, we'd taken over the College Republicans organization in DC, which was a very important steppingstone to the Young Republicans nationally.

(Within two years, I was running the College Republicans in DC, and emerging as my main opposition at the time was a group out of Utah being run by Karl Rove. Many of the emerging players of the next forty years of Republican Party politics—Charles Black, Roger Stone, Terry

Dolan—were all active then. Going into 1969, the main competition for the national chairman of the Young Republicans was a guy named Frank Fahrenkopf from Nevada, who ended up becoming the chairman of the Republican Party later in life under Reagan, and Don Sundquist, who ended up becoming governor of Tennessee. They were two consequential leaders and from an early stage, I found myself in the middle of the activity with many of the players I was going to be dealing with for the rest of my life.)

By this point, I had control of the College Republicans and I was a player in the national Young Republicans. I started getting really interested in the *politics* of politics, not just the governance of politics. While my friends were watching *Star Trek* and *Wild Wild West*, I was working the phones and going to all these College Republicans events. But there came a moment, at the end of my sophomore year, when I had to make a critical decision. I could run for chairman of the College Republicans for DC or run for president of my class at Georgetown. Silly as it sounds today, I thought long and hard on it, tried to imagine all the potential outcomes. Finally, I asked myself: Why do I want an office for one year, when if I win the College Republicans chairmanship, I could build on that role over multiple years? That was the deciding factor, and even though it was a silly decision matrix, it would change my life. We won the election for College Republicans and built a structure that would ultimately elect my friend and future partner Roger Stone chairman of the Young Republicans. And we would use that as a part of the launching point for Reagan's presidential campaign in 1980.

Law school was another stepping-stone to a career in Republican politics. It was something I could fall back on if need be—lawyers were still put on a pedestal in Connecticut in those days—and it would be helpful if I were to run for office in the future. I was accepted to Georgetown Law School and by the time I graduated, all the pieces were in place. My life in national politics was about to take off.

For all intents and purposes, the National Conservative Political Action Committee (NCPAC), or "Nic-Pack," was the first *real* political action committee in the United States. Ten of us, including Charles Black, Stone, Terry Dolan, Richard Viguerie, and Thomas Ellis, Senator Jesse Helms' right-hand person, contributed $1,000 each to lend to the new organization. So, in 1975, NCPAC was created with $10,000. Black then convinced Helms to sign the first fundraising letter. We sent the Helms letter to the Barry Goldwater lists and with a direct mail campaign, the PAC started to make a little money. Dolan, Stone, and Black went on the payroll, and I was back in Connecticut with my law degree on the family payroll, keeping busy and going back and forth to DC.

Around the same time, President Ford, who had taken over the Presidency when Nixon resigned, appointed his buddy Donald Rumsfeld to be Chief of Staff. Rumsfeld wanted to eliminate any political remnants from Nixon's White House. After the excesses of Watergate, he completely sanitized the White House. First, he brought on as his deputy a policy guy named Dick Cheney and Cheney brought in a friend of mine named Peter McPherson. McPherson got in touch with me not long after about a job at the White House. I was shuttling between Connecticut and DC, but really, I was in between law school and what I was *going* to do. It was a great opportunity for an ambitious twenty-three-year-old like me, but I was linked to the conservative wing of the Party through the Young Republicans and NCPAC, and with rumblings that Reagan was going to run against Ford, I found myself in an awkward position. I told Charlie Black about the White House job offer, but I said I would not take it if Reagan was going to run. At Charlie's direction, I reached out to call Judge Clark. I was told that Reagan had no plans to run—"maybe in four years." So, with that pressure removed, I took the White House job.

Of course, Reagan then changed his mind and decided to run. And by this point, NCPAC was starting to raise some serious money. I was twenty-six, Dolan was twenty-five, Stone was twenty-three, and Black was twenty-seven.

With Reagan's announcement, my friends at NCPAC told me I had to quit the White House. I couldn't do that. I'd made my bed and it would go against my conscience to leave. They insisted. For the first time, they said, there would be a real leader for the movement we had been building for the last decade.

But I couldn't do it. Which is how I found myself at the White House in the middle of a political fight with the very machine I'd spent my nascent career helping to build. Soon Reagan was really cleaning Ford's clock. Rumsfeld had political experience but had left the White House to become Secretary of Defense, elevating his deputy, Dick Cheney, to Chief of Staff. Unlike Rumsfeld, Cheney had little political experience, something that would change dramatically over the course of the next thirty years. However, as Chief of Staff, he was now the de facto manager of Ford's campaign.

The official Chairman of the Ford campaign was a very liberal, aristocratic congressman named Rogers Morton, an old-school, white-shoe Republican. The lack of presidential campaign experience was missing at all levels of the Ford campaign and the results were telling.

Reagan was beating Ford everywhere. Finally, Ford decided that he needed to totally reorganize the campaign. At a meeting with Cheney, Stu Spencer, a crusty seasoned political operative who had managed Reagan's two successful governor's races in California, and George Bush, an old friend of Ford's whom Ford had appointed Director of the CIA, it was decided that Spencer would take on a major full-time role and several people, including me, would go over the campaign to engage in the work of helping to build the convention delegates strategy. This was the same function that Trump would ask me to undertake in 2016. A major concern of the Ford campaign was who would run the day-to-day operations of the campaign. Bush said there was a friend of his who was a very good manager working for Ford in the Commerce Department, but he had limited political experience. His name was Jimmy Baker. Ford spoke to Baker and the new team was now in place.

It was a close race, one of the closest in history. With the revised political team, we were able to turn things around and narrowly win the nomination for Ford, who then went on to lose the presidency to Carter. For me, though, the experience was invaluable. And while Ford's presidency was short lived, I had achieved something very unique. I now had personal knowledge of how the White House worked mechanically and how a presidential campaign was managed. Plus as an added bonus, I now had strong personal ties with a group of people who would be a bedrock part of Republican Party national politics for the next forty years—James Baker, Dick Cheney, and George Bush.

On a more mundane level, however, as of January 20, 1976, I was twenty-six years old and out of work. It seemed like this was the right time to reconnect with my conservative comrades. This decision was the most important decision of my life. Plus, NCPAC had retired all of the $1000 notes except mine—my friends' way of expressing their disappointment in my decision to not quit the White House.

Even though they were still angry at me, I went over to NCPAC to try to rebuild those relationships. In the process, I built the foundation for the rest of my career. If that was not important enough, I met a girl named Kathy Bond who worked at NCPAC. She has been my wife for the last forty-four years.

While I was busy in the White House and with the Ford campaign, Kathy, who had a background in finance, had been hired by NCPAC to be the bookkeeper for the organization.

The way she tells it, I walked into the room at an event and both she and her friend spotted me and said, "I want to date that guy." I was there with political motives, to deal with my former partners, so I was looking right past her. I was still paying interest on the money I'd borrowed for NCPAC, and come January I wouldn't have a job. So my mind was elsewhere. But they started flirting with me and I liked Kathy right off the bat. She said she'd heard of me, but that my name always seemed to be attached to a string of expletives. In person, she said, she could see I wasn't really like that.

For our first real date, I took Kathy to The Palm Restaurant in Washington. I had my picture up on the wall there, which was sort of a badge of recognition in DC. There were two other couples with us, both a part of my political group, so they had nothing in common with her. And I was kind of "big dogging" it, even though I did not have a nickel to my name. I didn't even have a job.

As Kathy tells it, I looked at the menu and I said the lobster is really good at the Palm. Now, she had been dating a guy for the last year or so who also had a picture on the wall, and actually had a job. And she'd been having the lobster on that guy regularly for a while. So she thought, "Ok, big shot, I'm going to teach this guy a lesson. Besides I doubt I will ever see him again." So she ordered the lobster. I looked at her and I said, "You have to eat all of it, you know?" And she said, "Don't worry, I will." And with that insouciance, I was hooked. Her attitude has been the same ever since.

Truly pushing my luck, for our second date I took her to a State Department event. There were about two thousand people at a reception on the eighth floor. As soon as we arrived, I got distracted and started walking around, talking to people, losing Kathy in the process. I found her an hour and a half later and thought she'd be mad at me. She was, but she'd met some people, too, and was having a great time. She could really hold her own.

The relationship grew from there. We were engaged on Christmas of 1977 and married in August 1978 in front of 350 people at St. Ann's Church in New Britain. My mother had organized the whole thing down to the band that would play before we even told her that we wanted to get married. She'd probably been working on it for ten years.

There's no question that meeting Kathy changed my life. I have always been a self-starter and I've followed my instincts and ambitions to great success—largely without mentors save for my father and a few others. But the only figure close to me who was a real and deep influence on the decisions I would make in my life was my wife.

Not long after we were married, I became deeply involved in Reagan's 1980 presidential campaign. My future partner, Charles Black, was the political director of the Reagan campaign; John Sears was the campaign manager. Sears had a relationship with Reagan that could only be described as disdain, but he was a genius and Reagan felt like he needed him. As this new campaign was getting organized there were two distinct and disconnected factions in it. The first group was the California group, which was led by Reagan's California staff—Michael Deaver and Ed Meese and Judge Clark. The second group was the Washington group, built around John Sears, Black, and Jim Lake—all operatives of the 1976 campaign against Ford. I was associated with Sears's group.

Sears never paid attention to the details of structure and instead spent a lot of his time fighting Deaver and Meese and running a front-runner's campaign that didn't harness Reagan's value. The reason for this disdain was that Sears did not respect Reagan. Sears and I disagreed about Reagan. To me Reagan was an incredible candidate who connected with the American people. To Sears, Reagan was a novice surrounded by a California group that, at best, were amateurs and more likely just out of his league.

My friend Jim Baker was running George Bush's campaign, and Bush was beating Reagan by replicating Carter's strategy from 1976. He had used Iowa to set himself up as the front-runner going into New Hampshire with only four weeks left before the primary. Their strategy was to defeat Reagan in New Hampshire and deliver a fatal blow to his candidacy. After Iowa, Reagan realized he needed to run an aggressive, door-to-door campaign in New Hampshire. Ultimately, this change highlighted the magic of Ronald Reagan, which connected with the New Hampshire electorate. He achieved a landslide victory that righted the course and put him on a path to the White House.

Winning the New Hampshire primary became the catalyst for Reagan's nomination, but it was also the moment when he took control of his campaign. At the time, I was handling convention states for the campaign, which was a significant job.

On the day of the primary, I was driving from Montpelier to Manchester to be part of the Reagan victory celebration. According to our polls, Reagan was going to win big. On the ride over I was going over strategy with my Vermont campaign manager. We had the radio off and spent the three-hour drive engrossed in conversation. When I arrived at the hotel in Manchester, Jack Germond, the most preeminent political pundit at the time, grabbed me. He wanted to know what I thought about Sears, Black, and Lake being fired. I had no idea what he was talking about.

I went up to the second floor, where Governor Reagan and the campaign leadership were located. Reagan's closest adviser, Mike Deaver, came up to me, grabbed me, brought me into an empty bedroom and said to just wait there a minute. I had no idea what was going on. This was a time before cell phones. I couldn't reach Black. He was gone. Using the hotel room phone I called Roger, who was back in Washington at the campaign HQs. As best he could, Roger filled me in on some of the background, at which point Deaver and a gray-haired guy in a rumpled suit named Bill Casey came in. With them was Governor Reagan.

I didn't know it at the time, but there was a panic among the California group that I would quit. I had three of the next four states and they were worried that with Black and the rest of them gone, I would quit. Reagan explained to me what he did to Sears, et al., and why he had to fire them.

Before Reagan could go any further, I interrupted. "Governor, I want you to know that if you want me here, I am here. I'm committed to your candidacy, and I want you to be the president of the United States. I understand what you did, and it won't affect my support for you." Reagan looked at me and without saying anything gave me a hug.

After he left, Nancy Reagan came in. She said, "Ronnie just told me what happened. Thank you so much. I know you're close to Charlie, and we love Charlie, but he wasn't doing a good job. We've got to get Ronnie elected."

I said, "Mrs. Reagan, you don't have to worry about it. I'm here for you and the Governor."

When I finally got Charlie on the phone, he said he wanted me to quit, which I couldn't do. And which Roger wouldn't do, either. We decided it would work better if Roger and I stayed on the inside and Charlie on the outside. Charlie would go back to work with NCPAC. I told Charlie that when I got back to Washington, we would huddle up.

When Roger, Charlie, and I met later that week, we decided we would start a political consulting firm. It was still early, and no one was sure that Reagan would be the nominee. We had yet to win Florida. For all we knew, Roger and I would be out of a job that summer. So, we agreed to start a company. We wouldn't announce it formally until after the election, but we'd start taking a couple of political clients. Black would service them, and Roger and I would donate our salaries from the campaign to the company and then after the election we'd decide what kind of political consulting firm it would be.

When Reagan won the nomination and then the presidency, we saw the opportunity to broaden the scope of our work and formed a Republican Government Affairs Company. I didn't want to be just another political consultant. I enjoyed politics, but I was also interested in international affairs, and dealing with international organizations. I wanted to be more than a consultant and I felt I had the skills and the knowledge of how to build it, even if Washington hadn't really seen a business model at that time similar to what I was envisioning.

My business model combined the skills of political campaigns with the policy issues of Washington lobbying. At that point in time, lobbying was really lawyers practicing through their connections. Lobbyists/lawyers were law firms. There were no political consulting firms, and no one was practicing lobbying in the strategic sense. They practiced it in the back-room sense, but under the cover of the prestige of a law firm.

I saw the opportunity to have corporate clients because we were deeply embedded in the Reagan administration. Washington had been a Democrat town for so long that there was only one lobbying firm that had any serious Republican credentials, Timmons and Company, and it was a small-by-design, lobbying-only firm.

With the creation of Black, Manafort, and Stone (BMS), we became the second firm, but I saw a bigger opportunity. I believed the time was ripe to evolve the skills of political consultants to the needs of public affairs and lobbying into a new model. I convinced Black and Stone that we could do this.

In my model, instead of having clients paying us $2,500 to $5,000 a month for the limited period of a campaign—campaigns only lasted so long—we would get clients to pay us $5,000 or more a month for twelve months a year. Timing the announcement with the beginning of the Reagan administration, we began to attract a lot of interest from the New York financial and real estate communities. Stone was one of our key links to these communities. Roger had managed the Northeast for the Reagan campaign, and in that capacity had spent a lot of time with many of the business titans from New York City. One of those titans was Donald Trump.

In the 1980s, Donald Trump was not a Washington, DC, person. He had very little interaction with the Washington community other than to donate to various political campaigns. He enjoyed this dynamic because powerful Washington figures would be supplicants seeking his financial support. Most of Trump's business needs were in New York City, where his properties were located. Roger convinced Trump that we could be his "eyes and ears" in DC. Trump knew that Roger in particular, and BMS generally, had strong ties to the emerging Reagan administration and saw no downside to helping BMS as we built our business. He signed on and became one of our first important clients.

Roger was the principal link to Trump in those early days. Primarily, he would keep Trump in the political loop in both Washington and New York state politics. Knowledge is the coin of the realm in politics and Roger kept Trump informed.

During the first year of our contract with him, Trump began to pay more attention to Washington—to the senators and congressmen who solicited his financial support. The more he interacted with these people, the more he came to realize that they were not "special." Within that first year, we began to see a change in him. While his interest and focus remained on his real estate business, a growing fascination with Washington was emerging. Roger was getting several calls a week to discuss politics and what was going on in the mayor's office and in Albany.

Stone always believed that Trump was a special kind of guy, and Roger is very good at making those kinds of assessments. I could see a certain magnetism, but in those early years it was hard to see Trump as a serious politician, let alone president. This was before Ross Perot; the idea of a businessman as president didn't seem possible. I did believe that Trump, with his charisma, could be a Senator, maybe Governor of

New York, and then use those positions as a stepping-stone to the White House. But Roger made the point that Trump couldn't live in Albany, and he'd hate Washington. I couldn't see it without one of those stops. Though, frankly, it wasn't something I thought much about until I was running the convention for Bob Dole in 1996 and ran into Trump there.

By the mid-1990s, Trump's interest in politics had grown precipitously. He had watched Perot emerge as a serious candidate in 1992. To Trump, this was a sign that he could be elected president. Assessing the candidates in 1992, Trump felt he was much smarter than Perot and all of the others. Without question, Trump also believed he would be a better candidate. As he was walking around the convention floor in 1996 at Dole's nominating convention, you could feel his fascination with the pageantry and the spectacle. My wife Kathy, who was walking Trump around the convention floor, overheard Trump talking to himself. "This is what I want," he was saying. "This is what I want."

It would take another twenty years, but eventually, when the timing was right—and no one has a better sense of timing than Donald Trump—he'd get what he wanted.

CHAPTER 3

Donald Trump Enters the Race

E very year, the White House Correspondents' Association puts on a dinner that brings together the national media, Washington's political leadership, and the elected officials of the Executive Branch, the Legislative Branch, and the States. It is their way of honoring themselves as celebrities. The dinner is a way to meet informally, make new contacts, and to feel important.

The 2011 White House Correspondents dinner was to reverberate in importance far behind that night in April.

"Now, I know," Obama says, pausing for comedic effect, "that no one is happier to put this birth certificate issue to rest than The Donald."

Here the audience laughed, a little uncomfortably, since "The Donald" happened to be in the crowd that night.

"And that's because he can finally get back to focusing on the issues that matter. Like did we fake the moon landing? What really happened in Roswell?"

Trump smiled, content for the moment to be the butt of Establishment Washington's joke. He's never held these people in high regard, anyway.

But Obama continued: "All kidding aside, we all know about your credentials and breadth of experience. For example, just recently on *Celebrity Apprentice*"—boos from the audience—"at the steakhouse, the men's cooking team did not impress the judges from Omaha Steaks. And there was a lot of blame to go around. But you, Mr. Trump, recognized the real problem was the lack of leadership. So, ultimately you didn't blame Lil Jon or Meatloaf. You fired Gary Busey. And these are the kinds of decisions that would keep me up at night."

Laughter filled the room. Obama was clearly enjoying himself getting even with Trump for his "birther allegations."

"Well-handled, Sir. Well-handled," Obama said, looking directly at Trump. "Say what you will about Mr. Trump, he certainly could bring some change to the White House."

Typical of their fawning over Obama, the media-laden audience broke into nearly rapturous applause as Obama finished his public humiliation of Donald Trump. Later, some would point to that 2011 White House Correspondents Dinner as the moment Trump decided, once and for all, to run for president. Trump himself would disagree. After all, he'd been toying with a run for fifteen years at that point. But the sting was something Trump would not wipe away until Tuesday, November 8, 2016.

Personally, I believe that he committed to himself, that night, that Obama would pay for his ridicule, and the glory of November 2016 was payback time.

Even back then, Trump was sensitive to two facts that Obama and everyone else in the room that night seemed to miss: the first was that, while it was true no one in Washington or the establishment took him seriously, it was Washington that wasn't being taken seriously by the American people. The second was that Trump's outsider status, far from being a hurdle to overcome, was a formidable asset, one that would catapult him a few short years later into the presidency and—from Obama's mouth to Trump's ears—bring some real change to the White House.

Throughout 2015, I watched Donald Trump steamroll his way to the top of a crowded field of presidential candidates—some talented, some less so. Busy with other business, I watched from the sidelines. To anyone paying attention, it was clear that there was something extraordinary about candidate Trump. Everywhere he went, he seemed to resonate with people in a way that most politicians could only dream of. What was even more impressive was that he did it by being himself and speaking *what he believed*, not what he thought people wanted to hear. I knew from personal experience how charming and how magnetic he could be. So, while Democrats, the MSM, and nearly everyone in the Republican Party was quick to laugh him off, I wasn't so doubting. Was it obvious to me that he would win? No. But was he was an interesting candidate *who could win*? Absolutely yes, to say the least.

After a career in politics—both domestic and foreign—there's always an itch to get involved when a campaign begins. But in 2015 I was busy abroad, and while Trump was a special candidate, the US election wasn't compelling enough to me at that time. I understood that if you want to have influence, you need to be a part of the campaign from the beginning. You have to put in your dues if you want to be there at the end of the day. And I was busy elsewhere.

Besides, in the early months, Trump was doing very well on his own doing what he was doing. I couldn't see a clear role for myself in those early days. I was content to be on the sidelines watching to see how the field shook out. I had friends in almost every camp, people who knew my skill set. And they knew how to get ahold of me. I figured I might be a natural fit if there was going to be a contested convention. Or perhaps to help put the convention together for a presumptive nominee. On the Republican side, there were very few people who could do what I could do. So, I didn't feel like I needed to get committed early on.

In any case, I was busy in Ukraine helping to build a new party. Events in Ukraine had changed dramatically in 2014 when Putin squeezed Ukraine to refrain from joining the European Union, causing a revolution that brought down the Yanukovych government. These events changed the dynamic of everything I had worked to build over my ten years in Ukraine, causing the need to build a new democratic party in the country. I was angry about Yanukovych running from the country, claiming he feared for his life. But I was even more upset that the momentum that we had built up to get the European Union to accept Ukraine on terms that were not draconian to Ukraine had now been seriously damaged. It was one of the ironies of the revolution against Yanukovych: if the West had worked with him through that crisis, Ukraine would not have suffered the loss of Crimea or Eastern Ukraine and the mess of Putin's invasion in 2022 might never have happened.

I didn't know what direction the US presidential campaign was going to take any more than anyone else did, but I was watching it as a student of politics. I was paying attention to what was going on. After seven years of Obama, I believed that the country was ready for a change. The "Obama fatigue" was almost palpable, and there was the sense that fatigue could translate into the Republican Party taking control. They had taken over the House in 2014, adding it to the Senate. The Presidency was the last piece, and, for the first time in a long time, it seemed as if that piece was within reach.

Most of the media was laughing at the prospect of a Trump candidacy. But because of my relationship with Roger Stone, who was involved with Trump from very early on, I was aware that Stone and Trump believed very sincerely that this was Trump's time. Roger had been telling me this on a regular basis since early 2015. But I really began to pay attention when my cousins back in Connecticut—blue-collar working guys, businessmen who were not particularly political—started calling me to say how much they liked Trump. This drumbeat definitely got my attention.

Factoring these responses, I felt that Trump had a solid platform from the success of *The Apprentice* and that, if he worked it right, he could be a far more serious candidate than most people were giving him credit for. He was being underestimated, in my opinion, and from my experience with Donald Trump, it was always dangerous to underestimate him.

It was obvious that Trump, more than any other candidate, was successfully tapping into the voter anxieties that had been brewing over the last few years. It was clear from all the polls that the American people had lost confidence in Washington. But that wasn't a new finding. Voters had long believed that politicians did whatever they had to do to get reelected or elected, and once they got to Washington, they went local and forgot who had elected them until the next election. What *was* new was this antipathy was energized by a broad and deep sense that people had lost faith in the direction of the country.

The Tea Party had become a major mechanism for channeling this anxiety. When Obama had the IRS investigate the Tea Party and other conservative organizations, it created an even deeper sense of frustration with Washington. The Tea Party is often mislabeled as a right-wing movement. It wasn't a right-wing movement. It was a movement of populists who were upset with Washington. And within the populist movement, by 2015, you saw growing support for Sanders on the left and for Trump on the right. The phenomenon had nothing to do with idealogy and everything to do with a call to arms to "drain the swamp."

Shortly before Trump's June 16, 2015, presidential candidacy announcement—the famous escalator ride at Trump Tower—Roger called me to tell me it was coming. I congratulated him. Roger had been pushing the idea of getting Trump to run for president for years. I viewed this as a success on Roger's part. Trump had always said that he'd only run if he was sure he could win. He didn't think he could win before, but he did now. I was impressed by Roger and Trump's confidence. Many candidates want to win, but they don't always think they will win. Trump, from day one, knew he would win, and he knew he would not have to—in fact could not—compromise to do it.

This was something else that set him apart from regular politicians. Many people who don't know Trump believe that he acts spontaneously. This is incorrect. Trump doesn't do things spontaneously. He thinks things through. He follows his instincts, but his actions are almost always premeditated.

Likewise, when people said that on election night Trump was shocked to have won, I disagreed. If you look at his campaign over the final ten days before the election, he was in twenty states, doing multiple events each day. It takes an incredible toll on the body. But he was doing that because he felt like he was going to win, and he wasn't going to leave anything undone. He even went to Maine for one electoral vote. That was the focus he had on winning.

When Trump came down the escalator and said, "So, ladies and gentlemen, I am officially running for president of the United States, and we are going to make our country great again," he moved to the front of the pack in the political polls almost immediately. This surprised a lot of people, but it did not surprise Trump, Roger, or me.

From the beginning, Trump was doing what Trump does very well: he was defining the field. And he was defining the field as "me vs. them." He was on the side of the American people and his opponents were with the Washington swamp. Even though that distinction didn't fit all of the other candidates, it became the primary organizing mechanism used by the media to analyze the prospects of the various candidates. And it allowed Trump, with somewhere between eighteen and 23 percent in the polls when he announced his candidacy, to emerge as the front-runner.

The group of candidates—a record seventeen of them—was a mix of ideological people like Rand Paul, establishment people like Jeb Bush, Marco Rubio, and Ted Cruz, and outsiders like Ben Carson and Trump. Trump stood out—as Trump usually does—from the start. He and Carson were in a position by themselves. Carson coming from the religious right, and Trump being a businessman—they had something different. Trump didn't come from any partisan political bloc; he was just the independent businessman, and a successful one who got things done.

I saw all of those movements going on. And while most of the media were proclaiming Jeb Bush the front-runner, it was clear to me that the time had passed for someone like Jeb, someone who would be seen as just another competent, professional politician. The country was looking for an outsider, someone who would shake things up. So to me the more interesting candidates were people like Rubio, who was a new face, Trump, and Ben Carson.

What is not often understood about presidential politics is that it doesn't matter where you start, it matters how you are able to position yourself for when an opportunity or an opening occurs. If you have any kind of base, you position yourself to take advantage of that. Carson had that kind of base. But as is usual with candidates like Carson, if you don't have the depth to then take advantage of the opportunity to which you've availed yourself, you miss the moment. Which is exactly what happened to Ben Carson. He was not a traditional politician, and when his moment arrived, he could not pivot to handle the cascading events and challenges.

Trump ran that same risk. The difference was that Trump was much savvier politically than Carson. Trump had better PR skills, too. And Trump was a strategist. In many respects, the reason Trump succeeded as a candidate was that he possessed many of the skills that you would hire multiple consultants for. He had a very good sense of the country from a polling standpoint, even though he didn't use polling. Trump knew where the country was and understood it very well. As a communicator, he knew how to take advantage of the media tools and use them to his advantage. He was savvier on social media than anybody. He had taken that lesson from Obama, who used social media very effectively, and elevated it. So even though he had a team of people around him who were not very experienced, Trump emerged because he had tapped into the right channels using his unique range of skills.

Donald Trump had been famous in New York circles for decades, but to the broader American public, he was known, at that point, mostly for playing a successful businessman on TV. Projecting his image on TV, Trump could point to real-life examples, like the Wollman Rink, and say, "Look, Washington is always promising to get things done and nothing ever gets done. But I really *do* get things done."

The Wollman Rink in Central Park was closed in 1980 when its floor buckled. It was estimated that renovations would cost $5 million and take two years. By 1986, nearly $13 million had been spent and it was supposed to take another $3 million to finish it by the winter of 1987. Trump offered the city to rebuild it and to do it in under six months. "I have total confidence that we will be able to do it," Trump said. "I am going on record as saying that I will not be embarrassed. If Koch doesn't like this offer, then let him have the same people who have built it for the last six years do it for the next six years."

The city decided it had nothing to lose and gave Trump the mandate. He kept his promise and delivered the rink "two months ahead of schedule and $775,000 under budget."[1] So here was the perfect Trump story: "No one thought it could be done and I did it." He saw those openings and was able to take advantage of them.

When Trump said he would "drain the swamp" in Washington, he was able to articulate in three words the desires of millions of Americans. This was his particular genius: his ability to define issues and use a language that people could relate to. He could talk about bringing back American prestige, which he said was at an all-time low, without sounding like another phony politician. He could talk about the border, energy independence, the economy, and American greatness in an authentic way—as a businessman. He could discuss job creation from the perspective of someone who had actually created jobs.

Trump understood that first you have to establish the themes and then you establish the issues. Otherwise you get caught up at the micro-level before you've had a chance to define who you are and what you stand for. This understanding also allowed Trump to establish the agenda for the primaries—an agenda that played to his strengths and could not be used by his opponents.

From very early on, he was the one setting the agenda in the election. While it seemed counterintuitive to many in buttoned-up DC, Trump innately understood that his persona—the flamboyant, fabulously wealthy businessman—was integral to his appeal. He had *always* been Donald Trump. "The Donald," as Obama so smugly called him: successful, larger than life, a beautiful woman on his arm, a golden apartment. It conveyed a consistency that stood in stark contrast to regular politicians, who could change their minds on an issue at the drop of a hat depending on which way the wind was blowing. Trump had been outspoken and true to many of his core issues for nearly two decades.

I didn't always agree with how he handled things or with some of his more incendiary remarks. It certainly wasn't my style. It's not what I would have recommended. But Trump knew what he was doing. He knew how to use drama to bring attention to an issue and how to then dominate the conversation.

From early on after he announced his candidacy, Trump's strategy—a brilliant one—was to define his competition. He was able to do this quickly with nicknames: Little Marco, Sleepy Ben, Low Energy Jeb, Lyin' Ted Cruz. He was creating a shorthand for voters and that would be difficult for the other candidates to shake off. Normally, consultants would be telling a candidate not to do this, pollsters would be saying, "This is not good." But he didn't have consultants, and he didn't have pollsters. He was his own communications director, and he had the instincts to separate himself from the field.

At the first Republican primary debate on August 15 in Cleveland, Ohio, he made himself perfectly clear. "The big problem this country has is being politically correct," he said. "I've been challenged by so many people, and I don't frankly have time for total political correctness, and to be honest with you, this country doesn't have time either." To many Americans, this was both refreshing and effective. Trump's ability to define and dominate the conversation was captured perfectly by a *Politico* headline following the debate: "Yes, it's the Trump Show."[2]

I don't think that he ever worried about burning a bridge or ten. He was running as an outsider, and he understood that it was politics. It wasn't personal. He felt that once these people were no longer his opponents, they would be his friends. The day after someone would drop out, he would be on the phone with them telling them they were "great guys" and he was so impressed with them. Of course, all they could do was acknowledge he had whipped them.

In 2015, Trump used the media and his celebrity status to great effect. At first, the media thought it was interesting—this flashy businessman who they never thought could be president was out here beating all of these seasoned politicians, some of whom the media were fans of. Eventually the media would turn very quickly and very sharply against Trump, but it wasn't always like that. Jeff Zucker, who was running CNN, had been the liaison from NBC to *The Apprentice*. He had a relationship with Trump, and when Trump announced his candidacy, Zucker had special access. Even when CNN and Trump were blasting each other all day long, Zucker would call Trump or come to the office, and they'd yell at each other in person. But then they'd shake hands and laugh. Zucker was playing a little chess game. He knew Trump well enough to know how to piss him off. So Trump would attack CNN and CNN's ratings would go up. But Trump was getting near-constant press—for free—so he was happy too.

Trump understood the media on a level that was far above that of all of the other candidates. Throughout all of 2015 and into the early primaries, there was still no campaign structure, at least not in the professional sense. Trump was the campaign. He was the campaign manager, he was the pollster, he was the speechwriter, and he was the scheduler. There was a staff, but they were simply trying to implement what Trump was telling them to do.

Trump had developed a pattern with the media where he would start his day talking to *Fox & Friends*. Here, he would lay out a topic. The topic would become the issue of the morning. He was setting the agenda every day. In the pre-cable days, there used to be one news cycle in a day, but Trump understood that with social media he didn't need to limit himself to one news cycle. He could dictate three or four. It was a new model. He would define the topic of the day at 7:30 a.m., people would spend the morning reacting to it, Trump would react to the reactions, and suddenly he'd built himself into a 24-hour news machine. It was truly unlike anything anyone had seen before.

But for all of the campaign's success, it was a very small operation. Hope Hicks, the communications director, was essential here. She was able to connect Trump to any media outlet he needed to keep his finger on the dial. Corey Lewandowski, the "nominal" campaign manager, was dealing with structuring the speaking events. And Dan Scavino, an underappreciated but critical resource of the campaign, was dealing with the social media. It was a threadbare machine running mostly on the power of Trump.

However, despite achieving mind-blowing success at the polls, there was an organizational deficit that would soon become a serious problem during the nomination process. But until February of 2016 the cracks hadn't really started to show. Crucially, his team was collecting the addresses and email addresses of anybody who came to an event, which became very valuable later on.

Another important element of Trump's early campaign was that it was self-funded. He didn't have to raise money. It was, also, an important message to the electorate that nobody owned him. He was a billionaire. He didn't need a fundraising apparatus. So, while other candidates were spending half their time going to private lunches, dinners, and fundraising receptions, Trump spent none of his time doing that. He was doing rallies and dealing with the media.

Absorbing all of this at an arm's length, I was caught up in Trump's genius. For a veteran political consultant, it was truly remarkable to watch. Clearly, throughout 2015 and into early 2016, I understood that he was succeeding on almost all levels and doing it primarily on his own. He didn't need me. At the time, I didn't fully realize the lack of depth in the campaign structure and the totality to which the campaign was really just Trump. I was watching a brilliant execution of a strategy. And I was impressed.

At the same time, Roger Stone was telling me that Lewandowski was a terrible manager, that he didn't know what he was doing, that he was causing Trump problems, and that what Trump really needed was structure. I heard Roger but felt that it was usually impossible to come into the game in the fifth inning to revise everything. It just didn't work, especially when the campaign was winning. Despite Roger's deep concerns, I still didn't see a real role for myself.

It wasn't until I met with my good friend Tom Barrack in late February 2016 that the idea of getting in touch with the Trump team came up. I'd known Tom since the mid-70s, and we were very close. But he was not in politics; he was a brilliant businessman and a personal friend. Through the sale of the Plaza Hotel, a prized landmark property in New York City that Barrack had owned and sold to Trump in 1988, Tom had gotten to know the Trumps. Since that sale, the two of them had built a close personal and professional relationship.

While I was out in California visiting with one of my daughters, I called Tom and scheduled a coffee to catch up. During this visit, he asked me about the Trump campaign. He knew my skill set and was curious about my thoughts on the campaign.

Trump had started to hit some rocky ground and I gave Tom my impressions as to why. I explained how delicate the delegate selection process was and how I didn't think the Trump team was paying attention to it. Tom asked if I might be interested in being a part of the campaign. I said I might, but that the campaign was succeeding, for the most part, and I expressed my concerns about coming in at a late stage to suddenly become the expert that's going to fix everything, most of which still was not recognized as broken. While I knew Trump for a long time, I didn't have a personal relationship with him where I could simply move in and become a trusted aide. Plus, I hadn't been involved in US politics at the national level in several years. My work in Ukraine was not going to be the basis for Trump to reach out to me. So I said I didn't think there was a place for me. Tom disagreed and said he would feel out the Trump people. I found out later that after our meeting, he brought me up to Ivanka, who didn't want to rock the boat, and the idea died.

Then Louisiana happened on March 5. Trump was winning most of the early primaries, but Cruz was getting proportionately more delegates than he was getting primary votes. Louisiana made this crystal clear. Trump was looking at this contradiction and thinking, *they're stealing my election. I'm winning these primaries just to lose the nomination?*

But brilliant as he is, Trump didn't understand the rules. And Lewandowski didn't either, even though this was exactly what a campaign manager is supposed to know. Since neither Trump nor Lewandowski understood the problem, neither had any idea about how to fix it.

It is instructive at this point to explain how Trump was managing the structure of his campaign.

After a primary was over, the Trump campaign would shut the state down, take the volunteers, and move on to the next state. There was a movement of almost all of his paid personnel, which meant that once the primary was over, there was nobody as part of the Trump-paid organization in New Hampshire, in Louisiana, or in any of the states, dealing with the essential work of getting delegates, identifying people to be delegates, managing the local Party meetings to elect delegates who would go to the state convention to elect the national delegates. None of that was happening. Lewandowski didn't understand this concept at all. His assumption was that the local Trump supporters would get it done. But the local Trump supporters were outsiders who supported Trump because he promised to fight the establishment. Delegates were elected by the state party apparatus, i.e. the establishment. It was not a fair fight once Trump moved on. The system knew the rules and would dominate the process, including the campaigns of Trump's primary opponents that he had just beaten in the state election.

Clearly seeing what was happening, I called Barrack and I explained to him what was going on. Trump's success was being built on very shaky ground. Barrack asked me to write a memo that he could give to Ivanka and Donald so that they could understand this arcane problem and why I had the ability to fix the problem. I put together a two-page memo, thinking he was going to change it around a little and then hand it over to the Trumps.

Indeed, the family was starting to get nervous about the way the campaign was being managed, especially after losing the Iowa caucuses to Cruz at the beginning of February. They had gone out to Iowa to help mobilize for caucus night. Up to that point, Trump was the star at all events. To the family, who did not have a history in politics but understood the importance of organization nonetheless, they saw clearly the lack of organization and the lack of structure on the ground. They were very anxious. They could see for the first time that the campaign was not organized, that it was running on Trump and nothing else. They didn't respect Lewandowski to start with and began to believe that he was not up to the job. Iowa gave them proof, but it would take a couple more primaries before they could really see the growing division between the primary wins and the delegate operation—or lack thereof.

The memo I put together for Tom was nothing that required any research on my part. It was a subject I had spent my career understanding, and thus was straightforward in defining the problems and solutions. Around the same time, because Trump was feeling that his victories were being robbed, he set up a meeting with Reince Priebus, the Chairman of the Republican National Committee. Incredibly, this was Trump's first real interaction at national Republican headquarters, even though he was the front runner for the Party's presidential nomination.

Trump began by walking through his complaints about what was happening to him and how the process was "rigged." Almost immediately, Priebus, realizing that Trump didn't understand the rules, politely interrupted, and explained the delegate selection process. He emphasized that delegates were elected by the state party rules, not by the RNC. And more importantly, Priebus explained that every state was different.

Trump listened intently as if this was all new information to him.

Priebus further elaborated that in some states, when a candidate wins the primary, he automatically gets to select the delegates. But in other states, the delegates aren't tied to the results of the primary.

Furthermore, in some states, there is only a first ballot requirement on how the delegates must vote. In these states, if a primary opponent elected all the physical delegates in a state that Trump won, those delegates only had to vote for Trump on the first ballot. Furthermore, they didn't have to vote in favor of the Trump campaigns' position on any of the rules of the convention, the organization of the convention. In other words, other than voting on the first ballot they could completely ignore or work against the interests of the Trump campaign.

When Priebus explained this division of the nomination process, Trump realized that the physical delegates could totally undermine Trump's campaign, even though on the first ballot they had to vote for Trump. Suddenly, Cruz's second ballot strategy made total sense: keep Trump from winning an absolute majority of delegates and for Cruz to have a majority of the physical delegates of the convention be anti-Trump delegates.

After Priebus explained this to Trump, Trump turned to Lewandowski and asked, "Did you know this stuff?" Lewandowski said, "No," and Trump exploded. The one thing he was relying on his campaign to do, they weren't doing. In fact, they weren't even aware of the rules.

Meanwhile, my memo from Barrack had gone into the system, and Ivanka, seeing what was happening, thought it was worth passing to her father. Trump called Barrack and they both talked to Stone. Stone told Trump, "You've got to bring Manafort on. He understands this stuff. He knows how to deal with delegate selection. He understands what the rules are. He's got experience in the national campaigns, you need him to come in to be the delegate coordinator, convention coordinator."

In late March while I was in Florida, I got a call from Barrack.

"Trump is going to call you and he's going to ask you to get involved in the campaign," he said.

"What does that mean?" I asked.

"I don't know," he said. "Just talk to Trump."

Soon after, I got the call from Trump. He started off with a few Roger stories and then we got into what was going on in the campaign. I opened up by telling him how he was doing a brilliant job *doing what he was doing*. I then segued into the whole *other* part of the campaign. I told him that, based on what I could see from the outside, there was no structure to harness the wins he was getting. I didn't see a mechanism to deal with what happened when he left a state. I explained that it wasn't his job; it was the job of the campaign operation.

"Well, can you do the job?" he asked.

"I have a lot of experience," I said "But I have to tell you that I have a problem coming into a campaign in the middle, unless the campaign manager wants me involved. In order for me to be effective, not only do you have to want me, but your campaign team needs to want me as well. Otherwise there will be a lot of infighting and we'll spend more time fighting each other than doing our jobs to get you elected."

"That makes sense," he said.

"Well, do they know you are talking to me?" I asked.

"They'll want you because they need to get this job done."

"I would feel more comfortable if you told them first and got their approval."

"I don't need their approval," he said.

"*You* don't need their approval, but I need their approval to do the job you want me to do."

He said he would talk to the team and call me the next day. We left it at that.

Two days later, he called me again, this time to tell me everybody was on board. "We need you. We want you. When can you start?" he said. Since I was at my Florida home, he invited me to Mar-a-Lago for dinner the next night.

When I arrived, I met Hope Hicks and Corey Lewandowski for the first time. It was clear that neither had any interest in me being there. Lewandowski saw me as a threat from day one. I knew right away it would be a difficult relationship.

At Mar-a-Lago, Trump holds court. He has his meals in the middle of the dining room with all the members. The four of us—Trump, Lewandowski, Hicks, and I—were at one table. Don Jr. was at another table with his family. It was Easter weekend. Trump introduced me to everybody. We spent, all told, about an hour and a half together, talking over the campaign. I was impressed by Trump. His charisma and focus were overwhelming, plus his confidence in success filled the room. There was no fear in him, only fight. He truly believed that he was meant for this moment. He would clean out Washington and make the country great again. I wanted to jump up and start working immediately!

At one point, Trump left the table to walk around, and I said to Hope and Corey, "Look, I'm a team player. I only want to get Trump the nomination." I asked Lewandowski if Trump had talked to them about me coming on board. He soft pedaled it a bit, but the answer was no, he had not. So I explained to him what it was I was going to be doing. I could see the hair on the back of his neck go up. Lewandowski believed that I was being brought in to cut his wings. He saw me as one of Roger Stone's guys and he hated Stone. I could feel this anger and I realized I was going to have my hands full. I felt comfortable with Hope, but I also knew from Roger Stone that she was rumored to be very close to Lewandowski. So I didn't have any misapprehensions about where she would come down in a Manafort-Lewandowski conflict. But I did everything I could that night to let them know that I was there to work with them and that my first and only priority was to do what I do well to get Trump the nomination.

Driving home that night, I said to myself: *This is going to be exactly what I did not want it to be. It's going to be a war with Lewandowski.* So I decided that I would do everything I could to build a relationship with him, but that I wouldn't let it get in the way of doing the job. Roger told me I couldn't trust Lewandowski, that he was going to stick a thousand knives in me. But I was determined to do my best and see what developed. In the end, Roger was 100 percent right.

During the Mar-a-Lago meeting, we agreed that I would come to New York after Easter to see the campaign at its headquarters on the fourth floor of Trump Tower. But first I met with Trump in his office on the twenty-sixth floor.

A meeting with Trump is always a unique experience. I had been in his office briefly, in the 1980s, but this was different. Trump's office is enormous, far bigger than it needed to be for anyone but Donald Trump. But it was impressive.

No meeting with Trump is a private meeting. He keeps an open-door policy; anybody with any business can come in. Our first meeting, which lasted nearly two hours, was interrupted no less than half a dozen times by sidebar conversations, vendor bills, and anything else Trump was overseeing. But the thirty minutes we had to ourselves were extremely productive. First, Trump told me he was glad I was on board, that he had spoken to a bunch of friends since announcing my joining the campaign, and everyone said I was the right guy.

"You have a lot of friends," he said. "So what do I have to pay you?"

Before I'd even walked into the office, I'd made the decision not to take a salary from Trump. I knew that the moment he was paying me, he would look at me as staff. I understood his personality. If I didn't take a paycheck, he would respect me more and see me as a peer, as someone on his level (although never as an equal). I needed to be part of his group, not part of the campaign staff.

It didn't hurt that I had an apartment in Trump Tower. In the mid-2000s, my business was going well, and I decided to buy a place in New York City as an investment. It just so happened that the president of JetBlue, who had just resigned, owned a two-bedroom condo on the forty-third floor of Trump Tower. It looked out on Central Park and had a 180-degree view of the west side of New York City. My wife loved it and it was being offered at a bargain price because he needed to sell it. We bought it. It became our apartment in the city. I used it for my business, but also to allow my wife and I to spend time together while I was working.

So, when I joined the Trump campaign, I found myself living in the same building as the headquarters. Trump valued that. It signaled to him that I had succeeded in my life, that I was not looking to get something from him. When I answered his question that I didn't want anything for my help, he was surprised. He challenged me.

"Everybody wants something," he said.

I responded, "Maybe in the future I'll want something, but right now I just want to get you elected. I can afford it, so don't worry about it."

"I guess if you can afford a place in this building, you don't need to take my money."

I laughed.

"That's right," I said, "But I'm going to tell you what I think needs to be done. And I'm going to tell you, I need the authority to get things done." I wanted to protect myself in case Lewandowski turned out to be what I thought he would be. I got very specific in a way I could not get with Lewandowski sitting at the dinner table in Mar-a-Lago. "I don't want to be the campaign manager. I had asked you to talk to your campaign staff previously because I wanted them to buy into my role. You told me you spoke to them. Okay, but I don't think they have bought into it completely."

"Don't worry about my staff. You work with me."

"I understand that," I said. "But I have to work *with* them too. And I want you to know that I'm going to go the extra mile to make Lewandowski feel comfortable. But there are going to be places where I'm going to need authority to do what I need to do in the states."

I explained how, for example, in the upcoming Pennsylvania primary, delegates would be elected by name in congressional districts, and they didn't have to be associated with a specific candidate. Many of these delegate candidates would be local officials who were popular (and, at the time, uncommitted on the presidential election). I explained that while each congressional district elected three delegates, we had more than three professed Trump supporters running in many of the districts, thus running against each other. I explained how this risked Trump supporters splitting their votes and Cruz supporters, who were usually no more than one or two per congressional district, winning the delegate spots with small pluralities, all while Trump was winning the state primary by a big margin. We needed to take control over who would run as an official Trump delegate, otherwise his primary victory in the state would be meaningless at the convention. We needed to win the state primary *and* the congressional district delegates.

I said I was going to have to tell some candidates that the Trump campaign wanted them to drop out of the race and *not* run for delegate. Furthermore, I might need Trump or someone in the family to call some of these people to tell them to back off.

"I'll do whatever we need to do," he said. "You figure it all out."

I said, "Yes, but some of these people may have friendships with Lewandowski, and they're going to be upset."

"Don't worry," he said. "I'll take care of it."

I was trying to define for him the kinds of issues that could come up in the next month. I was going to have to focus on states that had not yet had their primaries, including developing the strategy of how we would run Trump's campaign in those areas. I told him that I would need to better understand the local issues that are going to select people. Which meant I would need to do some polling. I needed to start getting into how we were going to position ourselves with some of these potential delegates.

"Well," he said, "who would you want to do that?"

"Tony Fabrizio," I said. "Tony is the best in the business, and he knows you."

Tony Fabrizio had cut his teeth working with Arthur Finkelstein in the 1980s and 90s. Arthur was a renowned movement conservative poll-ster who knew how to analyze a poll and figure out the various ways to help conservatives win. Fabrizio brought these skills to a new level when he set out to open his own polling company. Over the last twenty years, we had worked together successfully in both US and international cam-paigns. I knew that Tony had the insight to help me target the votes we would need and would be invaluable in the general election. If anyone would be able to look beyond the common impressions and find a way to win, Tony was the man. I was confident that if Trump allowed me to bring Tony on, the combination would elect the next president, Donald J. Trump.

Fabrizio had been with Rand Paul, but Paul had dropped out of the race. Tony was from New York, and I felt he would be perfect for the campaign. But Trump didn't want Fabrizio. In 2012, when Trump was thinking of running, he had reached out to Fabrizio for his opinion. Fabrizio didn't think Trump was serious and never followed up, which is the worst thing you could do with Trump. So, Trump was very negative toward Fabrizio.

I did not want to bring on just any pollster. I felt I needed to bring on somebody who could help me understand what needed to be understood. So I pushed for Fabrizio. Trump said, "No."

I decided to move on and talk to the kids to figure out a way to bring Fabrizio on.

After the meeting broke up, I used the opportunity to lead myself for the first time to the campaign headquarters on the fourth floor.

I got off the elevator on the fourth floor and walked into what looked like a war zone. It was as if a bomb had detonated across the entire floor. The fourth floor had been the *Apprentice* studio. Trump Org. intended to reconfigure it for the new tenants. But no one had rented it when Trump decided to run, and when Trump came down the escalator on June 16, Trump Tower became the *de facto* headquarters. It became the most expensive piece of real estate to ever house a national presidential campaign. The problem was the floor was little more than a construction site with some card tables in the middle and a few desks here and there.

Lewandowski's office was a small build-out with walls that didn't even go to the ceiling. And there were about twenty people on the floor. This was the Trump for President national campaign and its staff. I laughed to myself and thought, *Well, at least I don't have to worry about moving people out of this campaign to bring my people in. There's nobody to move out, and there's nothing to move into.*

Once again Trump's unique genius was impressed upon me. Without any of the fancy offices, or high-priced consultants, or hundreds of staff roaming around, Trump had emerged as the clear front-runner for the Republican nomination. Truly, he was the driving force behind a movement that was on the verge of toppling the entire Republican establishment. I had never seen such a phenomenon in all of my years in politics.

While this approach had worked so far, I recognized that we were now moving into a new phase of the campaign, one that would require adding some of the traditional skills to complement Trump's genius. I realized immediately that in addition to bringing on a pollster, I would need to bring on my delegate operation as well as a media operation to deal with the delegate operation. I had discovered that there were some significant deficits in the organization of the campaign, but I could not have guessed the extent until I saw it with my own eyes. This was a bare-bones operation, and we were now heading into the most important part of the primary season. I had my work cut out for me, to say the least. But we had the best candidate, and that made all of the difference in the world.

Within the first few hours, in fact, it was clear that I was going to have to build my own campaign—a campaign *inside* the campaign—to do the job that I was brought in to do. I went to Lewandowski, and I explained to him what I needed. I wanted him to be a part of the process to avoid any conflict. I laid out exactly what I wanted and invited him to sit with me as I interviewed people. I wanted him to be comfortable. He agreed, but as I found out later, as soon as I walked out of the office, he was on the phone trying to undercut me.

I knew then that there would be a growing issue with Lewandowski on the campaign. But it would have to wait. The clock was ticking. I had no time to lose.

CHAPTER 4

Changing Directions

With the benefit of hindsight, I believe that I came on to the campaign in the nick of time. It was not difficult to imagine a scenario in which Cruz's delegate strategy would be successful. However, the costs of such a victory would be very high. If Cruz's strategy had been allowed to work, it would have resulted in a bloodletting that would have left the Party in shambles, and the Republicans would go into the general election very divided.

Did my involvement stop all of that from happening? No. But certainly my involvement contributed to maintaining the momentum of what Trump was doing. Trump's victories—before I came on and after—were still *his* victories. They were the result of his unique personality and his incredible skills. I simply gave him the structure he needed to protect his successes.

When Newt Gingrich—who has a lot of experience with campaign infrastructure—said that people don't realize how valuable I was to Trump's success, I believe this is what he was referring to. He understood the value of a structured campaign message, the organization to implement that message, and the utilization of the tools of campaign politics.

From my first visit to the "headquarters," I understood the need to systematize the messaging that was part of the politics of the campaign, not the politics of getting elected. I knew what the Cruz strategy was, and I knew what the "Never Trump" strategy was: to create a deadlock convention. The media, of course, would love a deadlock convention—for them it's as sexy as campaigns can get, and they were starting to understand what Cruz was doing and how it could cause Trump major problems.

"Bringing Mr. Manafort on board may shore up Mr. Trump's operation in an area where his opponents currently see him as vulnerable," ran a typical *New York Times* article from late March. "In an alarming tactical setback for Mr. Trump, *The Wall Street Journal* reported last week that he might harvest fewer delegates from his primary win in Louisiana than Senator Ted Cruz, whose campaign has aggressively picked off delegates who are uncommitted or apportioned to candidates no longer in the race."

"Too many missteps of that kind," the article explained, "could force Mr. Trump unnecessarily into a Cleveland floor fight."[1]

So my first priority was to defuse all of these possibilities early on and make it clear that there would be no such Cruz outcome. Publicly, nobody from inside the campaign, other than Trump, was dealing with the media. There was no face to the campaign other than the face of Donald Trump. While this was key to winning the outside part of the campaign, it was clear to me that we needed someone focusing on the "inside baseball" so that the operatives and the party officials, who were going to be important in bringing the party together *after* Trump became the nominee, would see something they could understand and be willing to embrace. It sounds logical today, but at this point in the campaign, they clearly did not understand Donald Trump and saw no basis for them to become involved.

I told Trump that I was going to start appearing on some of the talk shows to present this inside message. I wouldn't be talking about what he was talking about, other than to emphasize his message. But I *would* be talking about how he was going to win and why. He thought that was a good idea and told me to do it.

I then created the message: Trump was going to be the presumptive nominee. I knew that people—politicians especially—needed benchmarks against which to measure those kinds of statements. I had done my analysis of the primaries that were coming up and I could see that if we ran our races the right way, by the beginning of May Trump would have such a lead that, on paper, he would not be stoppable.

But we wouldn't have a sufficient number of actual delegates yet, and

I needed to make certain that the physical delegates on the convention floor would be 100 percent Donald Trump delegates. Otherwise, my narrative would be undercut by the second ballot narrative that Cruz and the Never Trumpers would promote. So in early April, when I started to appear on the talk shows, I gave the media a deadline. By the beginning of May—the Indiana primary—I predicted it would be apparent that Trump was the presumptive nominee.

Suddenly, the pundits and political cognoscenti had a measuring stick. They could follow my narrative and make their judgments of whether Trump was going to be a successful candidate or not. To his credit, Trump felt he would win, so he had no problem with me putting that message out there, even if it raised the stakes.

I was less worried about "Trump being Trump" than about the media and delegate operation. None of the controversies being promoted by his opponents that might have sunk another candidate—first time candidacy, narcissistic personality, the history of beautiful women, the bankruptcies—were getting in the way of his message. He was married to a beautiful and intelligent woman; he had a family he doted on. Nearly everything about Trump had been in the public consciousness for so long, the personal issues—good and bad—did not seem to matter. Everything could be focused on the issue agenda that Trump had established for the primaries, on contrasting his persona against his opponents', and on who best could deliver on that agenda for the American people. The media preoccupation and his opponents' attacks on his personal life would be noise. I decided I could ignore these stories, and I did.

Because Donald Trump is such a large and combative personality, observers often missed a central point about Trump. Donald Trump doesn't create fights, but he doesn't walk away from them either. He doesn't throw the first punch, but once you punch him, he'll punch back three times as hard. I tried to keep the focus on things that were important to the campaign. His image was now crystallized in the primary voters' minds in a way that between *The Apprentice* and the way he had defined himself in the early stages of his campaign for president—that was his image. Who he attacked was not as important as the message he was conveying in his attack. In my entire life in politics, I have never seen anyone who could benefit from this separation better than Donald Trump. I still laugh at the fact that only Donald Trump could attack the Pope and win the argument. Well, he did it and pulled it off.

So, when Trump attacked John McCain's war record, as unseemly as it sounded, it was his message that carried the day with his supporters, not the fact that he had attacked McCain. The reason he could attack the Pope and McCain was that his message always focused on a fundamental point: the interests of the people he was fighting for. The fact that he used the Pope or McCain as his target was not germane to the point Trump was making. Plus, both McCain and the Pope started the fight by unfairly accusing Trump of insensitivity on various subject matters. Instead of backing down, Trump doubled down. His supporters loved it. Finally, the people saw someone who would fight for them, even against a Washington war hero or the leader of the Catholic Church.

Right off the bat, my convention experience gave me enormous credibility and confidence. The job that Trump needed done was precisely the job I had built my career on. I had developed those skills in the United States, but where I really honed them was overseas—in Ukraine and elsewhere—where I had to understand and manage structures in languages I didn't even speak.

Having run conventions for Reagan, Bush, and Bob Dole, and successful campaigns for countless politicians, I was able to bring a lifetime of expertise to the Trump team when they most needed it. Such that when I came on to the Trump campaign, even though I came on for a limited role, I saw the totality, even in my limited role. And as the need required, I was able to expand my role to help Trump achieve his victory.

Here I had this unique candidate—unlike anyone who had ever existed before—who had all these skills, who had overcome the deficits of his campaign structure to become the front-runner for the nomination. I had never met a candidate who could do what he was pulling off. But there was a specific role that he needed help filling. I had the good fortune to have the skills for that role and he had the self-confidence to give me the responsibility to do this job.

Just prior to my joining the campaign, Ben Carson had dropped out of the race. Ironically, during the entire primary season, from the moment Trump announced his candidacy, the only person to ever outpoll Trump was Ben Carson. For one week, Carson led Trump in the national polls. The MSM, trying to make his campaign newsworthy, had pumped Carson's recent success. But once Trump focused his attention on Carson, this candidacy crumbled like all of the others.

Even though Trump was the reason Carson's campaign disassembled, the relationship between the two men was cordial, if not friendly. As a result, when Carson's staff went off his campaign payroll, the Trump campaign picked up several of Carson's key political operatives, including Barry Bennett and Ed Brookover.

Bennett and Brookover were long-time Republican operatives. They had been the principal consultants managing Carson's campaign. When they joined the Trump campaign, they were put in charge of the delegate operations, despite the fact that both had little real experience in convention politics. Brookover had once worked for the RNC, so he was given the added responsibility of dealing with the Party HQs.

This was the state of affairs when I attended my first official campaign meeting at the Washington offices of Don McGahn, the general counsel for the campaign the first week in April. McGahn was a former FEC Chairman and a partner at the prestigious law firm of Jones Day in Washington, DC. He was one of the sharpest minds in Washington when it came to federal election laws and his expertise was crucial to giving credibility to the early phase of the Trump campaign.

While it was not the sole purpose of the meeting, it was going to be my first opportunity to interact with the leadership and to get a sense from others as to their assessment of the state of the campaign, especially as it related to the delegate selection process. During the meeting, I asked for the upcoming local county conventions that would be holding their meetings to elect delegates to the state conventions. My request was met with silence. No such document existed. When I asked for the slates of candidates we would be submitting at the upcoming conventions, I was again met with silence. By the time I asked if we had a document that laid out how delegates were to be selected in the upcoming primary states, I already knew the answer.

What was obvious from this meeting was that Trump did not have a delegate operation set up. This was not Trump's fault. Campaign laws differ by state. Each state is different, and they all have their own particular quirks. Cruz and John Kasich, the Governor of Ohio, were running not necessarily to beat Trump, but to win enough delegates to force a second ballot at the national convention, where anyone could be nominated. Then they hoped lightning would strike and they could be nominated.

I remained quiet for the rest of the meeting and listened to Lewandowski manage the discussion. My concern became more acute when I realized that Lewandowski had no knowledge of the delegate selection in any of the upcoming states and, worse, little interest in acquiring the knowledge. He had set up Bennett and Brookover to fail and he would try to do the same to me.

After the McGahn meeting, I went to Trump and said I needed a separate budget to deal with delegate selection both going backward and moving forward. I tried to bring Lewandowski on board with it, but he wasn't interested in sharing power. I didn't want to have to keep going back to Lewandowski for approval. The budget I built that first week was a couple million dollars, a lot measured by the standards of the Trump campaign spending to date. But, as I explained to Trump, I needed to spend money to organize local county conventions, which elected delegates to the state conventions, which elected delegates to the national convention. It's a three-part process. Trump didn't like spending the money, but he understood. He wanted to know why it was so much money—but he understood the importance of what the money would be spent on.

During this conversation, for the first time, Trump was making the connection between winning the primaries and winning the nominating convention, rather than just being out on the campaign trail, doing rallies, persuading people, and winning the primaries. He understood that what I was trying to build didn't exist anywhere in his campaign structure.

Trump told me to take the budget, sit down with Allen Weisselberg—the CFO for the Trump Organization, but also, effectively, the CFO for the campaign—work out the final numbers, and make sure that there was no overlap between what I am spending money on and what Lewandowski was spending money on. I broke out the functions that were critical to my delegate operation. These were normally part of a campaign organization, but I knew that if I didn't have my own setup, Lewandowski would compromise me every step of the way. I had to have people working with me who I knew and who were experienced at this kind of work—results-oriented people. So looking ahead to upcoming primaries, I put people in New York, in Pennsylvania, and in West Virginia. I brought on Mike Caputo, who ended up becoming the assistant secretary of public affairs in the Department of Health and Human Services during Covid-19. He was from New York, and I trusted him. I brought on Dave Urban, a Washington lobbyist who was totally committed to Trump. I put him in charge of Pennsylvania, because Dave

knew how to put together the delegate operation and was the best political operative in the state, having proved himself by winning multiple
state elections for Arlen Specter. Susie Wiles, in Florida, was as good an
operative as existed there. Putting her in place was critical to the general
election, so I jumped the gun to move her into running the state.

With these people and my budget in place, I now needed to think
about scheduling. Again, this would normally have fallen under
Lewandowski's purview. We agreed to break it up. He would run the
plane and we would coordinate jointly on scheduling. A campaign schedule can be tremendously complex. It was important to run the primary
elections operation and the delegate operation in parallel, but they were
not the same. For example, I might need Trump in Erie, Pennsylvania,
not in Scranton, because that's where it's going to be more impactful for
what I'm trying to do—win delegates. A good campaign structure constantly juggles these needs.

The family—Ivanka and Jared, Don Jr., and Eric (Tiffany was in law
school at this time)—understood what I was trying to achieve, and they
could see the results almost immediately.

I had met Don Jr. at Mar-a-Lago that first weekend. But I didn't
meet Ivanka, who was pregnant at the time, until I attended my first
Trump rally on Long Island in early April. She spoke at the rally introducing her father. She impressed the hell out of me. Unlike most people
in politics, Ivanka would refrain from giving a response to a question if
she didn't know the answer. Instead, she would refer to an expert. She
was also an excellent manager. She was exactly the type of link to Trump
that I would need, and she had her father's total confidence. I decided
to set up weekly meetings with the family to build roles for them in the
campaign. Lewandowski had cut them out because he didn't want them
competing with him, which was stupid for two reasons. One: Trump has
a very special relationship with his kids. There was no way anyone could
compete with them. And two: they were an asset that had real value to
the campaign. They were articulate, smart, and willing to do whatever
was necessary—travel, make phone calls, go on TV. They were surrogates for their father in a campaign organization that had no surrogates.
So, I made sure the kids were formally at the top of the structure.

Not long after I first started on the campaign, Ivanka told me I
needed to meet her husband. At that time, Jared was working at his own
office a few blocks away and was not officially involved in the campaign.

When I sat with Jared, I saw someone who, like Ivanka, was incredibly impressive. Jared is like a sponge. He wanted to learn whatever was necessary to help his father-in-law get elected. Additionally, because he was of the younger generation, he understood and embraced the value of technology. I was trying to bring technology into the campaign in a modern campaign way. So when Jared asked me to let him take over the digital operation, I enthusiastically approved it. I had discovered, sitting in San Antonio, someone who was tangentially involved and could help me bring the campaign to the next level, Brad Parscale. I told Jared it would be great if he could undertake transforming Brad's San Antonio operation into a more central role in the campaign. Jared took on the project and almost immediately we filled the missing link in the national structure. Jared's involvement saved me weeks and cut through all of the campaign bureaucracy. Brad was such an impressive person that Trump actually selected him to be his Campaign Manager for his re-election campaign.

I now had a structure which—through the family—would help Trump build on his wins in a meaningful way *and* protect me from Lewandowski's spite. The more the family engaged, the more they could see what they had already felt from their time in Iowa, which was that Lewandowski was in over his head. This was critical to me because very soon after, Corey was fighting me on every major issue. There were some budget shortfalls, for example, that were clearly a result of the way he was mismanaging the budget. The family started to see this and helped me fix the problems.

Trump did not want to be involved in these details. He was happy with the direction of the campaign, and I was taking more and more responsibility, not just in the delegate operation, but in the upcoming state primaries as well. As long as we kept winning, the boss was happy.

It was with Ivanka's help that I was able to finally bring on Tony Fabrizio as the campaign's pollster. Ever since Trump had said he had issues with Fabrizio, I worked on the family to help me bring him on board. As I have mentioned, Trump didn't see the need to pay pollsters given all of the national polls and he was still upset with Fabrizio for not following up with him back in 2012. Notwithstanding these feelings, I knew that I needed polling data to confirm the narrative that I was laying out for the media, which was that Trump would be the presumptive nominee, and more importantly to target the voter blocs and districts where we needed to elect delegates. Fabrizio had come up in the Republican Party, but he was never part of the establishment. He was a maverick. To get around Trump's reluctance, I went to Ivanka, with whom I was developing a good relationship. I explained the situation to her, and I said that I needed her to come into the meeting with me to get Fabrizio approved. She said she would but for me to understand one thing: "Once the meeting reaches a point where my father is no longer opposed, stop. Don't try to get a sharper point on the pencil."

We went into the meeting and after a few minutes, I brought up Fabrizio. Trump said no. I moved on, but then came back to it, with a little less resistance from Trump this time. Finally, Ivanka weighed in and Trump said something like, "Ok, I can see where he might be useful." At which point Ivanka looked at me. I got her silent point and smiled to myself. She knew her father so well. It was all I needed to hire Fabrizio, though I knew that I would not have him doing any presentations to Trump for a while.

Now that Fabrizio was on board, I conducted specific benchmark surveys in all of the upcoming April and early May primary states. I started giving Trump the details of the polling—without identifying the pollster—and pretty soon he was buying into why he needed to say and do certain things. He saw his image improving across the board. To do this, the data was invaluable and Parscale's use of it in our voter outreach was critical. We were targeting the precise voters we needed and began to outperform all of the public poll's expectations of Trump's vote.

New York was getting a lot of attention because it was Trump's home state and delegates were elected at the congressional district level. The Republican Party in New York was an establishment party. This led Kasich, as the moderate in the race, to believe that he could exceed expectations. Cruz looked at the strength of the conservative party and targeted those specific districts. The initial assessment by the pundits was that Trump would be lucky to win sixty delegates.

Because expectations were lower than I thought they should be, I decided to make New York the first major primary using my team. I immediately turned to Michael Caputo, an old friend of mine and a friend of Trump's. Trump liked him, and I thought this would be helpful as we pushed aside the party malcontents who weren't lined up with Trump.

Caputo assembled a veteran team that included Carl Paladino, who had beaten the party in the last gubernatorial primary in 2014, and John Haggerty, who was viewed as the premier political operative in New York state. This team reassembled the 2014 Paladino County organization and when the dust cleared Trump had won eighty-nine of ninety-five delegates. Kasich won six delegates and Cruz was shut out.

Winning the New York primary on April 19 with almost 100 percent of the delegates completely surprised his opponents, the MSM, and the Republican political establishment. It also made Donald Trump a believer in the importance of what we were adding to his campaign. After New York, both the candidate and campaign organization were in sync and exceeding all of our marks in every state. For the first time, there was a convergence of the candidate and the campaign, working cohesively together toward a common objective.

When we met our benchmarks in New York, the media was shocked. No one expected those kinds of results. This both enhanced my credibility—and my vision for the campaign—and, more importantly, in the eyes of the media it undercut the credibility of the Cruz campaign, who had emerged by this point as our main opponent. Cruz was the only one with a real strategy taking advantage of the nomination process. He had a team of convention operatives who knew how to play the delegate game. Frankly, when it came to experienced delegate hunters, Cruz probably had a team equal to ours. However, being equal was not enough. We had a big advantage over his campaign. We had the better candidate.

After New York, I went on TV to build on the success. Using the polling data from Fabrizio, I was identifying, through my appearances, why we would win and how. Every time I did a talk show—I rotated between *Meet the Press*, CBS, ABC, and I was doing CNN a couple of times during the week—I put out the same message: if we continued to meet our delegate benchmarks, then by Indiana Trump would be the presumptive nominee.

I had never intended on being the face of the campaign organization. But I realized early on that there was nobody to do that job. The reason the organizational message was so important was that we would eventually need to get the structural support for Trump's candidacy from the party. They needed to see the nuts and bolts of it, not the politics. There was no one in the campaign who could fill that role. So, knowing it was a job that had to be done, I felt comfortable doing it. It wasn't going to be Lewandowski, who had never before been at a senior level of a national campaign, and it wasn't going to be Hope Hicks, who viewed her role as Trump's media assistant, not as a surrogate. My role lived in the shadow of Trump's media persona and targeted the inside players, not the voters. While secondary to his image, it was necessary.

While building all of the structure that focused on upcoming primaries and delegate selection, I had to, also, make sure that Trump's victories were not being stolen from him. I had to come in behind Trump with a structure and a strategy to protect what he won. To Trump, I was giving him what he wanted, but I was not the reason why he was winning. It was an important distinction to him, and it was one I was happy to make. I didn't want Lewandowski to be able to say that I was trying to take credit for Trump's wins. I didn't believe it was true, and I was not trying to look like it either.

But I knew Lewandowski was trying to protect his turf and would continue to undercut me in the process. Surprisingly to me, he did not seem to care when his self-interest would undercut what the candidate was doing.

The victory in New York on April 19 allowed me to go to Florida and attend the RNC's spring meeting the following week. This was where the RNC party structure would finalize many of the details for the nominating convention, which would be held in Cleveland on July 18. It was my introduction to the RNC as Trump's convention coordinator. Despite the victory in New York, the Party Establishment still did not consider Trump much more than a tepid front-runner. Thus, this meeting presented me with the opportunity to introduce the "inevitability" of Trump to the Party structure, and to let them know that Trump had an open door for all who had been involved in other campaigns.

This was relevant because Trump defined "draining the swamp" as getting rid of the Washington Establishment, which included both Democrats and Republicans. To him, getting rid of Hillary Clinton, Paul Ryan, and others was, by his definition of the swamp, part of his goal. Needless to say, the Republican establishment did not see things the same way. But, again, Trump's genius and his appeal to voters was precisely that *he did lump them all together*.

My goal in going to Florida was to start to pass these messages, informally. I wasn't speaking to the body. I would make an informal, closed-door presentation just for RNC members. Of course, there's no such thing as a closed-door meeting of one hundred and sixty Republican politicians, or any politician. I knew that whatever I said in that room would be in the media before I finished speaking. Which was fine. The message I was going to be pushing in the room was the message I was promoting on TV.

In the end, there were over two hundred people at the private meeting. Everyone who was invited showed up. No one wanted to miss it. I gave my presentation and opened it up for questions.

In response to a question of when Trump was going to stop criticizing Republicans, I made the point that during this phase of the campaign, Trump was running *against* Republicans for the nomination. I emphasized that the "swamp" that Trump was committed to changing included the Washington Establishment. While some in the crowd were uncomfortable with this statement, it was the truth, and I did not think I could or should try to downplay it.

"Well," they asked, "what does that mean for Republicans who support policies that aren't supported by Trump?"

I said Trump would emphasize the policies he supports. And it would be up to the people whose policies are different, as Republican officeholders, as to how they reconcile themselves with Trump. I explained: "It was Trump who was winning the nomination battle, he is the one who is putting himself out there. If the establishment leaders—senators or congressmen or party officials—have a different position on an issue, and they want it to be the position of the party, they need to run for president and win the nomination. Trump," I said, "is doing what he needs to do to build the direction of the party. And if he wins the nomination, that's what the party will stand for and that's what his administration will stand for."

It was my next point, however, that got me into trouble with my new boss. I said that after Trump became the presumptive nominee, he would be transitioning his focus to Clinton and the Democratic leadership in Washington. That was all I said. The media picked this up and began reporting, incorrectly, that I had said that I would get Trump to change his tone now that he is emerging as the nominee of the Republican Party.

Lewandowski, I found out later, had leaked this false message to the press before the meeting was even over. The *Associated Press* quickly ran a piece saying, "Trump's newly hired senior aide, Paul Manafort, made the case to Republican National Committee members that Trump has two personalities: one in private and one onstage."[2]

Trump, rightly, took great offense to the implication of this deliberate misstatement of my words. Unfortunately for me, the truth seemed like a very self-serving defense. Frustrating as this was, it gave birth to the "Let Trump Be Trump" era, which became a powerful narrative for the campaign. When Trump saw how well this narrative was working, I was able to get myself out of the bull's-eye that Lewandowski had put on me.

The national media ignored what I actually said because it was sexier to say that we were trying to change Trump. (This media tendency would grow even more intense during the Russian collusion hoax.) It appeared that I was making Trump look like every other politician—campaigning one way and serving another. The exact thing that Trump was promising to end if elected President.

In fact, I never wanted Trump to be anything but Trump. He had correctly figured out the angst the American people were suffering. He was articulating what everyday Americans were saying over their dinner tables. He was offering the forgotten Americans a voice and a champion. "Make America Great Again" was a call to arms by Trump, and the troops were the American people. But the Lewandowski lie had a real appeal to enemies of Donald Trump and they used the misstatement as a cudgel against Trump and, to Lewandowski's delight, me.

After the RNC meeting, it was important to pivot to the next phase of building the campaign structure. With the establishment's attention now firmly focused on Trump as the presumptive nominee, we needed to firm up his foreign policy credibility. Trump had a developed and deep understanding of foreign policy, and he knew where he had substantive disagreements with the Washington establishment. But, up to this point in the campaign, he only spoke of his vision in campaign terms. As he emerged as the presumptive nominee, we all felt like he had to make a substantive speech where we could put flesh on the bones of his philosophy.

This was a sensitive proposition. Trump's speeches up to that point were mostly outlines. He knew the subject matter but would speak off the cuff. That wouldn't cut it on foreign policy since he was on the doorstep of the presidency. Jared agreed to manage the process—everything from building the speech, to finding a location, to getting Trump to use a teleprompter. (Up until this speech, Trump had never used a teleprompter. It was a major undertaking to convince him of its necessity with a formal policy speech. In the end, he agreed, and from day one he looked like he had been using it his whole life—unlike Joe Biden who clearly can be seen reading the words on his teleprompter, including when the text says "stop for applause.")

Having Jared as a partner on this project was crucial. I didn't have to worry about getting undercut by Lewandowski. Lewandowski had worked so hard to keep the family outside in order to protect his turf. But it was a massive miscalculation on his part that ended up moving the family from what had been a skeptical but working relationship with Lewandowski to an increasingly unhappy one.

The speech also set the model for Jared's later work in the administration. He was always involved in Israel. It was important to him beyond politics. He's a very religious person, and he's very connected to the concept of a Jewish state. Anything I needed from Jared, however, had to be done before dusk on Friday, when he would disappear until Sunday morning. No matter how important the crisis was, he stuck to his religious practices. So, it was natural for him to engage on foreign policy issues that to a large extent related to the Middle East.

As we put the foreign policy speech structure together, we reached out to certain people who we felt might be helpful. One of them was Henry Kissinger, who gave us Dimitri Simes, president of the Center for the National Interest, a policy think tank created by Nixon in the 1990s.

At this time, Simes was the only foreign policy "expert" we had with any real expertise in foreign policy. We gave him the authority to build a foreign policy speech, which he did. We had our first practice reading of the draft speech with the teleprompter in the palatial ballroom at Trump's Manassas golf course on the Sunday morning before the speech. Trump was supposed to receive his copy of the speech the night before our practice session. Unfortunately while the speech was delivered to Trump Tower, it did not find its way to Trump. So when he showed up on Sunday morning, he had not read it.

Standing at the podium, having never used a teleprompter before, Trump started to read the speech from the paper. Then he started to edit it. After he'd gutted about 60 percent of the speech—not so much the substance as the style, which wasn't his—he handed it off to Stephen Miller, who was working with Simes. Initially, the speech was to be presented at the Washington Press Club, which had the formal ambiance we were trying to capture. But the attendance response was so overwhelming that the room wasn't going to be big enough to handle the press corps, never mind the ambassadors we wanted as staging for the event.

As we were running through the practice speech, the issue of the room at the Press Club came up and Trump, all of a sudden, in the middle of his practice, started to talk about the logistics of the speech. He was very happy to hear the room was too small.

"Well, he said, "this room could handle it. It would be great for my members. My members could sit in the audience. It's good for the club. It's good for me. It's a big enough room. It's a beautiful room. It looks out on the Potomac River."

I knew we couldn't have the first official policy speech at one of his clubs, which is thirty minutes outside of Washington. It would get very complicated. And it would look like a Trump Organization event. Meanwhile, Trump had called his club manager to open the folding doors expanding the ballroom. Now, instead of practicing the speech, Trump was directing the production, telling us where tables could go, where cameras could go, organizing an event, laying out where the press would sit, where his club members would sit, where the ambassadors would sit behind his members. Trump even focused on what kind of food the club could serve.

I had to laugh to myself—even as I was cringing—at the uniqueness of this candidate. *He does everything*, I thought. But I had to put a stop to it. I knew that the more he talked about it, the more likely it was that we would end up there. No one would pay attention to the speech. Everybody would be talking about how we had our first major foreign policy event at one of his golf courses.

Simes, meanwhile, was fuming that his speech had been gutted. I was worried we didn't have a speech at all anymore. We would have a great event at Manassas, but no speech. I called Jared and told him that we had to start over, and he said just have Miller do the speech. This became the first major speech that Stephen ever wrote for Donald Trump, a role he grew into over the next four years.

On Jared's advice, we got out of there and ended up finding the Mayflower Hotel, which is where on April 27, Trump gave his first major foreign policy speech: "Putting America First." Consistent with what he had been saying since he descended the escalator in Trump Tower, Trump called for a new foreign policy which was critical to his plan to rebuild the American economy.

"It's time to shake the rust off America's foreign policy. It's time to invite new voices and new visions into the fold, something we have to do. The direction I will outline today will also return us to a timeless principle. My foreign policy will always put the interests of the American people and American security above all else. It has to be first. Has to be."

"That," he said, "will be the foundation of every single decision that I will make. America First will be the major and overriding theme of my administration."

He went on: "No country has ever prospered that failed to put its own interests first. Both our friends and our enemies put their countries above ours and we, while being fair to them, must start doing the same. We will no longer surrender this country or its people to the false song of globalism. The nation-state remains the true foundation for happiness and harmony. I am skeptical of international unions that tie us up and bring America down.

"We have a massive trade deficit with China, a deficit that we have to find a way quickly, and I mean quickly, to balance. A strong and smart America is an America that will find a better friend in China, better than we have right now. Look at what China is doing in the South China Sea. They're not supposed to be doing it. No respect for this country or this president. We can both benefit or we can both go our separate ways. If need be, that's what's going to have to happen.

"The world is most peaceful and most prosperous when America is strongest. America will continue and continue forever to play the role of peacemaker. We will always help save lives and indeed humanity itself, but to play the role, we must make America strong again.

"And always—always, always, we must make, and we have to look at it from every angle, and we have no choice, we must make America respected again. We must make America truly wealthy again. And we must—we have to and we will make America great again. And if we do that—and if we do that, perhaps this century can be the most peaceful and prosperous the world has ever, ever known. Thank you very much, everybody. I appreciate it. Thank you."

It was a strong speech—a presidential speech. And Trump nailed it. After the speech we had a private reception for official Washington. Members of Congress, think tank leaders, Republican staffers all attended. Trump mingled easily and charmed most of them before he departed for his next political event in West Virginia. I could tell we pulled it off and I was thrilled by the response.

What I could not have known was that the event would come into my life again the following April. Because of the foreign policy topics, we had invited all of the Foreign Ambassadors to attend the speech. About half a dozen accepted, one of whom was the Russian Ambassador Sergey Kislyak. Senator Jeff Sessions, our Campaign National Advisory Committee Chairman, was also in attendance, and he spent a little time with all of the ambassadors. In 2017, Adam Schiff and the Democrats would point to this reception as a key moment in their Russian collusion conspiracy. This would have been laughable at any other time, but in the frenzied atmosphere of "hate" perpetuated by the Democrats, the media bought this hook, line, and sinker. The consequences, for me, would be severe.

But that was all in the future. By late April, we had a tremendous amount of momentum. Indiana was coming up on May 3. This was the primary, I had predicted to the MSM, that would make Trump the *presumptive nominee*. Indiana was a conservative state, and Cruz was favored. But I had a private poll from Fabrizio that told me that we were going to win that state by double digits. When I predicted Trump would win Indiana, the pundits paid attention. They thought we had made a major blunder and Cruz would capitalize on it, especially since they expected Indiana's conservative governor, Mike Pence, to endorse Cruz and turn over his organization to help Cruz win the primary.

Governor Chris Christie had a relationship with Mike Pence. Although Pence was viewed as a supporter of Cruz, he hadn't officially announced his support yet. I asked Christie, who had endorsed Trump after dropping out of the presidential contest in February and was now a surrogate for him, to set up a meeting between Trump and Pence where the purpose would be to get Pence to stay neutral, something I believed would remove Cruz's only chance for an upset. Christie set it up and the three of us flew to Indiana. Not surprising to me, Trump liked Pence. They agreed on a lot of the issues, which was very important to Pence, and when the meeting broke up Pence had privately agreed to not endorse Cruz.

The following week, Cruz got his own private poll in Indiana. He could see he was going to lose the primary. In desperation, Cruz put major pressure on Pence to endorse him, but Pence was reluctant. Pence's main financial supporters were the Ricketts family out of Chicago. They were also big Cruz supporters. Pence was looking at a close reelection campaign that November, and he needed the Ricketts to help him raise the money to run a very aggressive campaign. Knowing this, Cruz put the squeeze on Pence through the financial network. The Friday before the Tuesday Primary, Pence went on his regularly scheduled radio show. For five minutes, Pence talked about what a great guy Donald Trump was. He talked about all the issues that he and Trump agreed on, basically building Trump up to the sky. Then, he endorsed Cruz and ended the radio broadcast.

Trump called me immediately. "That was the best non-endorsement I ever got," he laughed. "But what's it going to do that he endorsed Cruz?"

"Nothing," I said. "Based on everything I am seeing, it's too late to help Cruz." This calmed Trump down and allowed him to enjoy the moment. Although he had endorsed Cruz, Pence had praised Trump in a way that the Cruz endorsement meant nothing. Trump enjoyed the absurdity of the situation.

Fabrizio's poll was right. Trump took every delegate in the Indiana primary. Trump was ecstatic, even praising Tony's polling. The strategy that we had laid out to him the month before, and the work that we had done in that month had allowed Trump to do what he wanted to do and keep the success that he had earned. Again, I made sure that he got all the credit. After all, he was the reason for his victories. My work only allowed him to keep the wins, not earn them. The new structure was invisible, except for the media I was doing—and the media now saw Trump as the presumptive nominee. All was good in the campaign.

Starting in mid-April, even before the Indiana primary, I had been meeting privately with Reince Priebus in Washington. First elected as Chairman of the Republican National Committee in January of 2013, Priebus had made it a key milestone of his tenure to build a more modern Republican Party. Having seen the Democrats and Obama use technology to gain competitive advantages that allowed them to raise more money, better target hidden voters, and organize the best ground game in American politics, Priebus committed his chairmanship to outdoing the Democrats in all three areas. I wanted Priebus to understand that once Trump was the presumptive nominee, he, as chairman of the RNC, needed to cooperate with us to bring the party along. Suffice it to say, the Party was not there yet. Trump was viewed as a truly insurgent candidate.

Before my first Priebus meeting, I sat down with Trump to make certain that he would not oppose this outreach on my part. I felt it important to do this because I was still feeling the sting of the Lewandowski-fabricated story that I was trying to change Trump.

Trump had nothing in Washington. Nobody knew him unless they had gone to New York for money. They knew of the *image* of Donald Trump—taking on Bush, taking on McCain, taking on the Pope—but there was no feeling in Washington for what kind of nominee he would be. Plus, none of them believed Trump could beat Hillary Clinton. To make things even more difficult for them, Trump was attacking Washington as an entity: Republicans, Democrats, think tanks, law firms, lobbyists. He never parsed the distinctions between all of these pieces. To him, it was easier to attack the establishment as a whole.

So, it became important to work with Priebus to build a road that Trump could get comfortable with reaching out to the establishment in Washington when the time came, without compromising his positions in the primaries. From the very beginning, I let Priebus know that I saw the general election as a collaboration between the Trump campaign and the RNC. I made it clear that if we worked together, I believed Trump would support us running a joint campaign. I valued how he had modernized the Party during his chairmanship and had built a technical infrastructure that was state of the art. I saw no reason why we should replicate it but first I needed his co-operation at this point in time in the nomination process to build the trust between Trump and official Republican Washington.

I explained to Priebus that if Trump didn't get the nomination after winning the primaries, the whole Party would blow up. Priebus would be a failed Chairman by virtue of not being able to hold the party together. I needed him to make sure there weren't any backroom deals being organized against Trump. And I wanted him to help me introduce Trump, to lay the groundwork for a successful convention.

Priebus's favorite candidate, Governor Scott Walker of Priebus's home state of Wisconsin, had fallen by the wayside so Priebus didn't have a particular horse in the race. He was letting the process decide around whom he would help galvanize the party. He appreciated my message to him, because it gave him a door to what he saw as the emerging winner.

None of this was being reported anywhere, but it was essential to start bringing the Republican establishment on board.

Trump authorized what I was doing, but he was still very wary about Washington and about the RNC. He was still running *against* them. Even though he was now emerging as the nominee of the party, he was basically campaigning as the leader of the campaign running against his own party. He felt the Party officials weren't for him. He understood that they may have to accept him because he was winning. But he didn't feel like there was anybody he could rely on. His instincts were not wrong. My job was now to bring that part of the party together. I knew that it was essential for a successful convention, and that was the hook I used.

But I also knew it was important for a successful general election campaign. We needed to have the RNC on board. Priebus was building a structure inside the RNC, both from a financial standpoint and from a grassroots standpoint. If we could work together, we would be able to run a large part of the general election from the RNC's digital media, advertising, and fundraising operations, rather than building those from inside the presidential campaign. I knew Trump would not be interested in building these roles into his official structure, and so the task of figuring out how to incorporate the RNC was a necessary job.

After we won Indiana, I called Priebus and said, "We are at that moment. And I need you now to start making phone calls to the RNC members. You need to start saying some positive things about Trump. I would like you to be talking about him being the presumptive nominee." He was hesitant at first, but the writing was on the wall. On May 4, 2016, he tweeted: "@realDonaldTrump will be presumptive @GOP nominee," effectively signaling to the Republican establishment that it was time to get on board with the Trump juggernaut.

CHAPTER 5

Keeping the Wins

With the Indiana primary behind us, the media finally began to get on board with the idea that Trump couldn't be stopped. This was welcome news—and proof that what we were doing was working—but it meant we needed to look further ahead into the future. I turned my attention to three things: the convention, the general election, and the RNC.

A small but significant part of the party was still made up of dedicated "Never-Trumpers," and it was essential that they not be allowed to gain momentum going into the convention. People like Mitt Romney, John Kasich, and Ted Cruz were promoting the idea of trying to nominate somebody else on the second ballot.

Romney hoped it was a way for him to use a backdoor into the nomination, which really angered Trump. When Romney had needed Trump's endorsement in 2012, even though Trump thought Romney was weak, he had endorsed him. And while he didn't expect Romney to be out there as a strong advocate, Trump saw Romney now as a traitor of the highest order. Romney was one of the former nominees of the Party; he understood the importance of folding your tent after you've lost and rallying behind the winner. Later, when Romney ended up voting for Trump's impeachment in 2020, it rankled Trump like very few things could. But it also proved Trump's point: that establishment types—and Romney was the epitome of them—only care about themselves. They didn't really care about the Party. It was this hypocrisy which Trump had seen in the system, and which caused him to run in the first place.

In this uncertain atmosphere, Reince Priebus would be *the critical link* to Washington. Priebus understood that if Trump won the White House, his chairmanship of the party would go down as one of the greatest in Party history. With this in mind, Priebus, despite the tensions between Trump the outsider and the insiders in Washington, came around to fervently supporting Trump, which opened the doors for us at the RNC and to its valuable fundraising operation—the Victory Fund.

A legal mechanism authorized by the election laws, the Victory Fund allowed the party to raise money in amounts that exceeded individual limitations to the candidate's campaign. The fund was not just for presidential campaigns, but for all party operations. So RNC members viewed the Victory Fund as something that they had an equal right to. This fact alone ensured that it would take quite a bit of negotiating to hammer out the details of a joint arrangement between Trump and the RNC.

Additionally, Priebus had spent years building up local field organization expertise, and at our first session on the Victory Fund, I told him I didn't want to recreate the wheel. We would build on what he had in place. I indicated that the Trump campaign needed to have control at the top, but that we would share decision-making in all states.

The one commitment I required, however, was that the people that we put in place had to be publicly and actively *for* Trump. It was critical that the joint operation with Trump be managed by solid Trump people. I also knew this was non-negotiable to Trump.

Lewandowski was taking the exact opposite approach. If he couldn't control it, he wanted to blow it up. I understood that his approach had a kind of appeal to Trump, as he had been campaigning against all these people. And because even in this moment of victory after Indiana, Trump still could feel the resistance within the Party.

Lewandowski played this up, saying we had to have total control. He was trying to have his person, possibly even himself, installed in the RNC as the deputy chairman, or to elect a national chairman. I knew this would not be good for Trump. And that although it might appeal to Trump's tendency to take control of something after he had won the right to have control of it, I knew that it wouldn't be in his best interest in a general election. Priebus had a huge amount of institutional knowledge, he had too much personal support at the state levels with the committee members, and he had an organization that Trump needed to tap into. The last thing I wanted to do was to replace Priebus. Using Lewandowski's aggressiveness as a tool, I urged Priebus to make the necessary concessions before it was too late and things got out of control.

The tactic worked. Our General Counsel Don McGahn, who was an encyclopedia on what we could structure within the FEC laws and in the best interest of the campaign, did incredible work in record time. He negotiated a framework that allowed the campaign to use the victory fund mechanism to build out the organizations for the Trump campaign in all of our targeted states. This structure kept all of our people active in their states, factored in the professional team that Priebus had built in the states, and allocated the full budgets we needed in the battleground states to build aggressive field organizations and voter contact operations.

One of the many false narratives of the 2016 campaign that the Democrats and the Clinton campaign put out—and that the media accepted—was that on election day they had the better ground game of the two parties. In fact, they didn't. And we knew they didn't. Thanks to the alliance formed early on with Priebus and the RNC, Donald Trump had a world class organization and a much better ground game.

It was important for the campaign to have a point guy inside of the RNC who we could trust and who was trusted by the RNC types. Fortuitously, we had such a person. Rick Wiley had come from the RNC world, had been the campaign manager for Governor Walker's presidential campaign, had been Trump's political director after I came on board, and now was back at the RNC. Wiley had excellent political skills, knew everyone in the RNC system, and most importantly understood the role the RNC needed to play working in concert with the Trump campaign. When Trump signed off on Wiley being the liaison, we had the structure needed to manage the joint operations in the general election.

By the second week of June, the campaign was humming. On May 26, Trump had passed the threshold of delegates required to guarantee his nomination. The final primary races were held on June 7 in California, Montana, New Jersey, New Mexico, and South Dakota. All told, Trump shattered the all-time record for votes in the Republican primaries.

On June 9, I had an important meeting scheduled with Priebus to discuss the convention, which was now a little over a month away. He was nervous because there was no convention program yet. I wasn't particularly worried because I knew Trump wanted to have a different kind of convention. But it was going to be a lot of work, so I wanted to meet with Priebus while he was in New York to discuss the details.

Before the Priebus meeting, however, I had agreed to sit in on another meeting at Don Jr.'s request. It registered—if it registered at all—as fairly insignificant at the time, though this would turn out to be very far from the case. Don Jr. had received a message from a man named Rob Goldstone, a publicist who knew the Trump family from the Miss Universe contest in Moscow. Goldstone said that one of his clients, Emin Agalarov, a singer and the son of a wealthy Azerbaijani real estate developer in Moscow, had information that "would incriminate Hillary and her dealings with Russia." Given the reputation of the Clinton Foundation for doing shady deals, as laid out in Peter Schweizer's *New York Times* best-selling book *Clinton Cash: The Untold Story of How and Why Foreign Governments and Businesses Helped Make Bill and Hillary Rich,* the Goldstone conversation rang true enough to Don Jr. that a meeting was agreed to.

Don Jr. asked me if I could attend the meeting and I said yes. I told him these kinds of things never pan out, so don't get too excited. I had a full day of meetings, but I was going to be in New York, so I said I would be there.

The meeting took place in the conference room on the twenty-fifth floor of Trump Tower. I walked in just as everybody was taking their seats. Don was sitting on the side of the table closest to the door. Jared was on the exact opposite end of it. On one side were a bunch of men that looked as though they were straight out of the Georgian mafia and on the other side was a woman. I decided to walk to the other side and sit next to Jared so that it was clear to the visitors that Don was the leader of the meeting.

We opened up with introductions. Goldstone was there, of course. He introduced a Russian-American named Rinat Akhmetshin, a Georgian-American, Ike Kaveladze, and a translator, Anatoli Samochornov, who barely spoke English. Finally, he introduced the lawyer, Natalia Veselnitskaya, who spoke English but said she would conduct her presentation in Russian. Her pitch to us—rendered in broken English by the translator—never mentioned Clinton. Instead, she was there to let us know that if Trump would endorse a repeal of the Magnitsky Act, this would be looked upon favorably and it could lead to a relaxation of the restrictions relating to Americans adopting Russian babies.

The Magnitsky Act was signed into law by Obama in 2012. Named after Russian tax lawyer Sergei Magnitsky, who died in a Moscow prison from Putin's brutality, the US law was adopted to punish Putin for a number of human rights violations. Among the penalties, the Act authorized the US government to sanction a broad range of Russian oligarchs who were close to Putin. In retaliation, Putin instituted a ban on the adoption of Russian children by Americans.

I was aware of the Magnitsky Act and the ban, but it became clear to me within minutes after Veselnitskaya began talking that the meeting was a waste of time. Normally in a meeting I take notes on my computer, but the meeting seemed so insignificant that I didn't bring my laptop with me. Instead, I took a few notes on my phone.

Jared, by this point, had texted his assistant to text him and get him out of the meeting. He got up to leave. After a few more minutes, Don and I looked at each other, Don looked at the visitors, who had nothing else to say, thanked them, and adjourned the meeting. The whole meeting lasted about twenty minutes. No one ever discussed Hillary Clinton.

I promptly forgot about the meeting. It emerged later on that the lawyer, Natalia Veselnitskaya, was active with Chris Steele and had met with Glenn Simpson of Fusion GPS, the firm hired by the Clinton campaign to do opposition research on Trump, both the day before and the day after the meeting at Trump Tower. This was discovered in the course of the Mueller investigation, along with the fact that Veselnitskaya and Simpson lied about what they had talked about.

For some reason, the Mueller prosecutors saw the meeting as a significant sign of the Trump campaign reaching out to Russia to help his campaign. They showed zero interest in the fact that the "Russian" who was the link to Putin had met with the dirty tricks team the Clintons had hired to create evidence of "Russian collusion." And even after these links between Veselnitskaya, Steele, and Glenn Simpson were uncovered, the MSM ignored them. Clearly, this was a setup by the Clinton campaign to trap the Trump team. And just like the Steele dossier, the black ledger, Stefan Halper's outreach to entrap George Papadopoulos, it failed. Why? Because the allegations were false. But as the Durham investigation is beginning to uncover in the cases it is bringing in 2022, the dots do connect to a conspiracy to collude with Russia. Except the dots connect the Clinton campaign, not the Trump campaign, to the collusion and the violations.

It is noteworthy, and symptomatic of the hypocrisy of Washington, MSM, and the Democratic Party, that in fact, in April of 2022, the FEC fined both the Clinton campaign and the DNC for illegally not disclosing its millions of dollars of payments to Perkins, Coie to conduct campaign research through Fusion GPS and Christopher Steele. No one in the media or Washington Democratic establishment seemed to care and it was a one-day story, even though it was the exact behavior the media had spent four years attacking Trump on, behavior that Trump did not commit.

I didn't see it at the time, but the Trump Tower meeting—soon to become a key moment in the fake Russian collusion narrative—was clearly a setup by the Clinton campaign, not by the Russians. It was set up to get us, but the Russians were so clueless they only focused on lobbying the campaign to be against the Magnitsky act.

No one in the campaign followed up on the meeting, or even discussed it. Trump was never aware it had occurred, and the campaign never opposed the Magnitsky Act. Yet, to this day, this meeting has an outsized place in all of the Democrat-driven fake Russian collusion narratives.

By the middle of June, the relationship with Lewandowski had deteriorated well beyond repair.

I didn't know Lewandowski when I got involved with the Trump campaign. I had to do a lot of research because almost no one knew him. He was a small-time operator. He became Campaign Manager almost by default. When Trump was looking for a campaign manager, he asked Roger Stone to assemble a list. Unfortunately, all the people Trump and Stone wanted were taken. Because the New Hampshire primary was one of the early state primaries, and Lewandowski was from New Hampshire and had done some work with Koch Industries, which made him sound important, he moved to the top of a very short list. He wanted the job and he got it by default.

But Lewandowski was never really the campaign manager. He was the guy who ran the plane. Trump made all the decisions. Trump was a one man show. In retrospect, of course, it had to be like that. No one with conventional campaign experience would have lasted. I probably wouldn't have survived if I had joined earlier. Trump had the vision, and he was going to do it his way. He didn't need someone with a lot of experience telling him how he was *supposed* to run *his* campaign. Trump needed a guy like Lewandowski who could take care of the bureaucratic details without getting in Trump's way.

But in June, Lewandowski had become a liability and even if Trump couldn't see it yet, I could. Around this time, I went to Trump to talk about setting up a mechanism to begin the process of selecting vice presidential candidates. I brought Lewandowski with me, even though I knew I couldn't trust him. I was still making an effort to work with him. After Trump asked for ideas on how to organize the selection process, I explained how the selection process could work, and that we would need to bring someone on board who could work with us to manage the process and vet the potential candidates. It was a complicated and delicate process. Trump didn't have any VP candidates in mind yet and there were a great many angles to consider when choosing one.

Lewandowski took great exception to this process. He wanted to be the one sitting at the table telling Trump who we should select. He had no thoughts about having a structure that was substantive and could deal with the vetting process in a professional way. He didn't like the fact that he had to share that authority as campaign manager with some third person.

One day Michael Cohen, Trump's personal attorney, came to me and said, "I've got the master code for the campaign server." Cohen had struck me as someone who craved Trump's approval, the kind of guy who would hang around to try to make something out of hanging around. He was never central to anything. But to make himself more important, he had taken control of the administrator's role for the server of the campaign. He had access to everybody's communications. He had knowledge and he would be sitting in his office, gaining knowledge by virtue of spying on the campaign.

I had a Trump campaign email address, which I used for general communications, but I kept all of my sensitive work on a different company's server. Beyond my communications, Cohen could see everything everyone was saying. He said, "Corey is undercutting you with the media. I see the emails he sends out." He asked if I wanted to see the emails, but I said no. I didn't need to see them. I had long suspected what was going on and Cohen's comments to me only confirmed what I knew already: that Lewandowski was hurting me and in the process hurting the campaign.

I sat with Lewandowski at this point, and I said, "Look, Corey, Trump can win this election. When he wins this thing, you're going to be in a very strong position as the campaign manager. So don't fight me. I'm not trying to eclipse you. You're going to be the campaign manager of a successful nomination. You're uniquely positioned. I'm talking to the same people you are. They're calling me after you call them. I know what you're doing. You don't need to look at me as competition. Ride the success, be on a plane with the candidate, do the things you're doing with it, and ride the success."

He said, "Of course, Paul. Of course. That's what we're going to do." But then he immediately went out and leaked something to the press about me. It finally got to the point where we had to have a session with Trump, who said he didn't want to break up the team. He liked the way everything was working. At the meeting, we agreed, again, on what the rules were for the two of us, what my responsibilities were, and what his responsibilities were.

Unsurprisingly, Lewandowski was breaking the rules again within a couple of days.

Something had to give, so I finally sat down with the family to talk about the situation. They could see what was going on, but more importantly, they knew Lewandowski didn't have the experience to do what needed to be done in the general election. They brought the issue to Trump. As much as he appreciated having competing voices on the team, Trump understood structure. He understood organization. He saw where we were and where we were going. He understood the value that I was bringing, and he understood the value Lewandowski had brought to the first part of the campaign. But he saw, clearly, that Lewandowski was now damaging the organization. So, he fully agreed with the family's assessment that it was time for Lewandowski to go.

Don Jr. met with Lewandowski the next day, June 20. He must have known something was coming, but I don't think he believed he would be fired. As soon as he was fired, his access was shut off and he was escorted from the building by security. No one trusted him at that point. The *New York Times* reported that Lewandowski "was often at odds with Mr. Manafort, who was brought on in March when the candidate seemed poised for a lengthy fight over Republican delegates," and that Lewandowski "was said to have resisted certain moves that would have increased the number of staff members, at times blocking Mr. Manafort from making hires or later undoing them. But the people briefed on Mr. Lewandowski's departure said the circumstances went well beyond any one episode or relationship. One stressed that the move had been in the works for many weeks, particularly since it had become clear that Mr. Trump would be the Republican nominee."[1]

At this point, Lewandowski did a very smart thing. He went on CNN that afternoon and praised Trump. "What I know is what we've been able to achieve in this election has been historic," he said. "[Trump] fundamentally changed the way people look at politics. And I'm proud to have been a small part of that. The voters have a binary decision coming up on election day. They can either vote for Hillary Clinton and her liberal policies or they can put someone in place who is going to change Washington. And I will do everything I can to make sure the latter of those two happens. Which means Donald Trump is elected president. If I can do that from inside the campaign, it's a privilege. If I can do that from outside the campaign, it's also a privilege."[2]

By saying this, he was able to preserve his role in the organization from the outside.

CHAPTER 6

Running Mates

With Lewandowski out of the picture, I was finally able to focus all of my attention on the tasks at hand. And the tasks were numerous and challenging. There was the vice-presidential selection, which was ongoing. There was a rapprochement with the Republican structure in Washington. Along with the RNC, we were building local organizations in fifty states. Tony Fabrizio and I were constructing a polling data strategy, which we'd need going into the general election. Brad Parscale was organizing a digital media plan that would be a critical reason for Trump's victory in November. And on top of everything, there was the convention, which, with a candidate like Trump, would have to be unlike any convention in history.

Trump had made it clear early on that he wanted a different kind of convention. He didn't want officeholders on TV. He didn't want to have people who had been against him in the primary race now having their moment in the sun at *his* convention. It was unusual, but it made sense to me. I understood Trump's mentality and it fit with his candidacy, which was always positioned against the swamp in Washington. It wouldn't make sense to have people from the establishment saying nice things about Trump on TV. He thought it would be boring, traditional, and dishonest. Once again, he was 100 percent correct.

He wanted a more interesting convention. He wanted to have people from the business world, people like Peter Thiel and Tom Barrack.

And he wanted his family front and center. I agreed with this whole-heartedly. The family knew him best, they were incredibly articulate, and they could each present a different side to Trump's personality, which would soften his image and attract voters who would, for the first time, be thinking about Donald Trump as President Trump.

The two most important moments for a candidate are when he announces his candidacy and when he's nominated. The difference is that at the announcement, very few Americans are paying attention, and for the nomination speech, everyone is. The convention is the moment to introduce the candidate in a way that summarizes who he is, and what the issues are going to be in the general election.

Over the last twenty years, the networks' nightly coverage of con-ventions had shrunk to about an hour or less, usually from ten o'clock to eleven o'clock. We began to build a framework where the nine-to-eleven hour would be composed of two groups: the family and Americans who represented the themes of the convention and the campaign: gold star families, people from the border, veterans who could speak on Libya and Afghanistan. Trump liked it.

I wasn't worried about the structure of the convention. But we needed somebody to manage the construction of the program and the details—the minutiae of it. It's an enormous undertaking that requires not just managing the speakers, but managing what they say, having the mechanics of getting what they say into the themes we want, massaging the egos, and getting it all to work on live TV, etc. Running a convention is a staggering amount of work that takes a great deal of experience.

A skilled program director is essential. The person I wanted was a veteran convention manager Bill Greener. Greener was the consummate Republican operative for this function. He was an expert who had spent years running the programs of national conventions in various roles and capacities. He and I had worked together on Bob Dole's convention, and I had been very impressed.

There was one small detail, however, that complicated the appoint-ment. In 2015, Greener had written an op-ed for *Inside Sources* that was not positive about Trump. (The headline: "Opinion: Donald Trump Is a Disaster."[1]) After meeting with Greener, I was comfortable that he was not only supportive of Trump but working to smooth over issues to help others come on board. While I had been slow in putting Greener in position until I felt comfortable that others saw Bill working publicly for

Trump, it was now or never. The meeting I had had with Priebus on June 9 was to discuss this issue. I had told Greener to get support from the RNC and we would find a way to put him in position. Once he had the RNC's support, Priebus and I met in Trump Tower to agree to recommend him to Trump. I then left Priebus and went to Trump, who agreed to hire Greener on Priebus's and my recommendation.

This was by far the most important issue that Trump was briefed on that day. Not the meeting with the Russians, but the fact that we now had a structure to run the convention the way Trump wanted it run.

The convention was set to begin on July 18, now a few weeks away.

As the convention approached, we still had not really bonded with the Congressional Republicans. It was decided that Trump needed to go to Capitol Hill. Three meetings set up for July 7: a meeting with House Republican leadership and Republican caucus, a meeting with all Republican Senators, and a meeting with Ted Cruz to negotiate his speaking at the convention.

The House meeting was very positive. The members were impressed by the beating down that Trump had inflicted on them. They recognize dominance and Trump had dominated them. With the members seated, Paul Ryan introduced Trump, Trump made his remarks, and then he opened the room for a Q&A. Trump is very good at these types of meetings. He makes everybody feel important. He's always very inclusionary. He answers every question on every issue. He took a few tough questions and handled them perfectly.

On the Senate side, I knew there would be tension in the room. Trump had been fighting with Ben Sasse and Jeff Flake. They were not important senators to his campaign, but they were part of Majority Leader Mitch McConnell's base. And Trump and McConnell were polar opposites. Trump was the consummate outsider to McConnell's "Mr. Insider of the Beltway" persona. On the way over, I reminded Trump that this meeting was going to be a bit more complicated than the last one. Already in Trump's mind, the Senate was a bastion of anti-Trumpism, and when we walked into the room, I could tell Trump was uncomfortable.

McConnell introduced Trump with a tepid endorsement. Trump used the clearly weak introduction to sarcastically suggest that this was the nicest thing McConnell had said about him to date. Then, he said he was looking forward to working with *almost* everybody in the room. For the first five minutes, Trump essentially let everyone know he expected them to work with him. The tone was very different from the earlier meeting. We got through it, but the feeling in the room was: Why did Trump attack McConnell and Sasse? While it was obvious to me why Trump defended himself in the room, it highlighted how far the divide was between our campaign and the den of Never Trumpers. Over time, the senators would have no problem answering their own question.

As challenging as the Senate meeting was, the Cruz meeting would be even more difficult. Typically, the losing Republican candidates for president have a spot at the convention podium. But there had been too many candidates, and most were part of the Establishment. Trump didn't want them speaking at the convention, taking up time. They'd been on the record opposing him during the primaries, and the media would highlight that. It would detract from the substance of what Trump wanted to communicate to the American people *at his convention*.

Cruz, on the other hand, was the "last man standing." There was a reason to allow him to be the only candidate to speak. Additionally, he was important to what we were trying to do to bring the party together. We told him that if he endorsed Trump before the convention, we would give him a speaking role.

Attending the meeting were Trump, Cruz, Jeff Roe, Cruz's campaign manager, Rick Dearborn, our Washington coordinator with the Congress, and me. Starting off the meeting, Trump made it clear that he held no animosity towards Cruz and wanted to work with him, but he also made it clear that Cruz needed to come on board now. Cruz vacillated.

Cruz started out by saying he would work with Trump, he would campaign for him, but that he wouldn't endorse him because his supporters didn't want him to. It was a forced justification for someone who is normally very logical. Trump didn't buy it. But, on his own initiative, Trump did apologize for saying some of the things he said about Cruz, which was unusual for Trump. He told Cruz he considered him an ally, not an enemy, and that he believed they could work together when Trump was president. Cruz did not have the same feelings at this stage. I looked to his campaign manager, Jeff Roe, who clearly was avoiding getting into the discussion.

After about twenty-five minutes and endless verbal jousting, Trump said we would send the language we wanted Cruz to say, and if Cruz could say it, he could speak at the convention, and if not, he would not be able to speak. As we were walking out of the room, I pulled Roe aside and asked him to call me later that day. It took me three days to reconnect with him; he was definitely avoiding me. The reason he was hesitant to talk was because he knew that Cruz had no intention of endorsing Trump and Roe wanted to completely avoid any role in the process.

When the meeting broke up, Trump turned to me and said, "I can work with Cruz, but he has to get on board. Make certain he knows there is no spot for him at the convention if he doesn't endorse me."

We now had eleven days to the convention. The Cruz situation was a real problem, but there was a bigger issue: we still needed a running mate.

I knew from experience that the most important thing in the vice-presidential selection process is that there's no negative reaction to the selection. The selection process of Dan Quayle by George H. W. Bush and Sarah Palin by John McCain were two glaring examples of how not to manage a VP selection process. While voters do not elect presidents based on who is selected as the running mate, the wrong pick can choke a campaign and create negative media coverage at the very time a candidate is being presented to the entire nation as one of two people to be the next president.

In Trump's case, I thought there was an excellent opportunity, with the *right* pick, to enhance Trump's judgment as a president. It was going to be very important that Trump have a vice president who was 100 percent loyal, but who had political experience and an ability to work Capitol Hill. By the same token, the worst choice would be someone who viewed herself or himself as an equal to Trump. That would blow up in a matter of days.

In preparation for the first meeting I had with Trump to discuss the vice presidency, I had called an old friend, A. B. Culvahouse, an attorney who had run the vice-presidential selection process in 2008 for McCain and had been involved in 2012. Culvahouse was very experienced in the technical vetting process. Other than the politics, the most important part of the vetting process is dealing with everything you never read about—the financials, the rumors, the skeletons in the closet.

Culvahouse said something to me that was very prophetic. He said, at the end of the process, what the candidate usually sees is all the negatives of the selection list. They're always looking for something different, something that's not on the final list of candidates. And that's how you get the Sarah Palins of this world—people who pop up out of nowhere. Going with the last-minute name is very dangerous.

That was one of my concerns as we sat with Trump and explained the process to him. "I need a list," he said. We sat together, and he began popping off names. From that session, we created a list of twenty candidates. Some were never going to be serious candidates, but many were. Pence's name was not on that first list.

From that initial list, we agreed that Lewandowski, who was still on the campaign at this time, and I would both come up with more names to add and then Trump would narrow it down to about ten names. We would then vet the ten, narrow them to five, and then look very carefully into whoever was left. I added Pence's name to the next list. Lewandowski was strongly promoting Richard Burr, the Senator from North Carolina, who went on to vote to impeach Trump in 2020.

At one point, Trump suggested Condoleezza Rice, the former Secretary of State. Rice was, in many respects, part of the Bush family. And Trump had spent much of the campaign fighting Jeb Bush. I said I didn't know if she would be interested, but if he was serious, I'd look into it. He said that he was. Trump believed she had "gravitas" and would bring together foreign policy and government experience to his administration. She would help with the phony racial attacks and the media would see her as very credible. In the back of my mind, I was wondering if she'd ever be able to work with Trump, but his head was in the right place.

I called Culvahouse and brought up Rice. As it turned out, she was one of his clients. He was very close to her. I said, "I don't want to embarrass her, and I don't want to embarrass Trump, but if you could informally approach her . . ."

Culvahouse reached out and Rice thought about it, but in the end, she wasn't interested. She was focusing on a different career at that point. But it showed me just how good Trump's instincts were. He understood the country; he was thinking very strategically.

After Lewandowski was gone, we narrowed the list to five names: Governor Chris Christie of New Jersey, Joni Ernst, a first term Senator from Iowa, Bob Corker the Chairman of the Senate Foreign Relations Committee, former Speaker of the House Newt Gingrich, and Indiana

Governor Mike Pence. Corker was the outlier, but he brought foreign policy expertise and Tennessee was still viewed as up for grabs at that point.

Chris Christie was very close to Trump. He had been the first to endorse Trump after dropping out of the presidential primary campaign. Gingrich was doing everything he could for Trump and Trump valued his opinion. Ernst was new as a senator, but she had been successful in the military, and was elected in a target state—Iowa—that we viewed as up for grabs. Pence checked the conservative box and the congressional box, having managed the budget process as part of the Republican leadership in the House. He was popular with the Christian constituency, and he brought significant governance experience. As governor of Indiana, his record and the issues that he was dealing with were almost the same issues that Trump was emphasizing. He was well thought of in Washington. He was well thought of as governor. He was assertive and strong, but he was not going to be challenging the president.

Pence and Ernst were the only two with personalities that I thought could work with Trump's. I didn't see Corker in that role. I knew Gingrich and Christie would argue regularly with Trump on everything. In the end, the shortlist was narrowed down to Pence, Christie, and Gingrich. Trump knew Christie and Gingrich, but he didn't know Pence outside of the one meeting we'd had with him about his endorsement of Cruz. Culvahouse began to compile information and I made sure the family saw it. I knew they would be instrumental in Trump's final choice.

The goal was to have a decision made around Fourth of July, which would leave us two weeks before the convention. But by the beginning of July, we still didn't have a decision. Trump met with Pence and his wife on July 2 at Bedminster, and Trump came away feeling good about him as a potential vice president, but was still undecided.

When we had not come to a decision by the Fourth, I knew we had to force one. Trump asked for one more round of meetings with the final three.

Christie's biggest problem was his relationship to Jared. As a US attorney, Christie had prosecuted Jared's father and put him in jail. There was no way Jared wanted the person who put his father in jail to be the vice president and potentially the next president of the United States. Trump decided that the best way forward was to air the issue. He called a meeting with Jared and Christie, which I attended. Ivanka was in the room for part of it, but she left. Trump started off by saying, "Well, I'm not going to say anything, but let's put it all on the table, and after it's done, it's over. We're not going to have this conversation anymore."

Normally, when somebody says that, both sides might go to the sidelines. Not at this meeting. They both got into it very aggressively. I knew right there it wouldn't work with Christie. Jared was never going to forget. It was one of the most uncomfortable meetings I have ever sat through. And it was one of the few meetings I ever attended where Trump's door was shut and stayed shut. I think it was clear to Trump, too, from that meeting that Christie could not be the vice-presidential candidate.

Gingrich brought a good amount of issue knowledge and experience to the table and obviously he knew how to maneuver around Congress. But he was as polarizing a character as Trump. Nevertheless, Trump trusted Gingrich, and he appreciated that Newt had been there for Trump in critical moments in the nomination process.

In his summary briefing of the final candidates, Culvahouse said Gingrich was trying to figure out how he can have his wife handle some of his current business if he was selected to be the VP. "I told him that he was going to have to disassociate himself from all that. It's an issue Trump will have to talk to Gingrich about." I think Gingrich understood this, but his head hadn't cleared as to how he was going to manage it. In the second week of July, Gingrich reached out and said he wanted to have one more meeting with Trump.

Trump had a campaign stop to make, so we flew Trump to see Pence in Indiana and Gingrich was going to see Trump the next day in New York. Trump was then going to make a decision the following Monday or Tuesday. We were now a week out from the convention.

Trump and his son Eric met Pence in Indiana. The meeting went well, but when Trump was about to leave for New York, the plane had an issue and couldn't take off. We found out it couldn't be fixed that day, so we made the decision to stay overnight in Indianapolis. The media was convinced that this was a sign that we were going to announce Pence as the VP in the morning. In fact, no decision had been made yet. All three—Christie, Pence, and Gingrich—were technically still in the running. Trump then said he wanted the family to meet with Pence, so we flew them in.

First thing the next morning, we had breakfast in the governor's mansion—Trump, the family, and Pence. It was a great meeting. Meanwhile, Gingrich decided that, due to the delay, he wouldn't be able to meet us in New York. Instead, he would fly to Indiana and meet Trump there.

At around eleven o'clock, we met with Gingrich. Trump was very comfortable at this point in time with the idea of Pence as VP. Christie's chances were dwindling because of Jared. But Trump really liked Gingrich. Gingrich started off the meeting by saying, "Look, I want to be on the inside." We could all see where he was going, that he was going to take himself out of consideration. Trump interrupted him and said, "You are part of the kitchen cabinet. You're going to be there every day. I want you. I need you."

After that, the meeting, including Gingrich, focused on how we were going to announce Pence. In Gingrich's mind, and in Trump's, Pence was the best candidate.

It was on me to call Christie and tell him. He didn't want to believe it. Especially when we had to postpone the announcement by a day due to a terrorist attack in Nice, France, which led both Christie and the media to speculate that we were going to choose Pence but were now reassessing.

The *New York Times* breathlessly—and falsely—reported that "late into the evening, Mr. Trump repeatedly hesitated over selecting Mr. Pence, according to people briefed on the tense deliberations, who insisted on anonymity to describe the confidential talks. Even as his emissaries reassured Mr. Pence, Mr. Trump considered a last-ditch appeal from Christie who once again pressed his own case."[2]

Trump called me and said, "Where is this coming from? I don't have any second thoughts."

I explained to him that this was normal rumor mill behavior at the end of the process, but that we had run out of time. We had to get the announcement out there immediately.

The next morning, on July 15, Trump tweeted, on his own initiative: "I am pleased to announce that I have chosen Governor Mike Pence as my Vice-Presidential running mate." Not the conventional way, but not the conventional nominee for President. Once again, Donald Trump made history and announced his choice "his way"!

The convention was three days away.

CHAPTER 7

"Collusion"

The Republican convention marks the end of the nominating phase of a campaign, but it also functions as the beginning of the general election. As we assembled in Cleveland, the once threadbare campaign organization was now a full-fledged national juggernaut. The synchronization with the RNC, the fifty state parties, the conservative grassroots groups, and the Christian right was complete. It took a great deal of time and effort, but Priebus wanted a winner, the state party operations wanted to return to the White House, and conservative groups worried about the Supreme Court, guns, and abortion. Above this entire network stood the most unconventional nominee in the history of the Republican Party, Donald J. Trump. This was now his party and his movement.

Not only had Trump triumphed, but he had done it his way. He had not compromised the core of his message. He had proudly attacked the Establishment, Democrat and Republican alike. Just four years earlier, the standard bearers of the party—people like Mitt Romney and Paul Ryan—were the epitome of the Establishment. In Cleveland they would remain on the sidelines with no role while Trump took center stage.

The national conventions are the responsibility of the Republican National Committee. It is their show even though the convention technically nominates the new head of the Party, its presidential candidate. Trump respected this distinction, but everyone understood that this was going to be *The Trump Show*.

The week before a national convention formally kicks off, the Convention Committees meet to do the technical work of the convention. One of those committees is the Platform Committee.

The party platform that we introduced at the 2016 convention was a decidedly Trump platform. Generally speaking, the draft platform document is submitted by the RNC platform committee to the convention platform committee, and they can then do whatever they want with it. They can change it, amend it, or totally throw it out. Generally, they usually only amend it on the margins based on the current issues of the day. That is what happened in 2016.

The platform is broken into sections—national security, the environment, economics—and then subsections of the committee debate and deal with those issues. They present to the full committee, the full committee presents to the convention, and the convention adopts the platform. This used to be a more important part of the process, but now conventions mostly do what the nominee wants. If they get elected president, they do what they want regardless of what the platform says.

The biggest goal of the platform hearings is to ensure that there is nothing that could create a negative media story that could affect the general elections.

In order to manage the deliberations and keep issues from getting out of control, we set up a pyramid whip political structure. I placed Rick Dearborn in charge of the overall platform deliberations. Rick was Senator Sessions's Chief of Staff and was the senior Chief of Staff of all Republican Senators. So, he brought experience, gravitas, and knowledge to the role. Under Rick's direction each committee was assigned a political organization of key Trump and RNC political organizers. Their job was to make certain that nothing was amended that was anti-Trump or could cause a problem in the general election.

During the Russian collusion investigations, an issue emerged on the language in one of the foreign policy subcommittees. A Cruz delegate from Texas did not think the language on Russia and Ukraine was strong enough. The issue was that Obama was refusing to give lethal assistance to Ukraine in its fight with Russia in Eastern Ukraine. Trump's position was that we needed to give lethal aid to Ukraine—blankets weren't going to cut it. Obama had not been giving weapons and Trump believed we needed to. This was, of course, an *anti*-Russian position.

In the bizzarro world of the MSM and the Mueller team, they saw the platform events as proof of Trump being pro-Russia, not tougher on Russia than Obama.

The Cruz delegate decided that that the platform draft language saying the US should give "appropriate" assistance to Ukraine wasn't strong enough. She wanted "lethal" assistance. The issue bubbled up to the convention platform manager, Rick Dearborn, who managed the people who were in charge of the subcommittees.

The platform committee political management structure was a pyramid. On behalf of the campaign, Dearborn was asked the Trump position. Dearborn decided that the language did not have to be amended, especially by a Cruz delegate. His rationale was that once you start amending every small request, it can create problems. And since "appropriate" included "lethal," and the fact that Trump was on the record calling for lethal assistance, the language was deemed sufficient. Besides, coupled with the rest of the anti-Russian language, it was clear that this position was stronger than the Obama administration foreign policy.

I never heard about any of this when it was happening. It was well beneath my radar. Hundreds of these issues arise during the platform committee deliberations. If it was a more serious issue, or a controversial request, the matter would have been brought to my attention. But Dearborn made the call and the matter never got to me. This logic made no sense to a Special Counsel who did not care about truth but only a narrative that fit his anti-Trump narrative.

Weissman decided that I, personally, was against changing "appropriate" to "lethal," and that this was more evidence of Russian collusion. It didn't matter that I'd never been aware of the issue in the first place, or that "appropriate" included "lethal." Nor did it matter that Dearborn and the subcommittee political whip said they never sent the issue to me. Nor did it matter that both Obama and Hillary were against giving lethal weapons to Ukraine. None of the facts were relevant. This was Weissman's narrative, driven by the media—that this was a very clear signal to Russia that Manafort and Trump were working with them in return for help in the campaign. Yes, that is how absurd things got as Weissman was desperate for any link, even if all of the evidence said otherwise.

When this "evidence" was raised to me in 2017, I didn't even know what they were talking about. I had to call Dearborn. He didn't remember it, either. He had to deal with someone—the Russia expert from the

RNC—who vaguely remembered. He went back and checked his notes, which he found. The real facts contradicted the Weissman narrative. The issue was a non-issue and it was nothing anyone was trying to hide.

From his days on *The Apprentice* and a lifetime in the spotlight, Trump had a finely tuned sense of what works on television. He also had contacts in the industry who he wanted to manage the convention. The problem was that these connections, like the producer of *The Apprentice,* Mark Burnett, did not want the association. After spinning my wheels for weeks trying to engage Burnett, I decided that it was not going to work out. I would need to rely on a more traditional cast of characters, but they would need to create a very different, very "Trump" program.

When Trump signed off on Bill Greener as the Convention Program Manager, we now had the experienced hand who could make certain that the program was well organized and crisp. The problem was there was no program. One of Greener's skills is that he does not panic and is able to work with all types of personalities to get the job done. "Take yes for an answer" is a Greenerism that helped me frame the program even while we were still trying to figure it all out.

Organizing a convention program is often a fight of egos for podium time. Normally, the stage is filled with Washington pols who represent one constituency or another. Trump wanted a different look in Cleveland. He wanted new faces and he wanted people who supported him completely. This reduced the list of almost all of the normal options, but it opened us up to some unconventional ideas.

While conventions will typically allot speaking time to a candidate's spouse or close family member, Trump took it to a new level. He wanted the convention to be a "family affair," with space for the entirety of the Trump family, from Melania on the first night, to Don Jr. and Tiffany on the second, Eric on the third, and Ivanka on the final night introducing Trump. As the nominee, his wishes were the command of the party.

The convention was also our chance to package Trump's agenda, to shift the focus from "Washington" to Hillary Clinton. Hillary Clinton was a career politician, so we were able to tuck her into the swamp with relative ease. The swamp could be the same, but the focus needed to be narrower and broader at the same time. And we had to be consistent with Trump's message.

We decided early in the planning stages that each night would have a theme that would allow us to build out our agenda on different issues. The first night would be "Make America Safe Again," the second, "Make America Work Again," and the third, "Make America First Again." Our position in the world was in tatters. We needed to talk about foreign policy and defense, and finally, Trump would bring it all together on the final night with "Make American One Again."

Technically, my role at the convention was that of manager, but in practice I was responsible for everything, and managing nothing. I had Bill Greener doing the RNC programming, and Rick Dearborn, who had managed our DC operations and was a detail person of extraordinary skills, working on the platform. Even though there was not a nomination fight, the campaign also had a floor operation. My job was to make sure the pieces were in place so that the program would go off the right way, that the speeches were in line with our platform, and that we were getting the right messages out. And when the time came, I was there, mostly, to put out fires, which always came out of nowhere. We'd spent countless hours in the weeks leading up to the convention preparing for it. I was confident that we would pull it off. But I knew that I had to be prepared for the unexpected.

Speaking to the night's theme of making America safe again, Melania kicked off the convention by highlighting her husband's lifelong patriotism. In many ways Melania is the steel that strengthens Trump. She is very intelligent and, although sitting on the sidelines, is aware of everything going on in Trump World. While not a politician, her instincts are razor sharp and her communication skills extraordinary, including the ability to convey them in five different languages. When she walked to the podium, she brought a presence and style that quieted the crowd as she spoke of her husband's love of our nation.

I have been with Donald for 18 years and I have been aware of his love for this country since we first met. He never had a hidden agenda when it comes to his patriotism, because, like me, he loves this country so much.

I can tell you with certainty that my husband has been concerned about our country for as long as I have known him. With all of my heart, I know that he will make a great and lasting difference. Donald has a deep and unbounding determination and a never-give-up attitude. I have seen him fight for years to get a project done—or even started—and he does not give up! If you want someone to fight for you and your country, I can assure you, he is the "guy."

If I am honored to serve as first lady, I will use that wonderful privilege to try to help people in our country who need it the most. One of the many causes dear to my heart is helping children and women. You judge a society by how it treats its citizens. We must do our best to ensure that every child can live in comfort and security, with the best possible education. As citizens of this great nation, it is kindness, love, and compassion for each other that will bring us together—and keep us together. These are the values Donald and I will bring to the White House. My husband is ready to lead this great nation. He is ready to fight, every day, to give our children the better future they deserve. Ladies and gentlemen, Donald J. Trump is ready to serve and lead this country as the next president of the United States. . . .

Thank you, God bless you, and God bless America.

It was a very good speech, delivered perfectly. Trump was supposed to be in New York, but he had come to Cleveland to surprise Melania. After the speech, they flew back to New York together.

Just as I was settling in for the night, around 11:30 Cleveland time, I got a phone call from Jason Miller, the campaign communications director. Jason is the ultimate professional whose skills blended a deep understanding of how to communicate with the media with a strategic ability to handle difficult issues without sacrificing our plan.

His message startled me back into crisis mode. The media had a story that Melania plagiarized some of Michelle Obama's speeches to the Democrat conventions. I couldn't reach Trump because he and Melania were on the plane flying back to New York, but I didn't believe that she would plagiarize a speech. I thought it had to be some dirty politics, another attempt to undermine Trump's win, take the focus off of the substance of the convention. I told Miller I would find out what happened and that he needed to engage the media to identify where this rumor came from.

By the time Trump landed in New York, the story was all over the media.

When I spoke to Trump and explained what was going on, he said he couldn't believe it. I agreed but asked him to ask Melania if she referred to Obama's speech when she was writing hers. She said of course they had looked at many speeches but didn't copy any language from any of them. I said, "Well, you have to think about this, because we can handle it a lot of different ways. But what I say coming out of the box next is going to be the story."

Trump was very irritated. I could tell he didn't know what to believe. But Melania was adamant that she didn't copy anything. So we put out a statement saying as much, which led to the media hammering me for refusing to admit that she had plagiarized a speech.

The controversy raged all night, and I was forced to defend myself and Melania on CNN the next morning. "There is no cribbing of Michelle Obama's speech. These were common words and values, and she cares about her family. To think that she would do something like that, knowing how scrutinized her speech was going to be last night, is just really absurd," I said.[1]

Finally, we said we would investigate what happened and ultimately, what we found was that the woman who drafted the actual words of the final draft had taken excerpts from different pieces of the various drafts. She had lifted some language without recording the source. When Melania gave the speech, as far as she was concerned, those were all her words, because she had polished the final result. She had not read Obama's speech. She didn't know what the media was talking about. But it hurt my credibility with the media because they thought I was lying when, in fact, I wasn't. I believed Melania. And she believed that she didn't lift the language.

Despite the bad press from Melania's speech, Trump stood firm in his belief that the family would be the centerpiece of the convention.

On Tuesday, Don Jr. got the convention back on track with a speech that spoke of the type of man his father really is.

As a proud son and family member, it was one of the great honors of my life to be able to put him over the top in the delegate count earlier today.

You want to know what kind of president he'll be?

Let me tell you how he ran his businesses, and I know because I was there with him by his side on job sites, in conference rooms from the time I could walk.

He didn't hide out behind some desk in an executive suite; he spent his career with regular Americans. He hung out with the guys on construction sites pouring concrete and hanging sheetrock. He listened to them and he valued their opinions as much and often more than the guys from Harvard and Wharton locked away in offices away from the real work.

He's recognized the talent and the drive that all Americans have. He's promoted people based on their character, their street smarts, and their work ethic, not simply paper or credentials. To this day, many of the top executives in our company are individuals that started out in positions that were blue collar, but he saw something in them and he pushed them to succeed.

His true gift as a leader is that he sees the potential in people that they don't even see in themselves. . . .

. . . The potential that other executives would overlook because their resumes don't include the names of fancy colleges and degrees.

He spoke of the risks of a Clinton presidency:

The other party is the party of risk. I've spent time with many great Americans who have served this country in the military, and they know what's at stake. When we have weak leaders in positions of power, Americans risking their lives for our freedoms are less safe. . . .

Let me tell you something about risk. If Hillary Clinton were elected, she'd be the first president who couldn't pass a basic background check. It's incredible.

Hillary Clinton is a risk Americans can't afford to take. She says she'll issue executive orders to take away Americans' guns. She wants to appoint judges who will abolish the Second Amendment.

And he spoke of what kind of president his father would be:

We're going to elect a president who will work with everyone to pass legislation that will make our country great again. . . .

A president who knows we can't simply delete our problems, but that we have to tackle them head on. A president who won't allow PC culture to put the safety and well-being of our children and our loved ones at stake. A president who won't bow and pander to nations that shudder at the very thought of America's existence . . .

A president not beholden to special interests, foreign and domestic, and one who funded his entire primary run out of his own pocket just to prove it. A president who will secure and defend the borders of the United States and who will appoint judges who believe that freedom requires a limited government . . .

A president who's actually created real jobs . . .

And when we elect him, we'll have done all that. We'll have made America great again, greater than ever before.

The convention was going very well with one exception: Ted Cruz. By the convention week, we had been in negotiations with Cruz for quite some time over the issue of endorsing Trump, which he did not want to do. I had been working with Jeff Roe, Cruz's campaign manager. While Roe was giving me "happy talk" about how he had Cruz in good shape to endorse, I felt like I was getting played.

Cruz had rejected all the language we gave him that explicitly endorsed Trump. Roe was double dealing and we needed to go beyond him to get Cruz on board or else Trump wanted Cruz shut off from the podium.

The deadline to send us the speeches was three days before a speech was scheduled. We needed Cruz's speech on Monday for his speech on Wednesday. By Monday, I still didn't have the speech. Tuesday—no speech. Wednesday, still no speech. We had not announced that Cruz was speaking yet, and we were not prepared to do that if we didn't get the speech and if it didn't say the right things. As chairman of the party, it fell on Priebus to try to smooth out the issue. But he couldn't do it.

With Cruz's speech now an hour away, Dan Patrick, the Lieutenant Governor of Texas and Cruz's national chairman, interceded. Patrick is a professional and an equal to Cruz. He agreed that Cruz should endorse. He replaced Roe in the negotiations and got Cruz to agree to say that he would campaign with Trump. It was a back-handed way of offering an endorsement without actually endorsing, but it was still more than the media was expecting. That was the final language we agreed on. We finalized the speech and put it in the teleprompter.

When Cruz started to read his speech, he moved off of the scripted text. "Don't stay home in November," he said. "Stand up and speak and vote your conscience." The message was clear: Republicans who don't trust Trump did not have to vote for him.

Trump was furious. "This is bullshit," he said. Once again, his instincts kicked in. Rather than just accept that Cruz had broken his word, Trump decided he needed to act in the moment. He knew how he wanted to deflect attention from Cruz at the podium. Moving from his convention holding area, Trump, doing something never before done at a convention, walked to the back of the convention hall and brought the pool of press with him, effectively pulling the attention away from Cruz and undercutting his speech. Cruz then got a message that there was a technical issue—a legitimate glitch—and the volume went out on his speech.

Cruz left very upset. It took months to bring that relationship back. But eventually Cruz came around to supporting Trump, and Trump harbored no ill will. He saw Cruz as an ally once there was no longer any fight. But the process of getting to Wednesday night was a very difficult one.

With Cruz out of the way, the convention got back on track with a speech from Eric Trump.

Thirteen months ago, my father sat my family down and told us the time had come. He could no longer sit idly by and watch our beloved country, the country that had given our family so much success, so much opportunity, crumble before our very eyes.

He confirmed to us that he was prepared to announce his candidacy for president of the United States. He made sure to acknowledge that ours would not be an easy path. That we should prepare ourselves for what was to come. That we'd quickly learn who our true friends were. Without hesitation, we each committed our unwavering support. . . .

A year ago, my father was a businessman.

But like many Americans, he simply could no longer stand to see what was happening to our great country.

"It's time for a president who can make America great again, ahead of budget and ahead of schedule too," Eric said. "Dad, you have once again taught us by example, you are my hero, you are my best friend, you are the next president of the United States."

Mike Pence brought the night's theme—Make America First Again—home. "You have nominated a man for president who never quits, who never backs down, a fighter, a winner. Until now, he has had to do it all by himself against all odds. But this week, with this united party, he has got back up." The crowd roared in response. "Let's resolve here and now that Hillary Clinton will never become the president of the United States of America."

Trump's own speech to the convention was of paramount impor-tance, as it would provide the opportunity to re-introduce Trump to the American voters and to the world.

Trump was adamant that he wanted to project a strong image on the very issues that won him the nomination. There would be no "going soft" in an attempt to make his image less strident. To Trump, this was his moment to double down on the contrast between his vision and Clinton's. The speech gave him the chance to compare Clinton's global village with his plan to Make America Great Again.

Often the acceptance speech is assigned to a speechwriter who has a gift for prose, perhaps an ear for soaring rhetoric. This wouldn't work for Trump. Among the many roles that Trump usurped from historical campaign structures was that of speechwriter. While he often did not pen the first draft of a speech, the final draft was almost always more Trump's words than any speechwriter's.

We knew that it was important to hit certain themes and using poll-ing data from Fabrizio, we presented to Trump key touch points for the speech: the nation was in crisis; crime was up and jobs were down. We had no respect abroad and the economy was in turmoil. The system itself was rigged to favor the establishment. What Americans needed, desper-ately, was change. Clinton would be more of the same. Trump was the only candidate for change. It was time to put "America First" again and "Make America Great."

This was Trump's core message. Rather than waste time and money, we did not even bother to reach outside the team. From the start we agreed to have Jared oversee the process and assigned Stephen Miller, Trump's emerging principal speech writer, to write the first draft.

Trump did not like to rehearse speeches. He thought rehearsals made speeches stale. But given the magnitude of this speech, I asked Jared and Ivanka to manage the practice sessions. My thinking was that they were the two best people to get Trump to practice. In the end we had two practice sessions, both in Cleveland, with Trump revising up until the very last min-ute. Again, Trump had upended the way things were done, and pulled it off.

Introducing Trump on the final night, Ivanka spoke of her father's work ethic and his ability to rise above party lines, to speak for all Americans:

> In the same office in Trump Tower where we now work together, I remember playing on the floor by my father's desk, constructing miniature buildings with Legos and erector sets, while he did the same with concrete, steel, and glass. My father taught my siblings and me the importance of positive values and a strong ethical compass. He showed us how to be resilient, how to deal with challenges, and how to strive for excellence in all that we do. He taught us that there is nothing we cannot accomplish if we marry vision and passion with an enduring work ethic. . . .
>
> My father values talent. He recognizes real knowledge and skill when he finds it. He is color blind and gender neutral. He hires the best person for the job. Period. . . .
>
> Like many of my fellow millennials, I do not consider myself categorically Republican or Democrat. More than party affiliation, I vote based on what I believe is right for my family and for my country. Sometimes, it's a tough choice. That is not the case this time. As the proud daughter of your nominee, I am here to tell you that this is the moment, and Donald Trump is the person, to make America great again.

Then Trump spoke. And as I watched him open his speech from the convention podium, I thought to myself, "this guy is the most incredible candidate I have ever worked for."

"Friends, delegates and fellow Americans," he said. "I humbly and gratefully accept your nomination for the presidency of the United States. USA, USA, USA. Who would've believed that when we started this journey on June 16th last year, we, and I say we, because we are a team, would have received almost fourteen million votes, the most in the history of the Republican Party and that the Republican Party would get 60 percent more votes than it received eight years ago, who would've believed this, who would've believed this?"

A month earlier, he had never spoken from a teleprompter. When I suggested he needed to get used to it for the convention, he put it off. Now, I watched him use the machine from the podium like it was second nature to him.

"The American people will come first once again. My plan will begin with safety at home—which means safe neighborhoods, secure borders, and protection from terrorism. There can be no prosperity without law and order. On the economy, I will outline reforms to add millions of new jobs and trillions in new wealth that can be used to rebuild America."

Ronald Reagan could not have done any better. I chuckled to myself and thought, "Look out Hillary, The Donald is coming."

The media said it was a dark speech, but it wasn't a dark speech. It was an *honest speech*. It focused on the problems facing the country. Trump spoke plainly and truthfully to those problems, and, more importantly, he offered the nation a framework with which to solve them. He gave people hope for something new.

"To all Americans tonight in all of our cities and in all of our towns," Trump went on, "I make this promise—we will make America strong again. We will make America proud again. We will make America safe again. And we will make America great again. God bless you and goodnight. I love you."

As I watched the waves of applause sweep the convention hall, I thought of the road ahead. To me, I had no doubt we had charted the right strategy, and now we had the organization revved up to take advantage of it. And best of all, we had the most incredible candidate leading the charge.

The convention was a success. Trump bounced in the polls establishing the campaign as competitive in the general election. Despite everything, he had a real chance to win. My attention had to now turn to the upcoming Democratic convention in Philadelphia.

Traditionally, both campaigns have a minimum presence during the week of the opposition party's convention. In the past, they would go completely dark. In recent times, however, a bracketing presence was employed by both parties, meaning that opposition parties have their own convention messaging operation in the midst of their opponent's convention.

The Democrats had a team in Cleveland and each day they would meet with the media to give their assessment of what we had done at our convention. Now it was our turn to do the same in Philadelphia. Making the matter more urgent, the Democratic convention was the Monday after our convention ended (on the previous Thursday). This meant we had the chance to boost our convention messaging by bleeding it directly into the Clinton convention.

Given the importance of building on our momentum, I had committed to Priebus, whose RNC was responsible for the Philadelphia bracketing operation, to kick off our Philadelphia presence with him at a press conference on Sunday. While it interrupted my weekend to recover, I felt I owed Priebus for being such a good partner to Trump at our convention.

We did the press conference at the 2300 Arena in Philadelphia, not far from the Democratic convention. It was well attended by the media, and Priebus and I took turns giving our impressions on what we had achieved and what the Democrats were facing as they started their convention the next day.

Near the end of the Q&A, I got a question from a reporter that, at the time, seemed completely off the wall.

The reporter said that Robby Mook, the Clinton campaign manager, had said that President Putin was pro-Trump, and that Russia was working with the Trump campaign to defeat Hillary Clinton.

Mook had gone on one of the morning shows with this, but I hadn't seen it. At first, I looked at the reporter to figure out why someone would ask such a stupid question. Then, I laughed and commented that while I had not seen the Mook quote, if he did say it, "they're pretty desperate pretty quickly. It's a far reach, obviously. To lead their convention with that tells me they really are trying to move away from what the issues are in this campaign."

It was a crazy claim, and it didn't really make sense. It was Obama and Hillary who had been soft on Russia in the past, not Trump. Afterward, I asked Priebus if he knew what they were talking about, but he didn't know either. I just assumed it was one of these oddball questions that campaigns get sometimes and dismissed it as that. It was the first time I'd heard anything pointing in the direction of the Trump campaign "colluding" with Russia. It was so ridiculous, I barely took it seriously.

As I left the podium, I thought to myself, "We must really have them on the ropes. This Russia angle is crazy." For a day or so, things quieted down. The Democrats had their convention, and the media was focused on that, as they should have been. But as soon as the convention was over, Russia came up again as part of the Democrat's campaign against Trump.

In hindsight, it is clear that Clinton was worried about her server issue. She knew it would dominate her campaign and she needed to muddy the waters. This was her way of doing just that. I don't believe she ever thought it would grow to the level it did, it was simply a way of deflecting some attention from her legal issues and dragging Trump down with her.

The Democratic convention ended on July 29. Within a few days, stories were cropping up alleging coordination between the Trump campaign and Russia to defeat Clinton. A *New York Times* story pointed to Mook suggesting "that the Russians might have good reason to support Mr. Trump: The Republican nominee indicated in an interview with the *New York Times* last week that he might not back NATO nations if they came under attack from Russia—unless he was first convinced that the countries had made sufficient contributions to the Atlantic alliance."[2]

I had no idea where this stuff was coming from. It was so outlandish that it didn't worry me.

When George Stephanopoulos asked me, "Are there any ties between Mr. Trump, you, or your campaign and Putin and his regime?" I said, "No, there are not," adding that it was "absurd" and that there was no basis to the allegations.

I said the same thing to Erin Burnett on CNN's *Erin Burnett OutFront*: "Donald Trump is talking about the failed leadership of the Obama administration . . . It is crazy."[3]

Because I knew there was nothing of substance behind the stories, I figured it would die down again when the next thing came around. Unfortunately for me, that next "thing" only sent the story into overdrive—and put me, for the first time, right in the center of it.

On August 14 the *New York Times* broke a bombshell story alleging that a Ukrainian government agency had uncovered a "black ledger" containing the names of people who had received "off the books" cash payments from the Party of Regions over the course of a number of years. "Secret Ledger in Ukraine Lists Cash for Donald Trump's Campaign Chief," went the headline.[4] In particular, the story said my name was on the list and that I had received payments totaling $12.7 million: "Handwritten ledgers show $12.7 million in undisclosed cash payments designated for Mr. Manafort from Mr. Yanukovych's pro-Russian political party from 2007 to 2012, according to Ukraine's newly formed National Anti-Corruption Bureau. Investigators assert that the disbursements were part of an illegal off-the-books system whose recipients also included election officials."

The story blew up in the media. It was the first major story since the Mook accusation that the Trump campaign was working with Russia to defeat Hillary Clinton. The ridiculous assertion that I had dismissed as laughable in Philadelphia was now on the front page of the *Times*, an indication that, far from being laughed off as it should have been, it was actually being taken seriously. Worse, it was gaining traction.

I didn't know how to reconcile the story and my role in it. My initial reaction was that this was part of the contact sport called presidential politics. But it smelled different. This was not a "drive-by shooting." Rather, it smacked of a deliberate, premeditated attack that showed a high level of sophistication. For the first time, I was genuinely concerned. To be active in politics, one needs to have a tough skin. But I had no idea just how tough it would have to be to endure the attacks that were about to come down on me.

The substance of the story was patently false. Yes, I had worked for the Party of Regions for almost ten years. I had managed the campaigns of three successful parliamentary elections in Ukraine, one presidential election, and multiple local elections. Part of what I did in Ukraine was to organize the best American political consulting talent and manage their services. Over the course of the various campaigns, the list of consultants included many Democratic consultants including an Obama pollster, Tad Devine, and Mike Donilon of the Kerry presidential campaign, and Republicans like Tony Fabrizio.

As the lead on the team, I billed for the services and was paid a lump sum. In turn, I would then pay my consultants. None of this was abnormal or improper. It was true that my political team and I had been paid millions of dollars for our services. But none of us received one penny in cash. All of our payments were invoiced and paid by normal bank-to-bank wire transfers. How the Party of Regions listed the payments was beyond my knowledge, just as how any of our Fortune 500 clients did their internal bookkeeping.

As for a ledger in the headquarters of the Party of Regions, I had no idea. I made a call to Ukraine to find out if such a ledger existed. I was told that it did not. Moreover, the "signature" on the small piece of the document that was exposed to the media was not my signature. I knew that it was fake, and I suspected right away that the alleged "black ledger" was the creation of one of my political opponents in Ukraine who saw the opportunity to cause problems for me. While this answer made me breathe a little easier, I was still shaken.

The Ukrainian who had released the "black ledger" at a press conference in Kyiv was not very sophisticated. His participation in this ruse was not something he would have thought up one morning. I reasoned that there was something larger and more sinister going on. It was no coincidence that the *Times'* story was a follow-up to the Mook accusation of collusion between Russia and Trump. I now understood that Mook's assertions were the setup for this story. I was beginning to piece it together, but what I knew then would ultimately only scratch the surface.

I had briefed Trump on Ukraine back when I first joined the campaign. At the time he listened but he wasn't interested. It wasn't viewed as controversial.

But now the implication of the black ledger was that there was illegal cash, and that I hadn't reported it because it had come from Moscow. Essentially that I was a connection to the Kremlin. I told Trump none of it was true. I told the media it wasn't true. "The suggestion that I accepted cash payments is unfounded, silly, and nonsensical," I said. I put out a statement denying everything.

In a follow-up article the next day, the *New York Times* admitted that "Ukrainian officials have emphasized that the appearance of Mr. Manafort's name in the so-called black ledgers does not mean he received the money."⁵

My suspicions would be confirmed later when the source of the black ledger was revealed. But in the hysteria of the times, the story was accepted as fact. Suddenly, there was nothing I could say to refute it. I could only deny it. But I couldn't prove the denial because there was nothing to prove.

This incident was the beginning of a pattern of circular reporting that would come to define the abusive way the entire Russian collusion narrative was reported.

First an unsubstantiated allegation would be provided, usually by an anonymous source. The media would repeat the allegation, and the repetition would then be cited as proof. This would go on to define the internal logic of the Russian collusion narrative. Small, insignificant pieces would be woven into the fabric. The pieces would be promulgated without a shred of proof. From this story, the conspiracy would grow

and the MSM, working Twitter world, and Democratic political operatives as well as unnamed sources in the government would expand it
to ridiculous levels. Leaks abounded during the course of the campaign
about linkages between Trump campaign officials, Trump, and Putin.
Not known to me at the time was the fact that there was a covert operation being managed inside the FBI, CIA, State Department, and the
White House promoting the idea that the conspiracy between Trump
and Putin was real.

When the *New York Times* story was printed on August 14, it
appeared to the public—and to me—that the reporting was in the early
stages of an investigation. In fact, a quiet disinformation campaign was
already months old. At the center of this campaign was a former *Wall
Street Journal* reporter, Glenn Simpson, who had formed an investigation company called Fusion GPS. I would later learn that Simpson had
first been hired by the *Free Beacon* to do opposition research on several
candidates in the Republican primaries, including Donald Trump. As
the primaries wound down, the *Free Beacon* ended its relationship with
Fusion. Simpson, however, had other ideas and approached the Clinton
campaign to be their outside "dirty tricks" consultant.

But all of that would come later. On August 15, the day after the article came out, the fabrication, the fake signature, and the incorrect details
all sounded very self-serving as far as excuses went. I'd been around long
enough to see where it was heading. Trump was busy fighting incoming fire over the gold-star family controversy that had emerged at the
Democratic convention. Now he was confronted by a growing Russian-
collusion story, built around me.

I sensed the seriousness of this fake narrative and concluded that I
wouldn't survive August. But I didn't want to leave without finalizing the
groundwork for the general election strategy. I had worked very hard for
Trump, and I believed deeply in his candidacy. I could see that I was the
victim of some dirty politics, but at the least I wanted leave the campaign
in a good position to beat Clinton. Fortunately, from my perspective,
most of the important functions to run a successful general election were
almost finished when the black ledger story broke.

I spent what would be my last official days in the campaign finishing
the budgets for each state and putting together what I would have overseen if I was still there in August and September so that the campaign
had a strategy in place. The schedule through the first debate, a social

media plan, and TV, radio, and digital ads all needed to be finalized. Only when that was taken care of did I feel I could step away.

On August 19, I had breakfast with Jared. The family was going off on a campaign event and I told Jared that I could see that the writing was on the wall. He agreed, which told me Trump agreed. I had to resign. I said I would submit my resignation letter that afternoon. We embraced and went our separate ways.

My resignation only deflected the attention from the Russian collusion story for a short period of time. Clinton was determined to keep the fire raging.

Knowing that there was nothing there, I figured it was a campaign issue and would die down after Trump won. While I was damaged to a certain degree, I felt like I was going to have access to the White House to be able to do the things that I would have done had I been able to stay on the inside. I had good friends in the campaign, and Trump and Pence both recognized the value I had brought to the organization.

By the Thursday before the election, I was convinced Trump would win. He had established the narrative that was a winning "close" to the campaign. Although it was a very close race, I believed that Clinton would have to do something dramatic in the last week of the campaign to change the momentum. When it didn't happen—when there was no "October surprise"—I was confident Trump would be the next president of the United States.

As confident as I was that Trump would win, I was concerned that the Democrats would try to steal the election, so I put together a memo highlighting what needed to be done to protect the results. "DT will be elected President on Tuesday," I wrote. "I believe that we are on the verge of a mandate size Electoral College victory. With the battleground states closing to within margins of error, DT is poised to win most of these states on Tuesday. I expect that this weekend, the Undecided voters will begin to break for DT. At this time HC is the incumbent in the race. This means that she has all that she is going to get on election day. The remaining Undecided will either stay home or break for DT."

But, I warned,

The electorate is not prepared for this result, nor is the media. I am concerned that the Clinton campaign does have an answer for this possibility. They will move immediately to discredit the DT victory and claim voter fraud and cyber-fraud, including the claim that the Russians have hacked into the voting machines and tampered with the results. As crazy as this sounds, it is not outside of their playbook.

It was crucial to build a strategy to secure the victory:

> Our plan to prepare the world for our victory is strategic. It is not just a communications plan. We need to define the strategy, build the messaging, organize the communicators, and brief friendly media. I know that we have all of our resources focused correctly on securing the victory on Tuesday.
>
> However, I can't stress the point enough—*It is just as important to build the plan to protect the victory.* We must start preparing the public for a significant DT electoral college victory, even if the popular vote is not commensurate.

I laid out several suggestions and ended by saying, "Clinton will never accept a loss without discrediting the process. The media cannot accept a DT victory as an uprising of the people. A DT victory is a repudiation of the entire "rigged system" by the people. This will never be accepted by the establishment."

I did not know at the time how prophetic my words would be.

I was invited to spend election night in New York with the campaign. During the fall campaign, I had stayed away, visibly, after I had resigned. That way no one in the Clinton campaign or the MSM could point to my presence and make an issue of it. Maintaining this approach, I stayed in Florida for election night.

On election day, everything seemed to be moving in a positive direction. The turnout in the key areas were indicating a strong Trump vote. But when the 5:00 p.m. exit polls were available, I became alarmed and confused. The five o'clock exits showed Clinton winning every major state by five or six points. Eight points in Michigan, nine in Wisconsin, five in Florida. It looked like Trump was going to lose—big! I couldn't believe these exit polls. They didn't make any sense. I was depressed that I'd been so wrong.

But when the actual polling areas began to close, and the actual votes were being reported, the picture showed a very different result from the exit polls. When Florida came in around 8:oo p.m. as too close to call, my confidence returned.

Around ten o'clock, Pennsylvania and Michigan were called for Trump, and it looked like Wisconsin was going to be the key. They called Wisconsin a bit later and I knew it was over. Clinton sent Podesta out around midnight. His message was, "Hang in there, it's too close, we're going to win this thing." But I could tell from the fact that he came out that they knew it was over.

All of a sudden, I started getting calls from all over the world. It was incredibly exciting watching Trump come on stage as the victor. Yet, at the same time, it was a bittersweet moment for me. I was happy to have been a part of something special, but it was hard not to be there. It was hard to be on the sidelines. And it was devastating to have been sidelined by such a blatantly untruthful attack. My life had prepared me for that moment, and I felt that I could have contributed in so many ways to the incoming administration. But I realized that for now, I had to sit patiently and let the storm pass.

I called Trump to congratulate him personally. "Congratulations, Mr. President," I said. "You did it. I knew you were going to win."

"We're going to make a difference," he said.

"You're going to change the world," I told him, the cheers in the background nearly drowning us out. "I am very proud of you."

CHAPTER 8

The Conspiracy Grows Legs

Before the black ledger story and before I resigned, my focus was on helping Trump win the general election. I was excited about the significance a victorious campaign could have on the country and my personal situation. While I never envisioned going into the administration, I could see how President Trump might see me in one of the only two roles that ever interested me in government, Chief of Staff to the president.

After I resigned from the Trump campaign, I could sense that I was damaged as far as joining the administration was concerned. But I wasn't particularly upset. I believed I would have access to the administration from the outside and that there was still a role for me to play, similar to what I did in the Reagan administration. I was not thinking then in terms of legal exposure because I knew the Russian collusion narrative was false, that the black ledger was a fraud, and that I had not done anything illegal. The stories were damaging, and irritating, but not necessarily threatening.

As time went on, however, I started to get a better sense of the sophisticated disinformation campaign at play behind the scenes. Like an onion, the more you peeled back, the more layers you would find.

The first thing to come out was the black ledger, which was totally false, and which the MSM made even more false. I knew I had never been paid cash for any work I did in Ukraine. We'd always used wire transfers and the payments were tied to legitimate invoices and receipts.

The money was from real donors to the Party of Regions in Ukraine, many of whom were Ukrainian oligarchs, none of whom were Russian. It was all Ukrainian private money which paid for services, fees I received for my consultants, many of whom were leading Democratic political consultants and lobbyists. This included people like Tad Devine, Tony Podesta, and Greg Craig. Most of the Ukrainian money was either in Ukraine, or more likely, in the Seychelles or Cyprus, which is where the Ukrainians did a lot of their offshore banking.

When the black ledger came out, the numbers were in the range of how much I had been paid, although the dates were not and the cash angle was clearly wrong. But the fees were public information, based on contracts. The way the ledger was presented made it look as though they were for secret services and in cash, the implication being that the money was either dirty, or that it was government money, or worse, Russian money that had been funneled through Cyprus to hide it.

This is an important distinction. One of the storylines was that cash money received from the Ukraine government through illegal means was used to pay me. The double whammy accusation was dirty money and cash money secretly routed to me. The accusations were false on all counts. I never received any money from the Ukraine government. I never received any payments in cash. All money was wired to me for legitimate services supported by documentation.

The accusations were so patently wrong that within a very brief period of time the ledger was discredited as phony and shown to be a setup, by the official body charged in Ukraine to investigate corruption, the National Anti-Corruption Bureau of Ukraine (NABU). NABU was a joint venture created by the government of Ukraine and the USG through its Kyiv Embassy. Its purpose was to investigate corruption in the Ukrainian government. The NABU quickly dismissed the black ledger as fake.[1] Unfortunately for me, the coverage of this finding was non-existent. No media outlet wanted to lose this "juicy" allegation as they built the fake Russian collusion narrative.

What I did not know at the time was the invisible force behind the NABU was George Soros. In 2014, accessing his contacts in the Obama administration, Soros's International Renaissance Foundation (IRF) and its grantees were active behind-the-scenes supporters in the creation of the Anti-Corruption Action Centre (AntAC) of Ukraine, a powerful NGO. This NGO was not only active in Ukraine but had total access inside both the US Embassy in Kiev and the Obama administration.[2]

As a part of this involvement, AntAC identified who should be investigated and who should not be investigated. In fact, when Yuriy Lutsenko became the Prosecutor General, replacing Viktor Shokin who was fired because of VP Biden's threat to President Poroshenko, US Ambassador Marie Yovanovitch presented Lutsenko with a list of people who should not be prosecuted, including people who were friendly to Soros, or supported the Clinton Foundation. Not surprisingly, Burisma, a corrupt Ukrainian energy company whose Board of Directors included the vice president's son, Hunter Biden, was on the "no investigation list."

Around the same time, the Soros-funded AntAC was looking to probe both me and my political allies and financial contributors in Ukraine. In fact, AntAC was a motivating force behind the "black ledger." Yet, the ledger was so patently false, even the NABU rejected it as a legitimate document, although not before the damage was done to me in the international media.

While all of this was going on, Fusion GPS started to conduct opposition research on Trump, and the DNC's Ukraine expert Alexandra Chalupa was searching for dirt on me in Ukraine.

In the course of the Mueller investigation, NACBU's clearance of my name was never mentioned. The Special Counsel knew the ledger was fake, but they no longer needed it to justify their investigation. The ledger and the Steele dossier and the myriad of unsubstantiated leaks from "anonymous government sources" had created the environment to have the Mueller Commission created. Now, it no longer needed either of these documents to expand its witch hunt into President Trump, his campaign, and me.

At the urging of the Democrats, led by Chairman of the Intelligence Committee Adam Schiff, who claimed to have seen damaging evidence that he could not at that time discuss and helped along by anonymous government sources now identified as Clinton operatives both inside and outside the Obama administration, the MSM began to go out of its way to exaggerate any relationships that might have tied me to Putin and the Russians, and to promote any inferences they could find into major potential clues to prove Russian collusion.

Given my work in Ukraine as well as work I did internationally for a

Russian oligarch, Oleg Deripaska, the media chose me to be the "poster boy" for links to Putin in the fake Russian narrative. As I said, I dismissed these early mischaracterizations as absurd. My work in Ukraine was very public and very anti-Putin and any Russian government interests.

As I would discover in my legal jeopardy, facts did not matter. Impressions and guilt by reference and association were enough to prove the accusation.

At this point it is necessary to review the work I was doing in Ukraine. Much of what I explain here can be found by just searching the web. The work was public and the goals clear. Once Viktor Yanukovych was elected president in 2010, everything was focused on preparing the way for Ukraine to become a part of the European Union (EU). The work required a total restructuring of the Ukrainian legal system, economic system, and regulatory bodies. I worked extensively with the Commissioner for Enlargement of the EU, Štefan Füle, the office of the President of the EU, José Manuel Barroso, the western embassies in Kyiv including the US Embassy, German Embassy, French Embassy, and with officials in the Obama administration. All of these touchpoints were engaged in the work that was emanating out of the Office of the President of Ukraine.

Yanukovych was from Donetsk, in eastern Ukraine. After the recent experience of Putin's invasion of Ukraine, people are somewhat familiar with the country, but I will digress briefly to provide context to my story.

Ukraine is really two different countries. In western Ukraine, from the capital Kyiv to the western borders with Poland and Romania, the heritage is European. The Church is the Ukrainian Orthodox Church, the language is Ukrainian, and, culturally, they are not Russian. Eastern Ukraine is predominantly ethnically Russian. Most people in this region belong to the Russian Orthodox Church, speak Russian as their primary language, and are culturally associated with Russian heritage. They also share a border with Russia.

While two distinct cultures, Ukraine is united in its desire to be one nation. Over the course of my ten years working in Ukraine, I conducted over one hundred and fifty opinion surveys on everything from politics to culture. In every one of my surveys, what stood out was that there was no difference between the typical western Ukrainian from the typical eastern Ukrainian on the issue of Ukraine being independent. Except for a small minority (less than 3 percent), eastern Ukrainians had no desire to be a part of Russia. Putin learned this firsthand from his recent invasion when he was confronted with the fierce resistance of the citizen militia.

While the issue of joining the European Union was more controversial, the elites in eastern Ukraine, who were the political and financial base for Yanukovych, were clear in their desire to be a part of Europe. To them, the future was Europe. Russia was the past and it was not a happy one. These ethnic Russian Ukrainians wanted to protect their Russian language, their orthodox religion, and their culture. But they also wanted to protect their freedom, and they understood clearly the difference between "freedom under Russian rule" and "freedom under a Ukrainian flag."

When I first met Yanukovych in 2005, I had extensive conversations with him. He had been Russia's candidate in Ukraine in the 2004 election but the reasons for it were more complicated than just the geographic issue. I was not involved in Ukraine at the time of this election.

After months of talking with him, it became clear to me that Yanukovych was a strong proponent of Ukraine joining the EU. As Prime Minister and later president, he would prove his commitment to this aspiration.

All of the background on the "why" would be interesting for historians, but for this book, suffice it to say that Yanukovych struck me as the right person for Ukraine for that assignment. As Nixon was the only one who could open up the US-China relations because of his anti-Communist past, I believed that Yanukovych was the key to bringing Ukraine into Europe. No politician from western Ukraine could accomplish this goal without creating such a serious schism that the country would be destroyed.

When Yanukovych was elected in 2010, the first trip he took as President was to Brussels, not Moscow. Controversial at the time, it set the tone for his presidency and pointed to the direction he intended to lead Ukraine. Each year, he built on this foundation to the point where Ukraine was poised to make a formal application in 2014. The reason it fell apart was because of the divisions in Europe and the US, not because of any Yanukovych wavering. At the critical moment, an ambivalent Europe blinked, and Ukraine's future was put into harm's way. The reason for Europe's ambivalence is instructive today.

My work in Ukraine, after his election, was in assisting Yanukovych to understand how to deal with Washington and Europe. When he became president of Ukraine in 2010, the focus was really more on Europe than on the United States. The United States government under Obama had basically treated Ukraine as within the sphere of Europe, and therefore, Obama supported what the Europeans were trying to do, or not do, with Ukraine.

Privately, the Europeans were not in favor of Ukraine becoming a part of Europe. But publicly, they had to say they were.

There were three components to this concept of Ukraine as a part of Europe. First was NATO. As is well-known today, NATO is the defense pact signed by western European nations to protect against any aggression from outside forces, mainly Russia. Russia is against Ukraine being a part of NATO because it would place NATO, and western troops on the Russian border. In the first phase, neither Europe nor Ukraine talked seriously about Ukraine joining NATO. While the Poles would have liked it, this prospect was looked at as something to consider after Ukraine was a part of the European Union club.

The second element was a trade relationship between Ukraine and Europe. This would be bestowed once Ukraine had signed a trade association agreement that conveyed special trade benefits and removed all protective barriers and tariffs. The adoption of such an agreement would significantly benefit Europe in the short and intermediate term because Ukraine's subsidies and protections would have to be removed, thereby opening up the Ukrainian markets to free open trade from European competitors. Only over time would Ukraine change this paradigm and it would trigger when Ukraine was formally admitted to the political union of the European Community, which was the third element.

The ugly truth is that the Europeans did not like Eastern and Central European countries coming into the EU. To them it messed up "the equation." The southern members (countries like Spain, Italy, and Greece) knew that Ukraine would tap into the subsidies they were getting from the European Union. In the long term, it would be a real financial drain on the European community.

Meanwhile, Merkel was in bed with the Russians. They were discussing the Nord Stream pipeline, which would bring Russian gas to Europe, and her mentor, Schroeder, was the chairman of that project. This pipeline would strengthen Russia's grip on controlling Europe's energy needs, while completely undercutting Ukraine. Nord Stream was vital to Russia and Germany had a major role in it. Merkel didn't want to do anything to disrupt that equation. But they couldn't say any of this out loud.

So publicly, Europe talked about how Ukraine should be a part of Europe. But in order to *become* a part of Europe, Europe stipulated that Ukraine would have to meet certain, stringent conditions. They would have to make significant changes to their legal system, their economy, and their society. The Europeans believed that Ukraine would never make these changes. So it was an easy thing to hold out the prospect of joining the European community.

When Ukraine was a part of the Soviet Union, eastern Ukraine was the major industrial center. A large share of the Russian oligarchs were in eastern Ukraine. That's where all the major industrial plants were. That's where the military plants were. Western Ukraine was the breadbasket. The wealth that developed as Ukraine became independent in 1990 was in the east. The Eastern Ukraine oligarchs were Russian-educated, often Russian-speaking and culturally closer to Russia than to Europe. But they felt that when they were matched up against Russian oligarchs, they were not just a junior brother, but a speck in the economic game.

They resented the way Russian oligarchs treated them. There was a jealousy and an unbalanced kind of competition. In the end Ukrainian oligarchs understood that any conflict with Russia would cost them an enormous amount of money in bribes to hold onto their business. So, it was the Ukrainian oligarchs in Eastern Ukraine who became the prime movers behind the idea of Ukraine becoming part of Europe. They believed it would free them from the yoke of Russian control. Yanukovych was their vessel to this end.

My benefactor in Ukraine, Rinat Akhmetov, was the number one oligarch in the country in the early 2000s. Before I went there in 2005, he was building a holding company structure that was very reminiscent of elite western structures. Working with McKinsey and Associates, Akhmetov was building a classic western model holding company organization. He saw the value in the west, and he brought in people who were educated in Europe, with MBAs from abroad. These were serious businesspeople. And they all tried to find a way, before I got involved, to move Ukraine closer to Europe. But no one thought Ukraine would become part of the EU simply because no one thought a Ukrainian politician would ever support the idea.

It was Oleg Deripaska who set up my first meeting with Akhmetov.

Deripaska was Russian. He was one of the top oligarchs there. His business was in the aluminum sector. His company, Rusal, was the second-largest aluminum company in the world. Deripaska was a brilliant businessman who would have succeeded in the western business world if he had born in Europe or the US. An engineer by training, Deripaska understood the importance of adopting western models to his business structures. His problem was that all of the various factories that supplied the resources necessary for Rusal were in former Soviet Republics like Ukraine, Uzbekistan, and Turkmenistan. Deripaska understood the need to modernize and diversify. He also believed that the future in these Republics was in moving them towards western models. He brought me on to assist in developing and managing some of the outreach and political work he deemed important to his future.

One of those places was Ukraine, where he had a number of plants.

In 2004, Ukraine experienced the political upheaval that Deripaska had presciently predicted. The Orange Revolution was the spark that ignited a movement led by politicians from western Ukraine challenging the Russian influence exerted by the outgoing President Leonid Kuchma. Kuchma was independent but aligned his policies within the Russian sphere of influence. Ukraine was looking to the presidential elections of 2004 to break out from this yoke.

I was not involved in the controversial 2004 Ukrainian presidential election, but came to understand that it was really a proxy election of Europe and the US against Russia. The European candidate Viktor Yushchenko was elected president over Yanukovych in an election that had significant charges of fraud by all sides. The MSM claim was that Yanukovych tried to steal the election. Since I was not engaged in Ukraine at the time, I had no basis to believe differently. That is until Deripaska introduced me to Rinat Akhmetov in 2005.

Very quickly I realized digging into the past election would not be productive. The evidence supported both sides being engaged in fraud. I made the decision to look to the future, not the past. As part of my agreement to engage politically in Ukraine, I made it a condition that we would have an election integrity component to any campaign I was engaged in. This was true for all of my election campaigns. We worked with western embassies, including the US Embassy to ensure the most credible elections possible. Again, this is not the book to discuss these efforts, but the approach has plenty of public evidence of how we oversaw election integrity initiatives and put observers in all of the places where corruption had flourished in the past. While the elections were not perfect, international election organizations accepted the presidential and Parliamentary elections where I participated as "fair and free" within western standards.

When Akhmetov engaged me, I came to understand the difference between the Ukrainian-Russian business model and the western business model. Ukraine's business model was simple: He who has the power owns the business. It has nothing to do with a democratic structure or honoring the rule of law. Whoever holds the power moves to take over the economy. With Yushchenko now in power, his government immediately began to transfer the industrial wealth to his supporters. The first step was to re-nationalize parts of the Ukrainian economy. This meant seizing the properties of the industrialists, who primarily lived in eastern Ukraine. Number one on this target list was Rinat Akhmetov, the leading industrialist in Ukraine.

Akhmetov hired Akin, Gump, a major Democrat law firm in Washington, DC, to protect his interests and to intercede with the Obama administration. When Deripaska introduced me to Akhmetov, he ran my name by Akin, Gump and they supported me being brought on board. Akhmetov explained that Yushchenko was seeking to illegally re-nationalize Kryvorizhstal, his steel company.

After many long conversations on a broad range of issues, including Ukrainian politics, he asked me if I might help in the upcoming Parliamentary elections. I said it depended on whom I was helping. He said, "You'd be helping the Party of Regions."

The Party of Regions was led by Viktor Yanukovych. I wasn't sure I could work for Yanukovych because all I knew about him was what I had read, which was that he had tried to steal an election and that he was supported by the outgoing president, Kuchma, as well as by Moscow. Akhmetov explained that Moscow supported Yanukovych in 2004 not because they liked him but because Moscow felt that Yanukovych was a way to destabilize Ukraine by pitting east versus west. To me that was reason enough not to engage. To get my support, Yanukovych would have to be willing to take on Moscow. Akhmetov said he thought Yanukovych would be very comfortable doing so as he had deep disdain for Putin. He encouraged me to meet with him first and then make a decision.

My initial sense of Yanukovych was that he wasn't comfortable with me. He was stiff and not open. As I started to do more research and talk to Deripaska, I understood that Moscow was supporting him insofar as Moscow was happy with the destabilizing that was going on in Ukraine. Russia didn't care about Yanukovych; they cared about chaos.

I ended up meeting with Yanukovych a number of times and it became apparent to me that, like Akhmetov, he saw the value in moving Ukraine toward Europe. He felt that he was being used by Moscow and that Putin had misled him.

After five or six months of research, I concluded that what interested me in Ukraine was its geopolitical importance. I did some polling and discovered that, given the regional breakdowns in the country, Yanukovych's Party of Regions could easily get up to 30 percent in a Parliamentary election. In a multi-party election, this was enough to form the government. My polls were more accurate than public polls, which showed the Party of Regions maxing out at 8 percent of the electorate. Again, Fabrizio was able to cut through the clutter, notwithstanding the language barriers, and lay out a detailed picture of the demographics of the electorate.

Part of the reason my poll differed from all public surveys was because of the internal factors I was probing. I found that in eastern Ukraine there was an undercurrent that Yanukovych was the only national political figure who was viewed as able to protect Russian culture, language, and heritage. This was a growing issue in 2005 in Ukraine. Yanukovych's rivals, President Yuschenko and Prime Minister Timoshenko, were trying to delegitimize Russian culture in Ukraine in order to rid the nation of feelings that they falsely claimed were dangerous to uniting the country.

The nuance here is critical. They supported Yanukovych to protect their freedoms in Ukraine, not to lead Ukraine into Russia. This nuance has been totally ignored by western media and politicians. It was also ignored by Andrew Weissman, Adam Schiff, and the "fake news media."

The Party of Regions used the anti-eastern Ukraine slant of the Yuschenko government as a rallying point for building political support in the east. This approach proved to be a double-edged sword because Yuschenko and Timoshenko used the Region's support for protecting Russian heritage as proof that Yanukovych and the Regions were pro-Russian, not pro-Ukrainian at all.

In fact, the issue was protecting the Russian heritage of Ukrainians living in the east, not opposing Ukrainian nationalism. This divide was buried in the propaganda. Protecting Russian language and culture became proof of being pro-Putin. This simpleton analysis, while laughable, was the same blurred conclusion used against me in the Russian collusion hoax twelve years later. I concluded Yanukovych was not pro-Putin or "pro-Russia." He was a Ukrainian nationalist who wanted to protect a multi-cultural society.

The background on my work in Ukraine and the misinformation that would come out later are foundational to the picture that was being painted of me in the media during the Russian hoax hysteria. The idea that Yanukovych was pro-Russian and that the Party of Regions was pro-Russian was categorically untrue. Yes, there were some in the Party who were pro-Russia, but Yanukovych and his team supported joining Europe and disliked Putin both personally and politically. His track record as president, if anyone cared to research it, showed this clearly.

Indeed, I had spent much of my career abroad—in Angola, in Afghanistan, the Caribbean—working against Russian interests. There was no way I was going to, all of a sudden, change a lifetime of work against communism, the Soviet Union, and now Putin.

There was more than enough information on the public record regarding my work in Ukraine to show that the idea of Russian connections was false. The US embassy in Kiev knew that I was there and knew what I was doing. I worked with them from day one. I was employed as a kind of back channel between the US government and the Ukrainian leadership to get done whatever the US wanted done.

Furthermore, my associate Konstantin Kilimnik, who would become Weissman's fake face of Russian collusion, was not only *not* a Russian agent, but he was a *US* asset. He was so important to the US embassy in Kiev that he had a code name to protect him in cable traffic between Ukraine and Washington.

This false narrative was based on two public facts. One, although he was a Ukrainian by birth, Kilimnik was Russian when he had to choose a passport after the demise of the Soviet Union. Two, as part of his mandatory military service, Kilimnik was trained as a linguist in a school that also trained Russian analysts who later worked for the Russian military intelligence. Because in past times this was one path for future intelligence officers who remained in the military, the MSM and Democrats used this historical connection to conclude he was a spy. But Kilimnik did not serve any additional time in the military. Unlike those who used this as a touchpoint, Kilimnik did not serve beyond his mandatory military commitment.

That is the sum total of any and all evidence that he was a Russian spy. Nothing more. The same anonymous US government sources who pushed this false narrative had access to the State Department files that identified him as a valued asset. They knew he was not a spy. But they didn't care. They needed a Russian, and unfortunately for this friend of the United States, he was their mark. Unconcerned with how it might impact Kilimnik and his family, they made him out to be a spy knowing it was a lie.

It might be useful to note that I was not the only Republican who valued Kilimnik's skills and pro-American attitude. Before he joined my staff, Kilimnik had worked at the Moscow office of the International Republican Institute (IRI). This was a Republican think tank that promoted democracy in developing countries. Kilimnik rose to be the number two person in the IRI Moscow office. The head of the IRI at the time was none other than Senator John McCain of Arizona. Again, the Moscow office of the IRI existed to "promote democracy in Russia," and Kilimnik spent several years doing exactly that. No one in that office believed he was a Russian spy.

But there was an even more important proof to me that the Weissman narrative was fake.

Yanukovych didn't speak English. In order to conduct our business, Kilimnik was the translator. Not my translator. *The* translator. When I would meet with Yanukovych, including after he became president, there were usually only three people in the room: me, Kilimnik and Yanukovych. In these meetings we would discuss how we were progressing in EU integration, Ukraine's nuclear policy which favored Obama over Russia, and many other sensitive issues. If Kilimnik had been a Russian spy, the Ukrainian security forces, the SBU, would have uncovered it in a minute. They thoroughly checked out Kilimnik and me. They would never have allowed official private meetings between the President of Ukraine and a known Russian agent or CIA agent.

So from the very first mention of Kilimnik as a Russian spy, I dismissed it as a total fabrication. I had worked with him for over ten years. I knew what he was doing and why he felt the way he did about Russia. At the beginning of 2017, I could see how the Democrats were trying to create a fiction out of minute connections which meant nothing. Yet, I also could feel the tension in Washington where everyone was afraid to say or do anything for fear of becoming the new "political piñata."

I accepted that it would be politically uncomfortable for me for the next couple of months. However, since there was nothing to expose, I believed the truth would eventually come out. I also felt that those in the media, many of whom were friends of mine, would ultimately get the story right.

I was wrong on all counts. No one protected me and the story continued to gain traction while simultaneously becoming more incoherent until it was essentially a fever dream conspiracy from the Democrats in which I acted as a direct Russian connection between Putin and the Trump campaign.

At the moment, however, in early 2017, with Trump heading to the White House, I felt that my "book of business" was about to grow substantially and quickly. I was prepared to make a trip to Europe when I started getting some phone calls from people in Asia saying that the South Koreans and the Japanese are scared to death of a Trump presidency. They were working off of headlines about Trump that Clinton had created during the campaign, most of which were untrue. A longtime friend of mine approached me to say that he believed it would be a good idea for me to take a trip to Asia to explain Donald Trump. This would be good for bilateral relations and good for my business prospects. I accepted the trip. I would go on my own without clearing it with anyone or coordinating with the Trump team.

I left just after the New Year and planned on returning home in time for the inauguration.

On January 10, 2017, while I was still in Asia, CNN reported that *classified documents* had been presented to President Obama and Trump which included "allegations that Russian operatives claim to have compromising personal and financial information about Mr. Trump."[3] These allegations "came in part from memos compiled by a former British intelligence operative whose past work US intelligence officials consider credible." CNN had reviewed the thirty-five-page collection of memos but did not report on the details as they had not independently corroborated the allegations.

Following the CNN report, *Buzzfeed* published the full dossier later that same day. "A dossier, compiled by a person who has claimed to be a former British intelligence official, alleges Russia has compromising information on Trump. The allegations are unverified, and the report contains errors," ran the article accompanying the dossier.[4] Additionally, the dossier included totally fabricated allegations against me, Michael Cohen, Carter Page, and Mike Flynn.

The dossier, the article claimed, made "explosive, but unverified, allegations that the Russian government had been 'cultivating, supporting, and assisting' President-elect Donald Trump for years." There were also "graphic claims of sexual acts documented by the Russians." The word "unverified" quickly became lost in the story. The crazy allegations were taking on a life of their own.

I could not believe what I was reading. I had hoped that the black ledger was a thing of the past. Now, my worst fears were becoming a reality. This was not going away. After I calmed down, I decided that I had to contact Trump. Since it was still morning in New York, I called Priebus, who had recently been announced as the incoming chief of staff to the president.

I ticked off all of the wrong information in the dossier as related to me, suggesting that I was certain the information on the others was equally as false.

"Why don't you tell Trump directly," Reince said.

I said, "I'm telling you so you can tell him."

"It would be better if you tell him yourself. Call him back on this number," he said.

So I hung up and called a different number and got Trump on the phone.

Knowing that I was on foreign soil, I understood that this call was really a public call. South Korean intelligence, North Korean intelligence, Chinese intelligence—they were all listening. I made certain that Trump knew I was overseas. He said he didn't care who was listening because this dossier was "bullshit." Using the same word, I walked him through all of the falsehoods. He interrupted to say how crazy the golden showers story was and that Comey himself had told him that there was nothing to this stuff. He finished by saying Clinton could not accept the fact that she lost.

As we hung up, I congratulated him on his recent appointments and said I looked forward to the inauguration. Feeling better that I had informed him that he had nothing to fear about the lies about me, I went to sleep.

Not long after, I got on a plane back to the US. But I was thinking still of my business. The trip to Asia had been successful and I was thinking of the work I could do advising foreign governments on how to deal with Trump. I looked forward to working in Europe, in the Middle East, and elsewhere.

But in the back of my mind, I knew on some level that this wouldn't go away. From the very beginning I suspected some involvement by the "Deep State," which would stop at nothing to destroy Trump's credibility, devalue his victory, and delegitimize his presidency. I was never so right in my life.

It seemed, at the time, as though the Steele dossier had come out of nowhere. But it had its roots in an earlier investigation dating back to the beginning of the Trump campaign when Glenn Simpson, a former *Wall Street Journal* reporter, was hired by the *Free Beacon* to do opposition research on several Republican primary candidates.

The *Free Beacon* ultimately ended its relationship with Simpson's firm, Fusion GPS, as the primaries came to a close, but Simpson knew that the DNC and the Clinton campaign were covertly compiling negative research on Trump personally and on his campaign officials, including me. He approached Perkins, Coie, a law firm that specialized in contracts with Democrat candidates, to do opposition research. Simpson knew that Perkins Coie was doing such work for the Clinton campaign, and he persuaded Perkins, Coie to hire Fusion GPS to continue the work. During their time together it appears that Fusion was paid over $10 million by Perkins, Coie—money that should have been reported on the DNC and Clinton campaign FEC reports but was not.

(In fact, finally in March of 2022, the FEC fined the Clinton campaign and the DNC for violating FEC rules and not reporting the illegal payments by Perkins, Coie. Yes, six years later, a slap on the wrist to the Clinton campaign. Justice really is blind when it comes to her illegal behavior.)

With this new contract in hand, Simpson hired Orbis Business Intelligence, a British firm, to uncover links between Trump and his campaign and Russia. Orbis co-founder Christopher Steele was hired as a sub-contractor. Steele created a series of memoranda that bordered on the absurd asserting that the linkages existed. These now thoroughly debunked memos would come to be known as the "Steele dossier" and it would drive the Russian collusion narrative through the early days of Trump's presidency.

For some reason, Simpson had this fascination with me. I had been on his radar from his days at the *Wall Street Journal*, where he'd written a front-page story sensationalizing the work that lobbying firms were doing in Washington. Among his targets in that story were Haley Barbour and me. Because of my work in the region, I was an easy target for the Clintons and for the non-probing MSM to push their narrative.

I knew the dossier was bogus from the beginning, but it would take years for the full extent of the lies and deception to come out. John Durham's investigation exposed the ugly truth the web of intrigue that the Clinton campaign deliberately wove.

The dossier was funded by the Clinton campaign, with assistance from the Soros Foundations. It's primary source, Igor Danchenko, was in regular contact with Charles Dolan, a Democratic consultant with close ties to the Clintons throughout 2016. Danchenko would later be indicted for lying to the FBI about his relationship with Dolan. According to an in-depth CNN article titled "The Steele dossier: A reckoning,"[5] the indictment raised "new concerns about the circular nature of portions of Steele's work, and how it fit into a larger effort by Democrats to dirty up Trump. Clinton's campaign funded the project, and we now know that much of the material in Steele's memos ended up being mere political gossip. Steele then sent his explosive but unverified findings to the FBI and State Department."

"While Steele was passing his tips onto the FBI in fall 2016," the article continues, "a Clinton campaign lawyer (Michael Sussman, who worked at Perkins, Coie) separately met with a senior FBI official and gave him information about strange cyberactivity between servers at the Trump Organization and Alfa Bank, the largest private bank in Russia."[6]

This lawyer has been charged by Durham with lying to the FBI. The same article indicates that "the Sussman indictment said Sussman peddled the same material to a *Slate* reporter, who published a story right before the election. The story said reputable computer scientists uncovered unusual activity between servers belonging to the Trump Organization and the Moscow-based Alfa Bank, suggesting a secret backchannel. The Trump Organization and Alfa Bank both denied there was a backchannel. The FBI investigated the underlying data and ruled out any improper cyber links by February 2017." (Note: Sussman was acquitted by a Jury that included "three Clinton donors, an AOC donor, and a woman whose daughter is on the same sports team as Sussman's daughter." If that was not enough to tip the balance of the scales of justice, the Judge in the case is married to a lawyer who represented Lisa Page.)[7]

After the *Slate* article, the Clinton campaign went crazy trying to tie Trump to Russia. Unknown at the time was the fact that the FBI had serious doubts about the credibility of Steele's contentions. In fact, they had dismissed him as a credible source based on his breaking of several rules that the FBI requires in order to be a paid informant for the agency.

It is important to note that while Steele was interacting with the FBI, John Brennan, the CIA Director, had briefed President Obama on July 26, 2016 that the Clinton campaign had "ordered "a campaign plan to stir up a scandal: by linking President Trump to Russia.

According to Brennan's personal notes that were released in October of 2020, he explained to Obama that Clinton's plan was a means to distract the public from her email server scandal during the fall election.

Yes, we now know that the CIA, the Obama White House and, according to information released by John Durham in his recent court filings, even the FBI all knew the Russian allegations were a Clinton campaign dirty trick. Yet, they lied to the media, misled the American people and allowed the destructive hoax to hang over the entire Trump Presidency.

The lack of confidence in Steele's reports, however, did not deter the FBI from using the contents to get Foreign Intelligence Surveillance Act (FISA) surveillance warrants on Carter Page. Page had been a member of the early Trump Foreign Policy Advisory Committee. He had no real profile in Washington and was not part of any particular DC think tank or policy groups. A graduate of the US Naval Academy, Page went to work for Merrill Lynch working out of its Moscow office where he interacted with Russian energy companies. Based on this background, he was appointed to Trump's advisory committee although he had never met or spoken to Trump. Steele included Page in several of the dossier's fake stories that sought to link the Trump campaign with Russia.

Also unknown at the time was the fact that on December 9, President Obama had convened a principals meeting of his national security apparatus. This is the most senior foreign policy body in the USG. It is usually convened by the president to deal with such foreign policy crises as 9/11, the invasion of Ukraine by Russia, and so on. The purpose of the

Obama meeting was to review what his administration should do regarding the raw intelligence they had been collecting on collusion between the Trump campaign and Russia. Raw intelligence that we know now that John Brennan had informed Obama in the summer of 2016 was a fake narrative being promoted as a political strategy by Clinton.

At the meeting, James Comey reported on the contents of the Steele dossier. Even though FBI agent Peter Strzok, who had been appointed by Comey to spearhead Crossfire Hurricane in August 2016, and Director Comey's FBI apparatus knew the contents were bogus, the dossier was treated as factual. In fact, at the time the dossier was being used as the foundation for securing the FISA surveillance warrants to spy on Carter Page and through him into me and the Trump campaign.

At the meeting, Obama ordered an accelerated, full-scale intelligence investigation of the allegations. While ordering it, he also issued new guidelines lowering the standards on the treatment of intelligence data that would allow the data to be more available throughout the US government. By ensuring more people had access to the data, Obama was confident the material would leak to the media.

The deadline for the National Security investigation to submit its final report was before Trump was sworn into office. Normally, such a review takes months to conduct. But Obama had a plan, and the clock was ticking. The report was finalized in record time for such an important document and released to the public on January 6 by the Office of the Director of National Intelligence. It was compiled in less than thirty days The report concluded that Putin had ordered a campaign to influence the 2016 US presidential election and had interfered with the election processes in a variety of ways, including hacking the DNC computer networks and leaking hacked material to WikiLeaks and other outlets for the purpose of helping to elect Donald Trump.

The leap to claim that the effort was to help elect Donald Trump had no basis in fact. Obama knew it. Brennan knew it. Nonetheless it became a foundation in all future narratives.

The Russian collusion narrative began to speed up as the remaining days of the Obama administration dwindled. This was not a coincidence. Obama was doing all that he could to protect his administration from potential damage of its unprecedented spying operation on an opponent's political campaign became public. Nixon had done much less in the Watergate scandal, and it had brought down his government.

But Obama had a big problem with the findings in the intelligence report. *The problem confronting his administration was that while there was some evidence of Russia interfering in the election, there was zero evidence of Trump or his campaign (and me in particular) colluding in the interference.* This did not stop the Obama National Security team, which included Director of National Intelligence James Clapper, and CIA Director John Brennan, from deliberately blurring the line between the two issues, thus implying linkage.

Notably, the DNI report contained no evidence of collusion between Trump, his campaign, and any Russians. This report was part of a general meeting that James Comey had with President-elect Trump and his National Security advisers, including Michael Flynn, on January 6 in Trump Tower. After the meeting, Comey stayed behind to brief Trump on the Steele dossier. This was the first time that Trump became aware of the dossier. Comey assured Trump that notwithstanding the salacious nature of the dossier, Trump was not personally under investigation.

The lack of evidence did little to slow down the collusion narrative. After a private meeting between outgoing Majority Leader Harry Reid and Comey, the dossier became public. This was not a coincidence. The Reid-Comey meeting was set up precisely to create the basis for the leaking of the dossier.

Lost in the aftermath of the release of the full dossier was the fact that the allegations were unverified and clearly contained information that was totally wrong. No media outlet focused on the discrepancies. Instead, the world was awash in black ledgers, golden showers, and other salacious and false storylines.

Once more, from CNN's "reckoning":

> It took five years of criminal investigations, civil cases and congressional reports to pull back the curtain on the flimsiness of the dossier. The big picture really came into focus in 2019 with the release of a Justice Department watchdog report.[8]
>
> That report described for the first time Danchenko's many walkbacks in his FBI interviews. It also said FBI agents gave Steele mixed reviews, with some seeing him as a "person of integrity," while others said he had a "lack of self-awareness" and was "underpinned by poor judgment," even if he was acting in good faith.

The report also said the CIA viewed Steele's material as an "Internet rumor."[9]

Last year's bipartisan Senate report said, "the tradecraft reflected in the dossier is generally poor relative to (US intelligence community) standards."[10] The blockbuster 966-page report also raised concerns that some of the material Steele put in his memos was Russian disinformation.[11]

In January 2017, even though I was no longer in the campaign, leaks about me being the link to Russia kept swirling in the news. A day after the Steele dossier became public, Ken Vogel of *Politico* wrote an eye-opening story that tracked the early phases of the investigation on me.[12]

The article laid out the case of how a DNC staffer, Alexandra Chalupa, working with the Clinton campaign, the Embassy of Ukraine in Washington, and a network of sources in Ukraine began to promote storylines of connections between me and Moscow, with Chalupa telling embassy staff that "if we can get enough information on Manafort or Trump involvement in Russia, she could get a hearing in Congress in September" before the election.

Additionally, the story highlighted the release in Ukraine of a ledger which alleged to list cash payments to me totaling $12.7 million. At a press conference Serhiy Leshchenko, an opposition party politician, claimed that the ledger listed payments the basis of which were "totally against the law." What the basis of this assumption was was never mentioned and the authenticity of the ledger was questionable at best. But the *Times* went with a front-page story. The *Times* story went further citing a meeting between President Yanukovych and Putin where Yanukovych told Putin the payments were authorized but there was no trail to worry about. This was totally made up. There was no basis for the allegation, but it was a good booster to the fake narrative.

The reaction in the political and media worlds exploded globally. Lost in the hysteria was the fact that there was no evidence to support any of these accusations. As noted earlier in this book, the National Anti-Corruption Bureau of Ukraine (NABU), an investigative body set up by the US Embassy in Ukraine and the Government of Ukraine to uncover corruption, dismissed the allegations as fake. The black ledger was totally discredited, as was the likelihood of a Putin-Yanukovych meeting about it. Unfortunately for me it was too late. I was a victim of the conspiracy to undermine the Trump campaign. Chalupa, the US Embassy in Kyiv, the Ukrainian Embassy in Washington, and the Clinton campaign had their scalp—mine—and with it the foundation for their narrative as laid out in the Steele dossier.

In 2022 Paul Sperry did an even more detailed dive which exposed how maniacal the Obama administration was in going after me.[13] And how they were trying to protect themselves from a growing "Biden problem."

These events directly related to a situation that happened pretty much exactly a year earlier. On January 12, 2016, a criminal investigation was opened on me that was being pushed by Ali Chalupa and various Soros-backed groups like ANTAC and Daria Kaluniek. Soros had been a big loser in Yanukovych's defeat of Timoshenko in the 2010 presidential election. His group of left-wing ideologues were trying to find dirt on me for the entire Yanukovych term, and failed to find anything. But it did not stop them from trying.

In late 2015 the Obama White House was getting reports on what we now know as the Hunter Biden Burisma "pay for play" scheme that included Vice President Biden's threat to withhold $1 billion in foreign aid unless President Poroshenko fired the Prosecutor General who was investigating corruption of Burisma and as such Hunter Biden's role on the board. Setting off alarms, an investigation was initiated to identify other American consultants who had been working in Ukraine. While there were many, including prominent Democrats, the White House meeting in January of 2016 fixated on me. Why? Because I was a Republican, and according to Chalupa was going to be involved in the Trump campaign. This was a month before I was even considering getting involved, but the Obama White House liked the narrative.

Ironically, I was the deflection for Hunter Biden in 2016. The various investigations came up with nothing, but they tried. In the end, this operation did create the black ledger.

A week after the opening of the political case against me, Andriy Telizhenko, various Ukrainian deputy prosecutors general, a special anti-corruption prosecutor, and the director of NABU met with Eric Ciaramella "the whistleblower" and other NSC officials plus Karen Greenaway at the FBI to discuss investigations into American individuals associated with the Party of Regions.

This is basically the genesis of the focus on me. The Ukrainian government working with the Obama White House to cook up dirt on me. Chalupa, the Ukrainian embassy, and Serhiy Leshchenko pushed this effort forward. This culminated with the black ledger being released by NABU to a reporter at the *New York Times* in August 2016 which started the chain reaction that led to my resignation.[14]

These activities were not happening in a vacuum. On a separate path but with links to the Chalupa activity was what had been organized inside the US government at the FBI. The USG activity centered around Peter Strzok at the FBI and his mistress, Lisa Page, who also worked at the FBI. The two lovers were hardcore Trump haters. If this was not enough to have Strzok disqualified from any Trump investigation, he was also the action officer, appointed by FBI Director James Comey, who wrote the exonerating memo of Hillary Clinton on the illegal server issue. Showing his bias, Strzok wrote the memo before the FBI even conducted their interview of Clinton.

Strzok had become the point man in an investigation that he opened on July 30, 2016, under the code name "Crossfire Hurricane." Crossfire Hurricane focused on contacts between the Trump campaign and Russia. Immediately upon opening the investigation, Strzok flew to London to meet with a US source who was on the USG payroll for a number of years, Stefan Halper.

Halper was an American living in London working at Cambridge University. In fact, he was a longtime intelligence source who networked in the twilight of national security and academia. It was Halper who reached out to Papadopoulos, Carter Page, and Sam Clovis trying to get them to provide incriminating evidence of linkages between the Trump world and Russia. Notwithstanding the fact that Halper's attempts were totally unsuccessful, these contacts were then fed into Strzok's Crossfire Hurricane FBI investigation to create a fictitious narrative of connectivity of the two spheres. Strzok used the storylines to keep the Crossfire investigation moving forward.

My conception of the legal dangers I was facing changed dramatically when *Buzzfeed* published the Steele dossier. Again, I knew the dossier was total misinformation, but everyone else was giving it credence. The more I cried "foul," the more the outside world wanted to believe the outrageous contentions.

When I hung up with Priebus and Trump on January 10, 2017 following the release of the dossier, my anxiety was off of the charts. Notwithstanding the complete lack of evidence, I had a strong feeling that the dossier story would have legs into the early days of the new Trump administration. I wasn't yet thinking about a special prosecutor, but I could sense the Democrats would not let this go and would demand investigations to keep it going. They were attacking Trump on Russian collusion and I figured it would be part of the political games they would play in Trump's first months in the White House. But the Republicans controlled both houses and the White House, so I figured I would just tolerate it until it died. I adjusted my personal plan looking to reemerge sometime around March. I was not hiding anything, so I didn't worry about anything coming out. It was simply a matter of enduring the attacks until they moved on to something else.

As the presidential transition wound to an end, the MSM was now moving into overdrive. The *Washington Post* published a story saying that, "According to a senior U.S. government official, Flynn phoned Russian Ambassador Sergey Kislyak several times on Dec. 29, the day the Obama administration announced the expulsion of 35 Russian officials as well as other measures in retaliation for the hacking."

What did Flynn say, the article asked, "and did it undercut the U.S. sanctions? The Logan Act (though never enforced since becoming law in 1799—yes 1799) bars U.S. citizens from correspondence intending to influence a foreign government about 'disputes' with the United States. Was its spirit violated?"[15]

The suggestion was that Trump was interfering with official US foreign policy being conducted by the outgoing Obama team and the implication being subtly promoted was that there was something illegal with Flynn talking to the Russian Ambassador—that it was a continuation of the collusion between Trump and Russia. In fact, it is totally natural for an in-coming National Security Adviser to open up lines of communication with Washington ambassadors prior to taking office. Flynn doing so was totally normal, just not in the supercharged atmosphere in DC.

Suddenly all of the traps that had been laid by Obama and the Clintons were creating a serious firestorm. These headlines were all meant to trigger a larger focus and, ultimately, they succeeded.

The reaction to all of this from Republican leaders was mixed. Because they did not know Trump, they didn't dismiss the allegations out of hand. Paul Ryan gave support to an investigation on the theory that it would be better to clear the air, but in the end, this only muddied the water by lending credence to the MSM's overtly false narrative. In reality, Ryan was leading the "swamp" (the Republican part of it), fighting back against Trump.

The clearest sign that the story would not go away any time soon came on January 13, 2017, when the Republican-led Senate Select Committee announced that it would investigate Russian activity during the 2016 elections including any links between Russia and people associated with political campaigns (i.e., Trump). On January 25, the House Permanent Select Committee on Intelligence (also a Republican-led committee) announced that it would conduct a similar investigation. Not by coincidence, the only activity they chose to investigate was the fictitious allegations against the Trump campaign. Ken Vogel's article in *Politico* set out a very detailed story of collusion between the Clinton campaign and Ukraine, a foreign power. This, however, was not where the two committees wanted to focus their investigations. So, the only *real* collusion between a US political campaign in 2016 and a foreign government was swept under the rug by both committees.

Again, while I was not worried about any particular investigation, I now realized that I would need to hire lawyers. Not knowing what I was going to be up against, other than a political propaganda tsunami, concerned me greatly. Recognizing that these investigations were totally political, I decided it made sense to hire a firm with strong Democrat Hill connections. I needed to have professional help that could cut through the legal issues and focus on the political ones. Since I knew there were no "Russian contacts" that interacted with me on the elections, I wanted a firm that could sit down with Senator Mark Warner, the ranking Democrat on the Senate Committee, and Adam Schiff on the House side.

I had known Warner personally for over ten years so I expected he would not require much attention on the issue. There was no way he would believe I was working with Russia against US interests (boy was I wrong on him). Schiff was a different story. He had no interest in truth or facts. All he cared about was a good headline. So, my law firm needed to be able to work with others on the House committee, including with House leadership.

I sought guidance from my longtime friend and legal adviser Richard Hibey. Dick had been a trial litigator on some of the most important cases in Washington over the past twenty years. He was also accustomed to the politics of the law having represented former President Marcos in his departure from the Philippines and settling into Hawaii.

It was Hibey who led me to hire WilmerHale, a major law firm in Washington with strong political underpinnings. One of the principal partners there was Jamie Gorelick, the former Deputy Attorney General in the Clinton administration. Gorelick was a skilled attorney, and she knew every important Democrat on the Hill. With WilmerHale, it was my hope that I was hiring expertise that would be able to communicate with the Democrats to deflect any misunderstandings and misconceptions about Russian collusion in general and my involvement in Ukraine specifically.

The lawyers, of course, saw it as an opportunity. Within a month, I had legal bills upward of half a million dollars, which was indicative of how Washington law firms work. Congressional investigations are a cottage industry in Washington and the law firms know exactly how to pump an investigation in the name of doing more research. I had not even had a meeting yet when I got this first bill.

I also knew that the DC political establishment never accepted defeat. The partnership of Democrats, the MSM, and social media would not give up, facts be damned. I did not know how they would strike back, and what made me uncomfortable was that I knew that I was the easiest target for the coalition to use. In the past I would have dismissed this fear as paranoia and moved on. But in the new world order, I feared that truth was not relevant. Even though I had spent my career fighting Russia and communism, including the last ten years helping Ukraine become a part of Europe against the vehement opposition of Putin, I believed I was vulnerable.

On January 20, Donald J. Trump was sworn in as the forty-fifth president of the United States. As I watched Trump take his oath, I flashed back to our many trips in the car where we would talk about why he was running. I remembered one day as we were returning from a day on the campaign trail in June. He had been to three states that day. His energy level was high from the rallies, but he was tired.

As our caravan was stopped in traffic returning to Trump Tower, I said to him that as president he would not have to wait for these lights. He looked at me and said, "Is this all worth it?"

Catching himself, he answered his own question. "You know I have to do this. Obama is ruining the country and Clinton will destroy what is left. We need to win."

I looked at him and saw the warrior. I said in a matter-of-fact way, "Donald, you are going to win, so get ready."

"I am so ready," he said as we pulled up to Trump Tower.

As I watched Trump being sworn in—saying the words that would give him the power to transfer his readiness into action—I smiled with a sense of satisfaction knowing that the country was going to be in a better place for the next four years. But, I wondered: would I be?

CHAPTER 9

The Office of Special Counsel

As the storylines grew during the first months of 2017, so did my exposure. Obsessed with trying to connect the nonexistent dots between Trump and the Russians, the MSM went into overdrive inventing a narrative that implicated nearly everyone in Trump's orbit.

While the focus never shifted away from me during the early days of the Trump administration, the heavy fire was aimed at Michael Flynn, Trump's newly appointed National Security Advisor.

The focus on Flynn centered on Flynn's interactions with the Russian Ambassador, Sergey Kislyak. Apparently, Flynn had not disclosed certain meetings in his government papers with Kislyak and then when he remembered and added the meetings, the substance was attacked. When Flynn met with Kislyak, it was after Obama had imposed sanctions on Russia for interfering with the 2016 elections, not for Russian collusion, but for cyber-attacks on election tabulations. Flynn asked Kislyak not to retaliate and to wait until the new administration started.

When the meeting became known the swamp attacked. They accused Flynn of violating the Logan Act, a law enacted in 1799 that criminalized negotiations between unauthorized Americans and foreign governments. It was meant to uncover behavior of British spies hidden in the US bureaucracy. Only two people had ever been indicted under the Logan Act. One in 1802 and the other in 1852. Neither was convicted. Flynn was not an unauthorized spy. He was the publicly appointed incoming National

Security Advisor to the president-elect. He was totally in his lane when he met with Kislyak, and their discussion was more than appropriate.

While the Logan Act violation was driving the news after the meeting between Flynn and Kislyak was exposed in the media, it was Flynn's meeting with Vice President Pence that triggered his resignation. When he briefed Pence, Flynn denied raising sanctions with Kislyak. This was the basis for which Flynn resigned his White House job in February.

It is important to note that Flynn had every right to have the conversation that he did with Kislyak. It is also not surprising in the hustle of building a team to work for him at the White House that he would not recall these details. However, in the frenzied Russian collusion atmospherics of Washington in early 2017, the telephone call and the failure to recall all of the details of it were fatal to Flynn. First, he was forced to resign from the White House and later Mueller indicted him for lying to the FBI about this call.

The FBI meeting was another of the Deep State setups. During Flynn's first days in office, Deputy Director of the FBI Andrew McCabe contacted Flynn and asked him to sit for a few minutes with some FBI agents. Flynn saw no reason not to meet. At that point the politicization of the FBI by the Obama administration and McCabe's partisan support for Hillary Clinton were unknown. It was a classic case of entrapment which Comey admitted at a later point.

That one call with Kislyak bankrupted Flynn and destroyed the reputation he had built up over thirty years of service in the military. It is important to note that just as they targeted me, the Obama administration had it out for Flynn. As Director of the Defense Intelligence Agency, Flynn believed that Iran was intricately involved in promoting terrorism and targeting Americans. His intelligence briefings were very different than the CIA briefings John Brennan was providing to Obama that were sympathetic to Iran. Obama believed that Brennan's view more closely aligned with his view and pressured Flynn to lighten up on the anti-Iran reports. When Flynn refused, Obama fired him.

In his first meeting with President-elect Trump right after the elections, Obama spent more time warning Trump not to bring Flynn into his administration than on any other national security subject. Clearly, Flynn was in the bulls-eye. When Trump appointed Flynn NSC Advisor on Nov 17, 2016, the die was cast, and the Deep State added Flynn to their list of targets. The Kislyak call was the tool they needed to bludgeon

Flynn. And bludgeon him they did. Flynn resigned on February 17, 2017, the second victim of the Russian hysteria narrative. I was the first when I resigned my official position in the campaign.

The third victim, and the one who made the Russian hoax the damaging political narrative it became, was Senator Jeff Sessions. Sessions had been chairman of the Trump for President campaign. His main role was to be the principal surrogate for the campaign and to be the official link to Washington, including the Ambassadorial Corps.

When Trump appointed Sessions to be his Attorney General, the swamp targeted Sessions claiming he was conflicted in representing the Department of Justice because of his political ties to the campaign. Of course, this was a joke. The attorneys general have historically been connected to the presidents in very personal and political ways. Eric Holder, Obama's attorney general, often proudly referred to himself as "the president's wingman." No one doubted what that meant, especially conservative political organizations like the Tea Party or anti-abortion groups, which were targeted by Obama's Justice Department.

Of course, the ultimate example is President John F. Kennedy appointing his brother Robert Attorney General. None of this mattered. The fix was in.

Most of Washington dismissed the "Sessions conflict" as just political rhetoric. Most, but not Jeff Sessions. The matter came to a head in Sessions' mind after a *Washington Post* story on March 1 reported that Sessions had two contacts with Ambassador Kislyak that contradicted his confirmation hearing testimony. For some unknown reason, the report was jarring to Sessions.

Based on this story and previous political attacks from the Democrats, Sessions believed he was conflicted from having any role inside DOJ on any investigations into Russian collusion. The story simply highlighted a spontaneous meeting between Sessions and Ambassador Kislyak at a public reception after the foreign policy speech candidate Trump gave at the Mayflower Hotel. It was very understandable why Sessions would not recall such a meeting. While the headlines blared conflict, no evidence of any improper behavior surfaced, just innuendo and the Democrat fake news narrative.

Despite this, on March 2, 2017, without telling the president or anyone outside of his DOJ staff circle, Sessions officially recused himself from participating in any investigations "related in any way to the campaign for president of the United States." While asserting that it was totally false to believe that Sessions had any interactions with "Russian operatives," he stated that he had decided to recuse himself from any matter relating to the 2016 campaign.

This decision united Nancy Pelosi and President Trump in a way that was unique for the entire Trump term. Both believed that Sessions should resign. Pelosi claimed Sessions could not preside over the Justice Department because he was conflicted on everything. Trump felt betrayed and while he would not fire Sessions, Trump effectively ended any useful role for Sessions in his administration.

The Sessions decision also pushed the swamp deeper in the collusion narrative. Paul Ryan, the Republican Speaker of the House, and Senator Lindsey Graham, congratulated Sessions. This infuriated Trump even more. These positive endorsements of Sessions's betrayal confirmed to President Trump that the Washington establishment, *meaning Republicans and Democrats*, was going to be united in fighting him for four years. Once again, Trump's instincts were 100 percent correct.

This decision by Sessions was the most consequential decision of the entire four years of the Trump Presidency. While it paled compared to the important substantive decisions Trump was making, it armed the swamp with the tools it needed to poison the atmosphere, and it created a toxic cloud over everything related to Donald Trump.

It also set the wheels in motion for the end game strategy of the Clinton/Obama/Comey/Brennan plan to appoint a Special Prosecutor. To this end, the Sessions decision enabled the corrupt Washington system to target anyone who was a part of the Trump world, simply because we believed he was the best man to be president.

When I heard that Sessions had recused himself, I said to my wife, "The ante has just been raised and I am now at risk." I didn't know the full import of what I meant but I did know that the swamp was coming for us, and I was at the very front of the line.

Already in the first forty-five days of his presidency, Trump was being isolated in his own administration. While it was not apparent yet, Comey was orchestrating a covert effort to create the momentum for the appointment of a Special Counsel. Typical of his duplicity, Comey was misleading the president, even while enabling the system to target his presidency.

Comey had already played a major role in undermining Trump. First, he oversaw the whitewashing of Hillary Clinton on the server issue that hobbled her campaign. Tasking Peter Strzok to draft an exonerating memo of Clinton's behavior, while giving immunity to Clinton staffers who had broken the law on destruction of evidence under subpoena, Comey provided Clinton with a clean bill of health. He had also appointed Strzok to oversee Crossfire Hurricane in late July 2016, worked with the Obama White House to get the Steele dossier into the public domain, and then worked with Clapper and Brennan to fast-track the Obama National Intelligence investigation that was meant to box Trump and put low-level, unverified data into the public domain.

Despite his insiders' role in plotting against Donald Trump, Comey continued to curry favor with Trump, pretending to be his friend in the bureaucracy. When Comey met with the president on February 14 to brief him on the latest developments, he made it clear to Trump that he was not a target in the investigation. This was a lie. The whole investigation was trying to figure out how to get a Special Counsel appointed with one purpose in mind: bringing down the president.

After the meeting, Trump pulled Comey aside to ask him to cut Flynn some slack. Later, Comey would misrepresent this aside to say that Trump was pressuring him to drop the Flynn investigation. It did not matter because three days later Flynn was asked to resign.

After Sessions recused himself, the focus returned to me. The *New York Times* published a story on March 20 presenting the black ledger narrative all over again. There were no new facts, only vague new allegations that a "member of Parliament in Ukraine released documents that he said showed that Mr. Manafort took steps to hide" payments. Again, it was all fake.[1]

Plus, NABU had already cleared me and declared the ledger fake. But that did not stop the MSM. Everything was presented as if there was new evidence, and the investigation was continuing.

The Ukrainian politician who leveled the original charges had another press conference and made the same claims. While the *Times* included my statement dismissing all of the facts, it was the story that was the story. This became a pattern over the next eighteen months. Anonymous leaks from government sources, coupled with partisan politicians repeating the accusations with no real facts, would appear in either *Buzzfeed* or the *New York Times* or the *Washington Post* or *Yahoo News* or the AP. There were a group of about six reporters who would get the lead and then the others would repeat the same story, making it appear as if there was this massive investigation going on. Sensationalizing the news, the headlines would be supplemented by MSNBC or CNN. The headline was the substance.

Manafort has ties to Russia. Well, publicly I did have a Russian client until 2009. The client was an informer for the FBI during the same time period I worked for him on his business interests, some of which extended to the US.

Manafort supported the pro-Putin Yanukovych administration. Yanukovych was not pro-Putin. Coverage of his time in office clearly demonstrated that fact.

Manafort was paid millions of dollars for his work in Ukraine. True. It was public information and many of those dollars were paid to me for the team of consultants that I was managing, including the Democratic firm that ran the presidential campaigns for Al Gore, John Kerry, and Bernie Sanders.

None of these stories had any value to the Russian investigation, but the sensationalism drove the churn on the media propaganda. Of course, Rachel Maddow, Chris Hayes, and the left-wing media spinsters would weave these headlines into a narrative that had me working directly for Putin and a traitor to my country. In fact, during my trial, George Soros was funding groups to have people stand in front of the Federal courthouse holding signs that said "Traitor," "Go back to Russia," and "Putin Puppet." Truth was not relevant. One-liners to tweet were the coin of the realm.

Once the media saturation created an image of me as connected to Russia in a shady or illegal way, the stories started to leak about possible financial improprieties. Some of the early stories centered on the existence of offshore accounts.

Without getting too technical, the stories focused on the existence of bank accounts in Cyprus. While the allegations scared me, I did not feel legally vulnerable. The reason for this was because the anonymous leaked stories dealt with information that I, and my junior associate Rick Gates, had *voluntarily* disclosed to the FBI in 2014. The setting of the disclosures was in depositions that both Gates and I had offered to the FBI in their investigation of corruption in Ukraine. The investigation was aimed at Ukrainian politicians. We were approached by the FBI to help them understand how business was conducted in Ukraine, and I volunteered wholeheartedly.

I started working in Ukraine in 2005. My contracts were multi-million dollar written contracts to conduct western-style political consulting in Ukraine. We managed three Parliamentary elections, two local elections, and a presidential campaign over the first five years. In Ukraine, we were averaging a national campaign every year. Our contracts were with the Party of Regions, a political party in the east. Donors to the Party would sign contracts with us to pay for the services. Normally, the payors would wire our fees from their offshore accounts, usually located in Cyprus, the Seychelles, or the Caribbean. In those early years the money was wired directly to one of my corporate accounts in the US. I would receive the money and pay the consultants. Everything was very transparent.

Around 2010 the USG ramped up their suspicious activities reporting on money from countries that had banking laws that criminals would use to their advantage. It is important to note that major worldwide corporations also used these tax havens to conduct their businesses. The mixture created confusion, and the USG started to monitor the wires going into and out of these accounts.

Since all of my money was for political consulting and in-country government advisory work, I did not worry about any review of my accounts or money movement. However, since large chunks of money were coming directly into my US bank accounts, the US Treasury began to monitor and issue SARs reports (Suspicious Activity Reports) on my transfers. These filings are not indicative of anything wrong or illegal. They are motivated by the sourcing of the funds coming from countries that are tax havens. Unfortunately for me, these reports had a chilling effect on the compliance departments of my banks. While there was nothing untoward about my receipts, the banks began to worry about getting pulled into something nefarious. Without any due diligence and with no warning, my banks started to shut down my accounts.

The net result was I was having trouble getting money into the US. This created a serious problem for me. First, I did not have money to pay my vendors because the transfers from Cyprus to my Wells Fargo and Chase accounts were being rejected. I found myself in a dilemma.

The solution sort of presented itself. I tasked my staffer, Rick Gates, to build a structure to avoid this problem. Gates contacted our lawyers in Cyprus, whom we had met when working for Oleg Deripaska in the late 2000s. They suggested a solution that made sense to me. Off shore companies are a cottage industry in Cyprus—a one-stop shop for creating legal books, filing with the government authorities, and managing the flow of money.

While working for Deripaska, we had created a business investment fund, Pericles Investment Fund. He was the 100-percent General Partner, and we were the Limited Partner researching and vetting possible investments. We were responsible for finding the deals, conducting the due diligence, and ultimately the plan was for us to manage the assets acquired.

In 2008 this fund purchased its first asset, a Ukrainian cable system. At the time Ukraine's cable TV businesses were locally run and owned. Our thinking was to do what John Malone had done at TCI in the late 1980s. Malone bought up local cable systems all over the US, rolled them into one entity, and took them public—Liberty Media. Just after closing on our first cable purchase, the world entered into the 2008–2009 recession, and Deripaska's financial condition was undermined. He had been building his aluminum empire by leveraging debt, principally Western debt. The Western banks started to cash in, since they were exposed from the recession, and Deripaska was on the verge of losing his empire. Who bailed him out? Putin. Putin saw the value of this asset—the second largest aluminum company in the world—just as he had seen the value of so many assets in Russia.

The oligarchs had underestimated Putin in 2000. They took him for a know-nothing guy out of the KGB. They thought they would own him, like they had owned Yeltsin. Well, Putin and Yeltsin are two very different people. The first thing Putin did as president was use the enormous power of the Russian presidency to tell the oligarchs, in so many words, that there was a new sheriff in town. He said, "You work for me. I own everything." He'd gotten away with it in many industries, but he hadn't done it with aluminum yet. He saw his chance with Deripaska after the recession and he ended up owning him around 2009.

When Deripaska nearly collapsed and no longer had the financial wherewithal to do these investments, which were not a part of his aluminum business, the $100 million he was going to put into the fund dried up.

At that time, we had identified several other cable systems to purchase. To facilitate the purchases, a series of Special Purpose Vehicles (SPVs) were created and "put on the shelf." As a purchase reached the point of closing the transaction, one of the SPVs would be used to do the deal. The ownership of these SPVs was a part of Deripaska's network of companies set up by his Cyprus attorneys.

Since there were no further cable purchases, the SPVs sat dormant. When the SARs reports caused my US banking problems, Gates discussed the options with Deripaska's Cyprus lawyers. The lawyers recommended that we use the SPVs to do contracts with the Party of Regions donors to move the received payments and then transfer the money according to a new framework. The goal was to limit the number of big transfers into my US accounts. This way the consultants were paid directly, some big-ticket investments would be paid directly, and money that was transferred directly to my political company would be much less. From my standpoint, it was perfect. Deripaska's lawyer would manage everything. (I was told by Gates that the lawyer's name would be the one on the SPVs, though this turned out to be a lie.)

The plan envisioned a year-end audit in Cyprus of all of the money movement and a netting out of fees paid directly to my US companies and US investments. This way any money that was for my personal use would be captured even if the money did not go directly into one of my US accounts. There was nothing funny about the flow of money and everything was transparent. We were not hiding the sources of money which were reflected in our accounting ledgers and my personal taxes. Payments to consultants would be captured in their annual tax filings outside of my filings since these were not fees to me. I was just the processing center between the client and the vendor.

Important to me was that the system be transparent. I was told by Gates, who dealt with the Cyprus attorney and with my US accountants, that as long as I did not own the SPV and had no actual control, I did not have to file the existence of an offshore account. There was a test for determining control and I was assured that I did not fall into this category. If I had been told that I did meet the definition of ownership, I would have disclosed the existence of these accounts because I was not hiding them. When you look at my bank ledgers you see the wires coming directly from the same offshore accounts to my personal bank accounts. The transfers were not hidden, and the money was identified by contract and wire transfer.

Rick Gates was my administrative person, and he was responsible for managing this setup. I trusted him to be careful, competent, and honest in his management of the money flows and record-keeping. Well, he was careful and competent, but not honest—something we shall discuss later in the book.

At the time, I felt that I was on solid ground. So much did I believe I was on solid ground that in 2014 when the FBI began to investigate corruption in Ukraine, they asked my attorney if I would be willing to explain how I interacted with Ukrainian contracts. The FBI told my lawyer that I was not a target or a witness but that I had information on business practices that could be helpful to their investigation. Thinking I had no legal exposure, I agreed to help the FBI.

Gates and I spent a day meeting with FBI agents. In the course of those depositions, I fully disclosed all of the details of the above setup. I had no knowledge of the names of the companies or the money flows, but Gates did. I had him organize everything and we presented it all to the FBI as examples.

I understood how the Ukrainian government worked and how business worked there. I thought I could be helpful. If I'd felt the least bit insecure in the legality of this network, I would not have volunteered to help and turn all my records over to the FBI. I cooperated because I believed I had no legal exposure.

Not being a target, I gave the FBI all of the SPVs. We provided them with the names of the banks and the companies, and Gates gave them the names of the accounts, so that they could better understand how the Russian model worked, how Deripaska worked, and how the Ukrainians worked—how money flowed from the Ukrainian oligarchs through these SPVs to Podesta and Mercury, or to whomever. The FBI took all this information down and that was the last I ever heard from them. They never followed up with me. Clearly, in 2014, the FBI did not think I had broken the law.

When I was indicted in 2017 for FBAR violations by not reporting the existence of foreign accounts on my annual tax statement, Weissman would make his case off of the very documentation that I personally had provided to the FBI in 2014. He knew that I contributed this information. He also knew that the FBI did not pursue any criminal actions for this "scheme" as Weissman called it. He also had the deposition that laid all of this out.

So even after I was indicted for these crimes, I did not think it was a criminal liability because if it was, the matter would have been the foundation of a criminal case against me in 2014.

Weissman saw the opportunity to build a media case against me for a structure used by mainstream Fortune 500 international businesses and me. There was nothing sinister about the accounts and definitely nothing criminal about them. They were a typical way of conducting international business. Weissman made them out to be a criminal conspiracy where I was hiding illegal money from Russians.

Rick Gates worked for me in a staff capacity. I never viewed him as strong enough to be my point in business, but I came to believe he could manage some of the day-to-day affairs. He'd started off at Black, Manafort, Stone, and Kelly as a gofer and evolved over time into being a research coordinator and then my administrative assistant.

When I created my firm, DMP International, in 2008, I needed a couple of assistants. I didn't want to build a big structure like the one I'd had in the 1990s. I just needed a few key people. I hired Gates because I knew who he was, and I trusted him. Over time, he emerged as my principal assistant.

By 2009, I was spending a lot of time in Ukraine, effectively living over there and coming back every few months. In this context, Gates evolved into a sort of CFO for the business operations. He was the one who managed the flow of money for my company; he dealt with my accountants, my CPA, and with a firm that handled all of my bill processing and other financial matters. Gates wasn't an accountant, so we had a firm that managed the bookkeeping operations and the payments at the direction of myself and Gates. But Gates always was the managing intermediary. He was the link between all of these aspects of the business, and he was my link to them. He was also responsible for managing the accounts receivable, billing clients, creating contracts, loan agreements, and payments to vendors—both corporate and in some instances personal, as well as the management of vendor needs like travel, lodging, travel itineraries, as he did with Tad Devine's media requirements in Ukraine.

There were two components to the accounting of my business. The first was business management firm NKFSB. Their role was similar to that of a CFO. They managed the business accounts, payment of bills, management of revenue, bookkeeping, etc. While I would sign off on the payments and billing, generally it was Gates talking to our account representative who prepared the lists that I would sign off on.

KWC was my accounting firm. They took the work product from NKFSB and dealt with the taxes, loans, and treatment of revenue from the multiple contracts we had and the multiple companies/LLCs that were a part of my personal financial life. Again, Gates was the link between the two firms.

I structured things this way because I needed to spend my time servicing the clients who were paying for me and expected me to be available. This expectation caused me to be on the road for over six months each year. It would have been impossible for me to service the clients and manage the finances of my business. Using two professional firms for the bookkeeping and tax filings made sense and having a CFO type to be the administrative link was necessary. I selected Gates for this role. It would turn out to be the biggest mistake of my life.

Because I was often on the road, I relied on Gates to manage the finances of my business. And because of the sensitivity of the work I was doing, we never spoke over the telephone or corresponded over email on the details. The threat of hacking from political opponents, especially Russian hackers, was very real. We were very careful in our discussions of sensitive business and financial issues. We had to be. So I would give Gates detailed instructions and he would get the job done. The only way this worked was with a great deal of trust. I trusted Gates with everything. This trust proved to be grossly misplaced. For this I took responsibility when convicted. However, this responsibility was not an admission of pre-meditated guilt. It was an admission of mistaken trust and approving the system that Weissman exploited, with the critical assistance of Rick Gates's lies, to send me to prison.

Should I have done a better job of researching my potential culpability for not filing the FBAR on my tax returns? In hindsight, yes. Relying on Gates' summary of the Cyprus legal structure and my full admissions in 2014 gave me a false sense of security. In normal investigations, like 2014, the truth would be valued and I would not be indicted. In a hyper-toxic environment like 2016 in the hands of a deceitful prosecutor who viewed facts as being malleable, my culpability became a key piece of a "gotcha" mentality that was central to the Special Counsel's mission to bring down Donald Trump.

Now that President Trump was a target and Russia was the angle, none of those facts mattered. Facts no longer seemed to matter at all. The Democrats were achieving their objectives. The MSM was blowing up any connection between the Trump world and Russia. One of my lenders on a home loan was of Russian heritage, so according to the MSM and Twitter stories, "I must have gotten the loan because I was working with the Russian government"; Michael Cohen's wife was Ukrainian, so that was the link; My longtime associate, Kilimnik, was part of the Russian intelligence operation because he was Russian and multi-lingual. The lengths they would go to find a connection were absurd and the stories ceaseless.

I was handling it on my end, but the relentless barrage of fabrications was distracting the president. Trump was being pulled into the vortex and he couldn't help but keep raising the stakes. Even on the outside, I recognized that Trump was going to be very difficult to manage during this cycle. Having worked under pressure with Trump, I knew that he would be totally fixated on getting himself exonerated by Comey and the FBI. I also knew the way investigations work in Washington, how they lingered on and on and on. Now that the media was engaged as intimately as they were, the narrative could only do one thing: grow and grow and grow.

Throughout March and April, a series of events would unfold which would only make things worse for everyone involved—Trump, Comey, the FBI, and perhaps more than anyone, me.

At a House Intel Committee hearing on March 20, Comey confirmed the existence of an FBI investigation of Russian interference and "the nature of any links with individuals associated with the Trump campaign.

Two days later, on March 22, Representative Devin Nunes, the Republican chairman of the House Intelligence Committee, held a press conference in which he revealed that communications of some members of Trump's transition team had been collected by the intelligence community. Nunes admitted that he had met his source at the White House, which led to a media outburst. It was later proven that Nunes was in a sequestered room looking at intelligence—the normal way such reviews are carried out as material could not be removed from the White House. But the damage was done. Adam Schiff, the ranking Democrat on the committee, called on Nunes to recuse himself from the investigation. On April 6, under pressure from Democrats and Republicans, Nunes stepped aside from the investigation.

On May 3, Comey disclosed at a Senate Judiciary hearing that the FBI had opened investigations on more than one US citizen in connection to an FBI investigation of any contacts between the Trump campaign and Russia. He declined to answer if Trump was under investigation.

On May 8, Deputy Attorney General Rod Rosenstein learned that Trump was planning on firing Comey. Rosenstein agreed with the move and wrote a memo outlining his concerns about Comey's leadership. The next day, Trump fired Comey based on the recommendations of Attorney General Sessions and Deputy Attorney General Rosenstein.

As the controversies surrounding Comey, the FBI investigation, Flynn, and Trump continued to mount, the media showed no signs of backing off. It was clear by the middle of May that these stories wouldn't simply go away, as so many surrounding the Trump team had in the past.

Finally, on May 17, the investigation moved into a whole new dimension when Rod Rosenstein appointed former FBI director Robert S. Mueller III to lead a special counsel investigation into possible collusion between the Trump campaign and the Russian government. In his statement, Rosenstein said, "It is in the public interest for me to exercise my authorities and appoint a special counsel to assume responsibility for this matter. My decision is not a finding that crimes have been committed or that any prosecution is warranted. I have made no such determination. What I have determined is that based upon the unique circumstances, the public interest requires me to place this investigation under the authority of a person who exercises a degree of independence from the normal chain of command."

In the first twenty-four hours, Mueller brought Andrew Weissman on board as the lead prosecutor. Weissman was known for, among other things, his prosecution of Enron and reputedly sometimes disregarding the constitutional rights of suspects in his investigatory tactics. He was a small, unscrupulous political partisan who would destroy lives to get what he wanted, justice be damned.

Weissman carried this unethical partisanship into his role in the Mueller investigation. I found it very ironic when I saw Weissman's book on his experiences as the lead investigator in Mueller's star chamber investigation. He titled it *Where Law Ends*. It was the perfect title for his book, because the law ended at the doorstep of the Office of Special Counsel. I was about to find this out big-time.

By pure coincidence, I ran into A. B. Culvahouse, my old friend who had worked with us on the vice-presidential selection process, at my local CVS the day after Weissman's appointment. A. B. was a solid member of the DC legal and political world as Managing Partner of the powerhouse law firm O'Melveny and Myers.

Pulling me to the side, A. B. told me he had dealt with Weissman in the Enron case. He told me that Weissman could not be trusted on anything. He will push beyond all legal and ethical boundaries and will create narratives that have no relationship to reality. Worse, he would demand that the defendants submit to his narratives regardless of how disconnected from the truth they may be. Finally, he suggested I read Sidney Powell's book on the Enron case, *Licensed to Lie*.

As I left CVS to get into my car, I thought to myself, "Great, the truth does not matter, my constitutional rights do not matter." The comfort of knowing there was no Russian collusion counted for less and less each day. If A. B. was right—and he was rarely wrong—this new Special Counsel only cared about scalps, not justice. And I was directly in their bull's-eye. The truth was that my life had just changed in ways I couldn't begin to imagine.

CHAPTER 10

A No-Knock Raid

It wouldn't take long for Culvahouse's warnings to—quite literally—hit home.

As a by-product of the "black ledger" story in August of 2016, the FARA (Foreign Agents Registration Act) unit at the Department of Justice began, in late 2016, to take an interest in my work on behalf of the Party of Regions in Ukraine. Initially I didn't think much of their inquiry because I didn't believe that my work fell under the purview of the Foreign Corrupt Practices Act that set up the FARA office.

FARA is a public-disclosure statute enacted in 1938 as a legislative response to extensive foreign propaganda activities in the US during the run-up to World War II. (The office of FARA is located in the Counterintelligence and Export Control Section (CES) in the National Security Division (NSD) of the Department of Justice.) The purpose of the law is to require foreign agents who are representing the interests of foreign principals, usually governments, in the US and engage in what FARA calls "political activities." If the lobbying firm or individuals are engaged in such activity, they must file disclosure forms periodically laying out "their relationship with the foreign principal, as well as activities, receipts, and disbursements in support of those activities."

The relevant definitions focus on foreign principals which the Act defines as:

1. Any foreign government;
2. Any foreign political party;
3. Any association, corporation, organization, or "combination of persons" that *either* was established under a foreign country's laws *or* maintains its principal place of business in a foreign country; and
4. Any individual outside the United States (other a US citizen who is also domiciled in the US).

The triggering element of the Act is if the agent is engaged in specified activity from the Act. Without getting too lawyerly, the Act defines an "agent" as

> an individual or entity that acts "within the United States" at the order, request, direction, or control of either: (1) a "foreign principal"; or (2) a person "any of whose activities are directly or indirectly supervised, directed, controlled, financed, or subsidized in whole or in major part by a "foreign principal."[1]

The law has been viewed as vague and unclear as to what activities would trigger an agent status. For example, acting within the United States at another's order, request, direction, or control is insufficient by itself to create "agent" status under FARA. In order to be an "agent," an individual or entity must also engage in FARA-registrable activity.

At the time of my indictment for FARA activities, work in a foreign nation or political campaigns in foreign countries were not considered "FARA registrable" activities. In fact, the FARA director at DOJ believed that my work was marginal, at best, as considered registrable. It was Weissman who twisted facts to build his own narrative that expanded the definitions. He had no authority to change the interpretation, but he did have the unchallenged power, in the Russian collusion hysteria, to expand its application to me personally.

The FARA law, historically, has been administered on the civil side, as opposed to the criminal side, although the law contains both options for the DOJ. For a criminal conviction of the statute, the USG must find that the failure to register and file the periodic disclosure forms was willful:

"a willful failure to register, a willfully false statement of a material fact, or a willful omission of a material fact." Through pressure on witnesses, Weissman constructed a criminal case that the office of FARA had totally rejected prior to the Special Counsel being appointed on May 17.

The law requires that any agent of a foreign government register their contract with the Department of Justice and then file quarterly disclosure reports of any activity on behalf of the foreign government with the United States government. I was confident that I had not violated the act by not registering. The reason for my confidence was that my work focused on managing elections in Ukraine, work that was clearly not covered by FARA. For US lobbying efforts, I had arranged for two prominent DC firms to be hired—Podesta Company, a powerhouse Democrat lobbying company, and Mercury Communications, a bipartisan government affairs and communications firm.

To manage the FARA inquiry that popped up after the black ledger stories emerged in the media, I hired the law firm of Akin Gump Strauss Hauer & Feld. This firm specialized in FARA registration laws and had represented me at Black, Manafort, Stone, and Kelly when I managed a large practice representing foreign governments in Washington. My attorney at Akin was Melissa Laurenza. She was an experienced FARA lawyer and had a good working relationship with the Director of the FARA unit, Heather Hunt.

Hunt managed the FARA office with a collegial hand. While firm in her expectation of disclosures, she listened when someone indicated why they did not believe they needed to file disclosures. My situation was one of those instances and she worked with Melissa to understand why I felt differently.

After the dossier story broke in January 2017, the tenor of the meetings between Laurenza and Hunt started to change. All of a sudden, members of the DOJ National Security Division started to attend the FARA meetings. Despite the very mundane nature of the administrative process, the list of attendees grew.

During this phase of negotiation, every time we thought we had an agreement that I wouldn't have to file, another negative story about me would pop up. But after extensive due diligence, Hunt told my lawyer that my situation was in a gray area. She divided my work into a couple of phases. The first seven years I was only doing political work in Ukraine and was not required to disclose that work. However, after my client was elected president of Ukraine in 2010, Hunt believed that I did have some disclosure duties. As far as I was concerned, having hired two DC firms to lobby the United States government, including Tony Podesta, the brother of John Podesta, who was chairman of the Clinton campaign, to do the actually lobbying work, they were the ones dealing with the US government, not me. I was dealing with them occasionally, but usually it was my staff person, Rick Gates.

Nevertheless, Hunt felt any work I asked the two firms to do "might" fall into the disclosure bucket. While I disagreed that I should file, my attorney persuaded me that I should do so just to get the controversy closed. It was difficult to argue. My overall situation was becoming increasingly political and despite my reservations, I wanted to be careful to dot my I's and cross my T's if only to protect myself from the growing political attacks.

When I hired the two lobbying firms, I told them that they should register under FARA to avoid any controversy. This instruction was written into their contracts in 2012 and 2013. Weissman had copies of those contracts. In fact, I made filing with FARA a requirement that was actually a part of the contracts I signed with the two firms. For their own reasons, the two firms preferred to register their work under the Lobbying Disclosure Act (LDA) which has a lower disclosure standard than FARA. I told them unless they could demonstrate otherwise, I believed it best that they register under FARA.

While the facts can get confusing, the setup was straight forward. The US consultants would be hired by an NGO that was set up to deal with Europe on issues that related to Ukraine making application to become a member of the EU community.

Mercury hired a FARA expert at the law firm of Skadden Arps. Based on facts that Mercury disclosed to Skadden, the law firm opined in a detailed legal memorandum that the contract did not trigger FARA and could be registered under the LDA. Gates was working with the two firms and informed me of this legal opinion. In another email, I registered mild objections because I wanted to be beyond criticism of the work the two firms would be doing in DC. But Skadden is one of the top law firms in the country, and they specialized in lobbying regulations and laws. So I backed off and agreed to let Podesta and Mercury file under the Lobbying Disclosure Act instead of the FARA act. This was a mistake that I would pay for later.

The records showed all of this, and Hunt was persuaded that it was a gray area. But given the increasing notoriety of the issue, she suggested a limited disclosure path for me.

Working with my attorney, we reached an agreement with Hunt near the end of April, just as the Russian collusion stories surrounding Trump were gaining serious traction, but before Mueller had been appointed. Melissa prepared my disclosure filings for the years of 2011, 2012, and 2013. In keeping with the way Hunt ran the office, we submitted a draft filing, which she then reviewed based on the verbal interactions that we had had with her office. This way if there were any issues, we could clarify them before submitting the final, formal official documents. Hunt had signed off on my draft filing. We formally submitted our final agreement with the FARA office and scheduled a final meeting with Hunt to wrap everything up in late May. We had our agreement in place. The agreement called for limited filing, no penalties, and no finding of wrongdoing.

The special counsel was appointed on May 17. One of the first things Weissman did after he was brought on by Mueller was call Hunt. He asked her the status of my FARA filings, and she indicated that we had reached an understanding and she would be meeting with my counsel to conclude everything. He told her she was off the case and that the filing was to be rejected. My meeting with Hunt was promptly cancelled and the filings, which had been meticulously reviewed and *finalized* with Hunt and my lawyers, quickly became the center of Mueller's criminal investigation.

I had never worked for Russia, but because I had dealt with Ukraine, Yanukovych, and Deripaska, the Mueller prosecutors, led by Andrew Weissman, saw it as a back door to get to the fake Russian Collusion narrative jump started in the first week of their tenure. FARA filings provided the atmospherics that Weissman would stoke to create the toxic misrepresentations that would color my image as the investigation grew.

Now, coupled with what Crossfire Hurricane was doing against Carter Page, and what the Steele dossier alleged (falsely) about how I was using Page to deal with Russia, all of a sudden, my FARA case became the "key" investigation. Never mind that I didn't know who Carter Page was, or that the FARA filings had nothing to do with Russia, or that this was an overt ploy to put pressure on me. FARA disclosure issues are civil matters. In the entire history of FARA there had only been one criminal action filed and it was for a unique case many, many years ago. Weissman taking over the case meant that my filing issue would be treated differently.

Weissman's strategy was to make my failure to file a conspiracy against the US government and my work for a "perceived" ally of Russia—the government of Ukraine—proved that I had links to Russia and was a backchannel in the Russian interference in the 2016 elections. This was the hook that would be used in the media to establish "clear links" to Russia. The fact that my work was managing political campaigns in Ukraine, and the fact that all of my work had been over for two years by the time I joined the Trump campaign—all of this was immaterial. I was holding the "smoking gun" and, in the "Weissman alternative universe" world where there was smoke, there was fire—even if he had to place the gun in my hand and create the fire himself.

In a sense, he had no choice.

By late May, the Special Counsel knew that the Russia collusion road they were trying to follow through FARA was a dead end. They knew it wouldn't lead anywhere. They had found out by then that I had never even met Carter Page. In fact, I didn't even know who Carter Page was. I had to research him to find out that he was on the first foreign policy advisory committee with Papadopoulos, whose emails to me urging a meeting between Trump and Russia I had rejected in a written response.

But anonymous sources were leaking that I was meeting with Page regularly. And that Page was reporting back to Moscow. Throughout May and June, in the early days of the Mueller investigation, that was enough to keep the salacious headlines about Russian collusion flowing on to the front pages. The implication, now, was that the reason I wasn't filing my FARA documents was because I was hiding my Russian connections from 2011 and 2012. Of course, this meant that I somehow knew years in advance that Trump was going to run for president in 2015 and that I would be his campaign chairman.

Absurd though they were, these "connections," which were pure fictions created by the Special Counsel, became the foundation not only for many of the headlines in the summer of 2017, but for the battles I would end up having to fight to keep my freedom.

From his first day on Mueller's team, Weissman made it clear that he would single-mindedly and without hesitation abuse the system to bring me down. Indeed, this was how the Special Counsel would work—less an independent investigation than a partisan machine hellbent on destroying Trump's presidency at all costs. Truth be damned.

When Trump heard that Deputy AG Rosenstein had appointed a Special Counsel to investigate Russian collusion, his immediate reaction was that it would destroy his presidency. Trump understood that Mueller's appointment meant there was no discernible end date for the Russian collusion conspiracy—that it would dog Trump through his entire presidency. Again, Trump knew there was no collusion, but he also knew that the Democrats didn't care. The conflict was simply the next round of the 2016 presidential election. The ballot box was replaced by subpoena and the winner would be based on if they could bring indictments or a collapse of Trump's support among the American people.

The danger of an Independent Counsel is that it is free to range into any area that it wants. This excessive latitude led Congress to refuse to renew the Independent Counsel forcing the office to sunset in 1999. Both Congress and the Executive Branch had seen the abuses of the Clinton Independent Counsel, the Iran contra Independent Counsel, and several others. Of foremost concern to Congress was the fact that almost all indictments brought by the various Independent Counsels were based on crimes that had nothing to do with the reason the Independent Counsels were appointed in the first place.

When Rod Rosenstein appointed Mueller as a "Special Counsel," he gave specific authority to Mueller to investigate "any links and/or coordination between the Russian government and individuals associated with the campaign of President Donald Trump; and any matters that arose or may arise directly from the investigation."

"If the Special Counsel believes it is necessary and appropriate," Rosenstein's appointment letter went on, "the Special Counsel is authorized to prosecute federal crimes arising from the investigation of these matters."[2]

But within the first month of his appointment, Mueller was already running far afield. A June 14 *Washington Post* story noted that Mueller had expanded his investigation to examine whether Trump had attempted to obstruct justice in his conversations with Comey about General Flynn. Trump took to Twitter to complain that Mueller had "found zero proof" on Russian collusion, "so now they go for obstruction of justice on the phony story." The *Post* went on to say that Mueller was probing Jared's finances and business dealings as well as mine, Flynn's, and Page's.

What caught my attention was a quote from Jaime Gorelick—my attorney at WilmerHale and also Jared's. She said it was "standard practice for the Special Counsel to examine financial records to look for anything related to Russia." While the logic of this made sense to me, the spirit of the comment caused me concern. I did not need Gorelick to tell me the logic of Mueller's behavior. I needed her to expose the unlimited latitude he was taking in his investigation. The FARA investigation of activity that took place long before the 2016 campaign was proof to me that he was going to open my entire life up for review.

While I didn't feel legal exposure, I did worry about how I was going to pay for the legal services that would be required to prove my innocence. By early June, my legal bills were already approaching a million dollars, and I had not even testified before Congress.

Summer in Washington is usually a quiet time, but this year the noise was already reaching a very loud decibel level and was climbing higher each day.

As an aside, it is relevant to note that Mueller was Of Counsel at WilmerHale when he was appointed by Rod Rosenstein, and several of the attorneys he appointed worked with him there. The fact that the MSM found no potential conflict about the firm representing me caused me further pause. Normally, the MSM was finding conspiracies of real estate agents who had worked for me and were Americans of Russian descent. They saw no conflict with Mueller.

With everything going on, my friends and family started to worry about me. No longer were the stories just about Russian collusion, but tax evasion, offshore accounts, large amounts of money floating around, cash ledgers. These fragments were being woven into the fabric of an image of me as a criminal. And it all tied to Russia. Rachel Maddow was on MSNBC saying that *"they had proof that I am a traitor to our country, that I'm a spy for Russia."*

I wasn't sleeping well, either—maybe two hours a night. And by July, my life was miserable. I found myself in a twilight zone. I was afraid to reach out to my friends or political allies. With the new government coming to Washington, it felt as though there was excitement all around. But I was totally isolated.

My business dried up and I was reluctant to develop new business relationships until I was out from under the cloud of suspicion. I could no longer tell how long that would be. Plus, the Trump administration was hiring people, many of whom were friends of mine. But I felt like I should keep my distance rather than embrace them and limited any even personal interaction.

And then on July 8, 2017, the *New York Times* ran a bombshell story under the headline, "Trump Team Met with Lawyer Linked to Kremlin During Campaign."[3] The article, full of anonymous sources and lurid insinuations, went to great lengths to portray the meeting, which we had a year earlier and which I had totally forgotten about, as some kind of secret backroom cabal between the Trump team and the Kremlin. Of course, it was anything but.

According to "confidential" records "described" to the *New York Times*, "two weeks after Donald J. Trump clinched the Republican presidential nomination last year, his eldest son arranged a meeting at Trump Tower in Manhattan with a Russian lawyer who has connections to the Kremlin."

The Trump Tower meeting was only discovered when Kushner's lawyers found an entry on his calendar while providing documents to the House Intelligence Committee investigation of the Russian collusion issue. They filed a revised security clearance form to include the meeting in his White House papers and disclosed the meeting to the committees. His lawyers called my lawyers and they all agreed that we had to disclose the meeting in my filings, too. The next thing we knew, anonymous sources were leaking distorted misrepresentations to the media about the nature of the meeting.

The MSM characterized this as evidence of some sort of cover-up, but the truth was that the meeting was so inconsequential that nearly a year after it had taken place, we had all forgotten about it. Regardless, we felt it was important to be clear on who we'd met with and what we discussed, so, on our initiative, we let the House Intelligence Committee know.

At the same time, the annual G20 meeting was taking place in Hamburg, Germany. The media chatter centered on what kind of interaction Trump would have with Putin. But the story did not get published until July 18 when it became public that Trump and Putin had spent an hour in a private conversation. While not unusual, to the conspiracy mob, this was proof certain that the links were real.

Once Weissman was on board with the investigation, he had the information that we had disclosed to the various committees. Suddenly, this information began to appear in news stories citing anonymous sources. I had no doubt Weissman was behind the leaks. These stories led to the *Times* story being published, which in turn caused the Intel Committee to request more information from me and in their expressing an interest for me to appear.

In preparation for document disclosures, my lawyers found a fragment of a summary from my metadata on my iPhone Notes that would prove to the world that the June 9 meeting was the *nothing meeting* Don Jr., Jared, and I had all independently told the investigators and media.

When my lawyers presented me with the obscure note, my recollection of the meeting was recalled in detail. The note confirmed a vague memory I had about the meeting—that it was about Russian adoption and the Magnitsky Act. I disclosed the note to the House counsel and the Intelligence Committee a day or two before I was supposed to testify to them. It blew up their theory of the meeting being a secret Russian collusion meeting. In fact, it was so impactful that when I met with the House Intelligence Committee staff on July 25, the meeting took less than half an hour. They simply weren't interested. They wanted to know if there was any discussion of Hillary Clinton. I said no, and that was it. They didn't ask me anything more, which surprised me. They could have asked me about the black ledger, about the offshore accounts, but they didn't. And there never was a follow-up request to appear before the full committee.

Weissman had this information and a text Jared had sent to his assistant to "get me out of this meeting, it is a waste." Yet, in this scenario, Weissman needed to have evidence and he kept coming up short.

Originally, I was supposed to meet with the Senate Intelligence Committee on Wednesday, July 26, after my meeting with the House Intelligence Committee. But the Senate called off our meeting at five o'clock on Tuesday. I did not know what the issue was, but my wife and I were set to travel to Florida on Thursday, so we were pleased to not have to go through the trauma of appearing. Little did I know that Weissman had a surprise scheduled for that day which was meant to raise the stakes sky high and to intimidate the hell out of me. It achieved both of his objectives.

At six o'clock Wednesday morning, I got out of bed and heard some noises coming from outside my bedroom door. It was dark out, so I couldn't see anything. All of a sudden, from the corridor inside my condo, I heard, "FBI. Hands up, we're coming in and we have guns out."

I didn't know if it was the real FBI or some criminal pretending to be FBI. And since the lights were out and it was six in the morning, I couldn't see anything.

"One minute," I said. I went to put my robe on. My wife was still asleep, so I woke her up to let her know something was going on. I walked to the door and looked down the corridor leading from my bedroom to my living room. The corridor was full of people: over a dozen agents wearing flak jackets, holding weapons, pointing guns. At this point in time, after months of pressure and harassment from the media, I was somewhat paranoid. I'd heard rumors of a lot of people trying to get at me, including the Russians. At an absurd and macabre level, it was actually comforting to realize this time it *was* the real FBI.

I said, "One minute, my wife is getting dressed."

"No," the agent said. "We're coming in."

"No, you are not coming in," I said. But they pushed the door in with me standing there, guns drawn. My wife was half-dressed. I was in a bathrobe.

"We have a warrant to search your premises."

"Let me see the warrant," I said.

My wife said she was going to the bathroom and an FBI agent said she had to leave the door open. But God bless my wife—she went into the bathroom, sent a dagger from her eyes to the female agent, told her, "No I will not," and closed the door. Everyone froze for a minute, like my wife was going to turn into a gun toting killer and come out blasting.

I looked at the lead agent and told him to "chill out. We will cooperate," I said.

That seemed to calm the atmosphere. I escorted them down the hallway back to the living room. Somehow, they had come into the building from the garage, up an elevator to the fourth floor, and down the hallway corridor where they somehow unlocked my condo door and marched into my home down a twenty-foot corridor connecting my living room to our bedroom. I shuddered to think that anyone in our condo might have witnessed this "no-knock" invasion.

I said I had to call my lawyer. The agent said that was fine and that if I wanted to, I could even leave.

"I'm going to stay," I told him. There was no way I was going to leave them alone in my condo. While I was confused as to why the FBI had to conduct this secret attack on me given that I had totally cooperated with every request that had been made to me and every document disclosure, I recalled my CVS happenstance meeting with A. B. Culvahouse. He had told me that Weissman loved these dramatic and scary invasions. To Weissman it was his way of showing his targets how vulnerable they were.

The experience was an out of body one. The team of agents was there from six o'clock in the morning until seven o'clock that night. They went through everything. They took all the electronics they could find—twenty years' worth of old computers, hard drives, and cameras. They opened up every cabinet, every drawer, every closet. They were sure they would find something. I can't imagine what, but they were determined.

Once again, my life resembled something I'd only ever seen in movies. The agents went from room to room in teams of two or three. I didn't care what they were doing in the guestrooms, but I did care about what they were doing in my office, which came at the end of the raid. In each room, one person wrote down everything they were taking, and one person went through all my belongings. It was an exhaustive search. They were clearly on a mission; there was nothing they wouldn't look at, including my underwear.

My lawyer sent someone over who stayed for a short time. But I stayed the whole time. Though the FBI agents were polite to some degree, it was offensive simply by virtue of the way they were dealing with my home. It was disgusting.

While watching the FBI agents tear my house apart, I knew things had moved to a whole new level. And this was exactly what Weissman was signaling to me. There was a real significance to this invasion. They could have asked for anything they took. They didn't need a raid. Nothing I had done triggered the raid, either. It was a tactic designed to scare me. The Mueller investigation was active for several months, but it had not achieved any traction yet. They needed to do something to create a sense of suspense and intimidation.

I was the person targeted to add that suspense. Mueller had secretly started looking for other ways of going after me prior to this raid. I had a storage unit in Alexandria where I kept family memorabilia, old business records, furniture, and boxes of my kids' things. At the time, the only person I had on my payroll was a very junior employee who could drive me around and run errands for me if I needed him to. He had access to the storage unit. The Special Counsel secretly subpoenaed him and told him that if he told me, they'd arrest him. They had him open the storage unit because they believed they'd find something in there. Of course, they found nothing, but, as I found out later, they used that to get a subpoena to do a "no-knock" search of my home. And then they scheduled the search for the day they thought I was going to be testifying in front of the Senate. They thought they'd have free access to the condo.

None of this was necessary. I had cooperated with every request. I had testified before the House and was prepared to testify before the Senate. There was no indication that they were dealing with a difficult subject. They did this because this was Weissman's way of sending a signal, and that signal was: We're going to get you. We've got you in our crosshairs. You better cave. You better cut a deal, or we will indict you.

Perhaps for the first time since everything started, I understood the message loud and clear. There were no lines they wouldn't cross. Nothing was beyond the pale.

The raid had a truly chilling effect on me. Again, I felt no legal exposure, but I felt politically and personally violated. I was especially incensed because they had violated my wife and her things.

I didn't know what *else* they could do. I wasn't worried that they would find anything in the raid. They ended up getting some communications on the FBAR case, but I'd given those documents to the FBI in 2014.

What I worried about were the headlines, how they would affect my ability to work, my reputation, how all of these tangential things were spinning out of control and becoming central to my life.

On the heels of the no-knock raid on my condo, the Special Counsel arrested their first target, George Papadopoulos, whom the FBI had interviewed back in January 2017 regarding Trump campaign connections with Russia.

Papadopoulos had been one of the early appointments to Trump's Foreign Policy Advisory Board on March 21, 2016. From that moment on his life was targeted by the Deep State. While the details of his adventure with Russian Collusion are a bit complicated, what has come out in the last several years is something we all should fear: a set-up based on his political views.

What is clear is that Papadopoulos was set up by the Obama administration prior to the appointment of a Special Counsel. In the years since his arrest, it has come to light that Papadopoulos was the victim of an entrapment operation run by various intelligence agencies used to justify surveillance of the Trump campaign.[4,5]

Anonymous sources came at me hard trying to link me with Papadopoulos. They had an email he had sent to me saying that he could set up a meeting between candidate Trump and Putin. Why he thought he could do this, I have no idea.

When I received the email, I had to first ask my staff who George Papadopoulos was. I had never heard of him. Rick Gates informed me that Papadopoulos was on the Foreign Policy Advisory Committee that I had dismissed. I sent Gates a note to reply to the email from the correspondent division, not from my office, and to tell him that we don't do those types of meetings and had no interest in meeting with Putin. That was the end of it as far as I was concerned.

Even though I treated the Papadopoulos request as inappropriate and dismissed it immediately, the Deep State jumped on the email, especially after his arrest.

Around this time, my situation was causing Mueller concern. His narrow mandate relating to interactions with Russians regarding the 2016 election restricted his ability to investigate me *before* I was involved in the campaign. Of course, the FBI raid on my home found nothing on Russian contacts. Clearly, there was concern in the Special Counsel. But to Weissman this simply meant he needed to figure out a way to force me to tell the Special Counsel what was really going on with Trump, Russia, WikiLeaks, and Guccifer—the Russian hackers of the DNC.

By the end of July, it was clear to those involved in the Mueller investigation that they were vulnerable. They weren't getting anywhere in their investigation into Russian collusion, because there was no Russian collusion, and they needed a new way in. This led to the *secret expansion* of the Special Counsel's mandate which allowed Mueller to investigate beyond the narrow issue of Russian collusion.

When Mueller was appointed, there was no Independent Counsel law. So, he had to act within Department of Justice guidelines for US Attorneys, which were narrower than had existed during the time of the Independent Counsel law. In the beginning, he didn't have a "witch hunt" kind of mandate. Rather, in the initial creation of the Special Counsel, he was given a very specific function by Rosenstein, which was to investigate all aspects of Russian collusion and crimes that grew out of the collusion—*not* crimes that came out of the investigation.

But as time went on, that language wasn't useful for keeping the investigation alive. They needed an additional, much broader mandate. This led to a confidential letter from Rosenstein to Mueller on August 2 broadening Mueller's scope in his investigation of me. "The May 17, 2017, order was worded categorically in order to permit its public release without confirming specific investigations involving specific individuals. This memorandum provides a more specific description of your authority," the letter read. "The following allegations were within the scope of the Investigation at the time of your appointment and are within the scope of the Order: Allegations that Paul Manafort:

- Committed a crime or crimes by colluding with Russian government officials with respect to the Russian government's efforts to interfere with the 2016 election for President of the United States, in violation of United States law;
- Committed a crime or crimes arising out of payments he received from the Ukrainian government before and during the tenure of President Viktor Yanukovych;
- Committed a crime or crimes arising out of his receipt of loans from a bank whose Chief Executive Officer was then seeking a position in the Trump administration;
- You therefore have authority to continue and complete the investigation of those matters. . . ."

This letter did not become public for over a year, but it became the foundation of his getting into bank fraud crimes that I was charged with based on actions after the presidential election. The letter effectively authorized Mueller to expand the investigation into my entire life. The basis for this expansion was justified because I had worked in Ukraine and had represented a Russian oligarch, Oleg Deripaska. (Only later did it become public that not only was he not a Russian spy, but he had been a cooperating witness for the FBI on a number of occasions. And one of the occasions the FBI asked him if Paul Manafort was effectively working for the Kremlin. Deripaska's response was to burst out laughing and then tell them that it was an absurd allegation.)

Obviously, the FBI and Rosenstein knew this about Deripaska, and they knew that my time in Ukraine had been focused on getting Ukraine into the European Union, something Putin vehemently opposed. So there was no basis for the need to expand the scope of authority to investigate me other than to find a way to break me and coerce me into giving up the president of the United States. If that meant going beyond the 2016 campaign, so be it. If it meant ignoring previous US Government investigations that had shut down without charging me for the very crimes they now wanted to investigate under Weissman, so be it, too.

In fact, this expansion was precisely the reason that Congress *had refused to renew* the Independent Counsel law. So now, the Special Counsel was being given authority that Congress refused to give to an Independent Counsel. And the expansion of authority was based on false premises about my life which the FBI knew were not true. The Steele dossier and black ledger had been discredited, but to Weissman these facts were not relevant. They needed someone to squeeze, and I was the candidate they had chosen.

If there had been any doubt as to Mueller's real mission of bringing down Donald Trump, after the August 2 memo, that doubt was removed. Now, Mueller had unlimited authority to look at all aspects of my life. The purpose was clear. It was not to identify contacts with Russia. Rather, he was fishing for anything he could find to "squeeze me" into becoming his number one witness to "get Donald Trump."

During this time, I had no way of knowing where I fit in with Trump anymore. I worried, even though I knew none of the stories were true, that Trump was thinking I might have been a Russian spy. The Court of Public Opinion had decided I had a direct link to Putin. Per Rachel Maddow, who knew nothing about me, I was regularly communicating to Moscow. Twitter had convicted me of treason. And the byproduct of all of this noise was keeping alive the narrative of Trump being vulnerable to the allegations.

His presidency was being undercut by *my* supposed connections to Russia, which didn't exist. I was sending messages back, but people were afraid to talk to me. They didn't want the exposure. After all, if you were only reading the front pages—many of which stories were being leaked by anonymous government sources—you could have been forgiven for thinking I had a network of connections with the Kremlin. No one knew where Weissman could take the investigation. Though I had played a pivotal role in helping Trump win the presidency, I was very worried about losing my cachet with the administration. Under a huge amount of stress and facing growing legal concerns, not to mention fatal damage to my reputation and business, I had no way of knowing whether they would simply let me walk the plank alone in order to save themselves. It was a terrifying time

CHAPTER 11

Indictments

With the raid on my condo, the stakes had changed. It was clear to me that Weissman was not interested in me as a Russian collusion defendant. He was on a broad fishing expedition to capture me, pressure me, and make me into his "star" witness against Trump.

As the nature of the fight continued to evolve after the Mueller appointment and over the summer of 2017, I felt that I needed a lawyer who could fight a different kind of fight. Where before the stories about me pointed to connections and collusion with Russia, now all of the media leaks about me focused on possible financial crimes. The *New York Times* was writing stories about me having offshore bank accounts, receiving millions of dollars from Ukraine, and doing large scale bank loans with my properties.

While many of the facts were correct, the inferences or outright accusations were not. For example, I was using offshore bank accounts to manage the flow of fees to me and consultants working for me. However, I believed that I did not own the accounts, and I had voluntarily told the US government about these accounts in 2014. Just as the FARA unit had determined that I had done nothing criminal or even wrong regarding disclosures, the FBI had determined I had done nothing wrong with the offshore accounts and moved on. I heard nothing about offshore accounts until the Special Counsel was appointed, Weissman was put in charge, and he decided to resurrect them.

So, again I was confronted with a situation where I did not think I had done anything wrong and had cooperated with the relevant USG agencies. Yet I was reading about nefarious criminal activity on the exact matters with which I had cooperated with the US government.

What I didn't understand was how Weissman could exploit salacious facts leaked to the media by anonymous sources intending to convict a person in the court of public opinion. Weissman would use the sullied reputation to indict the defendant, and through witness intimidation, selective use of facts, and distortion of events, and bringing "over-charged" case to the Federal Court, he would overwhelm juries with literally millions of pages of documents.

I did not know it at the time, but I had no chance in this game. I was focusing on innocence; Weissman was focusing on the abuse of my rights to turn me into the most heinous villain and traitor imaginable. And just in case it was not enough, when I was indicted, he got a gag order imposed on me which didn't allow me to respond to the anonymous leaks while they continued to frame the most unsympathetic possible picture of me.

I had hired WilmerHale to manage my political exposure in the congressional Russian collusion investigations. Gorelick was a Democrat, and she was tied into all the right people on the Hill on the Democratic side. But after Mueller was appointed on May 17, it became clear that I needed to have lawyers to deal with a legal investigation, not a congressional inquiry. In fact, the congressional investigations mattered less and less to me every day. Now, I was dealing with a rabid dog prosecutor who wanted to bring down a president and who saw me as the means to that end. He was going to create financial crimes that would send me to jail for the rest of my life unless I cooperated.

I was also, by this point, buried under legal bills from WilmerHale. I'd already paid over a million dollars, but I was feeling the pressure in a different way now that Weissman had stopped my deal with FARA. Even though everyone in my network was saying I was not a target, I was a target, and I knew it. I kept hearing that they didn't want me for me, they wanted me for Trump. But I knew Weissman was looking right at me, and I knew I needed a different kind of lawyer to manage this change. What I didn't know was what kind of lawyer I would need. The Mueller investigation was political, and I hadn't yet grasped Weissman's creativity with manufacturing financial crimes.

The last straw came when my lawyers at WilmerHale, who were also representing Jared Kushner, made it clear to me that they didn't know where my investigation was going. They told me that they had a "wall" set up where they felt comfortable representing both me and Jared, but if both of us were to get indicted, the law firm could only represent one of us. In that situation, I was informed, the partnership had decided they would go with Jared. I laughed to myself thinking how much they must be charging Jared.

Fine, I thought. I didn't feel that they had the expertise to deal with some of the financial issues that were being put into play. Plus, except for one of the attorneys, I didn't feel WilmerHale had the fight in them.

Following the FBI raid on my house, I wanted a pit bull lawyer to fight back, not a white-shoe firm. Again, I turned to my old friend Dick Hibey and again Dick had good advice. Dick was at Miller Chevalier, but he was retiring. He had been a top litigator for twenty-five years and had acted as a sort of corporate counsel to me. I'd connected him with Ferdinand Marcos when I had negotiated Marcos's departure from the Philippines, as well as referring a number of other international cases to him.

In July 2017, I talked to Dick about who I might bring on and he pointed me to Kevin Downing. Downing was a litigator at Miller Chevalier. But he was getting ready to leave to either join another major firm or set up his own shop—he wasn't sure yet which way he would go. But he was from the streets of Long Island and his Irish working-class roots had made him a street fighter who was not afraid of battle.

Downing was especially appealing after seeing how fast a corporate law firm can bill hours and burn through my cash. I was still smarting from the advice one of my lawyers at WilmerHale had given me. Reggie Bush was the Republican member of my team at WilmerHale. He was an affable, street-smart attorney who I came to value as a friend and lawyer. Reggie told me that in his opinion things were going to get very bad for me in the coming months. He said I had to be prepared to spend millions to defend myself and that I should liquidate my investments and be ready to use the cash to pay for my defense. I had already spent over a million dollars in legal fees that year. I gulped and realized even in winning I was going to go broke. Again, Culvahouse's warning about Weissman's tactics to destroy people flashed in my mind.

So, I met with Downing, and we talked about who I was and what was going on. He had come out of the Treasury Department, where he was the lead litigator on a number of tax cases for the US Government. He knew everybody in the system—at the Treasury Department, the IRS, the DOJ, the US Attorney's office. He didn't know Mueller, but he knew enough of the players. In addition to being a litigator, Downing was a CPA. So he had both sets of skills in case they were going to move deeper into the area of financial crimes, which is what the rumors were. I still didn't feel legal exposure on those things, but I wanted somebody with the expertise to handle it if need be.

He explained that we could build a sort of virtual law firm and bring attorneys on depending on the direction of the investigation. That made a lot of sense to me, and it meant I wouldn't be paying for the overhead of a large firm with a team of lawyers—at least until I knew where the investigation was going.

He would be joined by another partner who was leaving Miller Chevalier, Tom Zehnle, who had twenty-five years of experience in white-collar crime and had served as the Chief of the Criminal Enforcement Section (Southern) of the DOJ. The two of them came together and I would be paying them for the time put in, not on a retainer.

I made the decision to terminate my relationship with WilmerHale.

Kevin cut a deal for some office space up at the law firm of Kostelanetz and Fink on Capitol Hill and I used that as my office. Eventually, Downing and Zehnle brought on Jay Nanavati, who was a white-collar crimes attorney at Kostelanetz. A veteran trial lawyer, Jay had more than a decade as both a federal and state prosecutor. He'd supervised more than thirty federal tax prosecutors and had overseen tax enforcement in a region covering twenty-two states.

I worked with Jay on pulling together documents. We also brought on Rich Westling, a lawyer whose southern, folksy charm belied a deeply incisive mind. A liberal Democrat, he had worked as a deputy assistant attorney general in the Eastern District of Louisiana, where there were a lot of tax cases. Rich understood forfeiture law. He had a network in the tax attorney system, and he had practiced law for a while in the same firm as Judge Jackson, the presiding Judge in my DC FARA case. Downing, Tom, Jay, and Rich—that was my new team of legal counsels. Over time they melded into a cohesive team of seasoned professionals and friends.

In my mind, I was always going to be involved in creating the strategy with my team, but I knew enough to know what I didn't know. I had never been involved in this kind of criminal investigation. I didn't know the players. So I would defer to the experts on all legal decisions. But I would push in one direction or another, based on where I thought things should be going.

When I hired Downing, the rumors were related to FBAR violations, where I didn't feel vulnerable. I felt politically vulnerable, but not legally susceptible. When I explained the situation with the accounts in Cyprus, the SPVs, and the work Gates was doing for me, Downing felt comfortable, based on what I was telling them—which was all I knew at the time.

We were looking at this as a politically damaging case, but not one where I would end up in jail. They looked at the FARA documents, which was where the Special Counsel was putting a lot of the initial attention, and felt I wasn't vulnerable there either.

When I hired Downing, I had no idea what kind of timetable I was looking at. From a political standpoint, I felt the Special Counsel had to act in 2017. What I didn't know at the time was that they had indicted Papadopoulos in the summer, but it was sealed. He'd agreed to a plea deal, and Weissman wanted to keep it under seal.

In hindsight, it was apparent to me that Weissman believed he would be able to get more information from Papadopoulos with other campaign actors. In the end this was not true. But the important point was that with the Papadopoulos indictment, the Special Counsel had their first scalp. Like the entire investigation, the scalp was the product of a travesty of justice. Papadopoulos had been illegally entrapped by several government informants. In fact, Papadopoulos had rejected all of the overtures to have him do something to give credence to the false Russian narrative. His indictment for lying to the Grand Jury was a byproduct of the failed investigation. Like Flynn, Papadopoulos forgot something in his FBI depositions. It was a process crime, and more likely a Weissman process fiction.

One of the first things I asked Kevin to do was research the authority of the Special Counsel. Mueller was appointed as a Special Counsel, which was completely different than an Independent Counsel. His jurisdiction and his authority were directed by the rules and regulations that the US Attorneys operate under. Independent counsels had had much wider authority. Trump was questioning whether the special counsel had any legal authority at all.

Early on, I felt I didn't have any exposure on Russian collusion, so I figured any investigation of me would go nowhere. My concern was, what if they start wandering? When Weissman stopped the FARA Division investigation within his first week, I knew the Mueller team would get active in that space. But I knew they wouldn't find Russian collusion. Anyone reading the news from 2008 to 2014 would see Yanukovych was trying to move Ukraine into Europe, not toward Russia. I assumed, naively, that the media would report that correctly.

My nervousness came from a feeling that the Special Counsel would try to do something outlandish to pressure me to turn on Trump. So I wanted to know what their authority was. Clearly, Mueller and Weissman were nervous about this too. Which is why they had gone back to Rosenstein in late July to get a more specific mandate to allow them to expand the investigation against me to include fraud, taxes, and financial materials.

This led to Rosenstein's secret memo of August 2, expanding the authority of the Special Counsel in order to focus specifically on me. They claimed they needed to keep it secret to avoid tipping me off to the crimes they were investigating. This was a lie. The truth was they kept it secret because they did not want to make public that they were secretly expanding their jurisdiction when nothing was turning up on Russian collusion. If the memo had been public, there could easily have been a loud outcry against this improper expansion of authority. The precise kind of expansion that was specifically rejected when the Congress refused to renew the Independent Counsel law.

All of this was in my head as the summer gave way to congressional hearings, fake news stories, FBI raids, and arrests.

September saw even more increased activity. But for a while, the media was more focused on the Flynn case than on mine. Mueller was rumored to be targeting Flynn's son regarding work they had done in Turkey. Weissman's tactics were clarified once more: take down Flynn's son or get Flynn to testify against Trump.

A career military man, Flynn had just recently started to make money in the private sector. Having left the US Government because of a disagreement with Obama over the threat that the Iranian Shiites represented, Flynn had been active in campaigning against Hillary Clinton.

I first met Flynn when he reached out to me in May 2016. He wanted to give Trump his new book exposing the Obama/Clinton foreign policy disasters that he had witnessed as DIA Director. I didn't know him, but I agreed to meet him, and he came up to New York. We met in the atrium of Trump Tower, he gave me the book, and I liked what he had to say. As we left the meeting, I had it in my mind that he might be a good person to travel with Trump on some campaign trips, to sit with him on the airplane, so that Trump could mine him for information on what was happening in Obama's national security team. In that way, Trump could start to build his knowledge base. Because Flynn had been the Director of the Defense Intelligence Agency, I thought he might be quite valuable to Trump. I liked him and I felt that his experience and knowledge of specific Obama failures would be useful as we crafted the Fall attacks on Clinton's failures as Secretary of State.

So I asked Flynn if he'd be willing to travel with Trump. He said he would and ultimately, he went on to do at least two trips with Trump while I was still involved. I also put him on the convention program to speak. None of this—my role in bringing Flynn into the Trump campaign—had come out yet, but I was sure it was only a matter of time before people picked up on the fact that I was the one who brought Flynn into the fold. It wasn't hidden. But no one had made the connection yet. In my paranoia, I saw how it would only strengthen the Russian collusion story. When the stories about me had started to come out, we texted back and forth a few times. He told me how crazy the stories were. But when he became the National Security Adviser, he cut off all communication, which bothered me because we'd had a relationship of equals. Now we had no relationship. I wasn't comfortable with that.

His deputy, a woman named K. T. McFarland, had a place out in the Hamptons, near my summer home. When I would do Sunday morning talk shows from Long Island during the summer, K. T. ran a kind of back room set-up for the networks because there was no facility to handle the TV feed. Spending this time together, I got to know K. T. personally. So when K. T. was selected by Flynn as his deputy, I called her to congratulate her. Sadly, she did not return my calls either.

All of this contributed to a growing sense of paranoia—that there had been an actual decision to cut me out. There never was such a decision. People were protecting themselves. They were doing the natural thing and distancing themselves from me. But, I felt that I was being ostracized in a palpable way.

Then the Democrats began to attack Flynn. They said he met with

Kislyak, the Russian ambassador, during the transition. But once Flynn was designated the National Security Adviser as part of the transition, it was normal to meet with the ambassadors in Washington. I got reports that he said to Kislyak, something along the lines of, we would appreciate if you don't take any reciprocal actions to the sanctions that have been imposed until we come into office. Which is a normal thing to say, as the designated National Security Adviser, to an important ally. But it became a kind of dog whistle for the Democrats to use against Flynn saying that he violated the Logan Act, a law dating from the eighteenth century to deal with British Spies. It was madness.

This led to the FBI meeting with Flynn where the media reported Flynn had lied to Pence. This is what caused Trump ultimately to fire Flynn. I felt guilty about bringing him into the campaign. There was no way he had done anything wrong. And the threats to his son were the latest Weissman fairy tale meant to squeeze someone into accepting his crazy theories. I recognized the tactics and empathized with Flynn's plight.

In my due diligence, I could see that Weissman did not give any cover. This was a guy who had been charged with ethics violations in many of the major cases he had ever been involved in. When Weissman was asked what he thought about the Supreme Court overruling his actions in the Enron case by the vote of 8 to 0, he said *they* got it wrong. In other words, nothing he did was ever wrong. If the legal system didn't understand why he did what he did, that was their problem, not his. That was the arrogance of the man.

All of this was constantly running through my head through the summer of 2017 and into the fall. I was scared and felt alone. I didn't know where it would go. My wife and I had gone to our Hampton's property in August, but after Labor Day, we returned to DC and life was even worse. We needed to get out of Washington. It wasn't comfortable there anymore. I couldn't go to restaurants without being harassed. The media was tracking me from my condo in Alexandria to buildings around the city.

Russian collusion on the front pages daily. I felt the pressure of everybody looking at me. I was also being followed by the FBI everywhere at this point. They weren't even hiding it. Coming out of a parking lot one day, I bumped a car that was parked next to mine. I got out of the car and looked to see if there was any damage. There wasn't even a scratch, so I got back in my car and went to get my wife a coffee at Starbucks.

A few minutes later, an Alexandria cop stopped me and told me that there was a police APB on my car for a hit and run.

"What are you talking about?" I said.

"Were you just at a CVS?" he asked.

I explained what happened and he said they received an anonymous call that my car was involved in a hit and run. I had seen the agent in that parking lot, so I explained that to the officer. He had sympathy for me and let me go. "Just be careful," he warned me.

When I got home, I told my wife the story and she said, "let's just get out of here." We decided to go to Florida, where our house is in a gated community. Being away from Washington would be a relief. I could work out every day in the gym. We could go to restaurants. People knew me but they weren't consumed with politics like in DC. The atmosphere was totally different. It was still stressful, but I felt I could get some relief there.

We arrived on Thursday, October 26, and intended to stay for the winter.

In the land of unintended consequences, now that I had escaped Washington, I was confronted with a new fear. What would happen if I was indicted in Florida? Would they arrest me in Florida and then transport me in cuffs back to Virginia? Where would I be jailed in Florida? We spent Saturday working out a plan for me to have counsel in Florida if the arrest were to happen in Florida. Downing was confident that I would be allowed to self-surrender in DC, but we didn't know for sure. Weissman liked grand flourishes to get his headlines. Friday night I took my wife to a movie. As we were pulling out of my driveway, I noticed a dark sedan parked two houses away on the street.

Through September and October, Flynn was still the guy getting all the headlines. In October, we heard talk of a grand jury and the media was picking up on people who were tied to Flynn. So it looked like the first target would come out of the Flynn investigation. (Papadopoulos's indictment was still under seal.)

Even so, I was concerned. I didn't really think I was out of the crosshairs. Then I heard that they were going to arrest Gates. I couldn't figure out on what charges, but it made me nervous. I had never been arrested, so I didn't know what the process would be. I asked Downing what would happen if I got arrested, and he walked me through it.

There are two ways to be arrested, he said. You can either give yourself up—self-surrender—or they can choose to come to wherever you are. I knew the Weissman move would be to find me in the most public place possible to throw the cuffs on me and put me in the back of a car. Whenever possible, he would inflict the maximum damage through humiliation.

If I was arrested in Florida I asked Kevin where I would be arraigned in Florida, or if would I come back to Washington. He said I'd be arraigned in Washington.

"How do I get to Washington?" I asked. These logistical questions were weighing on me before anything had actually happened.

Downing said he couldn't imagine I would be arrested in a public place in Florida with a perp walk and everything. Well, I told him, I could. I had a sense for Weissman by this time.

With this in mind, we set up a process that would be triggered if I were to be arrested in Florida so that I would have legal representation down there. Downing knew someone from the US Attorney's office who practiced in Florida. Jeff Neiman was a highly regarded criminal attorney who had practiced as a US Attorney in the Southern District of Florida. He called me to explain what would happen and immediately calmed me down.

The practice of the Mueller grand jury was to indict on a Friday so that the paperwork could be done over the weekend and the arrests could happen early the next week.

My lawyers got a call on Thursday that the grand jury would be coming down with indictments, but we didn't know who would be indicted. Downing told me that he thought it would be Gates so that they could pressure him. But I felt differently. Weissman wanted me. The atmosphere was unbelievably stressful.

New movies are released on Fridays, so that night I said to my wife, "Let's get out of here, let's go to a movie." To myself, I thought, *maybe the last movie I'll get to see for a while.* As I was pulling out of my driveway, I spotted a sedan that was not my neighbors' car. The car began to follow us. I called Kevin to ask what he was hearing. He said they were still hearing about Flynn, but not about me. But any doubt was now gone. I was going to be arrested on Monday, if not sooner.

The next day, we plotted out all of the logistics if I were arrested. If it was self-surrender, I would go back to Washington to turn myself in.

Around five o'clock on Saturday night, Kevin got a phone call saying

I was going to be indicted but the Special Counsel would let me self-surrender on Monday.

The first thing I did was call Rick Gates to see if he had heard anything on his end. I didn't know if I should be calling him, but I was still a free man and I couldn't have my lawyers call his lawyers because Gates' legal representation had fallen apart.

"I got bad news," I said.

He said, "Yeah, so do I." He told me they were going to indict him on charges relating to FARA filings, which didn't make any sense. It's the firm that has the obligations, not the employees. And Gates was my employee. This was Weissman's heavy hand at work.

We commiserated as we professed our innocence to each other. He railed on how unfair this was to me and how I had no exposure at all. He told me all the reasons why I didn't have any exposure. He was right on all of it. Six months later, courtesy of Mr. Weissman's pressure, he had changed his views which he expressed to the Grand Jury and eventually to the Federal jury that was hearing my case.

I made arrangements to fly out on Sunday morning to Washington and then turn myself in on Monday. Downing called the Special Counsel's office to give them the flight information.

There are two wings at the airport in Palm Beach. We arrived at the airport around 8:30 a.m., early enough to have a coffee and breakfast. We were sitting in the restaurant, which was right across from the gate. Twenty-five minutes before the gate closed, one of the FBI agents who had been following me came up to us and said, "Mr. Manafort. We don't know what you're trying to do but you have to board your plane and it's leaving in twenty-five minutes.

"I know," I said, "the gate is two minutes away."

"No," she said, "you are in the wrong area. You have to return to the main terminal and go through a long security line." Feeling the pressure, I had misread my ticket and had the wrong gate number for boarding.

I had to laugh. They had been sweating, thinking I was trying to miss my flight.

So Kathy and I ran down the corridor to the main terminal, asked TSA to allow us to cut the security line, explaining that we couldn't miss the flight. We were followed by the two FBI agents who had been following me. Of course, I was convinced that everyone in the airport knew who we were as we did our O. J. Simpson airport dash. Getting to the gate with two minutes to spare, I smiled at the huffing FBI agents. They did not appreciate my smile. As they turned from me with disdain I said to Kathy, "Well, at least we are in better shape than the two agents." They were red-faced and out of breath from our little dash.

I went to Downing's office at eight o'clock the next morning, Monday, October 30, 2017. He drove me to the FBI building. The marshals picked me up and we drove to DC booking somewhere in Southeast DC. There were so many people being booked that morning I had to wait in cuffs for almost an hour in a van outside the building. When I was finally allowed in, I saw Gates. I could see the sadness in his eyes. We were both devastated—utterly shocked and exhausted by the turn the investigation had taken.

We were then taken to the DC magistrate's office, where the magistrate, Judge Deborah Robinson, read the charges. The indictment contained twelve counts including failing to register as a foreign agent, conspiracy against the US, conspiracy to launder money, making false statements, and failure to report offshore bank accounts. (It's important to note that there was no mention of Trump, collusion, or Russian meddling.)

I pleaded not guilty, and they posted a $10 million bond on me and $5 million on Gates. I was outraged and shocked by the $10 million bond. This was totally abusive. John Gotti's bail bonds were less than mine.

Downing was floored. "This never happens," he said.

"Kevin," I said, "you have to start getting used to this. Things that never happen, *do* happen to me."

On one hand, I wanted him to be right when he said the number, which was ridiculous, would come down. But on the other, I knew it wouldn't. I had to find a way to get that kind of cash. I knew Gates didn't have the money. His whole portfolio wasn't worth $5 million.

I then went to a DC correctional office where I had a leg brace put on me. I sat there for a couple of hours and then I went home, tired, humiliated, and emotional. I couldn't believe it. I had never been in this kind of situation before. I was very angry. Listening to the charges, I couldn't believe what I was hearing. I made a note of the fact that there wasn't a single charge—not one thing—that had to do with Russia. The only reason the FARA filings were used was because they allowed Weissman to make a Ukrainian connection and they could create a narrative of Russian back channels through Yanukovych. And these were the very issues that I had reached an agreement on with the FARA office in May with no penalties and no criminality.

The whole case was a fraud. But the fraud was by the Office of Special Counsel.

Over time, Weissman had put the Deripaska connection in the media and created yet another access point for Russian collusion. But I had been made a scapegoat. Weissman had no concern for my life, for my family, or for what was legal or ethical. Anything and everything would be used to bring Trump down.

Before the indictment, I felt myself being smothered under a fear of the unknown. My mind never stopped. Afterward, I felt that at least there was something definitive I could work with. The indictments, far-fetched, unfair, and fabricated though they were, were black and white, right there on paper. In this way, I attained a certain clarity. I could focus my efforts and attention on proving everyone wrong. I knew I was innocent, but I had to make everyone else see it as well. And I thought I could. That became my motivation every day. It was hard, but I was determined.

In the immediate aftermath of the indictments, on some days I woke up feeling I could beat the world. But on other days, I was sure I was done. It was over—impossible. Mueller, Weissman, the MSM—they weren't interested in the truth, so the truth could never get my life back. I would go to jail for the rest of my life because that's what they wanted. But I always came back to what I knew—that I was innocent.

It was one of the lowest points in my life and my career. My previous life was filled with daily meetings and phones calls and events to attend. Suddenly, all of these activities were gone, and I started to learn who my true friends really were. There were some surprises—people who just disappeared and others who were grandstanding in the press. But on the positive side, there were those who I had not heard from in years, who stepped up to support me. One of my friends, a trial attorney in Virginia, after Judge Jackson was appointed told me plainly, "You're fucked. Jackson's not a good judge. She's very partisan and this is the most partisan case she's ever been involved in." Out of self-protection, I protested as I defended her, hoping it wasn't true. I felt she was bound by the law and that she had no choice but to be fair. But by the time the first bail package was rejected and the $10 million was effectively made into a $17 million bail, I realized he was right: I was fucked.

CHAPTER 12

Allegations

Neither the District Court Judge nor the Mueller prosecutors were interested in figuring out a fair bail package. It was just a game to them. They wanted to keep me tied down in home confinement where they could monitor everything I was doing. Between the time of my first indictment on October 30, 2017, to the time of my first trial in July 2018, I spent hundreds of thousands of dollars trying to craft a bail package that the Judge would accept.

It started with the magistrate accepting Weissman's request for a $10 million bond. This is more than drug lords, mob bosses, or murderers have to post. It was as much if not more than Bernie Madoff or Michael Milliken or any of the Enron defendants had to post. Yet, for failing to file a FARA form, a violation that in the seventy-plus years of its existence had been used to indict someone under the criminal statute only six times with only one conviction, I had to come up with that kind of money.

Not only did I have to post the $10 million, but, confined to my home and with a GPS bracelet on my ankle, I was only allowed to go to church or see a doctor or meet with my attorneys. Every time I wanted to do one of those three things, I would have to notify the Special Counsel's office. They were tracking me everywhere. And they were truly tracking me. I was very careful because I did not want to lose home confinement and be sent to jail. Once, coming back from a visit to my doctor, my wife and I stopped at a Starbucks that was en route to our home. I stayed in the car while she got herself a coffee. While walking into my condo, I received a call from my lawyer saying the Special Counsel called claiming I had taken an unauthorized side trip. I told Downing, "I didn't take a side trip. I stopped at a Starbucks which was on the road home, and the stop took less time than a red light during rush hour."

They were simply trying to make my life miserable, which meant I'd have to be even more careful. I had a porch on my condo, which was on the fourth floor. They tried to say I couldn't go out on the porch. I ignored that.

After the indictment shock wore off, I was assured by my lawyers that this was an unprecedented bail package, and it wouldn't stand. (This was the first time of what would be scores of times I was to hear the word "unprecedented" applied to my case.) They all felt the bail would be reduced when I appeared for arraignment in front of the Judge who would be assigned to me in the US District Court of the District of Columbia.

I took some comfort in their words, but my comfort proved unwarranted. My bail situation only got worse.

In fact, ultimately, I would present four bail packages and two appeals over the course of the six months. Each of the motions failed due to my judge, Amy Berman Jackson. Jackson was a Harvard-educated, Obama-appointed, Trump-hating liberal.

Throughout my ordeal, she would repeatedly and shamelessly show her liberal political stripes by creating obstacle after obstacle for me. I am confident that she did this with the active encouragement of her friends and former colleagues in the Special Counsel.

My first bail package gave her a staggering $10 million worth of my properties. She accepted it but added a requirement that my wife and daughter set aside an additional $7 million in cash and assets as sureties. So, all of a sudden, with the wave of a judge's pen, my unprecedented $10 million bond requirement became $17 million. Jackson added that she thought this was only fair because she had to be assured that the surety had the assets in case I fled. The fact that she had the $10 million in properties provided no comfort to her as to my risk of flight.

Yes, you read correctly. The reason that I had such a high bond was because the Honorable Judge and the Special Counsel believed that I was a flight risk. Their reasoning was because I did business internationally, had two passports (which for international businessmen is very normal), three phones, and that I communicated on the internet using encrypted applications like WhatsApp and Skype. The fact that 1.5 billion people in the world use WhatsApp did not ameliorate my risk.

When I rejected her "generous" first bail package, I created a new package without any sureties. This way she would not have to do math that was too complicated for her. This time I used a property with a mortgage from one of my banks. The Special Counsel, under the pretense of confirming that all was in order, contacted the bank's general counsel. As a result of this "informational inquiry," the bank declared my mortgage in default. I was current on the payments, but they showed me in default—a default that no one in the bank could explain to me.

Two months later, after threatening legal action, the bank sent me a letter saying that I was in default because of the indictment. Generously, they offered to take me off the default list if I would get the indictment dropped. Of course, I viewed this generous offer to be the solution. I told my attorney that I wanted to immediately contact the Special Counsel to request them to drop the indictment so that I could have my mortgage placed back into a current status. Kevin suggested that the call would not be a productive call. Apparently, the Special Counsel's "informational inquiry" to the bank was more than just a routine informational communication.

The third bail package had a new configuration that the judge said used assets frozen by the Special Counsel's indictments. There is no case law that prohibited me from pledging properties that were frozen because until I was convicted, they were my properties. But again, the "Honorable" Judge Jackson claimed that she was concerned about me being a flight risk and needed more assurance than these properties. However, in a moment of "fairness" she listed the assets of mine that I could pledge and that she would accept. The problem was the total value of the assets was less than the $10 million I had to pledge. This third package was, unsurprisingly, rejected. The fourth and final bail package, which I will discuss later in this book, was dealt with differently.

Moving into December, I had very little confidence in the prospect of a fair trial. I am an optimist by nature, and perhaps in the back of my mind I could tell myself that I didn't do anything wrong and that we would figure out a way to make the jury understand. But the reality was bleak. The truth had done little thus far to change anyone's mind about me. Weissman was busy making me look as evil as possible in the media and the system was treating me like a hardened criminal before I'd been convicted of a single crime.

Downing felt that we had a strong case and, as he said, when we went to trial, we would only need one juror to believe us. He was confident that if we didn't win by outright acquittal, we would at least have a hung jury. So I was feeling that even though the deck was stacked against me, I had no choice but to believe in the system. That is what was motivating me to keep fighting every day—the belief that at the end of the day the American judicial process would win out over unethical prosecutors, politically motivated judges, and a corrupt media out for blood.

But then on December 4, another blow: the Special Counsel asked Judge Jackson to revoke my bail due to what they called a violation of the gag order that had been imposed on me.

After I was indicted, there was a lot of support for me in Ukraine. One of the people who supported me was somebody who had been part of the Ministry of Foreign Affairs and worked closely with me to help Ukraine become a part of the European Union. He wanted to write an editorial in support of me for the English-language *Kyiv Post*.[1] On his own initiative, he wrote an op-ed article, and he sent a draft of it to me as a courtesy. I looked at it and made several corrections and sent back my edits. Weissman submitted a petition in Jackson's court indicating that by editing the piece, I had violated my gag order. It was not my article; I had no input in the decision to draft it. My edits were to correct misstatements of the author's. Finally, the *Kyiv Post* has no circulation in the United States and very little in Ukraine.

In response, Jackson came down very hard on me. As I sat in the court listening to her raving partisan statement, I was worried she would put me in jail over this. It was astonishing to me that she could stretch the probably unconstitutional gag order all the way to a tiny newspaper editorial in Ukraine. But she did. She said I was a danger to the community. What community? I don't know. No one in her jury pool would be reading the *Kyiv Post*.

She knew that it wasn't my article and that I had only edited it. But she played along in the spirit of the Special Counsel. It was just more proof that she was never going to be an impartial judge. She was in on the game, and she was going to make my life miserable.

Her decision was that I should consider this as a warning to not challenge her rules. If I violated the gag order again, she said she would revoke my home confinement and put me in jail while my case was pending. I was shaken by her absurd ruling. How could anyone claim this was a violation of an unconstitutional gag order? Weissman was not happy, but tactically he had achieved his purpose—I was one step closer to going to jail.

I was trying to get my bail package submitted before the holidays, but I couldn't. I spent the Christmas of 2017 under house arrest, which is where I'd been since I was indicted at the end of October. I asked permission to go to my daughter's house, which was two miles from my condo. To my surprise, Jackson approved my request and my wife and I were able to spend the holiday with my daughter and her family.

But it was not a happy Christmas. I couldn't shake the thought that it might be the last Christmas I would get to spend with my family. If convicted on all the charges that were filed against me, I could go away for life. What was once an outcome so unlikely I'd hardly considered it was now a very real possibility.

What made it worse was that I didn't have any confidence in the judge to be fair. She had rejected all of the bail packages and put a gag order on me. The issue with the *Kyiv Post* did not help give me confidence. I was feeling very negative about my prospects. There was no definition to the range of accusations Weissman could fabricate, no end in sight, no shape to the life I might be living soon. I was seventy years old and facing a ten- or fifteen-year sentence. I could be eighty before I got out of prison. It was a terribly difficult Christmas.

In February 2018, the rumors were all over Washington that the prosecutors were getting ready to file superseding (the legal word for "more") charges against Gates and me. If they did, it would be a gamechanger in how we prepared our case. We sort of knew the direction the new charges might take because of the media headlines being generated by anonymous government sources.

As I analyzed the possible new charges I was still confused. Our strategy on the FARA charges was in good shape. I felt confident we would be able to show why I did not have to file. One of the areas rumored to be a part of the superseding charges was my failure to check a box on my annual tax filing saying that I controlled offshore accounts. There was nothing wrong with having the accounts, but I had to disclose them in my tax filings. Again, I was confident of my innocence because I had fully and voluntarily disclosed the existence of all these offshore accounts and the specifics on the accounts to the FBI in 2014. I could not see how this would be an issue. Again, however, I was assuming justice and fairness. Two words not in Weissman's vocabulary.

And nothing I was hearing about tax evasion made any sense. At the end of every calendar year, Gates, as a part of the scope of his work, would send the year's details directly to my accountants, who would capture any income and calculate the taxes I owed.

Then I got a shocking surprise.

Rick Gates had cut a plea deal with the Special Counsel. When I heard he made a deal, it made no sense to me. I couldn't figure out why he would do that. He knew the charges were political. He understood the Special Counsel was lacking the evidence to prove the allegations. And because he was personally responsible for managing the finances of the company and for me, he understood how strong our case was.

Well, the last point was the problem for Gates.

The day before the superseding charges were announced in court, the Special Counsel had preliminarily filed the paperwork for the charges in Virginia. In the Gates indictment laid out by the Special Counsel, there were several million dollars in unreported wire transfers into Gates' personal bank accounts. They didn't say Gates stole the money from me, only that he took it from the offshore accounts and didn't pay taxes on it.

Downing had gotten a copy of the paperwork before it was retracted after Gates filed his guilty plea. Being the sharp attorney he is, Downing put it together immediately.

He called me into his office and started reading off of a document he was holding.

"How long have you known about Gates stealing money from you?" he asked.

"What are you talking about?" I said. "Gates never stole any money from me."

I really had no idea. But from the paperwork of the Gates indictment, Downing had calculated that Gates had stolen about $3 million from me. It was only after he explained it all to me for the first time, that everything made sense.

Gates *had* to cut a deal. He felt the pressure because he knew there was exposure on "his" finances. Weissman knew that Gates had been stealing from me and that, with the theft, Gates had tax exposure because he had not reported the stolen money in his tax filings. Gates was vulnerable.

The Special Counsel worked him hard. During this time, before the indictments, I was telling Gates, "Hang in there. We are going to be fine. We haven't done anything that they could get us on." In response, Gates was telling me not to worry. "I am not going to cut any kind of deal. There is no reason to cut a deal," he repeatedly told me and our mutual friends.

All of the time I was assuring Gates that we were innocent, he knew that *he was not* innocent. He knew in the new charges his theft would be public and his failure to report the stolen money as income in his tax filings exposed him to Weissman's pressure.

Unbeknownst to me at the time, Gates had listed himself as the transfer agent for a number of the offshore companies we were using in Cyprus. And he was a part of my company. So now suddenly, because of Gates, I *did* have legal exposure on the offshore accounts. I could see where this was going. I would now have to prove that I had not authorized Gates to have control over the accounts.

It was part of Gates's job every year to take any money that flowed in the Cyprus accounts and any money that I had spent and report it to the accountants. He couldn't do that, because the accountants would need to see the ledgers, which would have exposed the money he was stealing. So he didn't report a number of transfers to third parties from the offshore accounts.

Since Gates was the one dealing with the bookkeepers, he was the one making sure that they only saw what they needed to see so that his theft wouldn't be exposed. I didn't know any of this at the time. However, as I have reconstructed my life in the aftermath of this mess, I have admitted that even though they were not my crimes, I had to take responsibility for this scheme.

I should have paid more attention. If I had done so, I would be $3 million dollars richer and I would not have been convicted of any tax evasion crimes. Ultimately, I did admit this responsibility. But I should never have been convicted for crimes I didn't commit. Willful deceit was missing. However, I had no doubt sitting in Downing's office how Gates would be changing his story.

What convicted me was Gates saying that I had directed him. There was very little evidence that I did direct him. Unfortunately, there was no evidence that *I did not direct him*. And it was my company.

Weissman understood how this would look to a jury. Getting Gates to turn against me put Weissman one major step closer to putting a noose around my neck. And now the noose tightened. I did have exposure and Weissman had the only witness who could prove me innocent on his side.

The prosecutors had cleverly built the public relations case against me, and now they had Gates in a position to authenticate the narrative that I had masterminded a corruption scheme. If Gates had never turned state's evidence, the case against me would have fallen apart. They would have convicted Gates because they had Gates taking money that he didn't report. The signature on almost everything was Gates' signature. Not mine. But with Gates in their corner, Weissman could now do whatever he wanted. Gates would say what they wanted him to say, and salute while saying it.

On February 22, 2018, the Office of Special Counsel filed a new indictment with eighteen counts against me ranging from tax evasion, to hiding secret offshore bank accounts, to submitting fraudulent applications to banks for loans on various investment properties of mine.

I was flabbergasted. I now had twelve charges against me in DC Federal Court and eighteen charges against me in Virginia. The overwhelming number of charges were meant to convey to the public a criminal scheme of epic proportions. In fact, it was Weissman's way of creating criminal issues out of a weekend rental on Airbnb of one of my properties even though the loan application stated that the property was for personal use. (It was for personal use; it was where one of my daughters lived before she moved from New York to California.)

The reason the second case was filed in Virginia had to do with rules governing where tax cases can be filed. Without getting into details on this regulation, we decided that it would be better to have the case in Virginia to have a different judge preside. There was no way that I wanted to waive my right and have the new charges brought in front of Judge Jackson. The Eastern District of Virginia was where prominent cases were often brought and had a rocket-docket which forced the parties to move quicker than usual to get to trial. This appealed to me because I was not anxious to have these legal cases lingering for a couple of years.

On February 23, Gates pled guilty to lying to investigators and engaging in conspiracy to defraud the US.

Gates worked for me from approximately 2006 to 2016. He started as a staff associate and by 2016, he had advanced to managing my business affairs and serving as my deputy in the Trump campaign. After the campaign, I had encouraged one of my best friends to take him on as his assistant. I had pretty much advanced Gates's business life for the better part of a decade.

I promoted him at all of these levels because I believed that he was honest, hard-working, and loyal. I was wrong on all three counts.

If this was not bad enough, once Gates did a plea deal with the Special Counsel to protect himself, over twenty people told me that they tolerated Gates only because he worked for me. They found him to be a liar, a cheat, an ass-kisser who would knife anyone in the back, hot tempered, unreliable, and generally despicable. Needless to say, it was a little late for me to find this out.

On March 8, I pled not guilty in Virginia. The trial was set for July 10.

We now had to turn to the case in Virginia which dealt with the financial allegations. Not one of the thirty-two charges brought by the Special Counsel to investigate Russian collusion had anything to do with Russia or even politics.

When I was arraigned in the Eastern District for these charges in March, the judge took note of the multiple charges of tax evasion, not reporting the existence of foreign bank accounts, and lying on applications to banks for loans on properties I own.

Where Judge Jackson was auditioning for further appointment, Judge T. S. Ellis III was a professional jurist. The difference between the two Judges could not have been more pronounced. Ellis was a serious District Court Judge. He understood what the Special Counsel was doing. He wasn't unfair to the prosecutors, but he didn't let them get away with their antics. With Jackson, it was like she had a direct line to the prosecutors getting her instructions before the court convened its sessions.

From the very beginning, Ellis was telling the prosecution that he was on to their game. "You don't really care about Mr. Manafort's bank fraud," Ellis said during one hearing. "You really care about getting information that Mr. Manafort can give you that would reflect on Mr. Trump and lead to his prosecution or impeachment or whatever."

"I don't see what relation this indictment has with anything the Special Counsel is authorized to investigate," he said.

When the prosecution said that the scope of the investigation covered the activity in the indictment, Ellis responded, "Bank fraud in 2005 and 2007? Tell me how!"

"What we don't want in this country is we don't want anyone with unfettered power," he added. "It's unlikely you're going to persuade me the special counsel . . . has unfettered power to do whatever he wants."

Judge Ellis was very experienced, and very well-respected. And he was a tough judge. He told the prosecution that he required a US Attorney from the Eastern District, someone who knew how he worked, to be a part of the Special Counsel team. He put them on notice from the start.

At one point, he looked over at the prosecutors' table and smiled a smile that said he understood what they were doing. He said, "I know why you're doing this," meaning bringing eighteen duplicate counts. "You're trying to squeeze the defendant. But you'll have to prove a lot more, which means you'll give the defendant more opportunities to disprove your case." I felt comfort when he said that. For the first time since I was indicted in October, I felt like I might actually get a fair trial.

While I took comfort in the fact that Ellis understood that Weissman was misusing the system for his political agenda, it didn't make me feel better. Being right did not stop the negative headlines or the enormous costs I was incurring to defend myself. I had no control over my life and the stakes were sky high.

We thought the DC case on FARA violations would be first to go to trial. I would have preferred that order because I was concerned about the complexity of the financial issues of the Virginia case confusing the jury. The FARA case was pretty straightforward and based on the interaction with Heather Hunt and the FARA office prior to the politically charged Special Counsel being appointed, I believed the professionals' understanding would be something we could persuade the jury to understand.

Weissman tried to put the heat on me to waive my rights in Virginia. He was banking on me thinking: two cases, more indictments, more lawyering fees. He was shocked when I wouldn't agree to the waiver. Yes, it would be more expensive to defend myself in two different courts, but if I consolidated in DC, I might as well have just surrendered myself to the Bureau of Prisons. The media destruction of my reputation had been so thorough that I felt there was no way I would get a fair shake from Jackson or a DC jury that read the *New York Times* and *Washington Post* while getting their TV news from CNN and MSNBC.

I should note that all of my court references to the prosecution center on Andrew Weissman and not Robert Mueller. The reason is simple: I believe that Mueller was totally disengaged from my investigation. Weissman made all of the decisions. He was in charge of the team that was investigating me. What he showed Mueller is what Mueller would know about my situation.

While I was confused at first, it all made sense to me after watching Mueller fumble his way through the explanation of his final report to Congress a year later. It was clear listening to Mueller that he was suffering through an advancing stage of dementia. This disease was something I had more than a passing awareness of due to my father and my mother-in-law both dying of this dreaded illness.

Watching his confused presentation to Congress reminded me of my *only interaction* with Mueller. It came during the time I was proffering to the Special Counsel during the summer before my sentencing. I was returning from the bathroom as Mueller entered the corridor from an office. He was alone, as was I. I nodded to him, and he stared a blank stare at me. He did not know who I was. He had been investigating and prosecuting me for over a year at that point, my face was all over the news, and he did not know who I was.

Seeing his presentation before the Congress, I realized that Mueller had been disengaged for over a year. It gave Weissman what he wanted: unfettered authority and the ability to do almost anything he wanted to get a president and in the process any of his friends and colleagues, including me.

It was rumored that we would be filing a motion to disqualify Weissman because we had evidence of how he leaked grand jury testimony to the press, which was a total breach of ethics. There was an independent IG investigation into leaks coming out of the DOJ and Special Counsel's office. We had evidence of information being leaked to certain AP and CNN reporters. Through a backchannel of lawyers Downing knew in the DOJ system, we found out about the investigation. The leaks were illegal. It was Grand Jury material. They were specifically investigating Weissman. We had enough material to file a motion to disqualify him in front of a non-partisan judge—like Ellis. But Weissman, sensing this exposure, distanced himself from Ellis's courtroom while attending every hearing in Jackson's. He knew how to read the two judges.

Ellis was by no means on my side, but he was fair. I believe he felt that I was a political defendant, not a legal one. Weissman was afraid that we would file the motion the moment he made a formal appearance in the Virginia court. We felt it would resonate with Ellis in a way it would not with Jackson. It was a tactic we were prepared to use and Weissman knew it. So while he appeared occasionally in Ellis's court, he removed himself from the position of lead prosecutor in the Virginia courtroom. Whereas in DC, he made a point of being at every hearing. It was clear to us that he was comfortable with Jackson and afraid of Ellis.

Throughout the winter, Weissman was busy playing the bail game in the DC court case, keeping me in home confinement for as long as he could. When it looked as though I would get my fourth bail package approved at a hearing set for June 15, Weissman shifted his strategy. He would now try to get me incarcerated.

Recognizing that I was on the verge of being freed, the Special Counsel played their next dirty trick. They invented a crime and indicted me on a new charge—witness tampering. He knew, too, that if he argued this in front of Jackson—not Ellis—she would be favorable.

On June 4, the Special Counsel filed court documents accusing me of witness tampering. The media smear campaign went into overdrive for four days. Making the situation worse was the fact that, due to the gag order imposed on me by the "Honorable" Judge Jackson in October (to keep me from using PR to taint a potential jury pool) I could not respond. I had to sit by and quietly watch as a host of new damaging allegations were hurled at me.

On June 8, the Special Counsel got their complacent grand jury to add two new charges to my indictments: obstruction of justice and conspiracy to obstruct justice: "The defendants Paul Manafort and Konstantin Kilimnik knowingly and intentionally attempted to corruptly persuade another person, to wit; Persons D1 and D2, with intent to influence, delay and prevent the testimony of any person in an official proceeding."[2]

A little diversion is required to explain the basis for this new charge. Without complicating matters too much, it is important to understand the nature of some of the allegations against me. The principal charge of the case in DC centered on the requirement to file a form with the US government by any person who is representing a foreign government or political party in the US. The Special Counsel claimed that I was in violation of this statute.

In the charging document, I was accused of trying to intimidate a potential witness identified as Person D1. The identity of "Person D1" became apparent to me. He was a PR person who lived in Italy but was an American citizen. In theory, he might have had a duty to file with FARA too.

Additionally, this person managed a group of esteemed former heads of three European governments who were active in Europe on the Ukraine matter. They were identified in one of the exhibits of the FARA charge. This additional charge to the DC indictment, identifying them, was filed on February 22, 2018, when the superseding charges were filed in Virginia.

Believing that "Person D1" would want to be notified on what was going on in DC and also wanting to suggest that he hire an attorney, I reached out to this person on February 24. When he answered the phone, I identified myself. He said he was driving and could not talk so I asked him to call me back. By the next day he had not called, so I sent him a message identifying the purpose of my call.

In that text message I pointed out that the superseding charges filed in the FARA case now included failure to file FARA reports for the work of the European leaders who he was dealing with, and I included a news article on the reporting on this new indictment.

I still did not hear from him, so I asked Kilimnik who worked for me and had been the firm's contact with the PR firm to reach out to his contact to ask the principal to call me. Nothing came of this either. After about six attempts between me and my assistant, we gave up. I felt I had attempted to do the right thing but for some reason I was being ignored.

I knew instinctively, of course, not to call someone who might be a witness, but I didn't know the person I called would be considered a potential witness. Normally, one of the early dictates from the bench is the demand on the prosecution to produce a list of potential witnesses and instructions to the defendant not to deal with these potential witnesses. We had been asking for a witness list instruction in both courts. While Ellis provided one, Jackson never did. Clearly Weissman had known about my call for some time and he was sitting on it until he could use it to maximum effect. This June bail hearing was his moment. He wanted me behind bars, plain and simple.

My lawyers thought the charge was absurd. But Weissman understood how Jackson worked. With the added witness tampering charge, the prosecutors filed a motion with the DC court now opposing my fourth bail package. This was after they had agreed on the phone to support it. Not only did they oppose my proposal, but they now were calling for the revocation of my current home confinement and they demanded that I be remanded to jail, pending trial, with no bail. The basis of this position was that I had attempted to obstruct justice by reaching out to a witness to suborn perjury. Yes, my eighty-four-second phone call and subsequent text message were cited as proof of my illicit behavior.

With the new allegation, in which the prosecutors would present a claim by "Person D1" that he felt intimidated by my eighty-four-second call (later I would learn that he was being threatened with a FARA violation and indictment and this simple admission of fear would prove to cleanse him of any guilt), the June 15 bail hearing now had the added purpose of determining if I should have no bail at all and be sent to jail.

The added value to the Special Counsel of these new charges was that it gave Weissman a real Russian to finally indict. Konstantin Kilimnik worked for me in Ukraine for ten years. He managed my Ukraine office and interacted with all of the consultants that I had hired on the Ukraine project, including the individuals referred to as D1 and D2 in the new counts in D.C. It was just another salacious point to push in media.

CHAPTER 13

Incarceration

By the time we submitted my fourth bail package, I was able to cobble together all of the pieces that Jackson had approved from prior packages. Eighty-five percent of the package had already been approved. The package totaled $11.2 million in assets, well beyond the $10 million requirement. And the last piece was a property that a relative of my wife had agreed to put up.

Weissman actually called the relative, who is a lawyer, to talk to the husband and wife separately. He tried to tell them I was a flight risk and that their property would be at risk if I violated any of the terms of my bail. The husband and his wife were tough people. They were not intimidated by him. Finally, after being briefed on the two calls, I believed that I was ready to end this torture and be released from home confinement.

The bail package was going to be submitted on June 13 and it would have been approved. That's why Weissman leaked that their new position was that I should be denied bail and sent to jail, pending trial.

He came to our June 15 hearing in Jackson's court and said he had a new indictment and that now I was a threat to the community, and I needed to be incarcerated. I was no longer a flight risk; I was now a danger to the community.

To be clear, Jackson had never prohibited me from interacting with witnesses. There wasn't even a list of witnesses. And there was no way for me to know "Person D1" was a potential witness. In fact, the USG never claimed that he was. He was never put on a list. This was all a charade. But the prosecutors knew Jackson would play ball.

The prosecutors and Jackson also focused on the fact that I communicated with "Person D1" in Europe using the encrypted app WhatsApp, as if this was some sinister method to evade being caught. In fact, she knew from the evidence presented that 1.2 billion people use this app and that is *the preferred means* of communication in Europe. There is nothing remarkable about using WhatsApp.

Culvahouse had warned me about all of this. He told me Weissman had put the senior staff of Merrill Lynch in solitary for over a year because they wouldn't cooperate. It sounded absurd at the time, but every tactic A. B. warned me about, Weissman was using on me.

With the indictment in hand, Judge Jackson, claiming that I would be a significant flight risk if I were free, said she could find nothing that would comfort her. While she proclaimed sadness, she announced that she "had no other choice but to send me to jail"!

And before I could even begin to process those words, she was instructing the US marshal to take immediate custody of me and place me in jail. In the span of a few moments, the unprecedented $10 million bond had cruelly morphed into an unprecedented incarceration—for a white-collar crime that was founded on a failure to file a form with FARA.

I looked back at Kathy before it was too late and before I knew it, a US marshal came to me at my seat in the court and took me to the side room where he cuffed me and tossed me into a jail cell.

I was in shock. Worrying about my wife had made me a mess. Suddenly, as I sat in the holding cell outside of the courtroom, I realized that I was going to be transported to the DC prison. While I did not know anything specific about the DC jail, I did know that the reputation was not good.

Northern Neck Regional Jail is an outpost in the Chesapeake area of Virginia. The local community is rural and Republican. The jail was a temporary stop for prisoners who had been indicted and either not granted bail or not able to meet their bail requirements. The facility was used by the US government for special cases and housed prisoners facing trial in DC and Eastern Virginia federal courts.

When I arrived, I was met by a kind woman named Sergeant Kelly for processing. She encouraged me to try to be calm and offered a kind of assurance. Her compassion was the first sign that the guards would not all be "tough guys." After seeing my "VIP cell" for the first time and calling my wife and lawyer, I expected to pass out from exhaustion. It had been one of the longest, most difficult days of my life. But I couldn't fall asleep. I didn't sleep for more than five minutes that night or the next. Later, I came to understand that it was the stress that was making it impossible. Finally on the third night I was able to fall asleep for about three hours as my mind and body began to catch up to the reality that I was "in jail." But I would not manage a full night's sleep for four days.

I was told that I would be briefed on everything on Monday when the Warden of the jail showed up, but the weekend felt interminable.

On Saturday morning, I was told that the director had decided that I would not wear the traditional jail "jumpsuit;" instead they were going to buy me some clothes to wear. This would not happen until Monday either. So they gave me some temporary clothes: a 4XL white T-shirt, 3XL boxer shorts, and a pair of gym shorts. I had to hold my pants up whenever I stood up. But my dignity was not being undermined by wearing a jail jumpsuit. So, I did not complain.

On Monday, after two excruciatingly slow days and three sleepless nights, I finally met the head of the jail, Ted Hull. He had a folksy, southern charm that immediately put me at ease.

After putting me at ease, Hull explained the "special conditions" he had created for me but made the point that I was still going to have to follow the basic rules of solitary confinement. During my stay I found these conditions to be onerous. (It wasn't until I was transferred to Alexandria jail nearly a month later, that I realized how fortunate I had been.)

The key to surviving solitary confinement is to build a schedule and keep to it. As crazy as it sounds, a plan makes time go quickly. Without one, your mind wanders and you feel the oppressive environment of the jail cell.

By the end of my first week at NNRC, I had built my plan to occupy my time. I had managed to persuade the Warden to let me access a jail computer. There was no internet access, but by allowing the laptop, the warden made my stay into a kind of work environment. Having the computer was the only way I could prepare for my case. He permitted me to keep it in my cell which allowed me to do my legal work whenever I wanted. This, coupled with a flash drive, meant I had access to hundreds of thousands of documents Weissman had produced to date.

Of course, cells do not have power outlets. This was a concern, but I solved the power issue by securing a thirty-foot outdoor extension cord that ran under my door to an outlet in the hall outside of my cell. I was told this was a jail first. Deputies would walk by my cell, see this cord sticking out from under the door, and wonder aloud what was "going on in there."

On Friday, one week after arriving, I received my first grocery delivery from the commissary. In addition to chips, Doritos, and jolly ranchers, I bought several items of clothing—T-shirts, socks, and underwear. My jail attire was now complete. These items complemented the clothes that the director bought for me: three white polo shirts, two pairs of gray sweatpants, and one pair of Dexter sneakers. Seven days in and I was the best dressed inmate at Northern Neck! To amuse myself I wondered how Weissman would reference my prison wardrobe in his next indictment.

By the second week, I had a real program working. I was only allowed out of my cell for legal meetings. So, I arranged to have a "lawyer/paralegal" visitor every day. This allowed me to get out of my cell for several hours. Working my plan, I scheduled "workdays" of eight hours outside my cell. I would exchange work material with my paralegal and get more discovery to review.

In order to make this program work, I hired a retired FBI agent, Ken Mikionis, to visit every day my lawyers/paralegals could not make it.

At first, we held these meetings in the GED classroom of the jail, a large room with four long tables and a great AC unit. Summer in Virginia is hot and the AC in prison was only partially effective. But the GED classroom had two powerful units pumping air. This was reason alone to rejoice when getting out of my cell. Of course, it was in a different part of the jail which meant that they had to clear all of the corridors so that I could travel the thirty yards from my cell to the classroom without anyone seeing me. Because this was so cumbersome and manpower-driven, they let me stay in the GED room for unlimited lengths of time. All of this made my solitary, windowless walled cell more bearable.

Throughout my time there, the jail staff was unbelievable. I had rarely met a staff as compassionate and professional. They made me feel like I was surrounded by friends, not guards. In particular, Lt. Luna and Lt. Burton demonstrated a compassion for my situation that I am appreciative of to this day. Their interaction helped me feel human in a very dehumanizing environment.

My lawyer, Kevin Downing, returned to the US on Friday June 22, and we were able to meet for the first time the following Monday, ten days after my incarceration. I wanted to file a reconsideration motion with Judge Jackson. In this motion, I would offer conditions for bail that would deal with her phony concern for the safety of the "administration of Justice." Downing had a different idea. He wanted to file an appeal to her order citing legal and factual errors on the part of Jackson.

My concern with Downing's idea was that it would take at least a month to have all of the papers filed. In the end, I agreed to his plan but not before my daughter, Andrea, used her legal mind to persuade me that my approach was not wise. She argued that my idea would allow "the B****" (my characterization at the time) to simply fix the record on her mistakes and still deny me my freedom.

On June 28, we filed the appeal motion to the DC appeals court. It was a two-part filing in which we asked for a temporary release from the jail back to home confinement and a full appeal review for release on bail. The compelling reason for the stay was to spend time with my lawyers to prepare for the EDVA case. That trial was set for July 10—later pushed back to July 24. Filing the appeal to the circuit court was a long shot—they would not even hear it until right before the EDVA trial began—but I hoped the higher-level court would make a decision based on the law, not politics.

Boy, was I wrong. The stay was denied citing no compelling basis for this action. Again, I realized how rigged the system was against the defendant. I couldn't imagine how prisoners with no resources must feel going up against the US government—a completely futile process, fixed from the start.

Northern Neck was my first experience of jail. I had nothing to compare it to, and I was in solitary confinement, which limited my perspective even more. But the warden was willing to mitigate the harshness by providing me with certain benefits, like an old computer on which I could type notes, and a folding table to use as a desk. Despite the circumstances, I was able to get a routine down.

A motion we filed to be released from jail to home confinement had an unintended consequence. When Ellis saw the motion, he agreed that Northern Neck was not a good situation for me to prepare for his trial.

Jackson had control over my confinement because she was the one who placed me there over her concerns that I was a "danger to the community." But Ellis had jurisdiction over my location since his trial was first.

He decided it wasn't fair that I was so far away—roughly three hours in each direction from his court. He instructed the marshals to move me from Northern Neck to Alexandria, which is five minutes from the courthouse.

I don't know why I wasn't sent to Alexandria in the first place. After Jackson ordered my incarceration, I was only hoping not to be sent to a DC jail. I didn't know anything about the prison system or where I should have been sent. But by this point, to the extent that it was possible, I had grown comfortable at Northern Neck. It was the devil I knew, so to speak. While I felt that I should have been released to home confinement since I never should have gone to jail at all, I didn't want to go to Alexandria because moving would mean starting the whole process over again. Downing put in a motion saying I'd rather just stay in Northern Neck, but it was too late. Ellis wanted me moved and that was that.

On July 12, the US marshals picked me up at 6:30 a.m. to transfer me to Alexandria—a "real" jail. I had been at Northern Neck for nearly a month, in which time I had come to figure things out and adjust them to meet my needs. In fact, I had the system working for me. TV twenty-four hours a day, seven days a week! Telephone from 8:30 a.m. to 10:30 p.m.! Books. Control over my schedule thanks to daily visits by Ken Mikionis! A computer in my room. Polo shirts, sweatpants, and no mug shots. And a great staff of deputies who liked me with a management team that was supportive of me.

All of that changed at Alexandria. For the first three days, I was in a processing area, which meant I had a single cell and no privileges—no phone, very limited access to see or call people.

The most exciting part of those first days was that the cell had a small window through which I could see the corridor. I lost that when they moved me to my permanent cell, a concrete cube with a metal toilet and a sink. The light was kept on twenty-four hours a day so that I could be monitored. It was almost POW-style solitary confinement, justified— deceitfully—by the need to "protect" me. And all of this confinement came long before I was ever judged guilty of committing a crime. The same confinement that the government uses for terrorists, murderers, and gang criminals. What did I do to get here? I failed to file a FARA form.

In Alexandria, I was to be in my cell, isolated, for twenty-one hours a day. I had a two-hour break before 6:00 p.m. and a one-hour break from 6:00 p.m. to 11:00 p.m. During these breaks I could use the shower, make calls, and watch the TV in a kind of central living area. I could have scheduled attorney visits for blocks of three hours in the afternoon and evening. Thirty-minute family visits were only allowed on Thursday and Sunday.

My first chance to meet Kathy and my daughter was in a visitation room with a glass partition. I was prepared to be brave but as soon as I saw them, I broke into tears. My wife tried to be brave for me, but I could see the pain in her eyes. When we touched hands through the plexiglass window, I could feel her love and hurt. I was both enthralled and depressed by the sensation. There was nothing I could do to ease her pain other than to beg her to understand that I was managing my situation and she should not worry. My daughter, who is an attorney, was loving and businesslike in assuring me that they were taking care of Kathy and she was keeping busy taking care of her one-year-old grandson. I smiled imagining her running around making sure any infant mess was immediately cleaned up.

Watching them leave was hard. The thirty minutes went by too fast before the guard came into the room and said I had to go. We did "air kisses" and as I turned to go, I felt tears flowing down my cheeks. I couldn't show Kathy these tears without causing her concern, so I deflected my face as I threw her a kiss and turned to depart the visitor's cell.

In this new environment, it was imperative that I find new ways of getting through the isolation. I found them in the strangest places. The first lifeline in Alexandria was a postcard-sized transistor radio which gave me access to two radio stations that became my daily links to the world: WMAL and WFAN.

WFAN accessed sports shows. The Sports Junkies, Amy Lawrence, Nationals baseball, and NFL Thursday night games kept me connected to the world of sports. WMAL linked me to my political life. My daily schedule would include Chris Pratt in the morning, Rush Limbaugh in the afternoon, and the "Great One" Mark Levin in the evening. I should note that I developed a real fondness for Dan Bongino, who seemed to be the replacement host for everyone.

These two radio stations became my world. I came to be able to repeat every word of the My Pillow ads. Mike Lindell became my surrogate family. In fact, each night as I fell asleep using a rolled-up wool blanket covered by a cotton T-shirt as my pillow, I dreamt of getting my four-pillow special. Ironically, the number one ad on the radio was for the one item I did not have in my cell. We had no pillows. They were forbidden. My only disappointment was that I could not find a station that carried my friends Sean Hannity and Laura Ingraham.

Books were available once a week on a library cart that came around to my cell. I could not have books sent to me via the mail, but I found a solution to get access to the books I wanted to read. On a regular basis, my wife would donate books that I wanted to read to the jail. I'd then have to wait until the weekly library cart came around to my cell and hope that my donated books were on it. By the time I left the prison I was the largest book donor in the history of the jail.

I became a fan of Walter Issacson. While his politics align with the liberal Washington establishment, his work as an author and historian became very important to me in jail. Not only are his biographies on Hamilton, Franklin, Kissinger, the Wise Men of the twentieth century, Einstein, and DaVinci well written and engaging, but they are also quite long. So reading his works helped fill my time with matters of interest.

Since there are no clocks in jail, the only way I was able to tell time was through the twice-hourly room check that the deputies would conduct. The entrance to the cell block made a very loud sound, like a car backfiring, when they came in, which let me know I'd moved on to the next hour. It was a very unique way of keeping time. The problem was that I would need a periodic orientation to know what hour I was in. Thus, the value of the radio.

My attorneys were also bringing me boxes of documents to review, so I buried myself in research. The USG exhibits filled hundreds of boxes. I was not allowed to have more than three boxes in my cell, and this was only thanks to the leniency of the sheriff and his deputies. This meant the contents had to revolve. I would review, make notes, and then return them to my attorneys for a new set of exhibits. During this time, my attorney Rich Westling often gave up his evenings to spend time with me so that I would not be alone. His humanity was incredible. I felt blessed to have him as my lawyer and my friend.

Weissman's strategy was very clear. Not only did solitary confinement dull my senses, but it also seriously limited my abilities to prepare for a defense. I was fiercely determined, and I made it work.

But perhaps the most important byproduct of my time in solitary confinement was the effect it had on my faith and my connection to God. Without question, my most important aid in getting through the day was prayer. I started and finished every day by reflecting on my life and my trust in God that he had a plan that was guiding me in prison. When I could not understand it, I turned to the Bible for guidance and comfort.

When I arrived in Alexandria—alone and anxious—I had persuaded a deputy to get me a bible and decided I would read it as a history book. I wanted to educate myself. It quickly helped me overcome my feelings of abandonment. I was amazed at how the Bible seemed to talk directly to me. I gained a new understanding of the importance of suffering and the use of faith to give meaning to suffering. I would revert to the Bible whenever I found myself getting anxious. At first, I read the Psalms and Parables, but over time I focused on St. Paul's letters, written to new converts in neighboring countries while he was in prison.

In fact, St. Paul became more than my namesake while in prison. His life became a guidepost for me. What he endured became a model that I tried to replicate. His acceptance of suffering as a means to strengthen faith gave me a new appreciation for the parables in the Bible and how alive they are today.

Over time, I came to read certain passages depending on my moods. I was amazed at how relevant the Bible still feels in modern times. While at Alexandria jail, Pastor Ken Babington of First Baptist Church in Cocoa Beach, Florida, adopted me as one of his missionary projects. I looked forward to the weekly passages from the Bible he would send, which he believed were important for me to read based on what he was hearing about me from the media and what I was experiencing.

I am confident that this new part of my life will be with me forever.

We wanted the DC case to come up first because we thought we could win in DC. But Virginia works on an expedited system, meaning that when prosecutors want a case to be tried quickly, they file it in EDVA (Eastern District of Virginia) because they know it will move quickly.

So the Virginia case ended up ahead of DC even though the DC case had been filed months prior. When it became clear that we would not have the DC case first, we moved our strategy to winning in Virginia to impact the jury in DC. We were always looking at the two judges in two very different lights with two very different strategies.

As part of my research, I reviewed the Jencks material provided by the Government. The Jencks Act requires the prosecutors to turn over the testimony of witnesses or potential witnesses who will testify. If a witness has appeared before the FBI, the agent summarizes the testimony in what is called a Form 302.

Reading the 302s of potential witnesses, I saw the impact of FBI intimidation on the witnesses. Some witnesses had appeared several times. Reading their testimony in the order in which the meetings occurred, it was clear to me that over time their stories had gone from the truth to whatever Weissman coerced them into saying. At one point in my preparation I was so freaked out by the clear intimidation tactics and changing of testimony that I called Downing to ask if we should seek a plea deal in Virginia before going to trial.

Weissman's strategy was not to win by presenting evidence that established guilt "beyond a reasonable doubt." It was clear to me that he was looking to win on intimidated witnesses and a preponderance of nuanced evidence that would be impossible for a jury to track. After hours of reading, I concluded that there was no direct evidence in their Jencks material. The direct evidence was from witnesses who had been broken down to the point where they would change what really happened into what Weissman said happened. Many times I put down the documents and thought to myself, *This case would never have been brought but for the politics.*

As the trial date approached, we asked Ellis for a continuance for one week to prepare, which he granted. In fact, I wanted to use the time to explore the possibility of a plea deal.

I told Downing I would not lie to get a deal, which would mean that Weissman would not get what he wanted from me. To Downing, the starting point for any deal had to be a ten-year cap, meaning that all of the charges we agree to cannot total more than ten years (with any sentencing in the DC case being concurrent). The plan would be to cut the deal in EDVA and then have the DC charges dropped. I told them I wanted to kill the forfeiture and if that wasn't possible, to switch out Andrea's house and stock portfolio for my Howard Street and Trump Tower properties.

We spoke about it for a day or two before I decided that I had come this far, and I would not back off. I could not live with myself if I gave up. The last-minute jitters confused me for a day but then I regrouped and decided I was going to beat the bastard or go down trying. Justice would not let an unethical prosecutor succeed, I thought.

Well, I was naive.

On July 23, I was woken up at 5:00 a.m. and told I had thirty minutes to shower, shave, eat breakfast, and wait to be prepared for transportation. They brought me breakfast, which was a bag with cereal and some milk. And there was a microwave, so I could heat a cup of water to make some coffee. After half an hour, three deputies arrived—one to guard the door as if I was going to escape, another to put cuffs on my wrists and ankles and a belt around my jumpsuit, and a third to stand guard while the second worked. Once that was over, I was led to a holding area where I waited for another twenty minutes.

Nobody could be in the corridor when I was walking. I walked about twenty yards from my cell to the entrance of an underground garage where the US Marshals took control of me, which triggered a process of transferring a human being from one law enforcement division to another. First, I had to take off the chains. Then, I had to strip all of my clothes off to make sure I didn't have anything on me. Then I got dressed again and re-shackled. Finally, the US Marshalls would walk me the remaining ten feet to be loaded into a van.

This was my first trip to the courthouse, and it would become something of a daily ritual—humiliating, sobering, and totally unthinkable just a month earlier. Over time, I learned to "zone out" whenever I had to present myself to be cuffed but these daily trips to the court were especially humbling. I started every day in a very difficult frame of mine. I couldn't walk twenty feet without a chain around my ankles.

Every day on that drive—it was always the same—we would pass a big office development, a movie complex, some restaurants, and my acupuncturist. Sometimes Kathy and I would go to the movie theater on that road. It was very difficult sitting in the back of the van and looking out of a caged window. It was always the worst part of my day, a stark reminder that I had no freedom and that my life might never go back to normal.

I would arrive at the courthouse in a protected area. Usually in the van with me were a few other prisoners who had court appearances that day. There was only one daily movement from jail to courthouse. So all prisoners with hearings, regardless of the time, were moved at once. It didn't matter when the appearance was scheduled. And they brought you back as a group at the end of the day. Sometimes you'd be there for ten hours for a thirty-minute hearing.

We would come into the garage and be lined up against the wall. They would take the leg shackles off, we would undress again, be checked, and then moved to the holding cells. Since I was in solitary, I was separated from the other prisoners and placed in a cell by myself.

At the courthouse, they kept the prisoners in a large holding area in the basement with several large cells. I was always by myself in the farthest cell, for my protection. I had to walk the whole walk from the entrance to the cell. I would walk by five cells that had a number of prisoners waiting their turn to be called to court. A few of them recognized me and gave me fist bumps through the bars.

There is a kind of camaraderie among prisoners. So they always wanted to cheer me up. While encouraging, I couldn't help but think how a few floors above us, people were walking freely. My captivity never felt more pronounced than in those moments.

I would be brought to a cell in the basement of the courthouse around 6:45 a.m. and kept to myself. I'd wait there for several hours. My lawyers would come down and we'd speak through plexiglass about any last-minute conversations. I couldn't bring any notes because I wasn't allowed to have anything on my person, so I would memorize what I wanted to say.

At 9:45, I would be brought into a room outside of the courtroom that was about five feet by five feet. They kept me handcuffed. The bailiff would deal with the Judge and would be informed when Ellis was ready to come onto the bench. He'd notify the marshals, and I'd be moved up to a small holding cell where I would wait to be brought into the courtroom.

Judge Ellis allowed me to wear suits instead of jail jumpsuits, but only if the jury was present. I had Kathy deliver three different suits, ties, and shirts. The US marshals took possession of the clothes. When I was placed in the basement cell they would bring me a suit, tie, and shirt for me to change into before entering the courtroom. As one of the marshals was leaving, he said, "Oh by the way, those are dope clothes. I bet they cost a lot?" I laughed and told him to come to court next week and he will find out exactly what they cost as the prosecution intended to show the invoices in the early part of their case presentation.

Once Ellis signaled he was ready, my cuffs were removed, and I was escorted to my table.

For security reasons, I was not allowed to look at the gallery where my wife was sitting. Because drug defendants and gang defendants could signal messages back and forth, the US marshals made all defendants look forward.

While I would respect this rule during the court sessions, when I first entered and during recesses, I would make eye contact with my wife and throw her kisses. It was important that she see me behaving as "normally" as I could in this absurd situation. I would try to smile and project a positive attitude. But I ached to hold her, and my heart would always be pounding in my chest when I would first enter and see her there.

Following my transfer to Alexandria from Northern Neck, our attention turned to jury selection. The Virginia jury selection was the first I'd ever been involved in. As we prepared for the process, we brought Brian Ketchum, a young partner from Kostelanetz and Fink who specialized in juries. I had been asking if we needed to get a jury consultant, but when Downing explained what a jury consultant did, I realized it was what I do. It's politics. It's assessing an individual's background and making judgements on how they'll vote. It's being able to read people. I decided I didn't need a jury consultant and that I would be totally involved in the selection process. In the EDVA case, we had a pool of forty potential jurors, twelve of which would be selected, with three or four alternates.

In the selection process, the prosecution and the defendant each get three strikes. Potential jurors had to fill out a questionnaire that gave us a sense of their background and family, and if they have any experience in law enforcement. We prioritized our picks, but we only had three strikes and there we many more than three that we were opposed to having on the jury.

There were very few definite yesses. Brian, our jury expert, and I got deep into conversation to put our list together. I felt I could get a fair jury in Virginia based on the material I had in front of me. But I was still nervous. There were many unknowns. My feeling was that the further the juror lived from DC, the fairer they could be. I wanted to have educated jurors. This was a trial that required understanding taxes, FBAR regulations, and bank fraud. I did not want an uneducated, high-school dropout. I found that men were better for me. I didn't want a thirty-year-old female lawyer who lived in Arlington.

It was very similar to what I do in assessing the data in a political survey. Once we'd built our list, we started the selection process, which took two hours. Ellis would ask the juror's name and if there was anything they felt would prohibit them from being fair and impartial. We used our "strikes" to knock out jurors we categorized as "bad." The Special Counsel was not as prepared as we were. They knocked out jurors who we had identified as pro-government. In the end we got about seven jurors that we felt comfortable with, four we felt were bad, and two of whom we were uncertain. And in theory I only needed one of the seven to believe me in order to get a mistrial. The prosecution needed all twelve.

The jury had a six-to-six gender split, was highly educated (four master's degrees, six college graduates, and two with high school diplomas) and came from the collar counties like Ashton, Purcellville, and Leesburg. Since we started with a jury poll of very few positives, lots of negatives, and a few "uncertains," we defied the odds by our preparation. I chuckled to myself at the end of the process thinking this type of preparation is also why I win elections.

After the selection was over and the jury was sworn in, Ellis called a recess before we returned for opening arguments. I was feeling confident. We had done our homework. We had a jury that could rule in our favor. We had a fair judge. But in the back of my mind, I was scared. I had learned not to get my hopes up. There were still any number of things that could go wrong.

CHAPTER 14

On Trial

In a strange twist of fate, my trial in the Eastern District of Virginia began on the morning of July 31, 2018, two years to the day from the press conference in Philadelphia where I first heard anything about Russian collusion. In a million years I would never have believed that two years later, I'd be taking center stage in what the media was calling "The Trial of The Century."

The Special Counsel's opening statement was built on the image of "Manafort the Liar." They cited all of the standard lines about corruption, how I was a tax cheat, a fraud, how I lied to banks and even lied to my own accountants. I had heard it all before, but that didn't make it any less devastating. To make me look as bad as possible, they emphasized how I was paid by "Ukrainian oligarchs" and had thirty bank accounts in three different countries.

They talked about my character, but I didn't recognize the person they were describing: "A man in this courtroom believed the law did not apply to him." Not tax law. Not banking laws. "The law."

"This man collected over $60 million for his work in a European country called Ukraine. But this man didn't want to report all of his income, so he used shell companies and foreign bank accounts to funnel millions of dollars of untaxed income into the United States concealing it from US authorities and bankrolling his extravagant lifestyle." I was sitting there thinking, *I don't know who this person is.*

Then they went through a long lifestyle presentation—the lavish houses, the clothes, the carpets. Ellis, for his part, tried to steer the prosecutor away from salacious headlines about me and focus on elements of the crime rather than my lifestyle. "It's not a crime," he said at one point, "to have a lot of money and to be profligate in your spending, so focus on the allegations in the indictment and the evidence the government intends to offer to prove those elements."[1]

I was scared. All of the confidence I'd had during the jury process disappeared in a matter of minutes. "Sitting in this courtroom today is the man who the evidence will show hid tens of millions in overseas income, the man who on his tax returns concealed his many foreign bank accounts, the man who evaded the report to the Treasury Department, the man who the evidence will show lied to the IRS about his total income. That man is the defendant, Paul Manafort. . . . In each of these crimes, ladies and gentlemen, the evidence will show that Paul Manafort placed himself and his money over the law."

By the end of the prosecutor's opening statement, I was a basket case.

"Ladies and gentlemen, none of this happened by accident. Shell companies don't create themselves. Neither do fake loans. Bank records don't falsify themselves. The evidence will show that Paul Manafort orchestrated these crimes. He submitted the false tax returns. He willfully failed to declare his foreign bank accounts. He committed bank fraud. So at the conclusion of this trial . . . We will come back to you, and we will ask you to hold this defendant accountable for his actions to make clear that he is not above the law and that the rules apply equally to him. We will ask you to find Paul Manafort guilty on each count of the indictment."

In our preparation for trial, Tom Zehnle explained that he wanted the jury to focus on "taxes, transparency, and trust." Besides the alliteration making it easy to digest, it made sense to highlight how there was always evidence that I was not hiding things. I had put my trust in Rick Gates and put him in a position where he could do the damage that he did. That was my responsibility, but the crimes were not mine.

I also wanted Tom to spend some time on my history, to humanize my image for the jury, which had taken a beating after two years of nonstop slander and lies from the Special Counsel and the MSM.

When it was time, Tom got up and made our opening argument.

"This case," he said, "this case is about taxes and trust. It's about taxes because, as the prosecutor just explained to you, my client, Paul Manafort, has been charged with willfully and intentionally signing false tax returns because he failed to check a box on a schedule that was attached to his returns and because they say he didn't report his income. They also say that he failed to file this foreign bank account report or FBAR, as you'll hear it described.

"This case is also about trust. Because the evidence is going to show you that in his business affairs, in his tax affairs, and that dealing with these mortgage lenders that the prosecutor was just talking about, that Mr. Manafort consulted and involved his employees, his bookkeepers, and his tax accountants. And he trusted them to speak with one another and to make sure that these things were done right.

"At its core, this case is about trust because it's about Mr. Manafort placing his trust in the wrong person. And you just heard the prosecutor mention his name a moment ago, Rick Gates. Rick Gates, you'll find out, was Mr. Manafort's business associate and essentially the man in charge of the day-to-day operations of Mr. Manafort's business. Mr. Gates pled guilty not more than a couple of months ago to actually lying to the Government, among other crimes. And this is the person that you will find the Government now wants you to trust. There are two sides to every story. It's an old adage, but it's true. The Government's story you've just heard: Mr. Manafort is a criminal. But that is simply not the case." His point was that I had trusted the people who worked for me, and I was deceived.

Next, Zehnle asked me to stand up. "Members of the jury," he said. "I'm proud to be here representing Paul Manafort today. Paul Manafort is a talented political consultant and a good man."

Zehnle's arguments were clear, concise, and well-presented. He focused on trust and explained the mechanism I had set up and the expectations I had that people interact with each other on my behalf. I had put my trust in the wrong person: Richard Gates. My lawyers laid out a case that I was the ultimate authority but not the person doing the job. *This was the key point of my defense.*

The foundation of the Special Counsel's case rested on the credibility of Gates, who was convicted of lying to the USG, whose story was constantly changing, and who had embezzled millions of dollars from me, didn't pay taxes, and got caught. To counter this, the prosecution turned Gates into nothing more than an idiot clerk incapable of thinking or acting without direction from me.

Zehnle also raised the 2014 FBI interview, in which I had given the USG all the details of how my business worked and all of the details of the foreign bank accounts that were now the basis of my indictment. If, as the prosecution wanted the jury to believe, I was now "willfully and intentionally" trying to mislead the USG, why would I have laid out those details for the FBI—for the very years that the USG had now indicted me?

I also wanted Zehnle to make it clear—especially for Trump to hear—that much of my work in Ukraine focused on moving the country closer to the west, closer to Europe, and *away* from Russia.

Tom answered for me and did an excellent job of countering the Special Counsel. The two opening statements took about two hours. Now, it was time for evidence to come out the way that we needed it. We had to simplify the case and destroy the credibility of my former associate, Rick Gates, to show his pattern of deceit and incompetence. That was how we would win.

The first witness the prosecution called was Tad Devine. Tad was the lead consultant and strategist for John Kerry's presidential campaign and had worked for Al Gore's and Bernie Sanders's campaigns as well. He's a partisan Democrat, but he worked for me as a media consultant in Ukraine. He understood Ukraine and he knew me as a person.

I couldn't figure out why they were calling him as a witness. I hadn't talked to him in a while, so I wasn't sure exactly what he would say. Answering the lead prosecutor's questions, Tad gave a character reference for me that was better than I would have given for myself. "My impression was that it was a really incredible operation. He had a lot of really good people in place, very well organized. And I was deeply impressed by him and the people around him," Devine said.

They were using Tad to establish how smart I was—too smart, in their portrayal. But what came across from Tad was that more than anything I was trustworthy. Tad also made the point that Gates was the one handling the business and that I was more the strategist: "I understood Rick to be . . . Paul's business guy. The one who handled the contracts, our travel," he told the jury. At the end of that first day, there was a glimmer of hope in my heart. I thought maybe we could pull it off. But it was a roller coaster and every up would have a down.

That night the jail did a random search of my room. I found it less than coincidental that my first room search at Alexandria was on day one of my trial. The deputies tore the cell apart and threw everything on the floor. It was utterly humiliating, demoralizing, and inhuman—exactly what Weissman would have wanted. They confiscated eight yellow pads as "contraband," as I was only supposed to have one. If Tad's testimony had given me some hope that—with the truth on my side—I might come through this ordeal in one piece, the search reminded me that at the end of the day I was just another prisoner with no rights.

The prosecution was relying on three witnesses to establish my guilt. Gates was there to say I had directed him to do everything he did, and my CPA and bookkeeper were there to talk about my personality, decisiveness, and control. There was not one bit of evidence of me telling them to do anything that was illegal. The prosecution needed to establish a chain where I gave the order to Gates and Gates gave it to the bookkeeper and CPA or bank official. So, all three pieces were critical to their case.

The history of the bank accounts was important because around 2010, my US banking had become very complicated. Because I was involved in Ukraine, and because the FBI was looking at corruption within the government of Ukraine at that time, my income from Ukrainian oligarchs kept ending up in SARs reports—suspicious activity reports.

Even though the money was clean, the fact that it was coming from Cyprus or the Maldives or the Seychelles made it suspicious. Without me knowing, the Treasury Department was tracking a lot of these payments into my accounts. But the important thing was that the Treasury, after monitoring, had concluded there were no illegalities. However, the monitoring caused the wire transfers to be flagged, scaring the compliance departments of my banks. Compliance departments of banks don't want anything to do with clients who are regularly popping up on suspicious activity reports. So without informing me as to why, banks started to shut down my accounts. I assumed it was because the money was coming from Cyprus, but I didn't know the government was filing SARs reports on me.

As I said previously, suddenly, it became difficult for me to bring money into the US to pay bills. We needed a system that would remove the complications and we devised one that we thought was proper and could work without too much difficulty. Gates would be the gatekeeper. Instead of moving the large amounts of money at once we would pay the European consultants directly from the Cyprus accounts, rather than move the money to the US banks and then send out to their banks in Europe. Second, we would move money to my business accounts in the US that we needed to pay normal administrative overhead and the invoices of consultants whose work was solely in the US. Finally, we would pay big bills of mine and investments from the overseas accounts and then capture the payments in the year-end accounting of revenues, expenses, and payments.

The next issue was how would we create accounts overseas to be the bridge banks. This is where the SPVs created in 2008 to service the investments of my then client Oleg Deripaska in the fund that Deripaska had set up came in. Since the fund closed after making only one purchase, there were a number of dormant, on-the-shelf SPVs that could be used to open accounts. Since I didn't own these SPVs we needed to get the permission of the lawyer who had set them up and who controlled them.

I actually asked Gates if we needed to report the existence of the bank accounts and was told by him that as long as we didn't control the accounts and the money is at risk if the owner wants to move the funds without our approval, we would not have to file an FBAR. Since I trusted the attorneys, I didn't care about this risk, and I signed off on the process. This was my mistake. I should not have relied on Gates's judgment. Thinking I *never had* control from when the SPVs were created in 2008, I was too quick to agree to the process. I rationalized it because we were not hiding the existence of the foreign bank accounts. Money was not being moved around to disguise the existence of the Cyprus accounts. Transactions were appearing on my company's ledgers and books, and we were capturing what I believed was all of the revenue flow each year.

What I did not know until after my indictment was that Gates had lied to me. While I was not listed as owning or controlling the accounts, Gates appointed himself as the agent of the accounts and since he worked for me that triggered my filing requirement. The reason Gates did not tell me he kept himself on the accounts is because he needed to be listed to achieve his goal of stealing from me. Over the course of the time he was in control, Gates stole over $3 million from me as set out in the superseding charges the prosecutors threatened to indict him on if he would not cooperate with them against me. I would never have known if I hadn't seen a copy of the superseding indictment that Weissman was prepared to file against Gates in February 2018. The indictment specified, with great detail, the wire amounts and dates to offshore bank accounts in Rick Gates's name.

What was even more brazen of Gates was that he never reported the stolen income in his tax filings. This was why he capitulated to Weissman's pressure. While I was telling Gates to ignore Weissman's pressure because we had nothing to worry about, he knew that he had plenty to worry about. He also knew that I would have plenty to worry about, too, once I found out about the way he mismanaged my finances.

Furthermore, in order not to be caught, Gates did not turn over all of the accounting to our CPA firm at the end of each year. The accountants would have uncovered his theft. So, he selectively gave partial information to my accountants while telling me he gave them everything. In the process, several transfers made on investments into real estate were not included. I never would have hidden these transfers because they were made directly into LLCs that I set up in my name to invest in properties. A criminal intent would have disguised these transfers in ways that the drug cartels and mafia do, creating LLCs in third party names disguising ownership. In my case, the money was going into LLCs that were clearly identified as mine and easy to track.

Weissman had done exactly that. In fact, I had made it easy for him. In 2014 I gave all of the offshore bank information that was now the foundation of my indictment to the FBI. Clearly, I was not trying to hide these accounts. This was critical to my defense. And if Gates was not trying to hide stolen money that he did not declare, the 2014 disclosures would probably have resulted in my acquittal.

As he was constructing my defense, Downing was convinced that we would be able to expose Gates as the architect and the manager of the structure. Downing's attitude was that if they try to prove I'm smart, they can't say I would have done it the way I was supposed to have done it. Because everything was so transparent, not hidden. If I wanted to hide my income and not pay taxes, Downing said, this would have been, "the stupidest way to do so." I laughed, but it made me want to cry.

So Weissman had to break these three people: my bookkeeper, my accountant, and Gates. They broke Gates and immunized him. They threatened the other two and nuanced their testimonies in ways that directed all attention to Gates who confirmed that "Paul told me to do this." I sat and listened to their testimony and tried to rationalize how the CPA and bookkeeper could believe what they were saying.

They knew I paid attention to details. They knew I was in control. They didn't know about the source of some of the funds. They didn't know we owned the bank accounts, but they did know the bank accounts existed. Because they didn't know that we controlled the accounts they made certain decisions. The complexity made it difficult to follow. So, when Gates said affirmatively, "Paul told me to do it," even though there was no evidence other than Gates's word, the impression was imprinted. Given that I had been convicted in the MSM as a tax cheat and bank fraud criminal for two years, these impressions had Weissman's desired effect on the jury.

My accountant ended up losing her job because they made her admit she knew about the offshore bank accounts and she knew that I was lying about income, none of which was true. After her testimony, which was really personally devastating for her, I told Downing to go easy on her during cross-examination. She didn't deserve what she had been put through. I felt terrible about how broken she looked. I didn't meet her very often, but I knew her as a person and there was no way she would have done the things they made her say that she did. She was a good person, churchgoing, conscientious. They made her into this conniving, cunning, duplicitous person and that wasn't her at all. But that was the strategy. They used my bookkeeper to claim that I had lied to everyone about the offshore accounts and the unreported income.

In the atmosphere of a trial, Weissman knew it would be too confusing, with all the documentation on the bank loans. He knew a jury would be buried under the details.

The real weakness in the Government's case was in the area of bank fraud, in which they relied on backroom clerks whom I'd never dealt with. Most of these witnesses were middle-America employees of banks, accounting firms, and construction companies. When the FBI approached them, they freaked out. The Special Counsel would then intimidate them to get what they wanted. They would threaten indictment or career destruction.

The most damning witnesses against me either had a plea deal—like Gates—or immunity. Or the person who interacted directly with me at the bank was not called. Those who could be helpful to me and had first-hand knowledge were either indicted or threatened with indictments so that we could not call them to the stand. Essentially, we had to win our case on cross-examination of the government's witnesses.

The bank fraud cases were complex and focused on loan applications. Typically, in a loan application process, the borrower provides the details to the loan officer who organized them on the application and then has the borrower fill in the blanks. The applications of various loans that were the subject of the case were done over protracted periods of time with items changing in the process. The process resulted in some errors and corrections. Nothing that was deliberate. The bank loan officers on the loans were intimately involved in managing the process. They were aware of everything.

Weissman's bank fraud cases centered on details that did not tell a full or accurate story. An example of his tactics focused on an Airbnb advertisement that was used as evidence that I'd committed bank fraud regarding a New York condo property that I had bought for my daughter.

The bank knew about the Airbnb rental. When the bank officer discovered that my son-in-law had listed it for rent when they moved from the New York condo to LA, he said that the condo could not be rented as an Airbnb and I removed it from the rental market. There was nothing deliberate or deceitful.

But the bank officer was threatened by the prosecutors and told that if he didn't cooperate, he would be charged as a co-conspirator. He agreed not to be a witness, which was as good as cooperating because I needed him to be a witness in my defense. My lawyers were telling me we could not call him because he would plead the fifth and make me look even more guilty. I was upset. I needed the jury to hear my full defense, but I couldn't get any witnesses because they were either threatened with indictments or actually indicted, like Steve Calk, the president of the bank involved in one of the main bank fraud charges.

The Special Counsel took information out of context, threatened potential witnesses who worked directly with me and could have explained the process, got other witnesses to change their original testimony to the FBI. And most of the witnesses who were called were not directly involved with me.

Instead of the loan officers, the prosecution called as witnesses the people who worked in the backroom processing offices. They got these clerks to say that the bank would never have handled things the way they were done with my loans and that the bank would never have approved the loans the way they were. The fact that the loans were approved with the direction of the bank loan officers got lost in the process. Impressions, not facts, were driving the prosecution's case. My reputation—destroyed in the lead-up to the trial by targeted leaks to which the gag order kept me from responding—was an easy target to make the impressions stick.

Oh, and by the way, the "alleged victims" of the fraud—the banks were not the ones bringing the actions against me. The banks were all making money off of the loans. The banks were not the ones who initiated the criminal actions. Lost in the drama of the headlines generated by the Special counsel, was the fact that the banks all were making money on the loans. The banks were happy with the loans.

In fact, all of my loans were performing and did not go into default until after I was indicted, the property was seized and my cash frozen. Yes, the victims were making money. The Banks never brought the actions against me and would never have done so. It was the Special Counsel who decided that there was bank fraud, not the banks. None of these charges would ever have been brought against me but for the creation of the Special Counsel and its interest in going after Donald Trump, through me.

Despite all of these obstacles to asserting my innocence, without Gates' testimony—which lasted three days—the USG simply could not have made a case against me. There was little documentation and it was confusing. For the most part there was nothing beyond Gates' word, that I had committed the crimes I was on trial for. And he was a professed liar and thief.

There was a point where the prosecution pressed Gates to admit that he had stolen from me. They knew it was coming when Downing cross-examined him, and they had to get it in front of the jury first. They tried to soft-pedal the impact, but their whole purpose of using Gates was to get him to say I had directed everything, that I had told him to do everything. This was crucial on all the points to get me convicted. There was never any paper trail; there was almost no inculpatory proof that stood alone to convict me without Rick Gates.

I sat there for three days and listened as Gates lied and twisted everything to make me out to be a criminal. "Mr. Manafort," he said, "over the years had requested that I make wire transfers from the off-shore accounts. That information was not reported to the accountants. The income was not reported as well. In addition, we did not report the foreign bank accounts."² It was true I'd had him making wire transfers, but it was not true that I told him not to report the income.

Gates testified that he had lied to the accountants and bookkeepers and kept income from them, which was true. But, he said, it was I who had told him "not to disclose the bank accounts,"³ which was a lie.

He said he lied to accountants about the foreign bank accounts, but only at my "direction."⁴ Another lie. In fact, Gates's testimony was full of lies, but the prosecutors were not going after Gates. They wanted me and they wanted Trump. Gates was their means to get both of us.

On cross-examination, Downing was able to quickly establish that Gates was a thief, that he was not trustworthy, and that he violated the responsibility I'd given him. And he even got Gates to change his own testimony from the day before when questioned by the prosecutors.

Downing did a very effective job of going after Gates's credibility. Gates' demeanor on the stand smacked of that of a guilty man. He looked nervous. His eyes shifted back and forth. He wiped his brow constantly. He tried to look straight at the jury to show he was in control, but he looked weak in doing so. He didn't appear trustworthy.

Right from the start, Gates lied to the jury when he said he didn't lie to the Special Counsel:

DOWNING: And prior to you entering your plea, when did you provide false and misleading information to the Government?

GATES: There were instances where I struggled with the interviews, certainly recalling details and facts about various questions that the Special Counsel asked. So there's no question that I struggled to get all the information out.

DOWNING: So it sounds to me, as you sit here today, you're not saying you knowingly, intentionally provided false and misleading information. You just had a bad recollection; is that correct?

GATES: To some extent, yes.

THE COURT: But I thought you said you pled guilty to providing false information?

GATES: I did, Your Honor, to one count.

THE COURT: All right. You just said you just had a bad memory. Did you provide false information or did you have just a bad memory?

GATES: Your Honor, I provided false information to the Special Counsel prior to my plea agreement.⁵

He then admitted to the fact that he "took unauthorized funds from Mr. Manafort":

> DOWNING: Now, please take a look at what's been marked Defendant's Exhibit 17. So, Mr. Gates, just take a minute to look over this exhibit, kind of look at the totals for years 2010 to 2014. Give me a ballpark total number for all those items, if you could.
> GATES: It looks like approximately 2.7, 2.8.
> DOWNING: It's about $3 million, correct?
> GATES: Okay.
> DOWNING: And about how many entries are contained on this document?
> GATES: I'd venture to guess somewhere around forty.
> DOWNING: Somewhere around forty entries? And do you recall this document being a compilation of unreported income that you had been initially indicted for in this district?
> GATES: Yes.
> DOWNING: And included on this . . . on this . . . in this document are some very large dollar entries that are coming out of various Cypriot entities; is that correct?
> GATES: That's correct.
> DOWNING: And each and every one of the transactions that's contained on this document, as included in your original indictment here, they were authorized by you; isn't that correct?
> GATES: Yes. Some were authorized by Mr. Manafort, but there were unauthorized transfers as well.[6]

At one point, Judge Ellis was so caught up he asked Gates to clarify that the money Gates was transferring to his personal accounts from the Cyprus accounts was not his money.

"Oh," Gates said, "the money came in conjunction to expense reports that I created in order to get the money wired out of the account.

"That tells me how you got the [money]—you say by using these false expense reports—but [I want] to know whose money it was," Ellis said.

"In this case it was Mr. Manafort's," Gates said.

"Next question."[7]

By the time I learned about Gates's betrayal, he had already cut a deal. So, at that point, I couldn't interact with him. I haven't spoken to him since about three days before he pled in February. But by the time he testified against me, I had already processed the stealing. Watching him, my focus was on how he was reacting to the line of questioning. I have been told that he tells people it really hurt him to testify against me. But I think he's just a liar. He would do and say anything. I was wrong on Gates. I value my ability to judge people and I was dead wrong on Rick Gates. The one time I put my life into somebody else's hands so that I could enjoy doing the things I enjoy doing, I ended up on trial looking at the rest of my life in prison for crimes I didn't commit.

Downing was also able to trap Gates into admitting that the $3 million that Gates kept calling "unauthorized transactions" taken from me was really embezzlement:

> GATES: I said it's unauthorized, that's correct.
> DOWNING: It's an embezzlement, is it not?
> GATES: You can choose—sure. You can choose whatever word you'd like.
> DOWNING: Well, why don't you use the word? It's an embezzlement?
> GATES: It is an unauthorized transaction that I took from Mr. Manafort.
> DOWNING: Why won't you say "embezzlement"?
> GATES: What difference does it make?
> DOWNING: Why won't you say "embezzlement"?
> DOWNING: It was embezzlement from Mr. Manafort.[8]

More crucially, Gates admitted that there is nothing in writing from me to him telling him not to file and he expects the jury to believe all of the discussions where Gates claims that I told him to do something are true:

> GATES: A lot of our communication occurred verbally, especially on subjects like this.
> DOWNING: Actually, it's interesting you raise that question. Because in direct, every time you wanted to say something that would make Mr. Manafort be involved with your activity, you said, "We had discussions." Every single time.
> GATES: Correct.
> DOWNING: And there's no record of any such discussions, are there?

GATES: I think there's a strong record that there are a number of discussions that occurred, but for the most part, Mr. Manafort would employ both phone and e-mail in those discussions.
DOWNING: So with respect to every time you said "discussions" on direct, this jury is supposed to just believe you; is that correct?
GATES: Yes, they are.
DOWNING: Uncorroborated believe you?
GATES: Yes.
DOWNING: After all the lies you told and fraud you've committed, you expect this jury to believe you?
GATES: Yes.[9]

Gates admitted telling LaPorta that I did not need to file FBAR reports:

GATES: Well, specifically what I recall telling KWC is the information that Mr. Manafort and I discussed is that it was unnecessary to report foreign accounts because, in his view, he did not have signature authority over the account.
DOWNING: And do you recall telling the Office of Special Counsel that same thing?
GATES: Yes. Initially in my discussions with them, I indicated to them that is why Mr. Manafort did not file his foreign accounts.[10]

The courtroom was set up so that the prosecution was on one side and the witness chair was on my side and there was a lectern between us. When someone was standing at the lectern, the prosecution table was obstructed from my view. I had to push my chair back to get a look at them. I did that twice during Gates's testimony. The first time I couldn't see anything, but the second, I could see they were anxious. Greg Andres, in particular, looked nervous. Ellis was paying close attention to Gates, making sure that the points Downing was eliciting were understood by the jury, often to my benefit.

I was also taking notes during the trial. If I wanted to emphasize a point, I passed a note to Downing or Tom. Sometimes they listened, and sometimes they ignored me. But that was how we communicated.

Gates admitted that the millions of dollars that went through the Cyprus accounts were to pay other consultants, and that the money was not mine:

DOWNING: And so all the money that came in was not the income of DMP International. It actually was the income of a lot of different consultants; isn't that correct?
GATES: That is correct.
DOWNING: And there were transfers made through those accounts into the United States to a lot of those consultants, correct?
GATES: Yes.[11]

Gates admitted that DMP was having banking problems, which was the reason some expenses were paid directly:

GATES: There was a period of time, I think, as I disclosed earlier, beginning in 2012 through part of 2013, when Cyprus had experienced a banking collapse. So within the country, internally, they put what were called liquidity restrictions. So you were only allowed to withdraw a certain amount of money from the country over a defined period of time. So that's why the invoices were broken up into various amounts.[12]

Gates admitted that I told him to take his name off of all accounts:

DOWNING: And with respect to your signature authority on accounts, were you instructed by Mr. Manafort at the end of 2011 to no longer be a signatory on the accounts in Cyprus?
GATES: Mr. Manafort had requested me to remove him in 2012.
DOWNING: And yourself?
GATES: Yes.
DOWNING: But you didn't?
GATES: I removed myself from some of the accounts; that's correct.
DOWNING: But not all?
GATES: Not all of them.[13]

Gates admitted that he had the authority to make all transfers from Cyprus including the $3 million that he transferred to himself.

DOWNING: And with respect to initiating a wire transfer, you clearly, with Dr. K's firm, had the complete authority to make any transfer that you had requested?

GATES: Yes. Mr. Manafort had given me the authority at the begin-
ning with Dr. K, so that's correct.
DOWNING: And with respect to the transfers that you've made, and
especially from Defendant's Exhibit 17, the $3 million, you were never
questioned about making those transfers, were you?
GATES: No.
DOWNING: Not until you came here?
GATES: That's correct.[14]

Judge Ellis got Gates to admit that I didn't keep close watch over Gates's
transfers and caught him in an attempted lie.

DOWNING: And Mr. Manafort wasn't keeping after you on this
stuff, was he?
GATES: Mr. Manafort, in my opinion, kept fairly frequent updates
on the information from the accounts. Mr. Manafort was very good
about knowing where the money is and knowing where to spend it.
DOWNING: So it's pretty—
THE COURT: Well, he missed the amounts of money you stole from
him, though, didn't he?
GATES: Yes, that's correct.
THE COURT: So he didn't do it that closely.[15]

The courtroom laughed, but it was a powerful interjection by Judge Ellis
and Downing didn't need to do anymore beyond that. It was Ellis who
drove the point home to the jury.

There was no way Jackson would have done that. She would have said
Downing was badgering the witness. She had her agenda, which was not
to give me a fair trial. But Ellis saw right through Gates' lies and wanted
to ensure the jury did too.

Gates admitted that I told him to be fully truthful in the 2014 FBI
deposition.

DOWNING: So, Mr. Gates, as part of the FBI interview, you had
disclosed that DMP and Mr. Manafort had been hired as consultants
to assist in campaigns in the Ukraine, correct?
GATES: That is correct.

DOWNING: And you also disclosed that payments that came into accounts that were set up in Cyprus were for the offshore consulting in the Ukraine; is that correct?

GATES: Yes.

DOWNING: And you also disclosed to the FBI that you had been told or Mr. Manafort had been told to open accounts in Cyprus for the ease of payment from the Ukraine; is that correct?

GATES: Yes, that was one of the reasons.

DOWNING: And you also indicated that invoices—you had prepared invoices for campaign assistance that were also paid into the accounts that were held in Cyprus by DMP International, correct?

GATES: That is correct.

. . .

DOWNING: So you and Mr. Manafort agreed to be open and truthful about the activities in Cyprus and in the Ukraine, correct?

GATES: Yes.

DOWNING: And you felt that the interview you gave in 2014 was a truthful interview about the operations of DMP in the Ukraine and in Cyprus, didn't you?

GATES: Yes.[16]

And then Downing got Gates to admit that he had misstated several things, that he had lied in his previous testimony in front of the jury regarding the secret life he had been living and the affairs he had been having.

Far from being an innocent clerk acting on my orders, Gates was the real criminal. He was living a secret life, stealing money to support a girlfriend in London, and keeping everything from me, his wife, and the accountants.

By this point I had stopped believing in the fairness of the courts, but I felt that Downing did a fantastic job of creating doubt. I felt good about getting Gates to admit what he admitted, but I cannot say it gave me any real confidence. The problem was always going to be the complexity of the case and the way the prosecution blurred the lifestyle and legal issues. My case was going to succeed if the Jury believed Zehnle's opening statement and Downing's cross-examination of Gates. Weissman's strategy was to overwhelm and confuse the jury with details, which is why the prosecution took three weeks to make their case.

When Gates came down off the chair, Downing was happy. I had wanted Downing to really pound the points home, but that wasn't his style. We had to make the point that Gates had the responsibility and the authority to manage the flow of money and that there was no evidence that I told him what to do.

Among the millions of pages of documents, there's not one page that shows me telling him, in an email or in any other correspondence, to do anything improper or illegal with the money. We needed to establish that I couldn't bring the money into the country, because of the banking issues I was having. So, we were paying things directly from offshore accounts that were listed on DMP ledgers. We needed to show that I was not trying to hide the income and thought that the end-of-year accounting managed by Gates with CPAs captured the unreported outflows.

I think we did this to the point where it was not that the jury had doubts about Gates. They had to rely on him as the only witness with first-hand knowledge, but they did not have to trust him. My concern was that there would be so much in front of the jury that the only way they could really understand it was through repetition.

It was my life on the line. I worried that we could have done more to clarify the bank fraud points, given all of the confusion the prosecutors were spreading. But Downing was comfortable that we had made our points and that the jury would understand.

The atmosphere surrounding the trial was as intense as it was absurd. From the first session until the last, the court was packed with people— standing room only all the way out into the corridors. A *Politico* article from near the end of the trial captured some of the madness.[17] "On Wednesday, Ellis was . . . dressing down prosecutors after learning that an IRS agent they called to the stand as an expert witness had been in the courtroom for the entire trial. Ellis argued that witnesses should be present only for their own testimony. Mueller's prosecutors protested that the judge had granted them an exception, but the judge . . . was having none of it.

"I don't care what the transcript says, maybe I made a mistake," Ellis said. "When I exclude witnesses I mean everybody, unless I make a special exception."

"Also Wednesday," the article went on, "Ellis asked whether snaking flow charts Mueller's team presented as evidence showing complex financial transfers funding Manafort's real estate purchases were meant to signify illegal behavior beyond a failure by Manafort to report taxable income. 'One can get lost in all these movements of money,' Ellis told Greg Andres, one of Mueller's most senior litigators and a former lawyer in the Justice Department's criminal division."

"And when Ellis asked Andres . . . one procedural question in front of jurors, the admittedly old-fashioned judge bridled when the prosecutor answered with a casual-sounding 'yeah.'"

"'What?' Ellis said, sounding incredulous and irritated. 'Yes,' Andres then replied."

"'Be careful about that,' Ellis told him. 'This is not an informal proceeding.'"

According to the article, Ellis "also complained about lawyers allegedly rolling their eyes at his courtroom patter."

The drama of the trial even rose to the level of threats to the court. At one point Ellis's life was threatened and they had to increase security around him. He was used to the media from his experience with high-profile terrorism cases, so he thought he could manage the process. But this was different. And there was no real way the jurors could stay outside of it; Ellis admonished them several times: don't talk to anyone about the trial. Each day he would ask if anyone approached them.

Still, I believe they were impacted to some degree by everything that was going on. They tried to be fair in what was an extremely complex case, but the atmosphere made it nearly impossible.

There came a moment three weeks in when we almost had a mistrial because one of the jurors went to the bailiff and said that they were concerned that another juror was not taking the responsibility seriously and that juror had already made up her mind.

We filed a motion for a mistrial. Ellis was sympathetic to the issue. Every day he told the jury that they needed to keep an open mind until all of the evidence was presented. They needed to not watch the news or talk to anyone, including spouses and friends. Finally, he told them they cannot even talk to each other about the case until both sides rested and the case was sent to the jury. Now, one of the jurors was telling the Judge one of the other jurors was violating these admonishments.

Ellis didn't want a mistrial; he felt it was important to finish the trial. He took it seriously. There was a closed-door session where each juror was brought in and asked questions by the judge. Finally, he made a judgment call that he felt the jurors could render a fair decision and he would not declare a mistrial. During this process, I kept thinking to myself that this is further proof that we selected a good jury. They were self-policing.

CHAPTER 15

The Verdict

Even if matters were largely out of my hands, it was essential that I felt engaged. I'd been given a copy of *The Anatomy of a Trial* by my attorney and read it in less than twenty-four hours. I think he regretted giving it to me, because I constructed my trial management off the recommendations I found in that book and gave Downing a lot of notes. He was polite and took the notes. During the trial I confirmed to myself that Kevin listened but had disregarded most of my notes. I laughed to myself and thought "Listen to your lawyers."

However, as great a job as my team of lawyers had done presenting my case at trial by ignoring my notes, I was adamant about being involved in the summary.

I had to sign off on the actual summation, so I gave them an outline of the points I wanted in the summation. Kevin had decided to break our summary presentation into two half-hour segments, which made sense to me. I felt it was impossible for one person to hold the jury's attention for an hour.

In our summation, we didn't argue the facts of what happened. We argued about what I knew and didn't know. We didn't argue that there were no wire transfers or that the taxes had been paid. We argued that I didn't instruct Gates to do it that way, that I didn't know what he was doing, and that had I known I would never have done it the way it was done. I was nervous, but it made sense to rely on these distinctions.

For example, we had emails showing that once I found out there was an Airbnb in one of my properties, I stopped it. Of course, the bank officer that I dealt with didn't testify in my defense because he was threatened with an indictment if he didn't cooperate with the prosecution. This nuance was critical to my innocence, but in the end, I felt it was an effective summary.

But listening to the prosecution made me angry. The way they distorted everything, the way they made Gates into a saint, the way they said I destroyed his life and the lives of other people—it made me incredibly angry. They made me out to be an evil person, and I am not.

The trial lasted for over three weeks, and this was just hearing the prosecutors' witnesses and cross examination. We felt we presented our case through cross examination of the prosecution's witnesses because the people we wanted to call we could not make testify thanks to the tactics of the prosecution.

Now, the case was in the hands of the jury.

It took the jury four days to reach a verdict. I started each day of deliberations nervous, and I ended each day hopeful because nothing had happened. The jury came back twice in the first three days with questions, which I felt was good for me. It meant there was a good amount of doubt as to my guilt. I can say I was optimistic, perhaps more so than at any other point in the trial.

On the fourth day, which was a Thursday, I started to think that if they went into the weekend, we might win—not just a mistrial, but an acquittal. But I knew enough to temper those hopes with reality—almost nothing had gone my way since this whole thing started two years ago and there was no reason to think it would be different now.

I think the jury dealt with the technical material first, and the FBAR charges second. And I think they were having trouble finding me guilty on the bank fraud issues. From the work we had done on jury selection, I was confident that there was enough education among the jurors that at least one person would understand my innocence. One person was all I needed.

On August 22, the jury reached a decision. As they came out into the courtroom, I had no idea what to expect. It was all new to me. I looked into the eyes of the jurors to get a sense of what they were thinking. And a couple of them looked at me in what I thought was a favorable way. I was feeling nervous, but still optimistic. The signs seemed to be pointing in the right direction.

Then I looked at the forewoman and she averted her eyes. That told me something would happen, that it wouldn't be all good news. I believe in my ability to read people's emotions, and I knew then it would not go my way.

The forewoman began to announce the verdicts. "We, the jury, find as follows," she said. I stared straight ahead, sitting very still as they read:

> "As to Count 1, subscribing to false United States individual income tax return for 2010. Answer: Guilty.
> As to Count 2, subscribing to false United States individual income tax return for 2011. Answer: Guilty.
> As to Count 3, subscribing to false United States individual income tax return for 2012. Answer: Guilty.
> As to Count 4, subscribing to false United States individual income tax return for 2013. Answer: Guilty.
> As to Count 5, subscribing to false United States individual income tax return for 2014."

By Count 5, I felt I'd lost everything. Then she skipped to Count 12: guilty.

I didn't know which counts she had skipped, but I felt a rush. I didn't remember which counts were which charges. I knew the first ones were the tax charges, but I didn't remember where the FBAR or bank fraud charges were.

She skipped again: "Count 25: guilty; count 27: guilty."

And then it was over. I felt shattered, but some relief as well. They had found me guilty on only eight of the eighteen counts.

We'd been waiting all this time. Now it was all over. I was convicted on some counts, but not others and I didn't know which was which. I turned to Downing, but he was trying to pay attention. I remember thinking: this is going to change the rest of my life, but I did not know how. I could still get a life sentence, I thought. I just didn't know.

Downing was feeling good about the results. It was all such a jumble. I knew I had only been convicted on eight of the eighteen counts. This wasn't the win I had wanted, nor was it the justice I deserved, but it *was* a clear loss for the Special Counsel. I looked over at their table and I could see the disappointment on their faces. They had lost their "solid" case.

All these thoughts were going through my head and suddenly the adrenaline evaporated. I had to lean on the table just to keep myself up. I was exhausted, mentally and physically. I wondered if I would ever be able to hold my wife again. I wasn't allowed to look at the audience, so I could not see her. But I wanted to give her some hope, so I turned—the marshal showed a little compassion and let me—as I smiled at her.

Her face was frozen. I could see the fear in her eyes. "Don't worry," I whispered, and she smiled back, which gave me a huge amount of strength in that moment.

From the bench, Ellis summarized what just happened, making certain that the public understood that I had hung the jury on far more charges than I'd been convicted on. I had been convicted on all five tax charges, one FBAR charge, and two bank fraud charges.

On the tax charges, the most damning evidence was that in his year-end accounting with the CPA, Gates did not include any transfers from offshore accounts directly to third-party vendors for my benefit (as opposed to consultants under contract for work to be performed in Ukraine). This made it look like I was trying to hide income by paying directly, even though there was evidence to the contrary. But Gates's uncorroborated testimony, coupled with the relentless stories about me in the MSM—about fraud, black ledger cash, and lifestyle excesses—was enough.

I was only convicted on the one FBAR charge because there was a record of my signature on one of the accounts for a very brief time. I did not authorize this and once I found out from Gates, I had my name removed.

Finally, the jury did not find me guilty of most of the bank fraud charges.

After summarizing the jury's verdict, Ellis declared a mistrial on the not guilty charges. "And let me be clear," he said. "The verdict form, of course, will be public, but it's for purposes of the public, Count 11, Count 13, Count 14, Count 24, Count 26, Count 28, 29, 30, 31, and 32, I have declared a mistrial as to those counts."

He had me step to the podium to explain how the sentencing process would work. "Mr. Manafort, you have been found guilty by the jury on a variety of counts, I think on eleven of the eighteen; is that right, Mr. Andres?"

"I think eight of the eighteen, Your Honor," Andres said.

"Eight of the eighteen, of course. Thank you. And the Court, at the appropriate time, will enter judgment on those verdicts. I'm going to order the preparation of a presentence investigation report. Now, this is a vitally important document because it's a document on which the Court will chiefly rely in imposing an appropriate sentence. You need to pay careful attention to the preparation of this document and, indeed, you have a role to play in its preparation. You'll be asked by a probation officer to provide information so that the report can be prepared."

I stared at him, and listened to him speak, but I was not really processing. He then adjourned, and the marshals came to get me. As I was leaving, I turned to look at Kathy once more, smiled at her, and blew her a kiss.

To this day, I believe I got a fair jury. It took four and a half days for them to convict me, and they convicted me on less than half the charges. I think they were overwhelmed with evidence. They were not sequestered, so they were going home at night and watching the news and reading stories online about, as CNN called it, the trial of the century. They had to overcome a tremendous amount of media pressure, and they did a pretty good job.

I believe my entire case came down to Zehnle's opening statement and Downing's cross-examination of Gates. The problem was that these two presentations were just a few hours of a trial that took three weeks. My defense was destined to be lost in the details and confusion. This was Weissman's strategy from the beginning.

We nearly prevailed, but the number of witnesses, the millions of pages of documents, and most importantly, the court of public opinion was too much to overcome.

I asked Downing to meet immediately afterward to figure out what it meant, and more importantly, what we needed to say publicly. Even if I had been acquitted, I would still have remained in jail on the DC. charges. There was still a gag order on me, but I wanted Downing to go to the courthouse steps and make an informal statement.

There were two main points we had to get across. The first was that everything I was convicted of happened *before* the Trump campaign and had *nothing* to do with Russian collusion or Trump. I wanted to be clear: no Russian collusion. It was important to communicate to Trump and to the world. The Special Counsel had no authority to bring these charges and in the frenzied atmosphere fostered by the prosecutors and the MSM, it was impossible for me to be viewed impartially or fairly.

And the second was that I was not convicted on a majority of the charges. And the ones I was convicted on, I believe, were simply too confusing. It was a complex case that took the jury four days to reach a verdict.

On his own, Downing added that the real criminal was Gates, that he should have been the one convicted that day.

I laughed to myself. I loved Kevin Downing that afternoon.

CHAPTER 16

Negotiations

Within half an hour of my conviction, the Southern District of New York announced a plea deal with Michael Cohen. The media, predictably, went crazy. The news cycle that day was totally jammed with Russian collusion information. But Cohen was the shinier object since he could potentially get Trump impeached and put him in jail—that was their hope, at least. I was convicted on tax charges that had nothing to do with Trump. So, as would be expected, the media really went into overdrive on Cohen, which gave me some brief relief.

But more importantly to me, Trump tweeted that he felt sorry for me and my family having been targeted in this witch hunt, and he praised me for being "brave" compared to Cohen. I could not have positioned myself any better. "I feel very badly for Paul Manafort and his wonderful family. 'Justice' took a twelve-year-old tax case, among other things, applied tremendous pressure on him and, unlike Michael Cohen, he refused to 'break'— make up stories in order to get a deal. Such respect for a brave man!"

Of course, the Democrats on the Hill jumped on Trump's statement in support of me and immediately started demanding that Trump acknowledge that he would not give me a pardon. It was always the same strategy—force Trump *not* to give me a pardon. Trump understood what they were trying to do and never went for it.

But as a result of the Cohen deal and my conviction, the Mueller investigation, which had been limping along, gained real momentum.

If I had won my case, it would have been difficult for them to continue. All their tactics had been tied to getting someone to turn. Now, Mueller had two candidates.

With the conviction in Virginia, the media became a distraction, but I still had to turn my attention to preparing for the case in DC. That trial was set for September. The issues in that case centered around my failure to file FARA disclosure reports regarding my work in Ukraine.

As a part of his overkill strategy, Weissman was operating on the theory that he could claw back all the income I ever earned in Ukraine going back to 2005 even though the alleged FARA violations occurred in 2012 and 2013. His plan totally ignored the fact that I had reached an agreement with the FARA unit on these specific matters before the Special Counsel was ever appointed.

What was equally disturbing to me was the fact that I had just been convicted of an FBAR violation for a matter that I had disclosed to the FBI and that they had shut down any interest, Additionally, the tax charges had been dismissed by the Treasury Department years before. Yet here I stood, convicted. So, having a defense of "I already reached an agreement with the FARA office at DOJ" was not so comforting.

The prosecutor's attempt to claw back all revenue ever earned in Ukraine was based on the legal metaphor of the "fruit of the poisonous tree." The logic of the terminology is that if the source (the "tree") of the evidence or evidence itself is tainted, then anything gained (the "fruit") from it is tainted as well. In Weissman's case, he claimed that since I did not file in 2010–2013, any money earned in Ukraine could be recaptured. Triggering anti-money laundering laws, Weissman was claiming that my failure to file somehow allowed him to capture all of the money I had earned in Ukraine regardless of when it was earned or what the money was for. It was one of his wild legal theories where he felt that if he just kept saying it to friendly reporters, the logic would become entrenched, and a conviction would facilitate his ability to wipe out my life's earnings.

Yes, this is the bizarro world of Andrew Weissman.

Weissman had added the money laundering charges so that he could seek forfeiture relief and seize all of the properties I had purchased during those years. This allowed him to attach properties I had purchased for my family, an insurance trust that I had set up to care for my extended family, and stock portfolios I had established for my kids and grandkids. Several of the properties had been purchased years earlier—Bridgehampton in 1997, Trump Tower in 2006, Baxter St. in 2007—far outside of the 2010–2013 timeframe in question. And of course, far before Donald Trump ever thought about running for President and when I joined his campaign.

The prosecutors knew that this was a serious overreach, but they also knew that the media had been so one-sided that the public was already putting me in the same category as people like Bernie Madoff and John Gotti.

Again, neither of my cases had anything to do with Russia, collusion, the campaign, or Trump. The goal was simple: to crush me into giving them Donald Trump. They wanted me to admit that Trump and the campaign had colluded with Russia—something that would have been impossible to admit because it wasn't true. I knew it wasn't true, and so did Andrew Weissman.

I was in a box. Once again, I knew that I was innocent, but with the Virginia case behind me, I knew that my innocence didn't account for very much. The Special Counsel was still able to get convictions on a number of charges. But at the same time, this also meant that I had a chance of being just as successful in the DC case as I was in Virginia. It was very difficult to know which way it might go.

The day after they read my verdict, I asked Downing what to do about DC. I had come to trust his judgment in these kinds of situations, and I needed an independent, informed opinion. To me, it seemed impossible now to get a fair trial. The Washington media market is the same geographic population base for both the DC and Virginia cases. In my mind, I could not believe that any one in the DC case could be an objective juror. I told Downing I thought we needed to either change our venue or cut a deal.

He didn't think Weissman would be interested, but my thinking was that in Virginia I prevailed on more than half the charges of what was, in reality, the more complicated case—EDVA—and the Special Counsel might not want to go to trial in DC either. I was seeing the world the way I wanted. Of course, Weissman would want to keep the case in front of Jackson. She was 100 percent on their side. Still, I theorized that "maybe we could get them to agree to move the venue." I mean, to me, this seemed objectively to be the right thing to do to ensure a "fair trial."

On the other hand, a deal with the Special Counsel could end this nightmare. I would not lie to get a deal, but maybe Mueller's team had what they needed in my Virginia conviction and could move on. I was trying to think through all possibilities.

I had personal reasons for reaching a plea deal, too. My family was suffering through this ordeal, and it was costing me a fortune. I knew that if I went to trial it would result in more convictions. A plea deal was looking more and more like the *only* way to truly protect my family. If I were to lose the trial, it would trigger automatic forfeitures of my properties and there would be no way I could get them back. I felt it was crucial to remove assets owned by my kids and grandkids from any negotiation. It killed me, but I knew I might be able to get a better outcome by cutting a deal. Even if I didn't like that they were going to demand that I *knowingly committed* the crimes that they accused me of.

I made it clear to Downing that there were certain red lines that I would not cross. I could not, and would not, give them Trump. And I was not going to lie. I was looking at spending the rest of my life in jail. I wasn't about to trust Weissman and his sidekick Amy Berman Jackson. And I was not going to give up Trump for things he didn't do.

So, we had to have an understanding that any deal would simply end the process for both sides. I wouldn't be their stool pigeon. Plus, now they had Cohen for that role. The timing was right. They got their pound of flesh in Virginia, and we could seriously plumb the waters for a deal and see what we could come up with in order to protect my family.

Downing agreed. I said he had to find a way around Weissman to the other senior people. I felt that Weissman would never go for it without demanding "I give him Trump."

Downing had heard there was some discussion inside the Special Counsel's office. Some attorneys in that office did not want another trial. They were not happy with the results of the first case either. They were nervous. Weissman had convinced Mueller that I was going to be convicted on everything. We heard there might be some division inside the group about whether or not they should try to cut a deal, try to get me to turn state's witness, or go to trial. If Weissman was the hard-charging warrior, Downing believed that Aaron Zebley, the number two, represented a more balanced approach. According to Downing, Weissman wanted to go to trial; Zebley felt it would be better to try to get what they could out of me. It was all rumor, but we agreed it was worth looking into.

That afternoon, Downing reached out and we began conversations.

Normally these negotiations revolve around what is called a 5k letter. This document is a submission by the prosecutor to the court stating that the defendant has cooperated with the government and asks the judge to take this cooperation into account in their sentencing decisions. I made it clear to Downing that I did not care about a 5k letter, although we should not concede it in the negotiations. I explained to my attorneys that I did not expect the Special Counsel would be happy with my "cooperation" because I was not going to give them anything that they could use against the president, his family, or his campaign. I emphasized that there was nothing to "give up" to start with, but that I was not going to play Weissman's game and give him circumstantial information that he could distort and weave into his crazy theories of collusion and conspiracy.

Downing was equally firm that, no matter what I pled to, the maximum sentence had to be less than ten years. Based on sentencing guidelines, I was facing over eighty years if convicted, although the expectation was that I would get no more than seven to ten years. The ten-year cap was crucial, however, because the length of the sentence determined the type of prison I would be sent to and when I would be eligible for parole.

Hearing him say this made me shudder. "Here I am negotiating to limit myself to ten years in prison," I thought. "*Ten years*." I could not believe this was real and it was my future.

Additionally, Downing was adamant about what crimes I would plead to because this affected a variety of things. What I pled to was a real sticking point for me. I was firm in my belief that I had done nothing wrong. The prosecutor's assertions were fictions of Weissman. While some of their facts were accurate, their conclusions were not. Core to their argument was the testimony that Rick Gates had provided to them. This testimony was a combination of lies and self-serving narratives that Gates had created to absolve himself. While there were no documents supporting my story, there were none supporting Gates's testimony, either. It was my word against his, and he was a self-professed liar.

To my surprise, the Special Counsel came back with a deal: I had to plead to conspiracy to defraud the government and to lying to the government. The trick was that Weissman had packaged everything into the "conspiracy": failure to file, criminal intent, money laundering, bank fraud. He made it sound like I'd been running some kind of criminal cartel for twenty years and I would have to plead to all of it.

My mind was mixed as to how far I should go in the concessions to Weissman. And adding to the pressure was the fact that while we were negotiating, the jury selection process for the DC case had started.

DC is a totally Democrat town. The voter registration is something like 92 percent Democrat. Worse, the town hated Trump and all things related to Trump. So even the remaining 8 percent were not going to be objective in analyzing my case. They got their news from the *Washington Post*, the *New York Times*, CNN, MSNBC, Twitter, Facebook. Every one of these media outlets had conducted a two-year "destroy Paul Manafort" campaign under the surreptitious direction of Andrew Weissman and the Never-Trumpers.

The MSM and Trump-hating social media crowd had accepted every negative comment about me no matter how outlandish, and the gag order imposed on me by Judge Jackson prevented me from responding to any of the lies. This was the "pool" from which a jury was to be selected.

Negotiations for a plea deal aside, we felt that the case needed to be moved, at least to Roanoke, in the Western District of Virginia, which has a federal court. It was far enough away that we could get a fairer jury pool, and I wanted the half of the country that was supporting me to see that I was fighting a corrupt system trying to use me to destroy Trump's presidency. We petitioned Judge Jackson to approve a change of venue claiming that I could not get a fair trial in DC.

It was impossible, we argued, in the aftermath of the trial in Virginia, in the same media market as DC, for any potential juror to not have an opinion of me given the daily headlines during the trial—all of which were negative.

We argued: "This prosecution involves the president's former campaign manager. As a result, for many Americans, Mr. Manafort's legal issues and the attendant daily media coverage have become theatre in the continuing controversy surrounding President Trump and his election. This controversy continues to engender strong partisans on all sides of every issue. As a result, it is difficult, if not impossible, to divorce the issues in this case from the political views of potential jurors."

Furthermore, I had become embroiled in a larger drama between Mr. Mueller and President Trump; the prosecution had been sensationalized and untethered from the facts of the case; and coverage of my case was *most* intense "in and around Washington, DC."

We also claimed that my Sixth Amendment right to a fair trial "free from outside influences" was impossible in DC so soon after the case in Virginia had ended: "Nowhere in the US was the bias against Mr. Manafort more apparent than here in the Washington, DC, metropolitan area." *Everything inside the beltway is political and this case was politics on steroids.*

No one could seriously disagree with the facts in our motion. But, this case was about politics. There was no better venue to try me than in Washington DC. if you hated Trump and wanted to use the trial to not just try me but also to magnify the political narrative. The only reason not to try the case in DC was to ensure that I had a fair trial. But that was not relevant to the Judge, the prosecutors, or the lynch mob media.

Of course, Jackson denied the request. But she recognized the merits of the argument, so instead of selecting twelve jurors and two to three alternates from a pool of thirty candidates, she constructed an initial pool of one hundred and twenty people. It was insane. When the venue is tainted as badly as Washington DC was, choosing from more people was not going to solve the problem. But, it gave cover to a Judge who wanted to look fair without being fair.

In fact, the size of this jury pool was more than the jury pools for all of the federal cases going on in DC at the time combined. Plus, interviewing more prospects was only going to mean interviewing more people who were prejudiced against me. This was not a solution; it was camouflage for a lynching.

The process by which a jury is selected is called *voir dire*. The candidates from the jury pool are randomly assigned a number, and once they have filled out a questionnaire that both sides have agreed to, they are called in to be interviewed by the lawyers. The questionnaire is meant to give some information about the juror to eliminate any who have a conflict or bias. Each side has three strikes, meaning that they can veto three jurors selected by the other side.

We petitioned the court to put together a very different questionnaire for DC than we did for Virginia. This time, the questionnaire dealt with political matters, given the political nature of this case.

When it came to figuring out the preferences and prejudices of the prospective jurors, I had a secret weapon. One of the attorneys on my team, Brian Ketcham, was an expert in the analysis of potential jurors. Brian organized a process which allowed me to focus on the answers the jurors had provided. Between Brian's insights and my experience in reading polls and attitudes, we built a matrix that allowed us to dig down on the attitudes and prejudices of the potential jurors.

In addition to questions regarding education level and work, we asked potential jurors questions like: "What is your main source for news?" "Have you, or any member of your immediate family, ever been employed as an auditor, mortgage officer, tax preparer, or accountant?" "This case has received significant publicity in the media," we explained. "Have you seen, read, or heard anything at all about this case in any form of media, including newspaper, television, radio, or internet?" "You may hear some limited amount of evidence that individuals involved in this case were associated at some time with the Trump campaign. Is there anything about that information that would make it difficult for you to remain fair and impartial to both sides and to return a verdict based solely on the evidence in accordance with the Court's instructions?"

But just like in politics, understanding the electorate—or in this case the potential jury—doesn't mean you will win. In this particular situation, it made it clear to us that *we would not win*. When Brian and I went through the results, we found one potential juror we felt *could* be favorable. Out of the one hundred and twenty in the pool, ninety-two admitted to being biased against me and or Trump. Another twenty lied and claimed they had never heard of my case while also admitting they got their daily news from CNN, the *Washington Post* and the *New York Times* (an impossible statement to make given the daily coverage of my Virginia trial). Six left important questions unanswered. Two may have been objective, but it was no guarantee. Based on our analysis, we had no confidence in anyone being objective.

I was sure another jury pool would have produced the same results. So, a week before the trial was supposed to start, I told Downing we had to cut a deal. There was no other option anymore. We couldn't go to a trial with a jury made from this pool. I wouldn't stand a chance. To his credit, Downing put pressure on some of the other attorneys in the Special Counsel who he knew were receptive to a deal and somehow generated a real conversation with them.

In addition to the personal reasons I had for cutting a deal, there were political considerations. I knew that the media would have used each day of the trial to generate new damaging headlines to hurt Trump and the Republicans going into the mid-term elections. I wanted to take the trial out of the equation.

Downing and the Special Counsel did their dance. We wanted a ten-year cap. Weissman wanted no cap. He wanted to give me a minimum of twenty years. We didn't think he was taking us seriously. Somehow, Downing maneuvered backchannels into the Special Counsel to let them know we were serious about cutting a deal and we sidelined Weissman's veto.

But before they were willing to make a formal offer, Downing told me that I would have to go in for a "proffer." I didn't know what that meant. I learned that they would get to question me on a range of topics, and I had to be truthful. I was assured that if we didn't reach a deal, they wouldn't be able to use my answers against me in the future.

Of course, I didn't trust them for one second. Weissman would find a way. But that was the demand. So, reluctantly, I agreed.

My biggest concern was that Weissman would try to trap me, to get me to say something I didn't mean or that wasn't accurate. My concern was not about telling the truth—I had told the truth every step of the way and would continue to tell the truth. My concern was being tricked and getting trapped.

Another thing that made me nervous was that I would have to do the whole thing from memory, without documents, and I was beginning to feel the wear and tear of solitary confinement and the protracted legal process. I had been in solitary confinement for half a year and my mind felt dulled. Now I would have to be dealing from memory in a stressful environment with laser-focused prosecutors, at least one of whom would be trying to trip me up. The whole thing made me very anxious. But it was this or a jury that hated me and, based on what I had seen in the questionnaires, already thought I was guilty. So, once again with great trepidation but no other options, I relented.

Downing explained that I would have to agree to say that I had done certain things. I had a real problem with this. I felt very uncomfortable lying. But I would have to lie to get a deal. This was the conundrum I faced. It was the hardest part of the entire experience. Harder than serving time, harder than the uncertainty, and harder than the FBI 6:00 a.m. raid on my home. I had to say what the prosecution so desperately—so feverishly—wanted me to say: I was a criminal.

Seeing no alternative, I agreed to this process and ended the negotiations. I was terribly worried about my family's finances. We had lost everything. We had no cash, enormous debts, and one home we could not afford. I had no choice but to avoid a trial. To me, the key to the negotiations was the ability to change the properties subject to forfeiture so that my daughter's assets were removed from the list of targeted assets in the complaint against me.

Technically, everything should have been a part of the forfeiture deal in Weissman's distorted view of the case. According to his charges, I had been masterminding a criminal conspiracy for twenty years, using illegal money to do illegal things because I was not filing forms with the FARA office. All of my work, most of which was political and not even covered by FARA, was blended by Weissman into one ball and all of my income going back to the 1990s was declared illegal because I did not file disclosure forms in 2010–2013.

When we discussed the plea, Kathy found a way to put me at ease. She made it clear that all she cared about was getting me back. "We started with nothing, and we can live with nothing as long as we have each other," she said. "Don't worry about me and don't worry about what they want to take from us, no matter how unfair it seems." Her words were a great comfort.

Still, I did worry about her, and I worried about my family. But by taking my daughter's assets out of the forfeiture agreement, my daughter and her husband could at least take care of my wife while I was in prison. And knowing that, I could sleep at night.

Weissman's reputation as a deceitful prosecutor had proven more than true thus far in our relationship. He was a reckless, abusive, dishonorable prosecutor at every step of the investigation. He did not disappoint when we met face-to-face for our proffer sessions. In the end, I spent over fifty hours sitting with the prosecutors answering their questions. Weissman had many crazy theories, and he would try to wear me down and then pull a Columbo-style "one last question" stunt to direct me into a lie or concession. I was very wary of not committing a lie, but my fear was the inadvertent mistake, misunderstanding, or fatigued half-answer.

In the first session, Weissman began referring back to emails from five or six years earlier that I thought he was making up. But I couldn't be sure that he was making them up because I didn't have them in front of me. He asked me about a meeting I had with Kilimnik in Madrid that I had no recollection of. I recalled the trip to Madrid and why I went there, but I didn't remember a meeting with Kilimnik. He said something like, "What if I told you I had a plane ticket that says he flew there and met with you?"

I said, "Well, if you do have that, I'm telling you, I don't remember the meeting, but if you have a ticket that could be evidence that we met in Madrid."

"What would you have talked about?"

"I don't remember a conversation because I don't remember the meeting."

I found out later he didn't have any ticket because Kilimnik had never been in Madrid. He was lying. On and on it went.

I tried to be as cooperative as I could, but I wouldn't lie, which made the proffer sessions difficult. I actually got into a conflict with Downing a few times because Downing felt I wasn't cooperating enough. I kept telling him: "They want me to admit to things I didn't do. How can I do that? I call that lying."

The classic example that led to a difficult moment centered on Weissman demanding that I agree with his distorted assessment of Kilimnik's mindset when he was trying to reach out to one of our European consultants. I refused to speculate on the mindset, causing Weissman to accuse me of violating the proffer agreement. Finally after about thirty minutes of wrangling over the mindset of someone who was not in the room, I begrudgingly admitted his mindset "could have been" what Weissman claimed it was. The room breathed a sigh of relief. Then, I added "but I don't know." Downing was not happy.

As I reflected on this interaction in my cell that night, I could see how Weissman would most likely attempt to use a similar approach when we discussed Trump and Russian collusion in upcoming sessions. I committed to myself that I would not let him create a false record through these types of tactics, regardless of the reaction of my attorneys. Weissman did make this attempt in several later sessions, But I kept my resolve and would not let him browbeat me into saying things that "might" have been but were not true.

Each night after a session with Special Counsel, I would focus on key areas of inquiry, try to remember what, specifically, I had said, and figure out where Weissman was trying to trap me. In the sessions, which went from ten in the morning to four in the afternoon, I tried to parse my words, to speak very carefully. It was a very contentious process. It didn't have to be, but they wanted something from me that I couldn't, and more importantly wouldn't, give them.

To this day, I still don't know how I could have done it differently. I don't know how to tell the truth by telling a lie. Later, I spoke to other prisoners who had gone through similar processes, and I found out that "lying to tell the truth" is the norm when dealing with prosecutors. Then, if the prosecutors don't like where the proffers went, they could use the misstatements to come after you. And that is not all. When they are finished with you, they share everything with state prosecutors, who can bring similar actions against you. They get you through the backdoor and then they just give the state prosecutors the information to pile on.

Many of these inmates I met in prison were kids. They are uneducated, from broken homes. The system doesn't work in general, and it certainly doesn't work for them. The power of the prosecutors and the way they deal—it's just a notch for them. They don't care if you are guilty or not. A person can end up in prison for many years in this process.

When I was first confronted with all of this, I thought, "I'm educated, I'm strategic. I understand what Weissman is trying to do." But even I didn't know how to handle it. So I would just let certain things go rather than fight tooth and nail over every little thing.

By far, the biggest point of contention was what I would give them on Trump. Weissman wanted me to be able to change the timelines of what Trump knew and when, what his mindset was during certain episodes, and give him a framework that he could use to coerce others. The timelines were relevant to how the Trump campaign conspired. But Weissman also wanted me to accept "his theories" on the events that provided the quid pro quo.

Weissman's Russian Collusion Theory was built on a set of "HIS" assumptions, not facts. And in all cases his assumptions were false.

Weissman's theory of collusion was as follows:

The Trump campaign had advance knowledge of hacks and leaks. Roger Stone told Trump that Wikileaks had the Clinton emails. Trump told Stone to engage with his contacts on the hack. The release by Wikileaks of both the Wasserman-Shultz emails and the Podesta emails was orchestrated by Trump through Stone. The Russian connect is through Wikileaks/Guccifer. Stone was talking to both of these sources and briefing Trump directly.

The Trump campaign in September and October was coordinating, through Stone, with Wikileaks/Guccifer to release the Podesta emails in time to affect the voting. The Podesta emails released on October 7, 2016, was timed to offset the release of the Billie Bush tapes. The Trump campaign accelerated the timing of the Podesta emails to blunt the very damaging impact of the Billie Bush tapes.

Trump promised Russia, through intermediaries, that he would lift the Russian sanctions. Flynn was one of those intermediaries. Trump made several public statements that were signals to the Russians of his involvement and support for the conspiracy. On June 8, 2016, Trump said there was going to be a surprise very soon on Clinton emails. On June 14, 2016, Wikileaks announced it had the Clinton emails. On June 16, 2016, Crowd Strike announced that the DNC had been hacked.

Additionally, Weissman had two major problems. First he had to construct a Russian link connecting to the Trump campaign, and second he had to figure out what Russia was expecting in return for "helping" Trump get elected. He had neither a link or a "quo."

For the Russian link, Weissman arbitrarily selected my assistant Konstantin Kilimnik. The only basis for this selection was because while serving his obligatory military service in the Russian army, Kilimnik went to language school. Apparently, GRU intelligence officers also went to language school. So, with no other evidence Weissman declared Kilimnik as "*possibly* linked to Russian intelligence."

Over time the media morphed this possibility into a certainty that Kilimnik was Russian intelligence. The fact that Kilimnik was a trusted US asset with a code name appointed by the USG to protect him did not matter. The fact that the Security Service of Ukraine, as a part of their duty to protect the President of Ukraine, had done a thorough investigation of Kilimnik and me to assure themselves that the President of Ukraine was not being exposed to a Russian spy or a CIA agent was ignored.

The next problem Weissman had was that he needed to find a reason for Russia to want Trump to be President. Again, Weissman just made stuff up.

Weissman's made up narrative focused on a pro-Russian peace plan for eastern Ukraine as the quo Russia was seeking. There were many peace plans circulating in 2016. The status quo in Ukraine, accepted by the Obama administration but not the Government of Ukraine, had the two eastern provinces of Ukraine in a "no man's land." Ukraine refused to recognize the autonomous governments set up under the military support of Russia. One of the peace plans being circulated was for these autonomous zones to be formalized as independent governments under Ukrainian leadership that was pro-Russia.

According to Weissman's theory, for Ukraine Government to agree to this plan the US Government would have to force it on them. This US demand to Ukraine was what Russia expected from Trump for helping him to be elected President.

According to Weissman, I was lobbying for this Ukraine peace plan. It was so crazy, I really didn't know how to respond. The theory was based on a question in a draft 2018 poll I was taking for a candidate in Ukraine's upcoming presidential campaign. Yes, the poll was being taken two years after the US presidential election. Weissman's theory was that my including a poll question on all of the options for peace that were being discussed in Ukraine was somehow proof that I was promoting a specific a pro-Russian peace plan.

The option he was crazed by was one that focused on creating an independent territory in the two eastern Ukraine oblasts that had become a "no man's land" after being illegally hijacked by pro-Russian paramilitary forces. This option was in the public arena in Ukraine. It was not a secret.

This theory of Weissman's was wrong on so many counts.

First: the poll was in 2018, two years after the US presidential election.

Second: the draft questionnaire included all the publicly discussed peace plan options.

Third: the poll was never taken as the candidate dropped out of the race.

Fourth: there was nothing secret about this peace option.

Fifth: I was under home confinement and then in prison when I was supposed to be promoting the plan.

Sixth: Trump had already signaled in the early months of his Presidency a US foreign policy that was markedly more pro-Ukraine than the Obama administration's policy, including sending lethal weapons to Ukraine to defend itself against the pro-Russian para military in eastern Ukraine.

I tried to explain to Weissman that I was not promoting any of the options in the poll and definitely not the one allowing for an autonomous regional government. Other than showing his ignorance of how polls are conducted, Weissman made it impossible for me to educate him.

The more I rejected his narrative the more crazed he became claiming that I was lying. He continued to push this story because he needed to say the Ukraine plan was payback to Putin for colluding. Then he could make Kilimnik an agent of Putin, and implicate the Trump administration.

The problem was that he had no evidence of me promoting with anyone about any peace plan, and I emphasized this point over and over again.

In fact, there was no proof the Trump administration ever considered such a plan. From Day 1 Trump changed US-Ukraine policy from the weak Obama administration policy. He put Putin on notice that he did not accept the annexation of Crimea. Additionally, unlike the Obama administration, the Trump administration actually gave lethal weapons to Ukraine to defend itself from Russia.

Nothing Weissman was pushing made any sense other than that he was desperate.

This idea was 100 percent a Weissman fiction. He claimed that, because I had added several different peace plans on a draft of a Ukrainian Presidential campaign survey in 2018, this was proof that it was my plan and the Trump organization plan in 2016. He ignored the fact that Trump was supplying lethal aid to Ukraine in 2017 and 2018 to protect Ukraine against Russia. Plus, he knew that being under indictment at the time of the questionnaire made it impossible for me to lobby Trump without Weissman knowing it. Finally, he was totally overlooking the fact that I was on the record as having totally rejected this particular plan.

There is not one shred of evidence anywhere that I supported this plan or that Trump supported this plan.

This was Weissman's lynchpin and he had come up empty. There was no foundation other than Weissman's delusions and desires. And his need to have a motive. He could not find a motive for cooperation and without a motive there was no basis for the whole Russian collusion narrative. He had no facts, no evidence, no motive, only his delusional theory.

The fact that Kilimnik came to New York on August 2 to see me to brief me on Ukraine was made into a cabal. Then, because he needed to create heft to a theory that had no evidence, Weissman lied to me and said I met with Kilimnik in Madrid. But, the meeting never happened.

That is the total case of Weissman. A meeting on Aug 2 where I gave Kilimnik an overview of the campaign—the same overview I was giving in all my public interviews which are available for all to see. A meeting in Madrid that never happened and a survey questionnaire in 2018 that tested all of the publicly discussed peace plans that were being discussed in the Ukrainian Presidential campaign.

The fact that Kilimnik was a US asset, with ample cable traffic between the US Embassy and the State Dept was buried in redactions so that the public could not be informed of the role Kilimnik played in support of US policy in the region.

The other major misrepresentation by Weissman related to the "secret internal" polling data that I supposedly gave to Kilimnik. The fact that the campaign polling that I supposedly gave Kilimnik *at the August 2 meeting* was not even completed until August 8 was ignored. Also, ignored, was Gates testimony in his proffers to the FBI that the information that he gave to Kilimnik was publicly available information. The significance is that the campaign did not have no polling data on August 2. Fabrizio had gone into the field in the battleground states on Aug 1 with the preliminary results not becoming available to me or Gates until Aug 8 and later.

Finally, Weissman's theories on the timelines on the hacked material being dumped by Wikileaks at propitious times to help Trump right before the Democrat convention and to offset the Democrat leak of the Billie Bush tapes on October 7 had no evidence to support his allegations.

It's an interesting narrative, but not one that happened. I had never spoken to Stone about his timelines. After I was pardoned, I compared notes with Roger. He had been pressured to admit to a similar story. His answers and mine seemed to be the same. Yet, we never spoke during the entire investigation. Funny, but the truth really hangs so well, even in the midst of such a pressured environment.

The releases of this material to the public had come at two critical times for Trump, and Weissman wanted proof that someone in the Trump campaign had orchestrated them. The first was the Friday after our convention and before the Democratic convention and the other was in October when the Billy Bush story hit. The leaks of the Podesta emails drowned out the Billy Bush story and put Hillary on her heels. The beneficiary of both leaks was Donald Trump.

To Weissman, this smacked of orchestration, and he wanted me to say that Trump had worked with the Russians to hack the material, get it to Wikileaks, and then Trump and Stone worked with Wikileaks to release the material at critical times.

It was all fiction, pure fiction. There was no truth to any of it. And there was no evidence of any of it either. They were trying desperately: Wikileaks, the platform changes at the convention, the June meeting at Trump Tower. And Trump's whimsical statement at the press conference podium telling Putin that if he's got the hacked emails, to please release them. To Andrew Weissman, all of this proved Russian collusion.

The problem was that there was no collusion, no orchestration, and no cooperation. None of it was true.

I knew none of it was true because I was there when the first leak hit in July. Trump was as surprised as anyone. He was happy, but he was surprised. He didn't know it was coming. He called me and said, "What is this?"

On that Friday, I didn't have time to engage in that conversation because I was busy putting out another fire. At a press conference on that same Friday after our convention, the newly nominated presidential candidate of the Republican Party attacked the swamp—the whole swamp—Hillary Clinton, Obama, Mitch McConnell, and Paul Ryan. At the time, that distraction was way more relevant to me than who leaked the hacked emails.

None of Weissman's theories or factual misrepresentations were true. The more I provided him with the real facts, the angrier he got with me. Finally, Weissman realized that I was not going to lie for him.

Not one iota of evidence supported any of the foundations of Weissman's Russian delusions. None. All of the documents, all of the testimony of witnesses, all of the investigations produced nothing to support his delusional theories.

In the end, even the Mueller Report rejected Weissman's view on Russian collusion.

In the Report, Mueller states clearly on page 9 that his investigation found no evidence "to charge that any member of the Trump campaign conspired with representatives of the Russian government to interfere in the 2016 election." That was the one finding I completely agreed with.

For my part, I saw a certain byproduct value in my proffer session testimony. It was a way to nail the coffin shut on the whole Russian Collusion farce. I knew that none of Weissman's Russian theories were correct. I also believed—and have since been proven correct—that there *had* been a Clinton conspiracy to create a false narrative. Insofar as there was

collusion, it was on the part of the Democrats and if there was any interference, it was what had happened in the interactions between the DNC,
the Obama White House, the Ukrainian government, and operatives
like Alexandra Chalupa and George Soros.

The January 2017 *Politico* article by Ken Vogel and David Stern was
once again fresh in my mind.[1] The content of that article should have
been earth-shattering because it identified actual collusion with a foreign
government (Ukraine), foreign national operatives (Chris Steele, Igor
Danchenko), and known lies given to law enforcement arms of the USG
(FBI, DOJ, Treasury, CIA, White House) by political party operatives
(Chalupa, Blumenthal, Glenn Simpson) with the intent to interfere in
the 2016 presidential election.

Instead, it was totally ignored. I intended to use these sessions to put
these actions back into play and insert these facts into the record of my
discussions with the Special Counsel.

An example was Weissman's crazy theory that I was lobbying for a
Ukraine peace plan that would be pro-Russian in its impact. It was so
crazy, I really didn't know how to respond. The theory was based on a
question in a poll I was taking for a candidate in Ukraine's upcoming
Presidential campaign. Weissman's theory was that my including a poll
question on all of the options for peace that were being discussed in
Ukraine was somehow proof that I was promoting a pro-Russian peace
plan.

The option he was crazed by was one that focused on creating an
independent territory in the two eastern Ukraine oblasts that had become
a "no man's land" after being illegally hijacked by pro-Russian paramilitary forces. This option was in the public arena in Ukraine.

There was nothing secret about it. Plus, I made the point to Weissman
that I was not promoting any of the options in the poll. Other than
showing his ignorance of how polls are conducted, Weissman made it
impossible for me to understand how he could leap to his narrative. There
was no evidence of me speaking with anyone about any peace plan, and I
emphasized this point over and over again. The more I rejected his narrative the more crazed he became claiming that I was lying. He continued
to push this story because he thought he could say a Ukraine plan was
payback to Putin for colluding. He could make Kilimnik an agent of
Putin, and he could implicate the Trump administration. But unlike the
Obama administration, the Trump administration actually gave lethal

weapons to Ukraine to defend itself from Russia. Nothing Weissman was pushing made any sense.

Another thing that upset Weissman was the fact that I had maintained my joint defense agreement with Trump's attorneys during the time we were working on the proffer. Most of the witnesses appearing before Mueller and the prosecutors had joint defense agreements with Trump's attorneys, which allowed the two sides to share information with the attorney-client privilege protected by the agreement. These agreements are typically terminated when a plea is entered into with prosecutors. Mine wasn't because I refused to do so.

Frankly, I was not a part of this process and so I had few details of the arrangement. This was an agreement that allowed the attorneys to talk to each other. I was occasionally informed of something, but Downing kept a wall up on his conversations with attorneys from other targets, including the lawyers for the president. Even the *New York Times* acknowledged that "Mr. Downing's discussions with the president's team violated no laws" But they did "contribute to a deteriorating relationship between lawyers for Mr. Manafort and Mr. Mueller's prosecutors."[2]

Weissman ignored my lack of information on the lawyers' agreement. He was upset that my attorneys could be telling the president's attorneys of my conversations in these sessions. I asserted again that I had no knowledge of the status of the conversations.

I never tried to hide this from Weissman, but he was still angry when he found out. Oh, well.

While the negotiations with the Special Counsel were happening, I was telling Downing one important thing that I wanted him to say in the media, to other defendants' attorneys, and to anyone of relevance. I knew from experience that the worst thing was fear of the unknown. So it was important to me that Trump and his team knew that there was nothing to fear. I didn't want the Trump campaign to be thinking the worst—that I would somehow lie and turn on them—when it was never a possibility that I would do so. I wanted to make sure they knew that even though I was cutting a deal, I wasn't going to make anything up. I knew that would be enough for Trump because he knew what I knew, which was that there was no *there* there. So, if I would not lie, there was nothing to fear, by anyone.

I do not know how Downing communicated this to Trump's lawyers or to anyone, but I was led to believe that it was communicated. And Trump did say a couple of nice things about me during the whole process. So, I felt that he was comfortable with where I stood.

This drove Weissman insane. At one point in our proffer sessions, he said, "Trump is only saying these things to influence you, so you'll think you'll get a pardon."

I said, "No, Trump is saying it because I am a nice guy, and I wouldn't do these kinds of things and he knows that." Weissman's face would turn purple with rage when I made these statements. Plus, I told Weissman that I hoped he was right and that Trump was signaling to me. I never ignored the elephant in the room which surprised Weissman.

But all along—from the indictments, through the Virginia trial, and to the proffer sessions with the prosecutors—my thinking was clear: I needed to get a pardon. I felt I deserved a pardon because I should not have been in prison in the first place. I wanted to make sure that none of the noise got in the way of getting a pardon. All my actions were calculated based on that. And I made sure my lawyers understood this as well.

They were empathetic because they didn't think I was guilty. It wasn't as if I was a criminal looking for a way to avoid responsibility, which is not always the case. Often their clients really are guilty. But I wasn't, and the evidence and the prior decisions by the government in 2014 and 2017, outside of this toxic political climate, made that clear.

Presidents usually issue pardons around Thanksgiving, Christmas, and New Year's. I thought my circumstances were so unique that Trump might do it before I was sentenced so he would not have to say he pardoned someone who was sentenced to twenty years or thirty years, or whatever outrageous sentence they would try to impose on me. I figured that no matter when he pardoned me, it would be controversial. So, doing it sooner made sense in order to stop the bleeding for everyone.

From my admittedly self-interested perspective, there was a benefit to Trump pardoning all of us in this quagmire (Flynn, Stone, Papadopoulos, Page), and then taking the hit and getting it behind him. Republicans still controlled both houses of Congress in 2018. There were a number of different times that I thought might have been good opportunities for pardons. But I was always wrong. I would get my hope up as we approached these self-identified moments, and then rationalize why he didn't do it when those moments passed.

My fellow prisoners in my Pennsylvania prison couldn't understand why I had not already gotten a pardon when I was finally sent to Loretto. To them, the worst criminal is not somebody who breaks the law, but a rat. To them, Trump should have made sure the family was taken care of—that I wasn't in jail anymore. They would ask me, "What's wrong with him? Why aren't you being pardoned?"

I felt a pardon was possible, but I also understood the system. I knew his advisers were telling him not to do it because it was not in his interest. Trump always acts in his interest. I was told several times that he was so angry with what was happening to me that he said, "This is ridiculous, I want one thing: to free this man up. He doesn't deserve it." Those stories kept my hope alive. Even if they didn't necessarily give me comfort.

It was only in the fishbowl of the Special Counsel's investigation into Russian collusion that I was suddenly guilty of so many things—many of which I had been cleared of previously. I had to rely on third parties, and on Trump doing the right thing. It was not comforting to have to rely on all of that attenuation for something that would have such a profound effect on the rest of my life. This was all in my head as I tried to work with Weissman in the proffer sessions.

When we finally received the formal plea offer from the Special Counsel's office, which was, essentially, a twenty-page admission of all of the crimes I was supposed to have committed, I could only read about three pages of the document. The whole point of the document was to admit that I had committed all of these crimes deliberately. I knew it would impact the rest of my life, but I'd seen enough already. None of it was true. It was sickening. It cut against all of my values. Yet I knew I had no choice but to agree. I was not satisfied at all with the plea agreement. The only value it held for me was that it allowed my kids to keep their properties and it ended the public trial.

Later, Weissman would use the DC court as a venue to take the unusual step of reading the entire document aloud for public consumption and drama. Not surprisingly, the reading of the document made me sound like the worst criminal the country had seen in half a century. I couldn't bear to listen to it. I hated the person the document described. Weissman gloried in the moment. But it was killing me.

And worse than Weissman reading it aloud in court, I had to get up and say, "Yes, I did all of those things." Again, it made me want to throw up.

After repeated failed attempts to get me to support their story, Weissman, in a contrived moment of anger, accused me of lying to them on a number of different issues. Each of his accusations were on topics that were critical to his theories that I refused to agree were correct.

On November 26, 2018, the plea deal blew up when the prosecutors accused me of lying to them on five different counts: on statements relating to a payment to a law firm that was working for me, on my interactions with Kilimnik, on Kilimnik's role in the witness tampering charge, on statements made relating to another DOJ investigation and on my contact with the Trump administration.

Weissman was frustrated that after more than fifty hours, he had nothing to prove Trump or anyone in his campaign had colluded with Russia. In fact, the record was even worse than when he started because through my testimony there was now a record establishing that all of the Special Counsel's key narratives were wrong. So, not only did Weissman fail to turn me, but now he had a higher mountain to climb with the facts that I put on the record in those proffers.

Weissman could have sought additional charges on the basis of my allegedly lying to him and the grand jury, which is what he claimed I had done when he terminated the plea agreement. But he did not seek additional charges.

He didn't do so for several reasons. First, he didn't have any proof that the "lies" were indeed lies. They were simply facts that went against his personal theories, which had no facts to support them. Second, if we had a trial on these claims, the fact that Kilimnik was not a Russian intelligence officer but in fact was a "valued asset of the US government" would have come out. To this day, the prosecution has refused to unseal State Department cable traffic that would dismiss this misrepresentation and show that Kilimnik was a valued source with a protected code name that the US government had assigned to him. Weissman had gotten these documents sealed so it wouldn't come out and ruin his Russian collusion narrative, and Jackson, as usual, just rubber-stamped his request.

While I can't go into the details, in the closed session, Weissman asserted that the Special Counsel would not be bringing additional charges but that my lies were so deceitful that the prosecution was breaking the deal with me and would not be offering a 5k letter to the court asking for leniency in sentencing.

"I find that the Office of Special Counsel made its determination that the defendant made false statements and thereby breached the plea agreement in good faith. And, therefore, the Office of Special Counsel is no longer bound by its obligations under the plea agreement, including its promise to support a reduction of the offense level in the guideline calculation for acceptance of responsibility," Jackson said.

As I sat in the courtroom, I chuckled to myself. I had never asked for a 5k letter, had not expected one, and couldn't have cared less that Weissman would not be announcing his intention to ask for leniency. I never had any expectation that Judge Jackson would show any compassion in her sentencing anyway. By this point, I knew what to expect—nothing. As the hearing ended, I leaned over to Downing and whispered, "The charade is almost over."

CHAPTER 17

Sentencing

Because I had two different trials, I was now going to have two separate sentencing hearings.

The first sentencing hearing was to be in Judge Ellis's court, on March 7, 2019, followed by sentencing in Jackson's court the following week. I had hoped the order would be different. I had no doubt whatsoever that Jackson would simply add her time to run *consecutively* with whatever Ellis gave me in order to lengthen my prison sentence. However, if Ellis was second, I felt he might show compassion and have the time run *concurrently* with Jackson's sentence.

Ellis would be sentencing me on the eight convictions from the Virginia trial. It was scary not only because my fate would be decided, but because it was my first sentencing hearing, and I didn't have a clue as to the protocols.

As a critical part of the sentencing process, a pre-sentencing agreement is drafted that, in theory, considers your history, background, good deeds, and enhancements. The court then takes the charge that you've been convicted of and, using a points system and a formula, comes to a determination for the pre-sentencing agreement.

It used to be that the enhancements were crucial, and the judge had very little discretion. The pre-sentencing arrangements were critical. Now, however, judges have total discretion. According to the guidelines, Ellis could have given me up to forty years.

But Ellis had a track record of ignoring the guidelines and meting out terms based on his own sense of justice. He had been vocally critical of both sides, but I believed he was more critical of the behavior of the prosecution. (In one instance, he actually caused the first lead attorney, Greg Andres, to break out in tears when he admonished Andres's court-room behavior.) But I was still nervous. I felt good about Ellis, but not safe.

Because the jury had been dismissed, I had to appear in the Alexandria prison jumpsuit instead of my suit and tie. We asked for permission to wear the suit, but Ellis denied our motion. Around two weeks before my scheduled sentencing, my body finally broke down from the solitary confinement and my legs swelled up to the point that I was not able to walk. When I made my appearance in Ellis's court on March 7, I had to enter the courtroom not only in a green prison jumpsuit but being pushed in a wheelchair. In a show of compassion, Ellis allowed me to stay seated during the proceedings and even to be seated while giving my allocution.

During his presentation to the court, Andres, on behalf of the Special Counsel, asked for the maximum sentence claiming that in having chosen to fight the charges, I had taken up the court's time and had never taken personal responsibility for the "consequences of [my] actions." I laughed to myself. This case should never have been brought in the first place. It was the Special Counsel that had "taken up the court's time."

When it was our turn, Downing made several important points: the special prosecutor had treated this case like they would have in an organized crime or drug cartel case; the case was overcharged and I was only convicted on eight counts; and because of the way the Special Counsel structured it, I'd had to endure two separate cases.

Then he noted that the case had nothing to do with Russian collusion which was the mandate that had created the Office of Special Counsel. Finally, Kevin noted that I had already suffered enough and the Court, following its own precedents in sentencing these types of crimes should not give me any more jail time than I had already served.

If Ellis's sentencing had been second, I would have taken a very different tack. But because DC was next, I was very contrite. I didn't have any animus towards Ellis. I took responsibility. And I apologized for the inconvenience. I admitted that I had created the environment in which the crimes were committed, and now I was suffering the consequences. Even though it was Gates who committed the crimes, I had put him in a position where he could do it. I felt responsible and I made it clear to Ellis that I was taking responsibility. I didn't feel that I should go to jail. I didn't think my life should be destroyed. But I felt responsible for what happened. "To say I feel humiliated and ashamed would be a gross understatement," I told the court.

For some reason, Ellis didn't think I took enough responsibility. "I listened carefully to your allocution," he said, preparing to bring the sentence down, "and I don't have any doubt that what you said was genuine, but I was surprised that I did not hear you express regret for engaging in wrongful conduct. In other words, you didn't say, I really, really regret not doing what I knew the law required."

My heart sank. It was true that I did not admit that I committed the crimes. But I did take responsibility. All I could think was that he must not have heard me. And now it was time for the sentence.

"It is the judgment of this Court," he went on, "that you be committed to the custody of the Bureau of Prisons for a period of forty-seven months. That term is to be served concurrently with the other terms. So you have a total sentence of forty-seven months. I took into account, Mr. Manafort, your personal history and characteristics. I think I might have been a little more impressed if you'd been able to resolve your IRS and other problems, but I hope you will still do that. . . . It's more severe than most of the cases cited by the defendant, significantly more. I've taken into account all of the criminal conduct that's been found by the jury and admitted by you, Mr. Manafort, and I'm convinced that's a just sentence for that conduct. The government didn't argue for a guideline sentence, which I thought was a good thing. Then I would have concluded that it was vindictive, because clearly the guidelines were way out of whack on this, as the history of the sentences in this area show."

Forty-seven months in prison—nearly four years. And I had to pay $25 million in restitution. He did, at least, acknowledge that I had lived "an otherwise blameless life" and "earned the admiration of a number of people."

Wanting blood, the media pounced on the sentence, calling it unfair and too lenient. Saying I could have been sentenced to twenty-four years, the MSM and Twitter world screamed that the nearly four-year sentence I got was "wrong." One former US attorney told the *New York Times* that the sentence was "atrociously low," and the leniency shown me by Judge Ellis "absurd."[1]

My reaction was just the opposite. I had half hoped for no time at all, or limited time with credit given for the time I had spent in solitary confinement. I thought if he'd give me any time at all, it would be a year. But in the end, the leaks from the anonymous sources had created such a charged atmosphere that it made it difficult for Ellis to be as lenient as he might have been otherwise. Now I was thinking Jackson would tack on the full ten years she was allowed under our plea deal, and I'd be in jail for fifteen years. I'd die in prison, I thought. My life was over.

At my urging, my legal counsel put out a statement condemning the vile media reporting. I wanted this statement to be public because I believed it was necessary to have Jackson understand that Ellis had *not* been lenient in his sentence. I had my spokespeople characterize the media assault as "an unprecedented smear campaign against Judge Ellis and Paul Manafort by the mainstream media, legal pundits, and elected Democrat officials." We made the point that the distorted attack on the sentencing guidelines, by these people, was knowingly false and meant to generate a negative narrative about me.

I also had Downing make a statement outside the courthouse. "What we say today," he said, "is the same thing that we have said from day one. There is absolutely no evidence that Paul Manafort was involved in any collusion with any government official or Russia."

In fact, my sentence was severe, not lenient, when compared to actual sentences in similar cases. Judge Ellis had clearly explained to all that the guidelines are only advisory and are outdated in dealing with present-day sentencing in tax cases. All lawyers, including DOJ attorneys, know this to be true. Yet after the sentencing, Democratic members of the Senate Judiciary Committee and many other legal analysts decried the sentencing. They were angry because the judge did not sentence me to twenty-four years. Such a sentence would not only be excessive, but it would also have been inconsistent when measured against the criteria that a judge must follow in sentencing. The judge is required to follow certain criteria in any sentence. Judge Ellis did just this.

What was not followed, however, were the precedents of sentences in similar types of cases. In a brief filed by my attorneys before the sentencing hearing, we identified a number of recent cases where Ellis was the judge and which clearly demonstrated that I suffered a severe sentencing that was above the norm in federal cases today. Below is a small sample of the cases we outlined in the brief:

- Ashvin Desai, who was convicted at trial of hiding over $8 million in an Indian bank account. The Guidelines called for a sentence of seventy-eight to ninety-six months, but the court sentenced the defendant to six months' imprisonment and six months' home detention. (Case No. 11-CR-846 (EJD) (N.D. Ca. July 7, 2014));
- Ty Warner, who was prosecuted for an undisclosed offshore bank account that held a high balance of over $100,000,000, which resulted in a tax loss of over $5.5 million, but was sentenced to two years' probation. (Case No. 13 Cr. 731 (CPK) (N.D. Ill. Jan. 14, 2014));
- Mary Estelle Curran, who owned an undisclosed $47 million Swiss bank account which resulted in a $21 million FBAR penalty, was sentenced to five (5) seconds of probation. (Case No. 12 Cr. 80206 (KLR) (S.D. Fl. Apr. 25, 2013));
- Josephine Bhasin, who had an account at HSBC in India that held a high balance of $8.3 million, and filed a false FBAR after being contacted by the DOJ, was sentenced to two years' probation, the first three months to be served in home confinement, and one hundred fifty hours of community service. (Case No. 11 Cr. 268 (ADS) (E.D.N.Y. Mar. 8, 2013));
- Ernest Vogliano, who opened UBS accounts in the names of Liechtenstein and Hong Kong shell corporations, and actively used funds and transferred some after learning of the criminal investigation, was sentenced to two years' probation. (Case No. 10 Cr. 327 (TPG) (S.D.N.Y. Apr. 26, 2011));
- Jules Robbins, who created a sham Hong Kong corporation to be listed as the nominal holder of his UBS accounts that held nearly $42 million. The court took into consideration his "otherwise unblemished life" in imposing a sentence of twelve months' probation. (Case No. 10 Cr. 333 (RJH) (S.D.N.Y. Oct. 8, 2010));
- John McCarthy, who transferred over $1,000,000 to an unreported Swiss bank account and communicated with bank representatives to orchestrate various transactions and who was sentenced to three years' probation with six months of home detention and three hundred hours of community service. (Case No. 09-CR-784 (VBF) (C.D. Cal. Mar. 22, 2010));
- Steven Rubinstein, who hid approximately $7 million in unreported Swiss accounts that he used to invest in real estate was sentenced to three years' probation with twelve months of home detention. (Case No. 09-CR60166 (MGC) (S.D. Fl. Oct. 28, 2009)); and

- Igor Olenicoff, a businessman and investor, held more than $200 million in undisclosed offshore bank accounts and owed $52 million in back taxes, interest, and penalties, but was sentenced to two years' probation. (Case No. 07 Cr. 227 (CJC) (C.D. Cal. Apr. 16, 2008)).

My attorneys made the case that I was only convicted on eight of eighteen counts—the rest had been dismissed by Ellis without prejudice—and that I'd already given up so much. "Even if there were not numerous other factors warranting a sentence substantially below the Guidelines in this case, sentencing Mr. Manafort to prison for many years would create an undeniable and unwarranted disparity in the sentencing treatment of other defendants in tax fraud and FBAR cases. See 18 U.S.C. § 3553(a) (6). This factor alone weighs heavily in favor of a sentence that does not include a substantial term of imprisonment, particularly in light of the time that Mr. Manafort has already served in solitary confinement and his agreement to forfeit a substantial portion of his assets."

The facts of those cases and the facts of my case did not matter. Once more, I was the victim of a very personal media "hate" campaign that had targeted me simply because I served as Donald Trump's campaign chairman. The attacks on my sentence as lenient were disingenuous and deliberately deceitful. The Democratic hatemongers, the woke Left fascists, and the MSM/social media partisans were in total lockstep. To them, I should have been sentenced to life imprisonment.

I believed that Judge Ellis, fair as he had been during the trial, had reacted to the pressure surrounding my case and given me a more serious sentence than he would have but for the political circus environment that surrounded it.

Ellis's experience in my trial was one of the most difficult cases he had presided over, and he had presided over many major terrorism cases, national security cases, and drug cartel cases. In my case, the media attacked him personally every time he rendered a ruling that was not pro-prosecution. When he chastised the behavior of the Special Counsel, Twitterworld went after him, and midway during my four-week trial, the US marshals had to provide increased security for him because he was receiving death threats.

I have no doubt that the severity of my sentence reflected his concern that if he gave me a "fair" sentence there would be an uproar. I could see the logic, but I felt totally devastated. I'd spend the rest of my life in prison for crimes I didn't commit. I worried my wife's life would be cut short, too. And that I'd never see my grandkids again.

The night of Ellis's sentencing hearing was one of the worst nights of my life. The only thing that got me through was the thought that the sentence was so unjust that Trump would never let me sit in prison for five more years. I wondered how many years I'd have to put in. Five? Six? Seven? After five more years, I'd be seventy-seven years old. I'd been in jail for two years and I could already feel the physical deterioration. I couldn't imagine what five more years would do to me.

I had one week after Ellis's sentencing to prepare for Jackson's. Prior to the sentencing hearing in her court, I had submitted a motion to allow me to have bail between the time of my sentencing in her court to the date of my entry into federal prison. I argued that given that I was unexpectedly jailed in June, I had not had a chance to prepare my accounts before going to prison. Since I was now convicted, there was no threat to the community and the USG had already conceded that I was not a flight risk.

I argued that I had to organize a series of medical, personal, and financial issues and if freed on bail I would be able to do so. I was overdue for a colonoscopy. (The last two colonoscopies showed polyps that had to be removed.) I have a history of pre-cancer growths and I had several growths that needed to be dealt with by my skin doctor. I needed my internist to run tests and prescribe a new regime of prescriptions to deal with gout and liver issues—both of which had shown up in the medical blood work in the prison. And I needed to see my doctor to discuss issues of anxiety, which I was sensitive to.

On the financial side, I wanted to make arrangements for Kathy's well-being. Kathy suffers deficiencies from a serious head injury, and I needed to set up a care program, including instructions for the family, and to get doctors organized and medications updated. The current temporary arrangements, I argued, were not sufficient for long-term care.

I also needed to organize the financial affairs of my family. As a result of the forfeitures and seizures of my properties and cash, my wife was not able to survive without family charity. I needed to rearrange my remaining assets in order to provide for my wife. I needed to re-structure and organize my business affairs to keep from declaring bankruptcy, and this would require a series of meetings.

And I needed to say goodbyes to family and friends.

— While I had no expectation that Jackson would do anything other than throw the proverbial book at me, I also felt it was necessary to frame my vulnerability with the facts that would have been a part of my defense—had I had the opportunity to present it.

The conflict with these requests was that, in my plea agreement, I had admitted to committing every crime imaginable short of blowing up the Twin Towers. While this was my statement to the court in October 2018, I had no part in drafting it. Weissman had drafted the document and included every one of his harebrained ideas and theories.

Now in appealing to the court for leniency based on the *real* facts of the case, I was saying something different. My lawyers suggested that I accept responsibility and ask for mercy.

Accepting responsibility was not difficult because I had consistently done so. I recognized that the crimes that I was accused of were really the actions of Rick Gates and his criminal behavior and sloppiness. I accepted the fact that as his superior, it was my responsibility to monitor him more carefully. In fact, if I had done so, not only would I not have been vulnerable to tax fraud, not reporting foreign bank accounts, and not filing disclosure forms for foreign representation, I would also be $3 million richer since that is what he stole from me when he had full control over my accounts.

I had already pled guilty to the crimes I was charged with. I wouldn't get up there in front of Jackson to lie and say I was a Russian spy or some backchannel to Putin. I agreed that I would be clear that I accepted responsibility for the actions that have caused me to be in court. I would ask for mercy, and I would be sincere.

I agreed to have the lawyers make a few additional points in passing. The first was that the case in DC related to a FARA failure to file and for lobbying that I did not even do. The firms that did the lobbying did file reports. The DOJ has a process to manage filing violations that almost never included criminal indictments. I wanted the record to show that I had entered into negotiations and reached a deal with the FARA unit prior to the appointment of the Special Counsel.

The second was that with regard to the obstruction of justice charges, I never made contact with a witness, I was never prohibited by the judge from communicating with witnesses, and the witness did not convey false information as a result of my attempt to contact him.

I decided to leave the cleaning up of the destruction to my reputation from the Mafioso-style treatment I had endured from the Special Prosecutor for another time. I knew that trying to resurrect my reputation in a single allocution was impossible. It would take a sustained effort over a long period of time. Trying to deal with it when I was focused on how long I was going to jail would be foolish. Plus, I knew that it would send Jackson into orbit. After all, to me she had demonstrated a clear bias towards the prosecutors, so in criticizing them, I would be attacking her behavior too.

As I have said several times in this book, in my opinion, Judge Jackson had been 1,000 percent in the tank for the prosecution the entire time. When it came to issuing rulings from the bench, Jackson had not only accepted the Special Counsel's arguments, but she also often adopted their language, too. The morbid joke on my side was that her chair should be moved from behind the bench to the table of the prosecution.

Not only was I worrying about the number of years she would impose, but the issue of concurrent or consecutive sentencing was very relevant. I wanted Jackson to treat the two cases as related and to understand that the only reason there were two court sentencing actions was because of the requirement that tax cases could not be heard in DC.

I was told that she was so excited that she had invited members of her family to the sentencing, which told me everything I needed to know. It was a show for her, to let the outside world know that she was going to stick it to Trump. To her, this whole farce was really just a very visible job interview.

With these thoughts in mind, I made my allocution to her.

The last two years have been the most difficult of years that my family and I have ever experienced. The person that I have been described as in public is not someone who I recognize. While I know that I am not that person, I feel shame and embarrassment for the suffering that I have caused for my family and friends and to all who have been affected by my behavior.

Let me be very clear. I accept the responsibility for the acts that have caused me to be here. Furthermore, I want to apologize for all that I did that contributed to these actions and to the affects that they had on both people and institutions. While I cannot undo the past, I can ensure that the future will be very different, and I stand here today committing myself to this change.

I am especially upset at the pain that I have caused my family and my friends. If nothing else, this suffering will be a major deterrent to any future behavior by me. As I have sat in solitary confinement for the past nine months, I have reflected on my life and what is important to me. I can see that I behaved in ways that did not always live up to my own personal code of values. I am upset with myself for these failures and understand that many of these mistakes are what has brought me here today.

Because of this new self-awareness, I can say with conviction that my behavior in the future will be very different. I have already begun to change and am confident that the lessons of the past two years will be the guide for my future. What has been uplifting to me during this crisis is the incredible support I have received not just from family and friends, but from so many total strangers. I have been strengthened by the letters I have received from them and have grown positively from their prayers and encouragement.

This exposure to the goodness of people has had an energizing impact on my life and my ability to cope with the difficulties of being in solitary confinement. Their encouragement has helped me discover how I want to conduct my life when this ordeal has passed.

I can stand here today and assure the court that I am a different person from the one who first came before you in October of 2017. I have had the time to reflect on my life and my choices, and the importance of family and friends. It has instilled in me a commitment to turn my notoriety into a positive and to show the world who I really am.

I see more clearly both myself and my life, past and future. I can tell you that I already feel the pain from this experience, and I know that it was my conduct that brought me here today. For all of this I am remorseful. With the power of prayer and God's guiding hand, I know that my family and I will emerge stronger from this ordeal and look forward to setting forth on this new journey.

Again, I apologize to all who have been affected negatively by my behavior. I take responsibility for the consequences of this behavior. In about two weeks, I will be seventy years old, and my wife is sixty-six years old. This ordeal has destroyed my life. I am most concerned about the affect my sentencing will have on my family. I am the primary caregiver for my wife's well-being. I have lost almost everything: my investments, my properties, cash deposits, my life insurance, and my children's and grandchildren's trust funds. I have suffered.

I appreciate the time that you have committed to this case and ask that you can find compassion in your sentencing. I promise you that if you do, you will not regret it.

Well, it will not shock you to know that Jackson stayed true to form. Following my allocution, we recessed for ten minutes before she came back and read a fifteen-minute prepared statement that made it sound like I was an evil person, a sinister criminal. As soon as she began to speak, I could tell by her preening that the only question was how abusive the sentencing would be. Not only did she proceed to attack me, but she also attacked my wife and daughter.

"This sentence will not be an endorsement or an indictment of the mission or the tactics of the Office of Special Counsel. That question is not before the Court either. Nor does it fall to me today to pass judgment on Paul Manafort as a human being, or to decide, as his daughter asked me to, if he is worthy of forgiveness under God. His life is not over and he's going to have the opportunity to make something positive out of this, as he's suggested he's going to do, and that's a question left for a higher authority at another time."

She said it was "undisputed" that I was part of "a conspiracy that involved money laundering involving millions of dollars," that I "hid millions of dollars," that I lied to my bookkeeper and tax preparers. "It is hard to overstate the number of lies and the amount of fraud and the extraordinary amount of money involved," she said.

She was putting on a performance and before we could be done with it, we would have to get through the act. Finally, after making the Special Counsel's case for them one last time, she reached the sentencing.

"It is the judgment of the Court that you, Paul Manafort, are hereby committed to the custody of the Bureau of Prisons for a term of sixty months on Count 1. This sentence is to run concurrent to thirty months of the sentence previously imposed by the United States District Court for the Eastern District of Virginia, which has already accounted for the credit you are due for the time served. It is further ordered that you are committed to the custody of the Bureau of Prisons for a term of thirteen months on Count 2, to be served consecutively to the sentence on Count 1 and the sentence imposed by the Eastern District of Virginia."

There it was, a sentence of seventy-three months, thirteen of which were for the bogus obstruction charge. Thirty months would run concurrently with Ellis's sentence, but forty-three would not. Thanks to her, I now had a sentence of seven and a half years. I laughed to myself and thought, "Well I guess she could not figure out how to get me to ten years." For this I sighed in relief. Downing knew what he was doing when he held firm on a maximum sentence of ten years in the plea bargain process.

All this for failing to file a FARA form—a "crime" for which no one had ever even been imprisoned in the entire history of the law!

The lawyers sitting at the prosecutor's table smiled to each other and smiled to the judge's bench. They sat in a kind of smug, self-satisfied silence—a far cry from what followed the Virginia sentence. Here they turned to the media in the audience and took a silent bow. Crushed, I looked at my wife. I was not surprised, only devastated. Again, I could not show my feelings, so I smiled weakly at her, blew her a kiss, and told her I loved her as the US marshal started to escort me back to my cell.

It takes about twenty minutes to get from the courthouse in DC to the Alexandria jail, where I had been since before the sentencing hearings. It's a trip I used to take as a free man every day to work. Now I was handcuffed, shackled, and freshly sentenced.

The radio was rarely on, but the marshals had it on that day. Just as we pulled out from under the courtroom and we were getting on 495 to head to Alexandria, a breaking news report came on.

"Paul Manafort has just been charged with sixteen counts of bank fraud and consumer fraud by New York District Attorney Cyrus Vance and the State of New York," the announcer said.

I had to laugh. The timing was not a coincidence, even if hearing it on the radio was. Weissman had orchestrated it so that as soon as my sentencing was done, they would drop new charges on me, which they had been sitting waiting for this moment to pile on.

The Feds and the State, working in concert, but not for justice. This was all just one gigantic political prosecution.

The marshals looked at me. They couldn't believe I was laughing.

"Just another trial," I said.

I wondered if it would ever end. I didn't know yet what the exact charges were, but they sounded like the ones I had already been convicted of, so I hoped the concept of double jeopardy would apply. I knew that I would need to contact my lawyers, once again, when I got back to my cell. I needed to understand how this all worked and what was next.

Again, I was hit with that uncertainty. And you always think the worst in dark moments: Maybe the laws are different in New York. Maybe they don't have double jeopardy. I didn't know. I was so worn down that I thought it was macabrely humorous.

When I got back, I called Downing, who told me that I would have to hire a New York attorney. "Ugh," I thought. But Kevin did give me some good news: New York had a statute that dealt specifically with my situation. Double jeopardy should protect me.

I said, "Does it talk about pardons?" I was broke, and now I had to get a new lawyer. It was just one more thing.

It was a cold day and I had just been rotated to a new cell, which had a window that looked out on the pod as opposed to a concrete wall. In a twisted way, this window was a new freedom. Even this good news, though, had a bad news component. The windows were not well insulated, and the winter cold poured in as if there was no window at all. I sat in the little bit of sunlight, shivering, while wondering, "Is this what the rest of my life will be like?"

CHAPTER 18

Life Inside

As crazy as it sounds, even though I was looking at seven and a half years—not to mention new indictments in New York—for the first time in two years, my future had some definition. The sentencing brought a sense of stability to what had been a deeply uncertain period, and that uncertainty was causing a huge amount of anxiety. With the sentencing finished, the anxiety seemed less oppressive.

The big question now was: When will I be transferred and to where? The "where" was the most immediate concern. The practice of the Bureau of Prisons is not to let prisoners know anything. They keep you in the dark and then one day they wake you up, tell you to pack everything you have, stick you in a van, and you're transferred. You don't know where you're going until you get there.

There are four levels of prisons in the federal system. There is a maximum-security level for the El Chapos, the drug lords, the terrorists, and the murderers. There is the medium-security level, which is usually where people who have committed violent crimes or egregiously bad acts are sentenced for the beginning of their terms. There is the low-security level where white-collar criminals and prisoners who had started in medium-security facilities but over time, and with good behavior, had transitioned to a lower-security prison. Many people start and finish their sentences in low security prisons. And finally, there are camps.

In a camp facility, there are no cells, you are not locked in, and you have free access to the grounds. Sometimes, you can wear regular clothes rather than lockup clothes. And you have unlimited visitation rights.

In my mind, I felt I would be going to a camp because I met all of the qualifications. My sentence was less than ten years. I was a first-time offender. There were no drug crimes or violent crimes. According to the BOP guidelines, a prisoner must have less than seven "points" to qualify for a camp. I had zero points. Also giving me confidence was the fact that Michael Cohen was in a camp at Otisville for similar crimes.

Typically, a prisoner would be sent to a camp within five hundred miles of their residence and family. But one of Weissman's more diabolical schemes was to bring the new charges in New York. As a consequence of these State charges, I would have to be detained for the New York trial. This would mean more time in a transitory jail like Alexandria, and the real possibility of solitary confinement for another twelve to fifteen months. He also knew that with a Detainer, I could not be sent to a camp.

I didn't understand any of this at the time. I was busy doing my research on camp facilities and I had determined that FCI Cumberland in Cumberland, Maryland, was the camp closest to my home. In my mind, I would be sent there or to Petersburg, Virginia, which was about four hours from my home.

A friend of mine who had been convicted of a white-collar crime about ten years earlier had spent some time in Cumberland. I hadn't spoken to him in eight or nine years, but he came to visit me in Alexandria. He wanted to explain what life was like in a camp because he assumed that's where I would be going.

After months in solitary, dreaming of and researching a transfer to a camp facility brought a certain measure of hope to my daily life. But on the other hand, nagging in the back of my mind was the stress of the pending New York case.

One of the reasons the case was filed, I realized, was that state convictions were outside of the power of a presidential pardon. A state conviction was subject to a governor's clemency. This was Weissman's game plan from the beginning. It cast a long, dark shadow over my future, as if, with a seven-and-a-half-year sentence, it wasn't dark enough already.

Since Downing had told me to get a New York lawyer, my son-in-law was busy researching the kinds of firms we should look at. He interviewed four or five of them for me. Eventually we landed on Todd Blanche, a partner at Cadwalader, Wickersham, and Taft.

Todd was someone who came out of the New York Southern District Attorney's office and was a very experienced criminal litigator. After I interviewed Todd, I hired him immediately. He had a stellar reputation in the legal community and extensive litigation experience in the exact areas where Vance had charged me with committing crimes. Todd had practiced in the US attorney's office in the prestigious Southern District of New York. At Cadwalader, Todd specialized in tax cases, financial crimes, and fraud, and was a top-notch litigator. Plus, he was a really nice person. I felt very comfortable with him from the first moment. He helped me to believe that I would not only win the motion to dismiss the case, but that we would "kick ass."

He was exactly correct on all accounts. The plan was for Downing and Westling to stay on to manage other legal issues—the forfeitures, the pardon, dealing with other lawyers on pending cases—while Blanche took on the New York case.

Even after she had sentenced me, Jackson teamed up with Weissman to try to stay relevant. While I was preparing for the New York case, Jackson convened a closed hearing on whether Downing had violated the gag order by talking to Sean Hannity. As proof, Weissman submitted a text from me to Hannity saying that Downing would be in contact.

At the hearing, no one from the Special Counsel's office was present. Instead, an attorney from the DC US Attorney's office appeared before Judge Jackson. Jackson, with her snotty attitude, accused Downing of violating her order. Downing said that he spoke to Hannity before I had even texted Hannity. He did this as client management but then never spoke to him again. Downing said he had his phone records if Jackson wanted them.

When Jackson turned to the Government for them to contest what Downing had said, the US attorney said they looked into the matter and had no reason to doubt Downing's story. Jackson was taken aback. She was expecting to have the US attorney attack Downing so that she could reprimand him. When the Government said it was fine with Downing's explanation, Jackson could do nothing but back off.

Because Downing said this was a client management issue, it allowed him to demand that the hearing either be wholly sealed or wholly made public. Since Jackson did not want to look like she had lost the argument in a public transcript, she agreed to keep the hearing sealed. Even after I was sentenced, she continued to slam me and my attorneys.

The New York indictment charged me with sixteen counts of mortgage fraud, falsifying business records, and other crimes in connection to loans I had obtained on properties owned by me and my family.

The concept of double jeopardy has been a part of our US Constitution from the very beginning of our nation. Originally included by the founders to protect against people being convicted of the same crime at both the federal and state levels, the double jeopardy concept functioned well for nearly two hundred years. For most of that time, federal laws were more limited to issues of national security. This left most other crimes to be prosecuted by the states. Most of the bank fraud crimes I was indicted on would have been dealt with at the state level in the past. The federal government would not have tried them. But the Patriot Act, signed into law in the aftermath of 9/11, changed a lot of that dynamic.

After 9/11, the authority of the Department of Justice was expanded to justify warrants that could uncover terrorism. It became a regular tactic for there to be a yin and yang of complementary federal and state charges to try to pressure defendants into giving up bosses up the chain of power.

Though the concept has eroded in the last twenty years, New York has a strict double jeopardy law. Unless the potential crimes charged fell within specific exceptions enumerated in legislation, the double jeopardy concept in New York state prohibited most crimes from being double charged. It was clear as soon after the indictments came down that the state case was built on shaky ground. As an article on the indictments in *Politico* pointed out: "A state law barring retrials on charges tried in federal court could pose a legal obstacle to the new prosecution. New York legislators have struck a deal to amend that law, but the new legislation has not passed. Legal experts have also said it may be unconstitutional to apply that law to past acts by Manafort."[1]

In my case, the DA didn't even try to pretend that the crimes I was being charged with at the state level were different from the ones I had just dealt with in the federal courts. That was the signal to me that Weissman was behind it. They knew their chances of prevailing were not good. It was a total longshot. If it worked, great. If not, it would cause me a lot of pain, suffering, and money—also great. There was no real downside for them. Only a political upside and the narrow chance of a legal win.

Once I understood this, it told me that if I got a fair judge in New York, I could win. Todd had done all the research. Based on his work product, I knew the law was in my favor. It was just a question of getting the right judge, something I had had mixed results on to date.

After the Federal sentencings had wrapped up, I began experiencing the negative consequences of my convictions, the most concerning of which were the foreclosures on my properties. To continue to make my life miserable, the Federal Savings Bank triggered a clause in our loan agreement for my Bridgehampton property which allowed the bank to take over ownership of the property if I was in default. Since I had not been able to pay because the US government had taken most of my cash, and I could not sell the property because the US government had taken it, I was technically in default.

I had agreed to list my Virginia home as additional collateral on the loan, never believing it was at risk when the loan agreement was signed in December 2016. I never anticipated being convicted of any crimes. My condo was only supposed to be the collateral for the Bridgehampton loan in a worst-case situation.

I never thought it was at risk because the property was valued at $11 million, and the bank held in escrow $2.5 million in cash. The loan was for $9 million. In my wildest nightmares, I couldn't have imagined being thrown in jail and having everything taken from me just a few years later. Now, all was gone and I was looking at the bank coming after my Virginia home.

In Virginia, unlike in New York, there is an expedited process for property foreclosures. In New York when you're foreclosed on, it will take at least a year, sometimes a year and a half to get through the courts and lose a property. But in Virginia, property can be seized within thirty days. So there was no question: the Bank would move quickly. I felt terrible. The Virginia property was my wife's castle. It was her refuge. She loved that place. Now she had lost me to prison, and she would be out on the street.

We had no money. Our home in Florida was protected by the Homestead Act, but my wife didn't want to live in Florida, separated from me and the grandchildren.

With limited options, Kathy moved into my daughter's home. Now, in addition to everything else, I had to hire a Virginia attorney to deal with the foreclosures. Even though I knew I was going to lose the property, I still needed to go through the process.

Kathy was overworked. All at once she was dealing with the foreclosures of three other properties and had limited time to move everything out of the homes with no place to put everything. Making matters worse, I had the added expense of moving all the furniture that was in those properties to a storage unit.

So while there was some relief knowing that the federal cases were over, I had this pending New York situation, and I had to deal with the consequences of the foreclosures. I had to think about our ability to live. They had taken all of our cash. Most of our securities had been sold to pay for legal bills. Our insurance policy, which was supposed to be an emergency pool that we could dip into if we had to, was part of the forfeiture.

Between the approximately $5 million I spent in legal bills and the foreclosures, I was broke. My cash had been seized along with my properties. And by taking my properties, not only did they wipe me out, but they also prevented me from executing a divestiture plan to pay off loans and keep the profits. The significance of this was to remove the assets but leave me with bank loan liabilities. The destruction of my life was so comprehensive I had to laugh.

The crisis may have brought us closer as a family, but at the same time, it revealed who our true friends were. I was shocked to see who disappeared—people who I'd helped over the years, whose families I'd taken on vacations, business partners I'd been very close to. They left. They were fake friends who had simply used me.

The true friends, however, stepped up and helped Kathy. Support came from many surprising places, and I will always be grateful for it. But it was another low point. I couldn't help but feel terrible for the position my family was in.

Managing all of this from prison was extremely difficult and my ongoing hope was I would be sent to a camp, which would make everything easier. Meanwhile, the media was still ecstatic over my being sentenced to prison. They quickly began to create their own narrative that the plea deal was a sign that I would turn on Trump. They were writing that Trump was a dead man. They were wringing their hands at the prospect of the New York case because it was outside of Trump's purview. They were gloating that I was going to spend a long time in jail.

➤ Schiff, of course, was talking about the "proof." He was now Chairman of the House Intelligence Committee. He announced that he had seen the "proof" that I was a Russian spy, that I was leaking information to a "Russian agent" during the campaign. It didn't matter that everything he had seen was already public information. There was no secret file, no silver bullet or smoking gun. Ultimately, Schiff's lies were exposed. Of course, no one cared to correct the record. His lies still stand on the record today.

Weissman had fabricated a ridiculous narrative about secret polling data and unsurprisingly the MSM bought it all and went wild. Since there was no direct link showing Trump or his campaign officials dealing with Russia, Weissman constructed the narrative that turned my assistant, Konstantin Kilimnik, who was a Russian of Ukrainian origin, into a Russian spy. That way, whenever I was talking to him or sending him anything, I was "communicating" with Putin and Russia. In Weissman's narrative, when Kilimnik visited me in New York, and I told Gates to give Kilimnik polling data, I was passing secret information to Putin. This, of course, was not true.

Weissman even got Gates—a known liar and thief—to back this craziness up. Immediately, the MSM went into overdrive, and I was convicted in the court of public opinion of being a spy—not alleged to be a spy but convicted. What everyone ignored was a very relevant fact: there was no polling during the timeframe that I met with Kilimnik on August 2 in New York when I supposedly gave him this secret polling data. We didn't start polling until the beginning of August, so there was nothing to give Kilimnik other than public information, which I wanted him to pass on because it was making the case that Trump could win. There was nothing secretive or highly confidential. In fact, my talking points to him on the "public" polling data that we gave Kilimnik was what I was saying in public during my interviews. Gates even said this to Weissman during one of his early interviews with the FBI.

But Weissman knew that public polling would not create the hysteria he needed. So, Weissman did what he does best: he exaggerated the facts to make it "secret data" at a "clandestine meeting," and he asserted with no evidence or facts that because, according to Weissman, when Kilimnik had served in the Russian military (which was compulsory), he was associated with Russian intelligence. With those two allegations,

Kilimnik became a Russian spy delivering secret campaign information directly to Putin.

These facts were never confirmed with evidence by anyone. Not the Mueller Report, not the Senate Intelligence Committee Report, not the House Intelligence Committee Report. Not one MSM investigative report. Yet, every single one of them asserted this fake narrative with conviction. In fact, their assertions were based on the assertions each of them was making quoting each other. Circular fake journalism!

This is important to repeat. Konstantin Kilimnik is not a Russian spy. No evidence has ever been presented by anyone to even link the idea, never mind prove it.

The total basis for which this falsehood is alleged is an April 15, 2021, press release from the Treasury Department.[2] The Treasury statement alleged that Kilimnik is a "known Russian Intelligence Services agent" who "provided the Russian Intelligence Services with sensitive information on polling and campaign strategy" during the 2016 election. No proof, just an uncorroborated statement.

As a *RealClearInvestigations* article from November 2021 makes clear, "Writing that same day, *Times* reporters Mark Mazzetti and Michael S. Schmidt declared that Treasury's evidence-free press release—coupled with an evidence-free Senate Intelligence claim in August 2020 that Kilimnik is a 'Russian intelligence officer'—now 'confirm' the *Times*' report from February 2017."[3]

According to *RCI*: "The Treasury announcement did not explain how the department, which conducted no official Russiagate investigation, was prompted to lodge an explosive allegation that a multi-year FBI/Mueller investigation found no evidence for. It also does not name the position Kilimnik allegedly held in Russian intelligence—much less say whether he was a senior official."

The Senate Intelligence Committee picked up on these two references that really were just one and asserted categorically that Kilimnik was a Russian intelligence officer. Mueller did the same. Again, no evidence, no facts, no storyline. Just a Treasury Department press release, coupled with a *New York Times* story that was clearly based on a coordinated leak from Treasury.

This is justice in the atmosphere of Russian collusion. Ignored was the public countervailing evidence[4]:

- that Kilimnik had shared this same, publicly available polling data with Americans;
- that the FBI still does not deem him a Russian intelligence officer, instead claiming that he has unspecified "ties";
- that he had long been a valued State Department source;
- that he traveled to the US on a civilian Russian passport, not the suspicious diplomatic one Mueller alleged without producing it;
- and that even the Senate Intelligence Committee was "unable to obtain direct evidence of what Kilimnik did with the polling data and whether that data was shared further."
- In addition, no US government or congressional investigator ever contacted him for questioning, Kilimnik told RCI in an April 2021 interview when he produced images of the civilian passport.

Kilimnik, of course, was not a Russian agent. He was a link to my business relations in Ukraine. I wanted him to communicate to our Ukrainian contacts that Trump could win and it was the public polls that were showing it. I suggested private polls would back up the public ones, but I didn't offer them to Kilimnik, plus they did not exist at the time we met. I was gone from the campaign by the time the polls were completed in mid-August.

One more fact is especially relevant here, and the Office of Special Counsel knew this completely. As I have discussed, Kilimnik was not only not a Russian spy, but he was a "valued US asset" by the US State Department, and the French and German Embassies in Kyiv. In fact, the US Embassy in Kyiv had assigned a code name to Kilimnik to protect him in the cable traffic sent to Washington. Over the ten years Kilimnik worked for me, he would meet regularly—usually once a week—with either the political attaché or the CIA attaché in the US embassy. They valued him and the information he gave them.

So why did Weissman label Kilimnik a Russian spy and ruin his life with an indictment for witness tampering that he knew was false? Because the Special Counsel had run out of fake links to Russia. Papadopoulos did not fall for the FBI-generated Halper overtures meant to entrap him to link him with Russia. Carter Page was a nothingburger from the illegal FISA surveillance. Flynn had no link to the campaign to cause his interaction with the Russian Ambassador to the US that would trigger any incriminating action. Christopher Steele and his hired Russian

Igor Danchenko had come up empty handed digging around for dirt in Russia and their Steele dossier had been dismissed as a fake. Finally, even the fake "black ledger" produced by the Clinton campaign alleging that I had been paid millions in cash had been debunked by the US Embassy-created National Anti-Corruption Bureau.

Weissman had no links to Russia. So he pressed Gates to lie and got him to say that "some people have said that Kilimnik had links to Russian intelligence." No facts. No evidence. No reference to who those "some people" were. No story. Only "Kilimnik was a Russian citizen and had served his mandatory service in the Russian military (technically it was Soviet military—a fact he has never hidden) when he was in his early twenties." Somehow, anonymously leaked information alleging this fake narrative began to appear in the same media outlets that seemed to always have damning information on anyone in the Special Counsel's crosshairs. And a narrative took hold.

It is important to note that, to this day, one of the few groups of documents still sealed is the cable traffic from the embassy in Kiev to the State Department. They were sealed by Judge Jackson for one very obvious reason: they will show that not only was Kilimnik not a Russian agent, but that he was a US asset.

Deliberately linked to this refusal to unseal is the fabrication that Kilimnik traveled to the US in 1997 on a diplomatic passport, which, from Mueller's standpoint, was proof of his work for the Russian state. The truth is that Kilimnik traveled to the US when he worked for International Republican Institute chaired by Senator John McCain, and had only an ordinary passport at that time. A copy of this passport was obtained by journalists,⁵ but not by Mueller, whose people never made a single effort to reach out to Kilimnik. They knew the real truth already and it was not convenient to their fake narrative.

When I was at Northern Neck, a Catholic priest would come by weekly to visit me. He would take my confession, give me communion, and discuss with me the Bible readings he knew I was doing in solitary. His visits had a major impact on me. Not just while I was in prison but to this day.

We often discussed St. Paul, my name saint. Through these discussions, he helped me to understand suffering and its importance to being a strong Christian. He made the point to me that St. Paul dealt with suffering as a gift, not as a penance. No matter the suffering, there was always a plan in God's eyes. Suffering had meaning.

I took those lessons seriously and I tried to use them in my personal dealings. It didn't always work, but the effort was important. Especially with everything I was up against—from Weissman and Schiff to the New York District Attorney's office and on down the line to a bitter prison guard doing what she could to make my life even harder. There was no shortage of suffering, but I was intent on learning what I could from the experience. I wanted to learn how to channel my suffering into a positive outcome. In this way, this priest, the Bible, and St. Paul were invaluable guides during my entire prison time.

As my life was seemingly spinning out of control, I would find myself in fake-narrative overload. It was a lot to deal with from behind bars and I think it affected the way I was treated. Most of the guards I had in Alexandria were nice people. They were young, on the starting rungs of the ladder in the Alexandria Sheriff's office. They rotated often so there was little familiarity between the guards and the prisoners. Throughout my ordeal, I interacted with many of them and for the most part, found them very supportive and compassionate.

To this day, I am appreciative of the way the sheriff and his staff of deputies treated me. They would chat with me when they could. It's a simple thing but to a person in isolation, it was a big deal. When the opportunity presented itself, they would let me out early from my cell for my free time or come back late to return me to my cell. These sound like little things, but when you have no freedom, these kindnesses go a long way.

I had one truly mean deputy during my entire time in Alexandria. It happened in my last month there. She made a point of letting me know I was a prisoner with no rights, and I was at her total mercy. While I had almost no freedoms, I had learned the system and cherished the few perks I did have. Clearly, this deputy knew who I was, and she found ways to deprive me of these limited perks. I'm not sure if she was just a partisan Democrat, or if she hated me for being Trump's campaign manager, or if she believed everything she saw about me in the news. But she clearly disliked me and made certain that I knew it.

Normally, I'd have two hours each day where I could get out of my cell. Those two hours were gold to me. I could talk to my lawyers and my family. I could take a shower. I could sit in a real chair as opposed to the concrete bench in my cell. She would be the one to come in during this block and she always came in late to let me out and early to put me back. She knew that time meant a lot to me, and she did it anyway. I never complained, which bothered her, too.

On April 19, 2019, a guard came into my cell at 5:30 in the morning, woke me up, and told me to pack everything. I was being transferred. I received no warning, no notice. After almost a year, I was being uprooted and sent to God knows where, where I would spend some untold number of years.

This was not an orderly, smooth departure. I was literally told I had five minutes to pack up. I had no idea what I could take, so I just piled everything that was not food into my laundry bag. In the end almost none of it went with me.

Once packed, I was shackled and escorted in my four-guard parade to the holding room where I was stripped, searched, and then transferred from the sheriff's control to the US Marshal's. I dressed, was re-shackled and then transported to the federal court basement cell for shipment to my final destination. A destination that I thought I knew but in the end was wrong about.

After I was brought to the court, I sat for about four hours in a different holding cell from where I had been during my trial. The marshal there was a friend by now, so I asked if he could tell me where I was going. He couldn't, but he looked at the paperwork and said the designation was LOR. He didn't know what that meant.

I got anxious. My surmise was that I was being sent to a camp in Cumberland, Maryland. But Cumberland wouldn't be LOR. Anxiety gripped me. "What new trauma is the system trying to inflict on me now?" I wondered. I couldn't call anyone to find out, either. No one knew I was even being transported, except for the marshals. The BOP (Bureau of Prisons) doesn't share the information with my attorneys.

Adding to the anxiety was the fact that I didn't know when I would be able to contact my lawyers or my wife. (Ironically, I found out later that the prisoners at my final destination knew I was coming. Because the system has to prepare for a new inmate, the warden is notified by the BOP. The final destination has to process me, put my name into the local prison system, assign me a cell, and prepare the name tags for my clothing. So the prisoners and the guards where I was headed knew before I or anyone else did.)

When the transfer van arrived, I was loaded in—handcuffed and shackled, as always—with about twelve other prisoners. There were four rows of seats, and I was placed in the very back. My claustrophobia spiked and I forced myself to meditate. I had to remove myself mentally from the situation. Departing Alexandria, we drove on I-95, which was the route to Cumberland—a good sign, I thought. But my reprieve turned to anxiety again when we turned off of I-95 and started to drive across Pennsylvania.

I asked the marshals where they were driving me, but they said they didn't know because I was going first to an interim jail. We drove for hours. Somewhere in Ohio we pulled into a massive transport hub located in a rural private airfield. I saw ten football fields with airstrips, planes, buses, and prisoners. It was like something out of a horror movie. Our bus pulled into a line of other buses. Prisoners were being herded in long lines and then separated into other buses and on to BOP prisoner transport planes (sarcastically referred to as "ConAir"). The imagery reminded me of movies about the holocaust.

I didn't know what was happening, but I was definitely anxious. A fellow prisoner explained that I was in a hub where prisoners were sorted into groups going to different places. The planes were bringing prisoners to other hubs. Many ended up going to Oklahoma to await being transported to their ultimate destination. If I was guided on to a plane, I thought, it would not be a good sign that I was going to be close to my family.

On top of everything else, my bladder was close to bursting. We were four hours into the journey and our destination was apparently still two hours away. Before they moved us to a different van to travel to our first destination, somewhere in Pennsylvania, I was about to literally wet my pants. I tried to get the marshals' attention, but they ignored me. We sat there for forty-five minutes before they came to let a few prisoners out, but not me. Finally I said, "Look, I have to go to the bathroom. I'm going to wet myself right here. I'm sorry, but I'm physically not able to hold it anymore."

So the marshal led me to a porta-john. It was freezing. It was April, but very cold. And the wind was blowing across the field, making it even colder. But I was just glad to get to a bathroom. They led me back across the field to the van. Again, I asked where I was going. They told me to get in the van.

This van was going to a penitentiary in northeast Pennsylvania, a transition prison that also held criminals who were serving long-term sentences for violent crimes. This is how the BOP works. There is no logic to their routing and definitely no concern for the welfare of prisoners. I traveled on a bus for eleven hours of which almost half of the trip was going back over roads I had just traveled.

When we finally arrived at the way station prison, I still wasn't sure if it was just a transition or if it was where I'd be located. I could tell right away from the barbed wire and guard towers that it was a hardcore place. I was nervous as hell. The guards called out the prisoners by name, gave them their papers, and walked them into a holding facility. I was the last one to be called.

As I was getting my papers, the processing guard looked at me and said, "Well, was there?"

I had no idea what he was talking about. I said, "Was there what?"

"Russian collusion," he laughed.

I said, "I'll never tell," and breathed a sigh of relief that this journey was over at least for the night.

After being processed through a total body scan, I was put into a holding cell with about twenty other prisoners, even though it could only fit seven or eight. I asked a few people where we were, and they explained it was a prison used for transiting prisoners. I asked a few what the designation LOR meant. They didn't know. But a couple of people said they were going to Loretto, so I was finally able to put it together that I'd be going to Loretto, a prison I had researched in Pennsylvania that had a camp and a low-security facility. Once again, I started getting my hopes up that I might be headed to a camp after all.

With new hope, I quieted down, I was processed into a cramped cell with a bunk bed and toilet. I had a cellmate who had been traveling for three weeks already to get to his endpoint. We were allowed one hour out of our cell on Monday and Thursday. During this time we could shower but also had to eat our lunch. We had nothing to read or occupy our time.

Fearing being stuck in this dank and dirty cell for a time uncertain, I volunteered for a work assignment to clean up the common area. To no surprise, I was refused because I was a "high profile prisoner" who was at risk in the facility. At first, I was upset and then I found out that in the last month a guard had been killed in the common area. From that point on, I sat in my bed quietly and waited to be transferred.

I was lucky. Normally, I would have been in this place for at least two weeks. But, the last two buses had been cancelled for some reason, so there was a backup. To alleviate the problem, they shipped two buses. One to take those prisoners going to Loretto and one to another prison in central Pennsylvania. My stay at USP Canaan, a high-security penitentiary, ended up lasting only four days, but it seemed like a month. This was truly the most horrible place.

FCI Loretto, when I finally arrived, looked very different from any prison I'd been in thus far. A former monastery, it was laid out with dormitory rooms that had been converted to cells with doors on them. There was a big track where you could run or work out. There was a weight room (which most prisons didn't have). It had different rooms for different activities and an enormous auditorium.

It was without question the best place I had been in the prison system. I could walk around. I had some freedom. Within an hour of my arrival, I was standing in line to get clothes around lunchtime when people started coming up to me to introduce themselves. I was wondering how they all knew, but they knew. One guy gave me a toiletry package with a razor and shaving cream, some shower slippers. My clothes were prison khakis and a sweatshirt rather than a jumpsuit.

At first, I was put in a large transition area while a permanent cell was being assigned. It was like a large dormitory with four rows of bunk beds. It was managed by a couple of the inmates. I walked in with my stuff to my assigned bunk.

Immediately, I was approached by several people.

"You're Italian, right?" an inmate named Ralph asked me.

"Yeah," I said.

"Well, you don't have anything to worry about. We got your back."

Up to that point, I didn't know I'd had anything to worry about. So now I was thinking, what exactly do I have to worry about?

"You're a good guy," he went on. "You got screwed. You're not a rat. You don't have to worry."

He then presented me with my first big decision at Loretto: who would I sit with for meals? My choices were: I could sit with him at the Italian table, I could sit at the white boys' table, or I could sit at the New York table. I don't know why the New York table was a choice, but it was.

I said, "If you have my back, I want to sit with you at the Italian table." This first decision positioned me in so many ways, including with regard to who would be my friends.

Now that I had arrived, I desperately wanted to call my wife to let her know I was ok, but it would take another twenty-four hours to get phone access. It was a violation for another prisoner to let me use his phone minutes, and they could track the call. Violating this rule could cause me to lose my phone rights, which I didn't want to do on the first day. But more than that, I'd just spent almost a year in the hole "for my protection," and I did not want to get sent back for a violation.

Needless to say, I did not call my wife. I just waited. I started to meet other prisoners and get a sense of how things worked. At my first real meal in the cafeteria, I sat at the Italian table with some real characters. Some of them were *real* criminals and some of them just had the bad luck to end up in the prosecutors' crosshairs. But they were all nice people. And they were compassionate. A few of them were older than I was. They had served in medium- or high-security prisons but over time, as they got older, they were moved to lower-security facilities. They were the real veterans, guys with twenty-five-year sentences. Seeing them still in prison made it clear that the system really does not have an offramp. They told me stories about real horror—medium-security prisons, where the gangs were. I realized that even if I wasn't in a camp, I was in a low-security facility, and it was significantly better than a medium-security facility.

Despite the reputation of prison in general, I never felt myself to be in any danger (except briefly when I was told not to worry). I had spent the previous ten months in solitary, so I wasn't thinking about danger. Loretto was more open, and I was out among the other prisoners. It was really the first time I had to think about personal safety. I was glad to be with the Italians.

I didn't get the sense that I had to do anything to keep the protection. I ended up counseling some people, but nothing was ever asked of me besides being a friend. It made me realize that solitary confinement "for my protection" was a fiction. Weissman did it to break me, or make my life miserable for resisting his demands. There was nothing inhumane he would not do to achieve his warped objectives.

I discovered that Loretto was also where the BOP placed a large number of convicted pedophiles. They were the lowest rung on the prison ladder. It took me some time to learn the protocols, but one of the rules was that you couldn't associate with the pedophiles. If you talked to them, it could get you in trouble. When I first arrived, I was taking one of my first walks in a year on the track. While enjoying the exhilaration of this new freedom to walk and interact with others, I was approached by one of the prisoners who came up and introduced himself. We talked as we walked. At that time, I had no way of knowing what a prisoner was in for, and pedophiles did not introduce themselves as such. Within minutes of getting off of the track, an inmate came up to me and said, "You can't talk to that person." When I asked why, I was informed that he was a pedophile and I cannot associate with them without risking being ostracized by the broader inmate community. Suddenly, I understood how I might get into trouble, but I had no idea how to tell the players without a score card. That would come later.

The other group that was forbidden to interact with were those who had cut cooperation deals with the prosecutors—people who did plea agreements, had been cooperating witnesses, and put other defendants in prison. *The rats.* Even though I had signed a plea agreement, mine was not one where I had agreed to cooperate. (This was well-known in the prison, although a little later, this agreement was used by a thug who was jealous of my friendships to try to isolate me.) Informed of this prohibition, I wondered how Rick Gates would survive if he was given jail time by Judge Jackson. I laughingly dismissed this thought almost immediately. There was no way Jackson and Weissman would sentence Gates to prison time. Too bad, I thought. He deserved to be treated with disdain. Then maybe he could understand what a pathetic person he had become.

When a new prisoner would come in, a sort of committee of inmates would research the inmate and, very quickly, the other prisoners would know if they were pedophiles or rats.

I didn't like the system. It bothered me that I couldn't form my own opinion of a person and that I had to treat them one way or another. But at the same time, especially in the first week or two, I had to build some credibility. I didn't want to create problems for myself by associating with people I shouldn't be associating with.

I wasn't afraid for my life. I was afraid of screwing up this code that I was expected to know and follow. It got to a point where I sat down with my friend Ralph and asked him to explain all the dos and don'ts. "You know," I said. "My inclination is to deal with each person as a human."

He laughed and said, "No, you can't do that." Over time, he educated me.

Billie J. was a hypocrite who managed the commissary and used his role there to get people hard to find commissary goods—for a price, of course. He liked to act like he was a big-shot, but really, he was just an insecure tough-guy who bullied anyone he could on the prison "codes," except when it did not suit his interests. Early on, I saw his true character. He would always be the first one to attack someone for talking to a rat or pedophile but would completely ignore the code if he needed something from one of them.

I refused to respect him which pissed him off. In retaliation, he accused me of being a rat, citing the fact that I had done a plea agreement. He knew the truth, but he wanted me to be ostracized. In order to "cleanse" myself of this accusation, I had to have my attorney send me my sentencing transcripts—"my papers." The prison hierarchy could read the "papers" and proclaim judgment.

Two of the credible assessors of the "papers" were my mentor, Ralph, and a prisoner named Vegas. Vegas was totally "tatted up"—a muscle-bound specimen of a man. He was also a gentle giant who helped me navigate prison from the first day I arrived. He became a very good friend.

They both knew the accusation was just jealousy on Billie's part, but they advised me to submit my papers. Once I got them, I asked Vegas and Ralph to read them. Of course, they immediately proclaimed me innocent of the Billie J. attack. I approached Billie with the result to which he harrumphed and walked off. We never spoke again. We would be in the same room and have conversations with the others, and just ignore each other. I thought it was very immature, but then again, this was prison.

I also knew I was still in the Special Counsel's crosshairs. I knew Weissman had engineered the indictments in New York. I don't think the New York DA would have brought them on his own because he understood how double jeopardy worked in New York and he knew the charges should never result in a conviction, or even a trial. But the Weissman approach is to throw everything at someone, scare them, and get them to cut a deal to avoid the worse possibilities. Innocence and facts be damned.

Plus at this time, Gates was still being used to target others. My biggest concern was not my innocence. It was that I didn't know what I didn't know. As far as I was concerned, more indictments were possible, even if they were made up. I no longer had any confidence in the justice system—which had proven neither just nor particularly systematic. It was illogical, easily abused, and totally unmanageable. I used to think that since I was innocent, I wouldn't get indicted, and I certainly wouldn't go to prison. But there I was: indicted, convicted, and locked up. So in the back of my mind, I was always waiting for another shoe to drop. And Weissman was always looking for allies to drop the shoes on me.

On my third or fourth day at Loretto, a lieutenant called me into his office, which scared the hell out of me. It's never a good thing to be called into a warden's or Lieutenant's office. It's done over the intercom: "Prisoner Manafort report to the lieutenant's office." No prisoner wants to be called this way and since it is on the intercom, the whole prison population is aware that something is up.

I was shaking in my pants. I got there and the lieutenant said, "Look, I'm going to tell you this as a courtesy. All of your messages, emails, letters coming in and going out, all of your phone calls—it's all going to be monitored." According to the prison rules, I had three hundred phone minutes a month and access to an email system with pre-approved recipients. "There's nothing we're not going to read. You're a very high-level inmate. We have to treat you differently. We've been given instructions by the warden."

The only thing that wouldn't be monitored were calls to my lawyers, as long as I scheduled the calls and used a separate phone. To do that I had to go to a kind of account executive to get approval and scheduling taken care of. The problem was that he was about to retire, so for most of my time at Loretto he was difficult to contact. He was very nice and set things up when I could reach him. But there were time-sensitive matters that I would have to speak to my attorneys about and Mr. Hite could take a week to set up a call.

In order to get around the scheduling complications, I organized a pre-approved time to talk to my attorneys on Tuesdays at 10:00 a.m. I would be brought to a private room with a landline and, technically, I could use the phone as long as I needed. But they didn't like you using it for very long. Because we were in Trump country, I had the benefit of preferential treatment, depending on who was at the desk, but still I was conscious not to abuse this privilege.

In the beginning, I had a lot of calls to make because of the New York case. I tried not to use my three hundred personal minutes to speak with my attorneys. Instead I husbanded them to use for my family. I had my wife explain to my friends that I couldn't speak with them very often because of this limitation. Thankfully, being true friends, they understood. The result was that I had limited access to my friends for almost two years, and I missed them.

With the three hundred minutes, I could call anyone that was on a pre-approved list, and we could talk for up to ten minutes before the call would cut off. When it cut off, you'd have to wait half an hour before making another call.

I tried to organize the calls, but there was always something going on. My daughter in California was going through a stressful time because she was being blacklisted by Hollywood for being my daughter. Hollywood, of all places, should understand how wrong blacklisting is, yet they tormented her even though they knew that she was not a Trump supporter. I was on the phone with her often.

There were emergencies with the lawyers where I would have to talk to them on a monitored call because I'd have to deal with something quickly. The three hundred minutes disappeared fast. Often, I would get to the end of the month with a minute left. My wife and I would try to talk for four or five minutes every day, usually around dinner time, to check in, say I love you and goodnight. But the limits were difficult. The policy of the BOP is to encourage contact and communication with loved ones and family members, as part of the rehabilitation process, but the call limits make it very difficult. And on top of that, I was only allowed six visits per month and only on Friday, Saturday, and Sunday.

My wife and I worked out a plan where she would come up on Thursday nights and stay in a motel near the prison. There was a Starbucks and an Applebee's nearby, so she could eat dinner Thursday and have her coffee in the morning. She would visit for four or five hours on Friday, from eight in the morning until about one in the afternoon and then drive home. I didn't want her driving the four hours at night, especially in the winter when it gets dark early.

We would sit knee-to-knee. I wasn't allowed to hug her, but occasionally, when some of the nicer guards were on duty, they let me. I'd whisper things I didn't want heard about the case, or the property, or some family issue. Or I would ask her to tell Downing what I meant when I said something on the phone earlier. Sometimes it was very crowded, so the people around us could hear what we were saying. There was no real privacy, but it was the only privacy we had.

In the beginning, my daughter Andrea and my grandson visited, too. I had spent a lot of time with my grandson before prison, especially when I was on home confinement. Unfortunately, he got carsick on even short rides, never mind the four hours it took to get to Loretto. I made a decision and told Andrea that I didn't want him visiting anymore. It was heartbreaking. As important as it was for me to see my daughter and grandson, I couldn't bear him suffering the ride.

I was also getting mail from all over the country—family, friends, total strangers. A lot of pastors reached out to tell me they were praying for me. Some became regular correspondents. I was probably getting thirty or forty letters a week from strangers in support of me. It was gratifying. It helped me believe that it wasn't just me who thought I was being persecuted.

I was conscious of not putting much into the mail system, since it was all being monitored, so I didn't respond to much of it. But occasionally I would send a note back.

In Alexandria, I had had access to a library, but there were not many of my kind of books—self-help books, trashy novels, some John Grisham. I preferred to read history. But books could not be brought for prisoners from the outside. They could only be donated and put in the library system.

Loretto had a much larger library, plus you could have books sent directly from the publisher's website or from Amazon. What I could not do was have my wife send me books. This was prohibited on the theory that she could put something in the book. But as long as it came from a bookstore and it was sent directly to me, I could receive it. Over time, I became a big contributor to the library at Loretto, too.

At some point—pending the New York case and a hopeful pardon—I realized that Loretto was going to be my home for the foreseeable future. I understood that I had a choice. I could rage and fight and be miserable over every injustice that brought me there and every indignity I suffered inside. Or I could try to put the bitterness aside and find a way to be comfortable, recognizing the lessons on suffering from St. Paul (while pressing continuously for a way out). I went with the latter. It was a difficult journey, but it was necessary for my mind and body.

This decision is why the system failed to break me, no matter how hard it tried.

CHAPTER 19

New York

Even as I was making progress in settling into life at Loretto, New York was still hanging over my head in a big way. My lawyers believed that I should not have any vulnerability because of the constitutional right against double jeopardy. The competing principle was what is called the dual sovereignty doctrine. This doctrine allows both federal and state prosecution of the same crime as the governments are "separate sovereigns and each has the right to prosecute someone who has violated their laws."

There was a case going on right around this time, *Gamble v. The United States*, in which this exact issue was being argued. In November 2015, a handgun was found in Terance Martez Gamble's car when he was pulled over for a damaged headlight. Because he was a felon, the handgun was illegal under both Alabama state and federal laws. He was convicted in Alabama and given a one-year sentence, but then was also prosecuted under federal law after the district court concluded that double jeopardy didn't apply in this case. He appealed to the Eleventh Circuit Court of Appeals, but they affirmed the district court's ruling.

The Supreme Court agreed to hear the case in 2018, and I was very nervous about the outcome. I was worried because I saw myself in a similar light to what happened to Gamble in Alabama. My lawyers, however, told me not to worry about it. No Supreme Court ruling on this case would affect me because the statute in New York took me out of harm's way. But, I rationalized that Gamble was a reason why the DA took the risk of working with Weissman. He could point to these benchmarks in the system to show he wasn't being political.

But it was political. And it was personal. The goal was to make my life more miserable than it already was. Bringing this case certainly raised my stress level.

Since the case was in New York, it meant that I would need to have my custody transferred from the federal authorities to the state authorities to be formally arraigned in New York. This set off alarm bells for me. I knew that if New York State took custody, I would be sent to Rikers until my trial was over, which could be more than a year. This was not somewhere I wanted to be for one minute, never mind a year or more.

This was a time for my attorneys. I pressed them hard to appeal to the DOJ not to release me into State custody. The rules allowed the Feds to keep control over me even though I was dealing with a state court. My warden, however, approved my transfer the day after she received the request from the State of New York. Fortunately, I had the right to appeal her decision and petition to remain in federal custody. This is precisely what I did.

The Department of Justice overruled the warden, which was a very unusual thing to happen within the Bureau of Prisons system. I was kept in the control of the US Marshals. Instead of being sent to Rikers, I was sent to the Metropolitan Correctional Center in the Battery Park neighborhood of Lower Manhattan. Even though I had heard that the MCC was a filthy, unruly jail—the final step for prisoners transitioning from multiyear sentences to probation—this was a major victory and I cherished it.

I ended up getting transported to the MCC on June 17, 2019. Happy as I was to be there, it was a total dump.

I thought I would go into general population, but right away I was sent upstairs to solitary confinement. There were four cells in this wing, a "gym" that was just a small room with a bike that didn't work and a TV. You couldn't see out of the windows, but you could at least see the light coming in through the frosted glass. It was a nice feature because my cell had no windows at all. It was a concrete box with a concrete slab for a bed, a one-inch-thick mattress, and a thin, threadbare blanket. It offered very little protection from the cold of the concrete. The shower only had cold water. In early April, when I was there, it was freezing. There was no heat.

For all I knew I was going to be staying at the MCC not just through my arraignment, but through my trial, the date of which was not even set. It could be a year away. It was a horribly depressing thought.

The phone policy at the MCC was such that if a guard wanted to, they could get a landline with a long cord and put the receiver through the slot. The slot was just large enough for a tray of food. But there was no contact between guards and prisoners. It was a very dark, very lonely, very cold place.

But because my arraignment date was set, I had a timeframe to work with. My lawyers knew that if they didn't hear from me, it meant I was en route to New York. At this point I was working with Todd Blanche of Cadwalader, Taft, and Wickersham. Todd, who has a great bedside manner, knew exactly how to calm me down. Plus, he is an excellent lawyer, always does his homework, and knows the answer to every question. But he didn't know I was going to be put in solitary. It was a worst-case scenario.

The guards were supposed to come through every thirty minutes, lift the hatch, and look into my cell to make sure I was fine. They never did. I would have to yell to get their attention, but I didn't want to be a jerk. I didn't know how long I was going to be there. At the same time, my anxiety level was such that I needed to reach out to my lawyers. I would yell and yell, but never got the guard's attention even though he was no more than ten feet from my cell. When he did come to check on me after a couple of hours, I told him I needed to call my lawyer. He said he would let me know. It was not very promising.

Finally, I was able to reach out and I got in contact with Todd, who said he was already dealing with somebody he had worked with in the US attorney's office. He told me I should not be in solitary confinement for more than two or three days. He also said he'd look into getting me into General Population (GP), but that it might take a while. I had nothing in the cell. No notebooks, no papers, no tablet. I just sat meditating. And this was before I was even good at it. It was a very difficult time.

Typical with my luck, I arrived on a Thursday. If I had arrived on a Monday, it might really have been two or three days. Todd came to visit over the weekend, but that only got me out of solitary for a few minutes. He gave up his Saturday for me and I will forever be grateful to him for this simple kindness that to me was so liberating for my soul. This was the kind of person Todd was. An incredible lawyer, but an even more incredible human being.

Across from the deputy's desk were four glass compartments for an inmate to meet with their attorney. Each compartment had a small table and three or four metal chairs. There was no privacy. You could see the other inmates meeting with their lawyers. During the few visits I had from Todd over that weekend, meeting with his attorneys in the next room was the notorious drug lord El Chapo. He seemed to know who I was, too, which surprised me. We nodded the prisoner nod to each other on occasion and I would wonder, "What does he think of me? I bet he is confused as to why I am up here?"

Even more humorous in a macabre sense: the other inmate meeting in the glass room on the other side of me was Jeffrey Epstein. Yep, El Chapo to my right, and Jeffrey Epstein to my left. Yeah, I felt real safe!

On Tuesday, I was finally sent down to GP where I was put in a cell with an inmate, a guy at the tail end of his sentence. He was a weird person, a scary person. I spent one day with him before I was able to get the guards to move me to another cell. He had sold ads for *Hustler* magazine. I was told that he was supposedly in prison for a sex crime, but I never knew what the crime was. Oddly enough, when he got out of prison, a couple of months after I left New York, he wrote several articles about our time together, making up total stories. He acted as if we had spent time together. In fact, after one night I knew I needed to get away from him. I'd made a point of being nice to him, but he never forgave me for moving out from his cell after only one night. When he wrote the articles, he created a fiction that got him published. There were no truths in them, but it got him his fifteen minutes of fame.

After my first day in GP, I got transferred over to a new cell with a new cellmate, Dan L. Dan had a couple of months left on his sentence for a white-collar crime. He had actually been roommates with one of the guys that I worked with at Loretto. He had seen my situation and, by the luck of the draw, became my new cellmate, along with two other prisoners across the hall—Ron and G. Again, I lucked out. These three prisoners were running the MCC. Dan ran the warehouse and Ron and G. ran the kitchen.

This is what happens in prisons—the prison deputies do not run the prisons, the inmates run them. And for the most part, the guards don't care because they are lazy. The prisoners create the systems to make it work. They manage it. And in the course of managing it, they get certain perks. If you're running the warehouse, you have access to commissary goods that you could not get on your own. If you're running the kitchen, you have access to food that is not part of the menu for prisoners but could be part of the kitchen for the guards. Real food like vegetables and fruit, and sometimes an ice cream sandwich!

The four of us became a clique and they took care of me, which gave me comfort. They had my back. Not in a physical sense, but if I had questions, they knew the rules and regs. I didn't have to eat the garbage that was normally served to prisoners. I could have vegetables—not the string beans that have been cooking for two days—but real vegetables. I managed to eat pretty healthy during the short time I was there.

But the facility was filthy. Each cell in general population had a small window and you would look outside waiting for lockout to be done. Staring out the panel, you would see rats running across the corridor searching for food hidden in the cells. My cellmate knew that if you used aluminum foil to block up the holes, you could keep your cell secure. And good fortune for us, Dan had access to aluminum foil because he ran the warehouse. These were the little things that sound silly, but they were meaningful in this decrepit environment.

Besides being filthy, the prison was very cold. The concrete walls held the cold. It was not a very healthy situation. In order to cope with this mess, I did what I had done in the previous three prisons I had been in. I created a schedule and lived by it religiously. In a typical day there, I would have breakfast then I would go to the library, but you could only go during designated times. I'd come back and read the bible, have my lunch, usually make a phone call or two, go back to the library, exercise while everyone else was eating dinner. Usually my cellmates would be back from work, and we'd have our own dinner. After, we would socialize for a bit and then I'd call Kathy before lockdown, say goodnight, and go to bed. It was not exciting, but it got me through the day.

The way general population was set up at the MCC was there was a general area that everyone had access to. Then there were wings off of a hub, like spokes, two floors on each spoke. This is where the cells were located. In the hub were a few phones, two TVs (one for the Blacks and one for the rest), an exercise room with a treadmill and pullup bar, some chairs—but never enough. It was a general social area.

Part of my daily routine was to sit before lunch and read the Bible or whatever I was reading at the time. Because we were on lockdown, anyone wanting to exercise had to use the corridors because you couldn't do it in general population.

During my MCC time the only episode that came close to an altercation occurred. While there was a small room with two bikes and one treadmill, most people used their own homemade weights of books tied to bars and would exercise in the hallways outside of their cells.

There was a group, one of whom was someone I had befriended from another corridor, who started working out in my corridor. Normally they would exercise before I came back from the library, but they changed the time for some reason. They started working out at the same time I was at my table. I tolerated it for a day since I didn't expect it would be a pattern. On the second day, I tried to encourage them to come at a different time. I got some happy talk in response. By the third day, I told them I didn't want them coming anymore. It was disruptive. I said, "Here's my schedule. Come when I'm not here. This is my time. This is my corridor. You can use your own corridor and work out if this is when you want to exercise." One of the guys who I didn't know and was sort of thuggish came over to me. I stood up. I wasn't planning on throwing any punches, but I wasn't going to just sit there, either. We started jawing at each other.

The guy I knew put the exercise bar down and said to the other guys, "This is a good guy, leave him alone." He sort of worked out a deal. I said, "You don't have to change today because you're already here, but I would appreciate it if you didn't come at this time." And that was it. It was the only time I really started something that I didn't want to start. The last thing I wanted was to end up in the hole again. I didn't need that reputation.

I had been at the MCC a little over a week when I had to go to court to be arraigned, which was a traumatic experience. Up until that point, there were no pictures of me in a jumpsuit because the only time I wore a jumpsuit was in court. There are no cameras in court, only sketch artists. I liked it this way. I knew a picture of me in a jumpsuit would only make me look more guilty to the MSM. When I was transferred to New York, I was convinced that the DA would find a way to get a picture of me in my prison garb.

In preparation, I asked Todd to work it out so that there would be a path from the van to the holding room to the court that wasn't public.

He was able to arrange it in such a way that I would go from the holding cell to the courtroom using only back corridors. As a courtesy, the marshals let me use their office as a holding cell. They even took my handcuffs off.

When it was time to be arraigned, we went out a back stairway, through a bunch of back corridors, and then into a vestibule that went into another corridor that led to the courtroom. As soon as I turned the corner to walk to the courtroom my heart sank. It was like a parade or a Hollywood premiere. There were crowds on both sides. It was three- and four-people-deep. The media had all been tipped off, not by my escorts. They were as surprised as me. I had no doubt whose doing this was.

I had to walk, handcuffed, while flashes were going on all around me. People were calling out questions. I kept my eyes straight ahead, my face expressionless. The marshals were on either side of me. They had promised to protect me, and did a decent job, but they backed off in the corridor so that there was an unfettered view of me. Everyone could take pictures. The DA-orchestrated "perp walk" managed to catch me in kind of a Lee Harvey Oswald moment, surrounded by deputies, in cuffs, my hair messed up. The pictures immediately went worldwide. To this day, they are still the only photos used to show me in prison attire.

I was led into the courtroom and seated at my table. The judge came out, the charges were read, I said I was not guilty, the lawyers talked about schedules, and then the judge adjourned the hearing. It took all of about ten minutes. I had traveled six hours from Pennsylvania to New York in a cramped van, spent several days in solitary and then in a filthy prison, for a ten-minute arraignment.

I was angry about the waste of time and the unnecessary stress. But now that it was over, I didn't need to be in New York anymore. However, I couldn't get confirmation that I would be sent back to Loretto. There was a chance I would be sent to a different federal prison. I did not want to be sent to a new facility unless it was a camp. I wanted to go back to Loretto for one simple reason: it was the devil I knew. I had friends there. I knew the system. But for about two weeks after the arraignment, I had no idea what was going on. I was still at the MCC, just waiting.

I ended up staying at the MCC for more than thirty days. On July 25, at four in the morning, a nasty guard came into my cell screaming at me. "Get up! Get packed! You are leaving now."

I was groggy, but I said, "Okay, Okay," and within two minutes I was packing a duffel bag with everything I wanted to take with me.

She came back and said, "What's taking so long?" She started grabbing things and throwing them in the bag.

I said, "Look, I don't even want some of this stuff, just let me do this and I can be done a lot faster." But she just ignored me and kept throwing stuff in the bag, which I had to then take out.

We then went down to the disbursement center, where they were supposed to document what was in the bag. That way when you get to wherever you're going, they document what is coming in and the inventories should match. But this guard didn't document anything.

When I asked, "Don't you need to document this stuff?" she growled, "No, you're fine. It's all junk."

Of course, when I did get back to Loretto, I was missing everything that was of any value. She'd stolen a pair of Timberland boots. They weren't worth much, but they were the boots I wore. A thirty-dollar Casio watch. My $20 transistor radio was missing. A light I used to read at night was missing. It was not random. The junk was still there. But the things I valued were gone—stolen by a guard.

I was worried that the ride back to Loretto was going to be as bad as the ride coming to New York, which had been miserable. But it was only me in the car. Because the US Marshals were controlling the transportation, someone in DOJ had arranged for me to have a single car on the way back. What a luxury!

But I had the mindset that I would have to go back to New York in a month or two when the motions we were filing to have the case dismissed were going to be heard. We planned to move to dismiss claiming double jeopardy protection. The DA would then move to continue the case. My hope was that the only future action I would have to travel to New York for was the court hearing when the judge would accept our motion and dismiss the case.

As the day got closer, I grew very anxious. My blood pressure was considerably higher and a fellow inmate who was a cardiologist advised me on what to do. I hoped that if I was still in this condition, the judge would allow me to remain in Loretto and avoid being transported to New York.

Back at Loretto, I created a scare when my blood pressure legitimately flared out of control. My anxiety kept it out of control as the date of the hearing approached.

My hope to remain in Loretto was dashed when the judge told Todd that he wanted me there in person. I took this as a bad sign. I could not imagine he would make me travel this distance again just to dismiss the case. My anxiety grew worse, as did my blood pressure.

My cardiologist advised me on what my real health issue was. He explained that my blood pressure was reacting to my stress and that I needed to control my stress if I wished to control my blood pressure. Honestly, while worried about my health, I liked the fact that I was having health issues which could preclude my having to travel to New York for the court hearing.

There was a doctor for the prison, but most of the interaction for the inmates is at the Patient Assistant or PA level. Some of the PAs were very good. Some of them are terrible. My PA, Ms. Golden, was excellent. Plus, she liked me. We never talked about it, but she understood why I was there, and she was empathetic. I was always very frank with my doctors but was not a hypochondriac. If something was concerning me, I would let her know. Usually, she took care of it.

When my blood pressure got out of control, she became concerned. And then when I was sort of describing my physical condition driven by the stress and high blood pressure, she brought me to the prison emergency room, which was just a different room on the medical wing. Finally, my blood pressure was at the point where they decided that they couldn't risk something happening to me.

This was the one thing I always had going for me: the warden did not want anything to happen to me on her watch. I was never a problem for her. So, she appreciated that she didn't have to deal with issues that might make her job harder. When I had this health issue, she recommended I be sent to the hospital for a more thorough medical exam and proper medical procedures. The prison doctor, prepped by Ms. Golden, approved it.

I didn't know where I was going, but they put me on a stretcher and into an ambulance. My hands and legs were cuffed, and I was tied down to the stretcher. The guard, sitting over me, holding a gun, looked down at me and said in a menacing voice, "If you try to run, we'll shoot you." At first, given my bound and shackled condition, I thought it was a joke. But then I realized that he was deadly serious. I told him to relax. "Even Houdini would have trouble escaping from this situation," I said. He scowled.

I was taken to Altoona Hospital, which is a part of the University of Pennsylvania medical system—a very good hospital. For the first time, really, since June 2018, I was lying on a real mattress and on a real pillow. I had a real blanket on me. There was no way I was leaving after 24 hours. I was gonna milk this thing for as long as I could.

They were concerned enough on the first day that they had me stay overnight. And that was a breakthrough moment. They wanted to do an MRI. They had to do an EKG. They looked at my lungs. They looked at my brain. Over the next forty hours, I basically got my annual physical. I was feeling really good about my health based on the reports. The only thing that wasn't good was my blood pressure, and the reason it wasn't good was that my medications were in conflict. My cardiologist inmate was confident of this, but neither the prison doctors nor the early doctors at the hospital had reached this judgment. *I, however, luxuriated in their confusion.*

My interest in avoiding being sent to New York over the weekend for the hearing seemed to be coming serendipitously true. However, I did have a problem. I had been at the hospital for several days. During that time I couldn't call anyone, including my wife or attorney. When the warden shipped me to the hospital, it was late evening. I assumed, at the time, that I would be able to call my wife from the hospital, but the BOP would not allow it. The BOP policy is to *not* confirm anything about inmates when they are in public facilities.

During my stay, my room looked like a fortress. I had two guards outside of my room, and two guards in my room. The newspapers were writing that I had experienced a heart attack and was in the Altoona hospital. So it wasn't as if I was being kept there in secret. All I wanted to do was call my wife and let her know that I was okay, that I didn't have a heart attack, that she didn't need to worry. But they wouldn't let me do that. On the sixth day, they finally let me call her. Of course, I was calling from an unknown number. During my trial, my wife had adopted the practice of not answering unknown numbers. So, she didn't answer the phone when I called her from the hospital. I was frustrated but in my mind's eye, I saw Kathy staring at her ringing mobile phone and refusing to answer it. If nothing else, when she was resolved on a course of action, she would not deviate. I knew she would not answer.

But the good news was that when I hit the weekend, I knew I wasn't going to New York! The hearing was set for Tuesday, and I knew they would not move me that close to the date in the condition I was in. I sighed with relief and expected to be sent back to prison on Monday. In fact, the paperwork ended up taking another day. So it was Tuesday morning, the day of my court hearing, when I was finally discharged. I had been in the hospital for eight glorious days. Pillows, soft mattresses, healthy food, and all the President's Cup golf I wanted to watch, something the inmates never let me watch back at Loretto.

When I arrived back at Loretto, I was greeted with applause from the prisoners in the yard. During my stay at Loretto, I was always well-treated by the inmates, but I had never gotten applause. I didn't know what it was about. I thought maybe they had heard that I was healthy, but I really was confused.

When I got into the prison, they took me directly to my PA.

"Congratulations," she said.

"For what?" I asked her.

"You won your court case."

The hearing had happened while I was en route from the hospital to Loretto. The judge had released his opinion and it was the top news story in the country that morning. He had ruled in favor of my motion and thrown the case out. I always felt it would come down to the judge. Would we get a fair judge or a political hack? We ended up with Justice Wiley of the New York County Supreme Court. He was a Democratic appointee, but a real judge. He was principled.

He wrote a very strong opinion concluding that, "given the rather unique set of facts pertaining to defendant's previous prosecution in federal court, and given New York's law on this subject, defendant's motion to dismiss the indictment as barred by state double jeopardy law must be granted." He also admonished the prosecutors for bringing a case that wasted the time of the court on something that was clearly inappropriate.

The DA would appeal anyway, first to an appeals court and then to the State's highest court. At each level my position was unanimously endorsed. The Circuit Court had a three-judge panel. They totally adopted the opinion of Judge Wiley. The highest court took several months but finally issued a one-sentence opinion saying certiorari (where a court agrees to hear an appeal) was denied. The DA's case was so lacking in merit that the court of final jurisdiction wasn't going to waste its time. They refused to hear any more on the matter.

Ultimately, I would end up with three wins in New York, each more powerful than the last. But it was never about winning for the DA and Weissman. It was only about using the justice system to make my life miserable.

Now that there was no detainer, I thought I would automatically qualify for a camp. Of course, nothing in the BOP happens automatically. But when I could finally contact my lawyers, the question was: how quickly can I get into a camp? All of the good news notwithstanding, I still had a long prison sentence ahead of me. I wanted it to be as comfortable as possible and as easy as allowed under the law.

In my head, it was as easy as walking through the gate into a different part of Loretto. But nothing in the BOP is that easy. When I finally heard from my case manager, she told me what she knew all along but never bothered to tell me: no one gets moved anywhere in the BOP system in their first year. I was stuck in Loretto for the time being.

Nevertheless, the difference between prison life after my federal the convictions and after the New York case was thrown out was really night and day. It was over. Before the New York decision, as I was falling asleep, my mind was always working on preparing for the next day, working out the strategy, the documents, the key points for Downing or Blanche. Double jeopardy and dual sovereignty. Weissman and the New York DA. Jackson and Ellis. It was a constant, never-ending train of thoughts running through my head.

Now that New York was over, when I went to sleep, I slept. It was a relief. I was, to some extent, used to prison life. The pressure of every day was gone. Now I was dealing with the lack of freedom and how to fill my days. I had been an avid reader before prison, but I became prolific. I wanted to educate myself. I learned about meditation. My goal became to learn to live with what I had for the time being. Loretto was a low facility, I would make it work for me.

When I got back from the Altoona hospital, they had me in an upper bunk (even though I had a doctor's certificate saying I should be in a lower bunk). I also had a new set of roommates. There was one sketchy roommate, a young prisoner from West Virginia who stole from me even though I constantly was gifting him food and clothes. Otherwise, my new roommates were wonderful people.

There are people in prison who deserve to be in prison. They committed crimes and they're not going to change, and if they get out, they would probably end up back in prison at some point. And then there are people who, for any number of reasons, made a mistake. But once they get out, they are committed to not being sent back.

The BOP does not do a good job of helping people prepare to reenter society. They have all the laws, policies, and regulations that say the right things, but the reality doesn't come close to what's in the book. Most prisoners are not ready when they leave. They get pushed back out onto the streets and fall back into their old ways. It's a sad reality—one of the saddest—of the mismanagement of the prison system.

In spite of everything, I was determined to find a kind of peace there. To that end, I developed a schedule: I would wake up at six, make instant coffee, and sit in the TV room to watch Fox and Friends while no else was awake. I would read from nine to eleven. At noon, I would work out for an hour and listen to Rush Limbaugh. At some point, I would go to the library to read, write, or teach. I would meditate or pray for an hour before dinner, call Kathy around six in the evening, watch TV—Carlson, Hannity, Ingraham—and then call Kathy again to say goodnight.

Every day at four in the afternoon there were mandatory room checks. But the guards also did unaccounted checks. This was an enforcement mechanism. They were looking for drugs and phones, but they would take homemade pillows, extra blankets, and food items when there was no contraband to seize.

Many of my follow inmates were very smart people who had the skills to manage business networks. They often came from broken homes and often had no father figure or role model. Many had admitted to committing crimes, repented, and were preparing to re-enter society and start over. The BOP, of course, did little to assist with this transition. So it was up to other inmates to help.

I came to be aquatinted with a number of them. There was Bobby K., the Albanian—a strong conservative who befriended me and would spend time helping me understand the system. Another friend was Billy A., an older man, convicted on burglary charges. He was bright and would offer me guidance as well as cook me prison pasta and make homemade ice cream (in a garbage can) on Saturdays. He always had my back.

Charles H. was in prison for mortgage fraud. His prosecutor manip-ulated his sentencing, and he was unfairly given a very long sentence. I put him in touch with Ms. Hashimoto at Georgetown Law's Public

Defenders program. They won his case and got him home years ahead of his unfair sentence.

Al R. was in prison for killing a small-time mobster who was threatening to kill Al and his mother. The prosecutor refused to consider any of the extenuating circumstances. He was given a ridiculous thirty-year sentence.

John G. was one of the leaders of the Italian community. He befriended me and I will always be appreciative.

John T. was one of my roommates. He was a sweet tough guy who doted over his young daughter. We would spend many nights talking about family. He should be sent home, but the BOP won't do it.

And there was Pino, who owns a small Italian restaurant where Biden frequents in Delaware. I am certain he is serving Uncle Joe on weekends, although I am also certain the president thinks he is dining there for the first time, each time.

In each of the cells I was in, there was always a cook. Prison cooks will use a garbage can with hot water, a wire that's been stolen from something, or a hot plate, and they'll make prison pizza with a tortilla, or tamales, burritos, cheesecake, and so on. They scavenge for food in the system, cook it, and then sell it. It's one of the ways they make money. Fortunately for me, I usually had a cook in my cell, so I usually had access to decent food. Not great food, but decent.

I didn't want to have a menial job at Loretto, because I was busy reading and writing. So I got assigned to a workshop. The guy who ran the prison yard equipment was a friend of mine. He assigned me to work in the warehouse. But I did not have to show up. Instead, someone would sign me in and out each day. I would give him my weekly three-dollar check. Somehow, I found a way to live without my weekly paycheck!

What I was trying to do was get assigned to the computer library. The computer library was the only place where there were computers. It was one of the few educational programs in prison and the prisoners running it were good people.

I knew the guy who ran the library—the so-called Mayor of Loretto, Mike S. He was a banker who got caught doing some things to help his clients, not himself, during the recession of 2009. Technically, he violated the law, but in his heart, he was trying to help customers from being defaulted. For whatever reason, the local prosecutor threw the book at him. He was very articulate, very compassionate. A good person.

Through him, I got access to computers. The computers could not access the internet, but I could type. It was where I started to organize my notes for this book.

Ed D., who I also worked with in the library, was one of the most educated people I have ever met anywhere. He knew every obscure person in history or sports and was an expert on cryptocurrency. The man's range was incredible. He helped change my view of life by turning me on to the works of Dr. Joe Dispenza and Gregg Braden.

There was also a doctor I would turn to for prison health check-ups, Atif M., and Barry, a pharmacist who got caught in the opioid crisis and was made the scapegoat for the entire industry.

These men all had stories. Most had long ago repented. They still had much to contribute to society and had learned their lessons. But, again, the BOP has no off-ramp for these types of prisoners. They are still wasting away in prison instead of making society a better place.

The guard who managed the library was a guy named Ron Gresko—a really nice human being and a very good person. He was approaching his twentieth year as a guard and was going to retire. He empathized with the plight of the prisoners who came from broken homes, usually without a father figure. To Ron, there was no way these men knew how to be a "dad." So he created a Parenting 101 course. It was the most valuable course that Loretto offered, and the only real course that helped the prisoners prepare for reentry into society. Ron believed that it was a big problem that many inmates had no role models. They didn't know how to be fathers. Gresko created a ten-week course and he asked me to help, which I did. I consider myself an educated, hands-on parent who was actively involved in my kids' upbringing. The course was so well-organized that even I learned a lot.

I also helped with a few education classes at Loretto and in the end, I was able to use the classroom for eight to ten hours a day. It was a place where I could read or just have normal conversations as I would typically have on the outside. On Sunday mornings, we could have egg and cheese sandwiches and talk sports and politics like normal people.

The access I had to the computer classroom got me through the day. I felt the loss of my freedom less acutely in there.

When *American Greed* ran its program on me, they talked about the $90 million in the bank accounts, the oriental carpets, and the expensive clothes. Contrary to what I expected, the show created a whole other layer of friends and fans. I became a kind of hero in prison, a role model for a lot of the younger guys. They all wanted to know how to be successful. I ended up becoming something of a business tutor. Some of the guys wanted to know how to run a legitimate business. It didn't take long for me to realize that these guys had enormous amounts of money hidden away—a couple million dollars, four or five houses. I had no money anymore, so I was teaching them thinking maybe I should have them teach me. They were able to go to prison *and* keep their money.

I got some real insights into some of the problems with the prison system and the biggest problem is the administrative staff just punching the clock. I had my counselor, Mr. Hite—the most important link for an inmate—but he was never there. These counselors had hardened over time and often seemed to do the bare minimum. They checked the boxes and let the prisoners run the prison. There was a total disconnect between policy and performance. It was a check-in-then-check-out kind of job. There were some really good people that were part of the system, but they were few and far between. While I suspect if I was working there for ten or twelve years, I might have the same attitude, it contributed to the failure of the system to help inmates prepare to return to the outside world.

The other problem was the gambling. It's pervasive in prison and for the most part the guards looked the other way. I stayed out of it, for the most part, because it was technically illegal. But it wasn't a secret, and it was very well-organized. Books of stamps were the currency. Each floor had a runner, and people were hitting two hundred, three hundred dollars per bet. Occasionally I would bet a couple of books of stamps on football and college basketball to earn stamps to pay for better food, homemade things like pillows and coffee mugs, and for buying shirts that fit better from the laundry. One time I hit for sixty books of stamps, worth about $400, on a longshot bet. It kept me from having to gamble for most of the time I was at Loretto.

By March 2020, I had been in prison for nearly two full years, and at Loretto for almost half of that. When Covid-19 hit, it changed everything. My mindset at the time was that I would be in Loretto until after the election, when a pardon might come down. Until then, I reasoned, I would have to endure.

In late March, Congress passed, and Trump signed into law, the

Coronavirus, Aid, Relief, and Economic Security (CARES) Act. The law was soon being used to get people who qualified out of prison. The BOP was not anxious to send inmates home before their sentences were up. But, they viewed Covid-19 as a potentially very serious problem. There was a lot of bad health from imprisonment, lack of exercise, and unhealthy food. And a large number of prisoners were older. Under the CARES Act, certain criteria was established for early release to home confinement. The act favored prisoners who were elderly, had health issues, were convicted of non-violent or non-drug crimes, and had served more than half of their sentence. They could be released to home confinement. Notwithstanding this compassionate release law, the wardens were dragging their feet. No one was being sent home.

The Trump White House put pressure on the DOJ to implement the new law and begin sending prisoners home. Attorney General Barr's office imposed an additional, internal rule stating that in some cases the 50 percent time served rule could be waived. The policy was loosened to allow more prisoners to be released on home confinement.

When the BOP changed the policy to allow prisoners to be sent home even if they had served less than 50 percent of their sentence, it put me in play.

I qualified legitimately due to my age, the crimes that I was convicted of, and my health issues. Staying in prison became a morbidity issue for me. I was seventy years old with high blood pressure. In general population, I really would be at risk. But at the same time, solitary confinement for the duration of the pandemic might kill me, and solitary confinement by floors is what the BOP was imposing.

The BOP is a regulated bureaucracy that ignores the rules and governs itself the way it wants. All of a sudden, wardens were being told to do things in a way they didn't like. The number of inmates in a prison can affect the budget. Losing prisoners is not something the system wants unless it's to other parts of the system. So even though I viewed my situation as clear-cut, and my lawyers viewed it as clear-cut, getting the approval for a transfer was not clear at all.

I went down to see Ms. Golden because I figured she would be a part of any release plan. And if she could support me being sent home, I could leverage that support with Warden Moser and with Washington. Moser was the key. I could qualify under the regs, but she could still say no.

This is where having a supportive White House was useful. The BOP sent a list to the warden saying that the DOJ was relinquishing control to home confinement of a number of prisoners who qualified under the CARES Act, including Prisoner Manafort.

The warden understood exactly what this meant. I had known for months, especially since she was overruled in transferring me to New York State custody, that the warden didn't want me at Loretto. She didn't want to be embarrassed a second time. So, she supported me being sent to home confinement. She wrote the paperwork saying I should be sent home and my attorneys started working on making it happen before anything changed.

The problem was that at this point, Western Pennsylvania had few, if any, cases of Covid-19. So there was no reason to move quickly. The prison was on lockdown, so I could no longer leave my floor, and my concern was that if I was there when Covid-19 started to hit they wouldn't want to move me out. The argument I had my lawyers make was that I needed to get out *before* Covid-19 happened. Any longer and it would be too late.

I told Downing, laughingly, "Look, this is like playing Russian roulette with my life." He understood the "Russian" joke, and got the point. At first there were just trickles from the BOP of people getting sent home. While it was not freedom, it was still home. I could hug my wife. I could see my grandkids. It was really important. I also felt that if I could get home, I could work the phones and engage the pardon process in a way that I couldn't from inside prison.

In the middle of April, my case manager, Ms. Spielvogel, informed me that I was approved to be released to home confinement. No one in the system knew exactly what that meant. Only that I was one of four people to get a letter from the warden saying that I had qualified. I was given a date—April 28, about two weeks from when I received the letter. According to BOP policy, I would first have to quarantine for fourteen days.

Of course, this restriction made no sense. We had been in lockdown since the end of March. Being quarantined for fourteen more days merely meant that I would be in the same lockdown for an additional two weeks. BOP logic is often illogical. But, it did not matter. I was going home in two weeks. I was ecstatic.

Then on April 24, three of the four people who had been approved for release to home confinement had their applications rescinded. No explanation. Suddenly, I was waiting for the shoe to drop.

In a bittersweet moment, I found out my release date was no longer going to be April 28. Now it was May 13. They said I had to quarantine for even longer, even though we had been under lockdown for nearly a month. I knew that it was only a matter of time before there were cases in Loretto, and I was anxious that an outbreak at the prison would jeopardize my release—not to mention my health. Still, I had learned by then that there was no logic, and you couldn't fight it. So, I did what I had become very good at doing: I waited.

CHAPTER 20

Going Home

Before I could actually leave, the BOP had to approve where I would be going. They needed to see what the home environment was like. There was not a system in place to do this in the Covid-19 environment. But I could not complain because it was Covid-19 that was triggering my early release to home confinement.

The re-entry office finally decided they could do a virtual tour of the home with my wife and proceed with the approval process that way. Kathy walked around the apartment on FaceTime with the re-entry office, showed them where I would be living. Finally, they signed off on the apartment.

Although this minor review was critical to my release, it was not a priority for the court. Nor was it a priority to the prison system. Neither cared about prisoners being prematurely released for any reason. But it was a super-priority for me. I knew the BOP was rescinding approval letters, not only in Loretto, but in other prisons as well. There was a significant conflict within the BOP over how to handle these transfers. Everything was unprecedented.

At the time, Loretto didn't have a single Covid-19 case, so there was no real pressure to get me out immediately. From my perspective, though, once there were cases, it would be too late. It would spread like wildfire in a prison environment. The reason for my transfer to home confinement was that I was a health risk. So the logic didn't make any sense. Waiting too long could kill me.

By sheer force of will working the warden, the re-entry bureau, and my attorneys working with the DOJ, I finally got my release date: May 13, 2020, at 10:00 a.m. As soon as I had the confirmation, I called Kathy, who would be picking me up. She asked if I wanted her to bring me anything. "A pizza," I said. I hadn't had a real pizza in two years. She laughed, but she understood.

I did not tell anyone in Loretto the date that I would be going home. But the word somehow got out. The prison administrators were nervous that there would be all kinds of media at the gate. A day before my release, the lieutenant called me to his office again. I was thinking he was about to rescind the transfer. He sat me down. My stomach was in knots. I could see everything about to go up in smoke. I imagined having to stay locked down in solitary, and it would only be a matter of time before the prison was overrun with Covid-19.

"We have a problem," he said.

"Damn," I said. "What is it?"

"Can you leave earlier?" he said.

I was stunned. Of course I could leave earlier. I offered to leave right then.

"Not that early," he laughed. "Just don't tell anyone. Could you leave at 6:00 a.m. instead of 10:00 a.m.?"

I said I'd have to call my wife and let her know. He told me to call her now from his office to make sure everything could be sorted out.

When I called Kathy, her initial reaction was the same as mine: she said she would come immediately and pick me up that afternoon. After we laughed, we agreed that she would leave Northern Virginia at 3:30 a.m. Amidst this growing excitement, I was concerned about her driving that far at that hour and suggested maybe she should come that night and stay at the hotel. She said that she would figure it out and not to worry.

That night I tossed and turned all night. I couldn't fall asleep. I set my alarm to wake me at 5:00 a.m. After my previous departure experiences at Alexandria, Loretto, and the MCC, I wanted to shave, shower, and be ready for any sudden arrival by a guard.

At 5:45 a.m., a guard came to my room to escort me to the departure area. I said goodbye to my roommates, turned, and walked the long corridor to the sign-out area. For the first time in two years, I was walking away without chains on my ankles and around my waist.

Although I had dreamt of this moment for so long, it still felt surreal. I half expected to wake up at the last minute, back on my concrete bed. I thought of all that I had been through in the five prisons. My hands were shaking but my steps were purposeful and deliberate. Several guards on morning duty came by to say good luck. One of them came up to me and whispered, "I hope Trump pardons you right away." I smiled at him, but honestly, my only thought was of hugging my wife—a real hug, for the first time since June 15, 2018.

As I was about to go out the door, I had a problem. I had four bags of stuff with me—some books, my legal papers, some clothes, a few possessions. Most people leave with a duffle bag; I could not carry everything in one trip. But the guards were friends of mine by now, and they offered to help me one last time. When my wife and son-in-law saw me coming, I wasn't carrying any of my stuff; the guards had all my bags. They both laughed.

When the gate opened, there she was—my wife—smiling the biggest smile I had seen on her face in over three years.

As soon as I got in the car, my son-in-law turned to me and said, "They treat you like that all the time?" I laughed. I was so caught up in the moment I had not noticed the guards were carrying my bags for me. It was very emotional to hug my wife and then step into the car.

As I settled in, Kathy was focusing on something more important. From the back seat, a hand came over the armrest holding a large slice of a sausage mushroom pizza from Papa Johns.

They had brought me some clothes, and not long after we left, we pulled over so I could change out of what I was wearing and put on my own clothes for the first time in over two years. I'd also told my wife that when I got home, I wanted to cook her dinner and start repaying her for all the sacrifices she had made for me over the last three years. God bless her, she had it all set up for me to cook her dinner.

I was nervous that I was supposed to report somewhere as part of my release package, but I didn't know where or when because it wasn't on my release paper. I called back to Loretto and found out that I had to check in by four o'clock the next day at the office that manages former prisoners, probation, and home confinement in DC.

I checked in as soon as I could. I met my case manager, and he gave me the rules. I told him where my apartment was and that my daughter's home was close by. It was larger and had an office, so my office would be in her house. It was five blocks away. I gave him the address and he signed off on it. Or so I thought he did.

I went directly to my daughter's house to see her and my grandkids. She had a three-year-old and a newborn. Unbeknownst to me, some photographer was following me and monitoring her house. The media did not know where I was going to live since it wasn't public information yet. The photographer took a picture of me with my grandson on the swing in the backyard and the photo went viral. The headlines read that I was violating my home confinement because I wasn't where I was supposed to be. The media, always out for blood, was thrilled to have "caught me," even though I wasn't doing anything wrong.

The clerk managing my case was embarrassed. Either he had not been paying attention or he just didn't care. Either way, according to the media, he now had a high-profile prisoner supposedly violating the rules in his first hours of freedom.

He called me and told me to get to my home right away. I walked him through our understanding and what he had authorized me to do. He had the address listed. I had been very clear about everything. But I was not his typical parolee. He was definitely out of his league trying to figure out how to manage me.

Unfortunately, this rocky start ended up defining the relationship from then on. He informed me in no uncertain terms that he was the boss. To prove it, he constantly created silly or just plain dumb rules to manage me. He wanted me to understand that I was in prison STILL. He would go on to change the rules regularly to try to make my life more difficult.

The rules of my home confinement were essentially the same as they were during my pre-trial period. I could go to work, to church, to my doctor, and to my lawyer. I couldn't go to the gym or to the grocery store.

My mindset when I was released was that it would be another six months before Trump pardoned me. I was thinking Thanksgiving—after Trump was re-elected. Maybe it would be the week after the election, but most likely it would be Thanksgiving. I was feeling decent about a pardon, and I was home with my family. It was wonderful, really.

Normally, I would have to report in once a week with the case officer, or they would send someone out to check my condo. But, they were not scheduled appointments because of Covid-19. They were spontaneous to make sure I wasn't doing anything I shouldn't be doing. I was very, very careful. There was no way I was going back to prison. I could sense that my clerk wanted an excuse to send me back to Loretto. I was always anxious he would make up a reason.

It was a challenging environment. I tried not to let it bother me, because it was so good to be out of prison, but it hung over me like a cloud. I would do anything not to go back. Especially with Covid-19.

Within two weeks after my release, Loretto was the most infected prison in the system. It came in and spread like wildfire, like we all knew it would. And they didn't come out of strict lockdown until Christmas. Lockdown at Loretto was brutal. No access to the outside. No access off your floor. The corridors were cold and drafty. There was no natural light. During the winter I would sleep with three blankets and still feel cold. I couldn't imagine what life was like during the worst of the pandemic.

There's no question: I got out just in time.

There were, of course, certain adjustments to life back on the outside after very public investigations, trials, convictions, and a couple years in prison. A lot of people disappointed me.

Throughout my life, I was always taking care of people. Not because I needed to, but because that's what I did. We had a group of friends, all very close-knit. I would schedule trips around the country and overseas and Kathy and I would bring groups of eight or ten people with us. I took care of the housing and the transportation. I never asked for anything. I had the means, and the memories were important to Kathy and me.

Plus, I was always there to help someone start a business or work through problems when they were having difficulties. I never expected anything in return, but I always assumed that they would be there for me if I ever needed them.

There was a strong feeling of family among us. When we went through this crisis, I just assumed my friends would step forward and help Kathy cope with the mess she had done nothing to create. Yes, I knew anyone associating with me was subject to being linked to us. It was not fair for the media to chase them, but I expected these friends to be there for Kathy. She was on the outside and she needed friendship more than ever. I expected more from some people. Some came forward, but others did not. While I rationalized it all, it pained me to see my wife suffer these disappointments. More than anything else in this horrible experience, this pain she suffered was the worst for me.

The condo we rented when our home in Alexandria was foreclosed was about half the size of what we had lost. Again, it fell on Kathy to deal with closing out the foreclosed property, moving things into storage, and using some of the furniture to furnish our new apartment.

When I came home from Loretto, I was shocked at what I saw. Somehow, Kathy had transformed this place that was totally different in size, layout, and location from our home into a replica of the Alexandria condo that we had lost. The new place looked exactly like our previous condo—but smaller. The living room looked the same. My office was set up. She wanted me to feel like the memories were still there. Her attitude was that we had each other and that's all that mattered.

She was so right, and her attitude transformed my return into a non-event.

Between her incredible preparation of the new place and her emphasis on us and not on our stuff, I made the transition in a seamless way. None of the adjustment issues I had heard stories of in prison existed for me. There is no question that when I came out of prison my wife's sensitivities in helping me return to life helped me in more ways than I could ever imagine.

As a person, I was different from the man who went to jail. I was stronger in my belief in myself. I was more aware of who I was as a person. My faith was deeper. I'd found a way to manage my life in positive ways, regardless of how much pressure I was facing. The key to this transition was learning how to live in the present. I gained this perspective and ability from books that had been recommended to me at Loretto, in particular those by Gregg Braden and Joe Dispenza, which dealt with the metaphysical and the impact of quantum physics.

I truly believed that I could change my destiny, and that if I focused on the present, not the past, I would be in a higher place. I live this way to this day, with no rancor or anger over what happened to me over the last six years. People who have known me for a long time see this change. They don't understand it, but they recognize in me what I feel every day.

There was no contact from anyone in the Trump orbit when I was in prison. And I didn't want any, especially if it could be exploited by the MSM.

But when the re-election campaign started kicking off, I was interacting, unofficially, with friends of mine who were very involved. It was killing me not to be there, but I was advising indirectly from my condo.

I didn't have any prohibition against it, but I didn't want it to become an issue. So I was very careful. If word got out that I was anywhere close, it would become a campaign issue and I didn't want anything to get in the way of the president's re-election or, importantly, a potential pardon. I still had no promise of a pardon, but I had an expectation. My fear was that if I got in the way of the campaign and Trump lost, he might blame me, and I did not want that to happen.

In analyzing the 2020 race, I could see what they were confronted with. Biden was the only Democrat I ever worried about. He was the only one who could project an image different from Trump's. The MSM was defining the race in stark terms based on the personalities of the two candidates. This was a contest between "Uncle Joe" and "nasty, disruptive" Donald. Recognizing the media support, the Biden campaign did a very good job of projecting his strengths and hiding his weaknesses by keeping him in the basement.

While Trump rarely started a fight, he often doesn't know when to stop punching back. Hillary didn't understand this in 2016, and she kept playing to Trump's strengths. Biden understood it better and his campaign made a strategic decision, which turned out to be correct.

Covid-19 changed everything, too. It made it easier to vote without ID cards or even turning out. States loosened the rules in key states to allow harvesting of ballots, thus increasing fraud issues. But, most importantly, Covid-19 allowed Biden to make the election about Trump's personality rather than his record.

A portion of the electorate—a key portion—was exhausted by Trump. Biden made them feel relief. As I sat watching the Biden strategy being implemented, I felt sick. The election was never going to be covered fairly. Trump was never going to be able to expect an inquisitive media to do their duty to expose the faults in Biden's candidacy. Even having the best candidate, the Trump campaign was still limited by the toxic anti-Trump environment that the media was exacerbating daily.

Trump had been a good enough president to deserve re-election. But if people were not enthusiastic Trump supporters, they didn't appreciate the importance of his presence in the White House. These swing voters celebrated the benefits of his presidency pre-Covid-19—no inflation, economic growth, rising wages for all but disproportionately favoring those at lower income levels, energy independence, border security, a world at peace, and prison reform.

There was increasing peace in the Middle East, something every president for forty years had tried and failed to achieve until Trump. Farmers benefited under Trump. Latinos grew out of poverty.

But the female, suburban swing voters disliked the turmoil that seemed to follow Trump everywhere. With Covid-19 confining them to home, the stress and anxiety were too much for them to bear. Uncle Joe seemed safe, a return to a less tumultuous life where people could exhale when they saw their neighbors instead of girding themselves for unpleasant political confrontations.

Notwithstanding these warning signs, I could rationalize a narrow Trump victory. But unlike in 2016, I was not certain. I knew it would be close. The early returns were very strong. But the risk was always going to be the early voting where the Democrats had pulled out all stops. There was no way to judge. It was going to be another close election.

When they weren't calling North Carolina, or Ohio, or Georgia, I started to get nervous. Ohio should not have been close. Georgia should not have been close. When Arizona was still in play, I got very nervous. I went from not knowing exactly how the election could turn out to suddenly realizing he could actually lose.

When Fox called Arizona for Biden, I felt like throwing up. Trump was going to lose. There weren't enough ways for him to come out the winner on election night. It would have to be something that happened after. But I could see all the complications involved in trying to overturn multiple states. In one state, maybe. But in two, then three states, using a legal process that would take months—I could not see how we could overcome all of this, especially with the MSM promoting the narrative of President-elect Biden.

Watching the other elections results, I could see a pattern developing that was not healthy. Trump was losing by close margins in the very areas where we had organized voter protection teams in 2016—Philadelphia's suburbs, Pittsburgh, Milwaukee's suburbs, Detroit. Republicans were winning big almost everywhere. Instead of Pelosi increasing her House majority she was now in peril of losing it. Republicans exceeded expectations across the board—state legislatures, governors, local offices, and school boards. The only election Republicans were not leading was the race for the White House.

Trying to analyze the results that night, I was concerned. I believed there were patterns that were irregular. The results in battleground states were close enough that the fraud could be the difference between winning and losing.

My mind started to hope that the RNC had organized election security teams that could quickly identify the fraud and alert the public to what was happening in real time. I waited and worried.

With the country moving quickly to confirm Biden's victory, I saw the hypocrisy at work again. The same people who for four years refused to accept Trump's victory were now calling for "all Americans" to accept this questionable result.

I felt horrible. The country could survive Joe Biden, but at what cost? I knew Trump must be furious. He expected to win. He deserved to win. But Covid-19 had changed the paradigm.

Now the country was going to see the difference between real leadership under President Donald Trump and left-wing woke failed leadership under Biden. If Biden veered left, the Sanders/AOC wing of the Democrat party would be happy, but the mainstream Democrats would be marginalized.

Of course, the main thought going through my head that night, once Biden was called the winner, was: What does it mean for me? With a little bit of luck, it might mean that I could be pardoned around Thanksgiving. I couldn't see a reason why Trump wouldn't pardon me.

If Trump had won, I would not have had any problem making phone calls the day after to start working for a pardon. But with the loss, the timing wasn't good. They were deluged with the shock of losing.

Plus, Trump refused to accept defeat. In these difficult moments, despite the pain of the last six years, I could not focus on my pardon. I was mired in the mess the country had just put itself in.

The moment was another bittersweet one. I could see the pardon, but, once again, I had to be patient. I'd been patient for three years and I would have to be patient for two more months.

I didn't reach out in November and Thanksgiving passed with others being pardoned, but not me. I was hoping to be on the list, but I wasn't shocked. I set my sights on Christmas. I would have to bide my time, but

I did not want to miss this list. So, I called my lawyers and asked them to start making soft contacts.

Behind the scenes, I pursued two different tracks. Todd Blanche, my New York attorney, had friends in the US Attorney's office. They were able to keep the lines open. Kevin Downing was dealing with some of the president's lawyers. All of these efforts weren't getting anything. We weren't getting any negative feedback, which was good, but there was no confirmation either.

I did not think it was wise to have any paper trail in the White House system. I kept telling myself "Donald Trump will do the right thing." I felt I had a perfect case for a pardon, and it was a case I could make if given the chance. But that's not the way it works. I would never get in front of Trump. So I had no choice but to wait and hope my contacts were making progress on my behalf.

Even though I was out on home confinement, I was still a prisoner, and my sentence had many years left. If the situation with Covid-19 changed, I could be sent back. It was a very real possibility. So I was always focused on a pardon. It was incredibly nerve-racking. I'd lost my freedom. I'd lost my life. I hoped it was temporary. But it was always in my head that if I didn't get a pardon, I could be eighty years old before I got out of prison. And at that point, my life really would be over. In prison, I saw people's health deteriorate very rapidly, people much younger and stronger than me.

I was assessing things on a constant basis. What was Trump's position today? What is the mindset of those around him? I knew that there were those around him who wanted me to be pardoned. But I never thought anyone would put my interests above Trump's at any point. I didn't want that either. But now we were down to his last sixty days in office. I didn't have four years to make a case anymore. Suddenly, time was running out. I only had one shot; if for some reason Trump didn't pardon me, that's it—game over.

I have a very good doctor friend, Ron, who is also very close to Donald and Melania. He knew Trump from the Miss Universe pageants. My friend was always one of the judges. His relationship with the Trumps was personal, not political. He could pick up the phone and call Melania. He was invited to all the parties.

He was my safety valve as far as a pardon. If I ever needed to call in a last resort, I felt I could ask him to reach out to Melania. I knew he was keeping Melania informed about my situation, not talking about a pardon, just letting her know what was going on with me. He was going over to the White House all the time. The staff got to know him. He was a doctor for a lot of them.

In December he was invited to the White House Christmas party. Without any prompting from me, he approached Kellyanne Conway, who had been with the president that day talking about the pardons that were coming up. Somehow my name came up at the party and she told Ron that I was going to get a pardon. But that I was not in the next wave.

After the event, he called me up and told me what Conway had told him. I was really upset. "What do you mean, 'not the next wave'? I have to wait until after Christmas?"

Now I was being pushed to the very end—January 19. Doing it at the last moment put everything, including my life at risk. What if they messed up the language of the pardon? I was nervous that if they did the pardon the wrong way, it could create all kinds of problems in terms of getting my properties back or even keeping me on parole.

But at the same time, it was the first real indication, from anyone who would know, that I would actually get a pardon. It was the first time I felt certain—not totally certain, but more certain—I would be free again.

An announcement was made on December 22, and I wasn't on the list. But neither was Jared's father. Stone wasn't on it. Bannon wasn't on it. So it seemed to me that they were saving some of the more controversial names for the very end.

Since I would not be getting a pardon before Christmas, I called my case manager to ask approval to go to my daughter's house on December 25. He said no. Right to the very end, he showed no compassion and did what he could to make my life just a little more miserable. The family decided that we would celebrate Christmas at my apartment. It would be a different kind of Christmas, anyway, just marking time. I was starting to condition myself to be a prisoner for a little longer.

Early the next morning, December 23, I got a phone call from a friend of mine, a producer at NBC. He said he was calling to congratulate me.

I said, "John, I wasn't on the list."

He said, "No, no. You're being pardoned today."

"What are you talking about?" I couldn't imagine Trump would announce pardons on the 22nd *and* 23rd. "How do you know that?"

"I got it from the White House operation. It's on the board and it's over at DOJ as well."

"Is it public?"

"No, not yet, but it'll be posted. You know how it works."

"Well," I said, "you're the first one telling me. Even my lawyers don't know." I thanked him and said I had to tell my wife.

Before I did that, however, I called my lawyers, and asked them to call the White House to get confirmation. I did not want to wake Kathy with wrong information.

Almost immediately, Todd called me back. It was true. But it wouldn't be posted until five o'clock. By this point, the calls had begun. I shut off my phone. Kathy was still sleeping. I sat alone for a few minutes to let everything sink in. After two and a half years, I was going to be a free man again.

I teared up and thanked God for his strength. I didn't think about the past. I did not miss any of my possessions. I felt no anger or bitterness or regret. I had everything that mattered to me: a deeper faith in God, the love of an incredible wife and family, and my freedom to live again.

At around eight o'clock, I woke Kathy up and told her. I saw the stress vanish from her face. She screamed in joy. And then we just held each other. She had suffered in so many ways. But she never wavered in her belief. She never doubted. We were quiet as we hugged and cried. In this moment I felt a rush of energy that connected me to the force of the universe. It was as if the positive force that I had relied on to bring me to this moment suddenly surrounded and lifted me.

It was like a switch was pressed.

We hugged and cried.

I was free.

Knowing that the pardon was coming, I began to reorganize my schedule. One of the first things I wanted to sort out was getting the bracelet off my ankle. I couldn't do anything until the official announcement that evening, but I was anxious to start living my life again and this was a symbol that had to go.

I didn't know if the pardon took some time to go into effect, or if I

had to do anything after the pardon. My lawyers said it happened immediately upon being published. From the moment it was posted, I would
be a free man. So even though I had the bracelet on, I was no longer
under the authority of the BOP.

On December 24, I sent an email to my case manager to let him
know that the president had pardoned me the night before.

> As you know, last night President Trump issued a full and complete
> pardon for me, thus, freeing me from home confinement. I have been
> advised by Legal Counsel that this pardon was effective immediately
> upon signature by the president. While the paperwork may be lagging
> because of the holiday, I am forwarding a copy of the pardon to you to
> confirm what the White House and the media have reported.
>
> Now that I am free from incarceration, I will be going to my
> daughter's home for Christmas. As a courtesy, I am sharing below my
> schedule for the next two days.
>
> I intend to depart my condo around 4:30 p.m. today to go directly
> to my daughter's home. I will remain there tonight and tomorrow. I
> expect to return to my condo sometime in the evening of Christmas
> Day.
>
> If you have any questions, feel free to contact my attorney Todd
> Blanche, who is copied on this email.
>
> Finally, I would like to have the bracelet removed from my ankle
> on Saturday. At that time I can sign any paperwork if there is any asso-
> ciated with my release. Could you please contact me with a time that is
> convenient for me to come to the DC Core office to have this done and
> if there is someone else I should be in contact with to have this done?
>
> Thank you and have a very Merry Christmas.
> Paul Manafort

I was not surprised that my handler didn't respond. In my first act as a
free man, I drove to my daughter's house to play with my grandkids.

Two days later, on December 26, I sent another email.

> I tried to reach your office today to set up a time to remove my bra-
> celet, but was unable to make contact. I will wait until Monday to
> reach out for this to happen. It is time sensitive because I have travel
> scheduled for next week.

When I finally got my case manager on the phone that day, he told me that I couldn't get the bracelet off until he'd been officially notified by the BOP. I informed him that was not how it works. "Call your supervisor and ask when the pardon takes effect, and they will tell you it is effective immediately upon publication," I said. I offered again to come down so he could take it off, or I could cut it off. I also wanted a formal document from him.

It took me four days to get that appointment. When I arrived at the time he set for me to meet him, he wasn't even there. I didn't want a junior staffer to take it off. I knew the game he was playing so I waited. I wanted him, my case manager, to do it. I didn't want him to come back later and say he hadn't approved removing the bracelet.

So I waited. I waited about an hour when he finally walked in. He was not a good actor. I could see the shock on his face. He had been avoiding me, hoping someone else would take it off and he could sign off later.

Reluctantly, he oversaw the bracelet being removed and signed the paperwork. I wished him good luck in his life and drove home.

Driving back to my condo, I passed Capitol Hill, my law school, Congress, the Memorial Bridge connecting DC to Northern Virginia. Over the last three years, I had driven on these roads, seeing the monuments through a metal screen cuffed and shackled. Never again. I lowered my window and enjoyed an unfettered look as I drove by them. Now I was free, free from prison, from ankle bracelets and bitter case managers, free from the whole BOP and the Special Counsel and all the fake narratives of Russian collusion.

Free. It felt great!

At five o'clock on the afternoon of December 23, 2020, the announcement was made with no fanfare. I was a free man again. I poured my wife a glass of wine and myself a double Bombay martini and saluted her for her steadfast support, unswerving loyalty, and for being the best partner a man could ever wish for. I sipped my martini and once again broke down in tears of joy and relief.

One of the first calls I made was to Roger Stone, who had been pardoned as well. It was the first time I had spoken to him since October 2017. I congratulated him on his pardon, and we regaled each other with stories of the travails we had endured. I wanted to call the president but decided I would wait until after Christmas to do so.

On Christmas eve, around six o'clock, my phone rang. I didn't recognize the number, but I picked up anyway. "Paul Manafort. The president would like to speak to you," an operator from the White House switchboard announced.

Coming on the phone, President Donald Trump's first words to me were, "I've been wanting to do this for a long time," he said.

I wanted to ask why he hadn't! But refrained.

"You are a man," he said. He kept repeating that. "You are a real man. My friends have been calling all day to tell me how happy they are that I did this."

"So is my family," I said.

I told him I was sorry about the election, but he wanted to know how I was doing, and how I had been over the last couple of years. He cursed what I'd gone through. He told me I was important in getting him elected in 2016 and that he was really sorry I didn't get the chance to participate in the fruits of our success. I had heard that over the years he would see something on TV about me occasionally and explode that it was happening.

"We need to get together at some point," he said.

"At your convenience, Mr. President."

"I'll be down in Florida for the season," he said.

He got emotional near the end of the conversation, and he thanked me again for being the man that I was and for handling the crisis the way I had handled it. He said a lot of people would have caved with that pressure, but he always knew I had character. I later found out from Jared that he really was looking forward to that call.

I thanked him and wished him a happy holiday.

I joked to my family that I was usually Santa Claus for family and friends, but this Christmas Trump was Santa, and he gave me the best present ever—my life back.

Four days later, Kathy and I got on an airplane, flew to Florida, and spent the winter there.

CHAPTER 21

Final Thoughts

Once the post-pardon honeymoon was over, I was in survival mode—reconnecting with family, reconnecting with friends, trying to start a normal life again. Everything was a challenge.

First, I had to deal with the financial issues hanging over me. I had to handle the return of some of my assets and their loans. I had to get credit cards again. I had to get bank accounts. I wanted my passport back.

I needed to get my life back in order and under control. There was a lot of motivation to do this, and I felt a huge amount of energy. My goal was to be ready to turn the page and start a new chapter of my life by the end of 2021. And it's exactly what I did.

I have had a lot of time to reflect, and I am a stronger person than I was. I have a greater ability to live within myself and live in the present. I am no longer absorbed with the past or focused on the future. Prison helped me achieve that. I am not resentful about what happened. I have to live with the consequences, but I'm not bitter.

Working on the Trump campaign and playing a role in his election was the pinnacle of my life's work. I thought I could help him be elected president. I thought he was the kind of president that the country needed. I saw how he would change the system. I felt that way about Reagan, too. With Reagan, there was a philosophical change, but with Trump the change was structural. He was going to drain the swamp, and he had the capacity to do it.

My life has been directed, in many respects, by trying to make a difference in cultures and structures—in Democracy. And I thought Trump was going to be the right person at this critical time. It was the reason I'd spent my life in politics.

I do believe if Trump had four more consecutive years, a lot of the changes would have been instituted. Not surprisingly, in the 2020 election, the American people opted for the non-Trump as president. Biden is everything Trump is not.

He is weak and soft—qualities that may feel comforting until you realize a president must be strong and aggressive to bring real change to government. He is for a left-wing agenda that puts wokeism in power at the expense of the power of the people. He is for failed ideological programs that have enslaved America's needy for over fifty years and never improve their lives. He is for lawlessness at the borders, and in our cities. He mindlessly spends money with no regard for the impact on inflation. He is for making the US energy-dependent instead of energy-secure in order to promote a green agenda that has no credibility as a stand-alone policy. He believes the US should be one of many nations at the table of a global village, instead of the leader of democratic nations in the world.

Today, fourteen months into Biden's term, the American people have seen enough. They now understand the difference between a President Trump and a left-wing non-Trump president. The comparison of the records makes the case without the personality. There is a difference, and it is obvious. Trump promised to drain the swamp and incredibly, in only three years, he did it.

I usually don't talk about politics with friends. But I have had friends with whom I cannot even mention Trump's name. They go crazy—Democrats and Republicans. They like me, they respect me, but they don't understand why I was with Trump in the first place. They don't understand why I'm not angry with him right now. But I have a different filter than they do.

I have dedicated my life in a way they have not. Trump was a vehicle that made a great deal of sense to me. When you're dispassionate about his personality, and you can objectively look at policies, depending on what your own philosophy is, what he wanted to do made sense. The nation is in a better place today than before Trump was president.

Forget the rhetoric. Trump unleashed the power of freedom. The rich got richer, yes. But the poor got richer, too. And the middle class got richer. Lives changed for the better under Trump at all economic levels. There was real, positive change.

I dealt with a lot of the Black pastors in the campaign in 2016. And I have interacted with them since I've been free again. They talk about how their constituencies benefited. And they tell me about their worries that under Biden things are retrenching again.

I saw these changes abroad, too. Trump pounded his friends and his allies, but they needed to be pounded. Merkel was not good for democracy. She helped Putin get a foothold in making Europe energy-dependent that caused the Ukraine invasion. Trump didn't care that our friends would criticize him. But today, in talking to some of my friends in Europe, they are already wishing for Trump back. Under Trump they knew where the United States stood with them. Trump got out of Iraq because he thought heavily positioning troops around the world is a bad thing, that it should be our shared responsibility, not a US responsibility.

The world respected us even if they didn't like us as much. Now they don't respect us. We were exporting our energy, which gave us tools to control Russia in a way we can't now. I got to know the leaders in the Gulf, and they are scared of the leeway being given to the Mullahs in Iran. Under Trump, the world was a safer place, the country was improving at all levels. And when those changes became more structural, the rising tide would have lifted the country in significant ways.

My friends who hate Trump, and people who are not my friends who hate Trump—they're not going to listen because they can't get past the personality. I get that. I used to try to make sense with them. But I learned that you have to look through the veneer and see what's underneath. With Trump that's especially true. His depth is amazing, you just have to plumb for it.

Also, he gave voice to the forgotten Americans. True, the elites, especially on the East and West Coasts, despised him, but they also despised the forgotten Americans, the ones Clinton and the Democrats called the "deplorables."

Trump gave these people hope again. He made them understand that they mattered. More importantly to the poor and underprivileged, he made their lives better even though they did not vote for him. To Trump, they deserved the same opportunities that the elites got. For years, the Democrats promised relief, but never delivered.

That is why Trump promised to "drain the swamp." He understood that he needed to bring real change in order to "make America great again." But he did more than promise. In four short years, Trump delivered.

The hope that my cousins spoke to me about in 2015—that Trump was a candidate who understood what working men and women wanted, and that he would really deliver on his promises—was fulfilled during Trump's term. If Covid-19 had not happened, he would have been re-elected in a landslide.

A friend of mine, a sixty-year-old woman—liberal, not political, but politically knowledgeable—hates Trump. She can't stand him. Well, the last couple of times we were together, she was complaining about grocery prices, gas prices—basically making the case for Trump. I didn't want to engage her and say, "Well, why do you think that is?" But not long ago she made the connection on her own. She admitted that Biden's policies—the policies of the left—were hurting her and everyone. I didn't say anything. I just nodded.

I'm seeing more and more of this understanding in some of the polls—people who would not have been for Trump in 2020 coming back to the concept of Trump, not necessarily to Candidate Trump yet. But the idea.

People often ask me if I regret working for Trump. I don't regret the work I did for Trump even in light of everything that happened to me. I do regret Rick Gates. If I could change one thing, I never would have had Gates working for me. It would have changed the last five years. That is my biggest regret from this experience.

But I've always said: you make your luck, you pick your breaks, and you make your problems. I made my problems by giving Gates control. I don't wish him ill. In fact, other than in writing this book, I don't think about him, or Weissman, or any of the other left-wing hatemongers.

I read a lot in prison—history, self-improvement, biographies of great leaders, serious books. But what really changed my life was learning to live in the present as opposed to living in the past or pondering too long about the future.

I wouldn't wish what I went through on anyone. But I'm not bitter. I'd rather focus on being positive and on doing things I care about than on trying to get even. This is not a vengeful book. It's a way for me to do one thing and one thing only: tell the truth.

Epilogue

I am an optimist by nature, but I am nervous about the future of the United States. I'm nervous about the woke culture that reminds me more of a fascist world than the nation our Founding Fathers created.

I am worried about Big Tech using their platforms to promote censorship.

I am worried about Gen Z—the young people who are the products of the woke education system—a generation that does not understand that debate is founded on dialogue and difference of opinion. Freedom of speech and association is our most cherished and endearing constitutional right. But in the new woke world, it is despised and rejected. It is this woke attitude that created the environment for the witch hunt that dominated not just my life for the last five years but the entire Trump presidency.

Journalism has changed during my life in politics. When I was beginning my career, CNN kept us informed with what was happening in the world. I could turn it on anywhere I was and get a quick sense of the news. I depended on CNN and I made decisions based on their reporting.

However, with the emergence of social media and Twitter, the nature of the news business has totally changed.

The business of the news and the creation of media stars in the ranks of journalists have merged into a new type of journalism. Digital media reporting has changed the way stories are developed. Social media aggregates stories from other news organizations. They don't need to create a story. Rather these reporters track other stories, aggregate them, and drive news based on the aggregates. The Drudge Report is the classic magnet but Twitter, Facebook, and Google have defined the universe, too.

For reporters in traditional news outlets, it is imperative that their stories get picked up in these news aggregates. The more likely a story is to be reposted or retweeted and shared with larger social media audiences, the more likely a reporter is to ascend to the top ranks of journalism and political punditry.

For the news organizations, the key to their growth is the star power of their reporters. In order to track the top advertisers, the publishers must have their stories being promoted in the larger social media universe. Thus, there is a convergence between the interests in publishers and reporters—the stories going viral.

Today, journalism has morphed into a political dialog that is driven by clicks, not facts. Today, the most important thing for a reporter is to author a story that gets retweeted and liked. Cachet is built on how many followers media reporters have. Punditry and taking sides are what drives the clicks. The problem is that in order to get clicks, stories need to generate "heat." Heat means controversy.

Even the stalwarts of journalism like the *New York Times*, the *Washington Post*, and other major dailies pay more attention to clicks than facts. This in turn drives the subscribers which, based on the quality of the subscribers, drives the advertising.

And what makes a story go viral? In politics it is emotion—identity media is the audience and outrage is the coin of the realm. People don't share stories that don't evoke intensity. Thus, hatred and anger are key magnets for social media. Emotion promotes retweets and sharing.

In this new world, the *New York Times* and the *Washington Post* no longer are the drivers. Twitter, Facebook, Vox, Buzzfeed, and even TikTok are the venues, and outrage and hate are the currency. In fact, the audiences are a narrow field—elite, East Coast, educated, and young. The woke world.

Ironically, the fuel that drove this new media into overdrive was Donald J. Trump. When Trump first demonstrated a mastery of the new digital media world after he announced his candidacy for president in 2015, the audience watched in awe his ability to define his candidacy and his opponents. But soon the tides turned on him and all things Trump.

In the Introduction to this book, I quoted an article by Jim Rutenberg, which appeared in the *New York Times* on August 7, 2016, and identified the new moral code for reporters—partisanship and identity/advocacy journalism; the front pages replaced by editorial pages; news coverage focused on promotion of advocacy stories. And, where opinions differed, the woke culture practiced censorship journalism.

The idea of including stories, even if newsworthy, that conflicted with the advocacy was dismissed. As a result, all major media outlets chose to ignore the Hunter Biden laptop. Even now that the laptop has been proven to be real, the news media has refused to acknowledge a mistake. This is true even though legitimate public opinion surveys have shown that upwards of 19 percent of people who voted for Joe Biden have said that if they knew about the Hunter Biden laptop it would have affected their votes. Relevancy, accuracy, and importance don't matter if they conflict with the woke mentality.

The MSM journalists and the dominance of social media completely dominated the way the Russian collusion story was covered, shaped, and promoted. In the old days of Joseph Pulitzer–style news reporting, that narrative would have not survived a few weeks. Facts mattered then, but only emotion and going viral mattered in 2016.

The fact that I had made a lot of money, worked for a Russian oligarch at a time when the US had close relations with Russia in 2005, and had a real live Russian working for me for ten years set off a craze that was so supercharged that I was convicted in the court of public opinion before the Special Counsel was even appointed. That atmosphere made it possible for the prosecutors to promote theories that had no relation to facts for one simple reason. Driving this approach, the prosecutors understood (as did the Democrats) that the more outrageous the investigation, the more vitriolic the reporting and the more viral the clicks and retweets, the more coverage they would get. It created a symbiotic relationship between prosecutors, Obama/Clinton partisans, and social media and mainstream reporters.

Anonymous government sources could leak a provocative and unsubstantiated story on the black ledger to Michael Isikoff, who wrote a story in Yahoo that was provocative and even unsubstantiated. It entered into the Twitter world and went viral. MSM reporters would then pick it up and either retweet it or recraft it into their own story. Not relevant to the process was veracity or fact-checking. Then the *New York Times* would do their version and the cycle would repeat itself again.

When I would object, I was ignored. Facts were not relevant. The story was emotional, filled with charged accusations and promoting the anti-Trump narrative. All of the ingredients in the new world of Woke Journalism. Stories went viral. My responses went nowhere.

Instead of being the liberator it was originally intended to be, the internet became a vehicle of censorship. I'm nervous about surveillance. I am nervous about a woke culture that is fascist and destructive of all things American. It's all connected, and it is not good for our country. I felt its venom personally and intimately.

They were surveilling me and Carter Page and everybody else in Trump world. I am nervous about that and worry that the people who orchestrated this intrusion on our constitutional rights are back in power under Biden. So I pray every night, and I worry. I'm not negative about the future, but I'm cautious. I will feel a lot more comfortable when Republicans retake the Congress in 2022, which I believe they will.

One of the things I did when I was in prison was reread the Federalist Papers. I had read them many times in my life, but I was reading them in a different light while in prison. I was newly struck by their brilliance. They put protections into the system that spawned this enlightened governing structure that created the greatest democracy in the history of the world.

This system is now under attack. It is incumbent on all of us to rise up and fight back. We cannot lose this fight to the woke left-wing crowd.

I do not feel good about the court system right now. I had a naive attitude toward the court system before what I went through. But now I see how prosecutors have too much power, how they measure themselves by the notches on their guns, not by doing the right thing. They take political cases they know they cannot win, but which they feel will promote their left-wing ideology. Their strong-arm tactics are terrifying.

I listened to stories of prisoners, kids who got caught up in drugs or did something wrong. They would be persuaded by the prosecutor to plead guilty. They would plead guilty based on a deal with the federal prosecutors. But then these prosecutors would slip the information to the state district attorneys and suddenly the deal these kids made with the feds for a five-year sentence became a twenty-year sentence. I saw so much of that at Loretto.

The people who suffer the most are the ones who can't afford a good lawyer. You have public defenders, but the practice of public defenders, from what I saw, was often disconnected from justice. They work with the prosecutors and the lines are often blurred with the accused having no basis to make an informed decision on matters that will affect the rest of their lives. Typically, the public defenders would persuade their indigent clients to plea to some charges they did not commit and take the time. The deal cleared the docket, but the defendants' lives changed forever.

I heard many stories where these public defenders sounded more like they were the court's lawyer. That's an abuse that needs to be fixed. I'm not saying this is true of the whole system, but it is a problem in the system.

The legal system from the prosecution of criminals to the management of inmates does not make sense. If you read the statutes, if you read the codes, it says all the right things. But when you walk the walk, it's not the same. I don't think the solution is to have a lawless society. But ideology is driving those issues, not justice.

It is time that the champions of civil liberties and prison reform "stop talking and start walking." I found it noteworthy that in prison the champion of the downtrodden was Donald Trump. Politicians spent a lot of time talking. Then, Kim Kardashian and Kanye West focused a president who took decisive action. Trump enacted the first meaningful prison reform in modern history. The beneficiaries were the poor, Black, and Latino communities.

Prison inmates and their families took notice. Trump didn't do it for votes. Prisoners cannot vote. He did it because it was the right thing to do. Yet the Democrats, who did nothing, and the media accused Trump of being racist. In prison, the Blacks and Latinos overwhelmingly favored Trump over all Democrats who ran for president in 2020. They knew he was not racist, and they appreciated that he fought for them.

I find it absurd that the woke crowd can talk about defunding the police but do nothing about helping the prisoners who need assistance and education. Trump understood that you could reconcile criminal behavior and prisoner compassion and he did.

For years, the left has talked about re-education programs and early release of prisoners convicted of non-violent crimes. But it took a President Trump to make the changes. It told me that it can be done if the right people are in office.

Cancel culture is poisonous. Wokeism is a danger to our Constitution.

The Swamp is fighting for its life because its fascist ways were unveiled in all of their ugliness in their Covid overreach. I see pathways to fixing these problems, and that's where my optimism is.

Elon Musk took a major step forward in our fight to return freedom to speech. In his move to buy Twitter, he vowed to challenge the suppression of debate. He did not claim to pick a side. He said he was engaging to make Twitter the public square for the free speech that it should be. CNN is coming under new leadership with Discovery taking over ownership. This new leadership has stated clearly they want to see a return to the CNN of the Ted Turner days, the CNN that I grew up viewing. I hope this turns out to be true.

Of course, immediately the forces who championed censorship went crazy. Why? Because they could not stifle dissent. The Biden administration fearing its loss of this tool of suppression immediately responded by creating the ludicrous Disinformation Governance Board at the Homeland Security Department. No one was fooled by this craven last grasp to control the flow of facts and debate.

And this is why I am most confident about our future. I believe in the American people. Not the people of the coastal elites, but the people of the great heartland of our nation. The elites have nothing to fear because Elon Musk, mainstream Americans, and even the basket of deplorables will protect their right to be heard. I am confident that the more the elites and the woke Gen Z crowd objects, the more they will isolate themselves.

The voter tsunami is growing. The American people understand what is happening.

Donald Trump was elected in 2016 to drain the swamp. The American people understood this as a change to the agenda of government: from an autocracy of elites to a democracy of the people. It sounded simple, but it was a revolutionary call to arms. Biden's administration, in just thirteen months in office, has sounded the clarion call again.

My journey over the last five years has taught me more about the strength of our nation than I learned in the entire forty years of my career. As difficult as the experience has been, it has renewed my hope in the strength of the American dream. I believe that the excesses that I endured will generate a response that will be a renewal of the hope inspired by our Founding Fathers.

In his 2016 acceptance speech to the Republican National convention, Donald Trump identified our path to reclaiming our country. "America is a nation of believers, dreamers and strivers that is being led by a group of censors, critics and cynics. Remember, all of the people telling you, you can't have the country you want… No longer can we rely on those same people, in the media and politics, who will say anything to keep our rigged system in place. Instead, we must choose to believe in America." Well, notwithstanding all that I have been through, I choose to believe in America.

Postscript

As this book goes to print, there are a number of matters discussed in these pages that are prominently in the news. All of these news events point in one direction.

The Russian Collusion hoax was a political lie told to the American people by the Clinton campaign and the Obama government. The real collusion was between the MSM and the Democrats to promote this lie and keep the truth from being heard by the American people.

Eighteen months into his presidency, Joe Biden's administration has lost the confidence and trust of the American people.

The American people are witnessing a fact that got lost in the five-year effort to destroy the Trump candidacy and presidency. Who is president matters!

Russian Collusion Was a Hoax

John Durham's investigation is presenting its case against Michael Sussman, the Clinton campaign attorney who was indicted for lying to the FBI about the Trump campaign colluding with Russia. The testimony of the witnesses in this case is clearly establishing two incontrovertible facts that point to the most incredible fraud in US political history.

It is now clear that the entire Russian collusion narrative was a deliberately created hoax by Hillary Clinton and her campaign to deceive the American people. Her own campaign manager, Robby Mooks, admitted under oath that he spoke with Hillary Clinton, and she approved the campaign to promote the false narrative that Donald Trump was using private banking channels to communicate with Vladimir Putin and that the Trump campaign was colluding with the Kremlin to hurt Clinton and elect Trump president. Yes, the Clinton campaign manager said under oath that even though the Clinton campaign could not verify the collusion narrative, it still pushed the story to deflect from her own legal issues.

What is more incredible is that, even with this firsthand testimony of Clinton's campaign manager, the MSM is not reporting the story. The media continue to cover up for Clinton because the truth—that their complicity in 2016 and during the entire Trump presidency was based on a deliberate lie by their preferred candidate—is too painful. Even now, with no doubt remaining, the MSM refuses to acknowledge the truth. There is no investigative reporting required. There is no second-hand knowledge making the allegation. Clinton's own campaign manager admitted the truth.

Yet, the silence in the media is deafening.

The second revelation is even more frightening. John Brennan's *personal notes* of a meeting he had in July of 2016 with President Obama *state without equivocation* that he briefed the president that the *Clinton campaign was going to promote false propaganda against Hillary Clinton accusing Donald Trump and his campaign of colluding with Russia.*

Yes, the president knew in July 2016. So, the entire Crossfire Hurricane investigation by the FBI, the entire FISA surveillance of the Trump campaign, and all of the investigations by the Obama National Security apparatus and the Congressional Intelligence Committees were conducted *after* the White House and CIA knew of the Clinton campaign's dirty trick. Yet, knowing this fact did not prevent them from undertaking an illegal campaign to not only destroy the campaign of their political opponent but to take down a legally elected president of the United States.

This was the most dangerous political coup attempted in the entire history of the United States.

Hypocrisy
Except for the Durham investigation, the Biden White House has returned to the police state policies of the Obama administration.

Hunter Biden's laptop has been authenticated. This is not new news. The *New York Post* uncovered this in the fall of 2016. Hunter Biden's partner and CEO of his venture with China, Tony Bobulinski, admitted this and stated clearly that Joe Biden was the "Big Guy" referred to in the emails on the laptop.

Except for the *Post*, the entire MSM ignored this story. Today, the *New York Times* and *Washington Post* have acknowledged that the laptop belongs to Hunter Biden. However, the contents of the laptop, which is the story, have been ignored.

The reason for this media malfeasance is clear. If the contents of the laptop were truly investigated, the Biden presidency would never have happened.

Additionally, the laptop exposes the hypocrisy of the DOJ, FBI, Democrats in Congress, and their allies in the media.

First-hand admissions in emails by Hunter Biden and his partners expose their violations of the Foreign Corrupt Practices Act. Andrew Weissman had to rely on the false testimony of an admitted liar, Rick Gates, to indict and convict me. The Department of Justice has all the first-hand evidence it needs on Hunter Biden's laptop to convict him. But they refuse to even look at the contents. They are ignoring it because the Democrats and the MSM have two standards—one for Republicans and one for Democrats. Unfortunately for me, I was a part of the Republican standard.

The hypocrisy of DOJ is palpable and totally un-American.

With the likelihood of a Republican takeover of the Congress in November 2022, these contradictions will see the light of day. Already Republicans are saying that, when given the authority by the American people in the elections, they will commence investigations to uncover these abuses and, in some cases, crimes.

The police state policies are not restricted to unequal application of the law. Biden has tried to impose an unconstitutional censorship program. It created a Disinformation Bureau inside of the Department of Homeland Security. The mission of this office was to shut down any criticism of the Biden administration's policies. Biden appointed Nina Jankowicz as the Disinformation Czar.

Ms. Jankowicz's public record on disinformation clearly qualified her for the job. She was one of the biggest spreaders of disinformation against Donald Trump and his administration. The attempt to stifle free speech and criticism of Biden's failed policies was so apparent that within three weeks the bureau was shelved and Jankowicz resigned. But not before the MSM tried to defend it and her. Yes, the protector of free speech, our valued independent media, cheered on the creation of a government bureau meant to stifle debate and eradicate opposition thinking.

Thank God for the American people who understood and vociferously rejected this threat to their right to free speech.

I could write a second book on all of the unconstitutional and hypocritical policies of the Biden administration.

The point is that today the "swamp" is in full force as it seeks to grow its power at the expense of the constitutional and legal rights of the American people. But their efforts are failing because the American people, thanks to the leadership of Donald Trump, are rising up in opposition. The silent majority has become engaged.

The Biden Administration Is Imploding

On the first day of Joe Biden's presidency, he revoked a number of policies of the Trump administration, including the Trump policies on energy independence, border security, and economic regulatory matters that were the foundation of the Trump economic successes.

When he did this, President Biden set in motion a new direction that has resulted in inflation at record levels not seen in over fifty years, gas prices at historic highs, and an open border that is allowing hundreds of thousands of illegals to enter the US every month. Yes, every month.

Additionally, the US has moved from an energy-independent country to one that relies on foreign oil, including billions of dollars being paid to Russia that is being used to fund Putin's invasion of Ukraine.

If this is not enough, the US is experiencing historic supply chain problems in food and basic goods. In the last month, a baby formula crisis threatening American families was foreseen—and ignored—by the Biden administration even though its own Department of Health and Human Resources admitted to being alerted to the potential crisis months prior.

The world has not been spared from the failed Biden policies. The US withdrawal from Afghanistan was so disastrous that even the MSM could not ignore it. Today, thanks to Biden's lack of preparation, Afghanistan is an unstable nation in the hands of a government that is a haven for terrorists.

Ukraine is a mess from a Russian invasion that destroyed the country. But for the ferocious response by the Ukrainian people's militia, the freedom of 55 million people would have been quashed by the megalomaniacal ambitions of an out-of-touch Russian despot. Furthermore, empowered by a weak US president, North Korea and Iran have resumed their nuclear ambitions.

Biden's repeal of Trump's "America First" foreign policy has left the world more unstable and dangerous. Leaders who felt the wrath of a US president for failing to live up to their commitments are now yearning for the return of a strong US president.

I could go on but suffice it to say that as a result of these and other Biden policies, the American people have already deemed the Biden presidency a failure. Two-thirds of all Americans believe Biden's economic policies are a failure and disapprove of his presidency.

2024 and the Prospects of a Trump Candidacy

Even worse for Biden personally, less than a third of his own Democrats want to see Biden run again in 2024.

The 2022 mid-term elections are shaping up to be a disaster for Democrats. Republicans are looking at historic gains as they are forecast to take over both the US House of Representatives and the US Senate.

The political prospects are so damning that Democrats running for re-election are quietly urging Biden to not come into their states.

As Republicans are looking to the November elections, they are seeing that the Hispanic vote is galloping over to their side. This is not a coincidence. Donald Trump saw this possibility in 2016. He campaigned for president promising to deliver for the oppressed and lower economic Americans. Then, as president, Trump delivered on these promises.

As president he implemented policies that focused on improving the job opportunities for minorities. During his presidency, job growth and real wage increases were felt by Hispanics and African Americans at historic levels. These same groups today, based on the Biden administration's economic policies, are suffering real wage losses. These voter blocs understand the difference in the economic policies of the Trump and Biden administrations on their livelihood.

The American people are seeing a very clear picture of two presidencies. When a simple chart is created to compare inflation, real wage growth for all income levels, consumer prices on staple goods like food and gas, the flow of illegal immigration across the southern borders, and supply chain metrics, a picture is vivid and undeniable.

These findings are pointing to two clear understandings. The Biden administration is failing in the very areas where the Trump administration was successful.

All of these failures have generated a growing loud demand for Donald Trump to run for president in 2024.

The question of the day heard in all corners of the US is being asked more loudly every day: "Will Donald Trump run for the presidency in 2024?"

I believe the answer is *yes*.

Donald Trump understands that his promise to "drain the swamp" remains incomplete. If he had served a second consecutive term, the mission would have been ingrained in the bureaucratic system. Washington politicians would have accepted the Trump changes if for no other reason than the American people would have demanded they do so.

This would have been clear from the sustained economic and cultural benefits that would have been bestowed on the country from the Trump policies.

That mission remains incomplete.

However, Donald Trump's resolve remains steadfast.

For this reason alone, I believe Donald Trump will run in 2024. And if he runs, there is no doubt in my mind—he will win!

The American people will demand, and Donald Trump will once again answer the call to Make American Great Again!

Appendix

TPs for Trump Conversation

My role
1. I am not looking for a paid job; but the role would be established inside of the Trump for President campaign.
2. ROLE—Trump campaign National Convention Manager
3. In this role, responsibilities typically include
    a. Oversee the interests of the Trump Campaign in organizing the both the official program and the political organizations of the National Convention.
    b. Organize the mechanisms to manage the interactions between the RNC and officials of the Republican Party and ensure that the National Convention is organized into a Trump controlled convention.
    c. Organize the Delegate Co-ordination and Communication operations leading up to the Convention
    d. Manage the interaction between the various convention committees, most importantly the Rules, Platform and Convention Program committees
    e. Organize the media presentation at the convention—linking Positive messaging, Trump

political image, and anti-Democrat messages, especially as they relate to the podium program, floor operations and off site events in Cleveland.
4. I have served in this role
    a. 1996—Convention Manager for Dole for President
    b. 1988—Convention Manager for Bush for President
    c. 1984—Convention Deputy Manager for RR Re-election (actually performed all of the roles of Convention Manager)
    d. 1976—Floor leader and Delegate Co-ordinator, Ford for President
5. Over the last 20 years, I have managed Presidential campaigns around the world but have not been active in any US Presidential campaign since 2008. I can channel my strategic skills, tactical abilities and knowledge of modern political campaign tools into the demands of this specific convention job but also will be available, if desired, to apply these skills in helping to shape a national campaign working for the team that Trump has organized.

Not a Part of the Political establishment
1. I have not been a part of the Washington establishment since I de-registered as a lobbyist in 1998.
2. I have had no client relationships dealing with Washington since around 2005.
3. I have avoided the political establishment in Washington since 2005.
4. I have not been partner with Roger Stone since we sold Black, Manafort, Stone and Kelly in 1992.
5. At the same time, I am familiar with the players today and the way in which all matters work regarding the transition of the campaign of a Presumptive Presidential Nominee with official Washington.

6. I have not been active or passive in any of the current Presidential campaigns, and have been promoting Trump for President in my communications with media and business leaders I know.
7. My blood enemy in politics, going back to College in the 1960s, is Karl Rove.

Political activity
1. Background provides me with the experience, knowledge and skills to deal with the upcoming issues Trump will confront as the presumptive nominee in dealing with the convention and the transition of the RNC into a Trump for President structure. At the same time I will not bring Washington baggage.
2. Since I have not been active in the Washington political scene for over 10 years and really closer to 15 years, there will be no surprises about Trump capitulating to the Washington establishment by bringing me on board.

Trump Link—non political
1. I live in Trump Tower on 5th Ave—43G
2. When Black Manafort and Stone worked for Trump, I managed the Mar a Largo FAA problem Trump had. Kathleen Casey was as my link to Trump.

SECURING THE VICTORY MEMO

To: Reince Priebus
Fr: PJM
Re: Securing the Victory

State of Race
DT will be elected President on Tuesday.
I believe that we are on the verge of a mandate size Electoral College victory. With the battleground states closing to within margins of error, DT is poised to win most of these states on Tuesday.

I expect that this weekend, the Undecided voters will begin to break for DT. At this time HC is the incumbent in the race. This means that she has all that she is going to get on election day. The remaining Undecided will either stay home or break for DT.

I suspect that on election day, the voting Undecided should be enough to give DT victory in most of the battleground states where the race is even or DT is slightly ahead.

In addition, I do believe that in most battleground states the enthusiasm factor will be strongly in DT's favor. This means that soft DT support will vote while soft HC support will vary in turn-out. Also, any Clinton GOTV advantage, which I believe is over estimated based on my analysis and phone calling, will still have a hard time turning out black vote and millennial voters. The only voter group exception that I have seen that is motivated to vote is in the Hispanic community in Florida and Nevada.

The cumulative effect of these factors is that it is likely that DT will win most, if not all, of the close battleground states.

This is great news but it also poses a challenge that we need to be prepared for.

CLINTON Reaction to Losing Election Strategy
The electorate is not prepared for this result, nor is the media.

I am concerned that the Clinton campaign does have an answer for this possibility. They will move immediately to discredit the DT victory and claim voter fraud and cyber-fraud, including the claim that the Russians have hacked into the voting machines and tampered with the results.

As crazy as this sounds, it is not outside of their playbook.

Because neither the public or the media (or even some of our supporters) is thinking we can win all of the states, we are vulnerable to this Clinton attack. It shouldn't affect our victory but it could seriously impact our mandate (think how GWB was affected by Florida controversy and magnify it).

Building DT Strategy to Secure the Victory

Our plan to prepare the world for our victory is strategic. It is not just a communications plan. We need to define the strategy, build the messaging, organize the communicators and brief friendly media.

I know that we have all of our resources focused correctly on securing the victory on Tuesday.

However, I cant stress the point enough—***It is just as important to build the plan to protect the victory.*** We must start preparing the public for a significant DT electoral college victory, even if the popular vote is not commensurate.

The plan should include, at a minimum, the following elements:

1. Starting Sunday, campaign and Republican leaders, like Preibus and Conway—should background the media walking through the prospects of the way DT will win on Tuesday. The media should have a perspective of what can happen. It doesn't matter if they agree, only that they are aware of it.

2. Talking Points should be distributed for Monday and Tuesday raising the possibility that DT can win all of the close states, that the election momentum now favors DT, that he will attain a sizable Electoral College total, and compare the rapid change to the 1980 RR victory with the electorate breaking 10 points in the last 4 days.

3. Republican State Election officials (Secretary of States), key state officials (Governors, Attorneys General) and

campaign election integrity lawyers who have media and political smarts should be organized to go on TV on Election night attesting to the credibility of the election results. This needs to be prepared in advance.

4.   We need to identify Democrats who would step forward after the election and call for closure and recognition of the election. This will have to be implemented after the election but we should identify now Democrats who we believe would be potential candidates for this role—Sen Leiberman, Sen Joe Manchin etc.

The point is we need to organize our plan now.

Clinton will never accept a loss without discrediting the process.

The media cannot accept a DT victory as an uprising of the people.

A DT victory is a repudiation of the entire " rigged system" by the people. This will never be accepted by the establishment.

We need to understand this fundamental point. Recognizing it, we must apply the same focus as we have in this incredible campaign to secure our victory. Preparing the mindset on Monday and having our plan ready on TUESDAY night to immediate implementation is vital.

PRESIDENTIAL PARDON

Executive Grant of Clemency

DONALD J. TRUMP

President of the United States of America

TO ALL TO WHOM THESE PRESENTS SHALL COME, GREETING:

BE IT KNOWN, THAT THIS DAY, I, DONALD J. TRUMP, PRESIDENT OF THE UNITED STATES, PURSUANT TO MY POWERS UNDER ARTICLE II, SECTION 2, CLAUSE 1, OF THE CONSTITUTION, HAVE GRANTED UNTO

PAUL J. MANAFORT, JR.

A FULL AND UNCONDITIONAL PARDON

FOR HIS CONVICTION in the United States District Court for the Eastern District of Virginia on a superseding indictment (Docket No. 1:18-cr-00083-TSE-1), charging him with violations of Sections 2, 1344, and 3551 et seq., Title 18, Section 7206(1), Title 26, and Sections 5314 and 5322(a), Title 31, United States Code, for which he was sentenced on March 7, 2019, to 47 months' imprisonment, three years' supervised release, a $50,000 fine, $25,497,487.60 restitution (as amended by order on March 21, 2019), and a $800 special assessment, and in the United States District Court for the District of Columbia on a superseding information (Docket No. 17-CR-00201-1), charging him with violations of Sections 371, 982(a), and 3551 et seq., Title 18, and Section 2461(c), Title 21, United States Code, for which he was sentenced on March 13, 2019, to 73 months' imprisonment, 36 months' supervised release (concurrent), $6,164,032 restitution, a $200 special assessment, and forfeiture of $11,000,000.

I HEREBY DESIGNATE, direct, and empower the Acting Pardon Attorney, as my representative, to sign a grant of clemency to the person named herein. The Acting Pardon Attorney shall declare that her action is the act of the President, being performed at my direction.

I ALSO DIRECT the Bureau of Prisons, upon receipt of this warrant, to effect immediately the release of the Pardon recipient (Reg. No. 35207-016) with all possible speed.

IN TESTIMONY WHEREOF, I have hereunto caused this Pardon to be recorded with the Department of Justice.

Done at the City of Washington in the District of Columbia this twenty-third day of December in the year of our Lord Two Thousand and Twenty and of the Independence of the United States the Two Hundred and Forty-fifth.

DONALD J. TRUMP
PRESIDENT

Endnotes

Introduction

1. Jim Rutenberg, "Trump Is Testing the Norms of Objectivity in Journalism," *New York Times*, August 7, 2016, www.nytimes.com/2016/08/08/business/balance-fairness-and-a-proudly-provocative-presidential -candidate.html.

Chapter 3

1. David Freedlander, "A 1980s New York City Battle Explains Donald Trump's Candidacy," *Bloomberg*, September 29, 2015, https://www.bloomberg.com/news/features/2015-09-29/a-1980s-new-york-city -battle-explains-donald-trump-s-candidacy.
2. Kyle Cheney, "Yes, It's the Trump Show," *Politico*, August 6, 2015, https://www.politico.com /story/2015/08/republican-debate-donald-trump-121114.

Chapter 4

1. Alexander Burns and Maggie Haberman, "Donald Trump Hires Paul Manafort to Lead Delegate Effort," *New York Times*, March 18, 2016, https://www.nytimes.com/politics/first-draft/2016/03/28 /donald-trump-hires-paul-manafort-to-lead-delegate-effort/.
2. Steve Peoples and Thomas Beaumont, "Trump Team Tells GOP He Has Been 'Projecting an Image,'" (Correction: Campaign 2016 Story), AP, April 22, 2016, https://apnews.com/article/97ff2c296579425 c9825d6ea79aa2363.

Chapter 5

1. Maggie Haberman, Alexander Burns, and Ashley Parker, "Donald Trump Fires Corey Lewandowski, His Campaign Manager," *New York Times*, June 20, 2016, https://www.nytimes.com/2016/06/21/us /politics/corey-lewandowski-donald-trump.html.
2. MJ Lee, Dana Bash, and Gloria Borger, "Corey Lewandowski Out As Trump Campaign Manager," CNN, June 21, 2016, https://edition.cnn.com/2016/06/20/politics/corey-lewandowski-out-as-trump -campaign-manager/index.html.

Chapter 6

1. Bill Greener III, "Donald Trump Is a Disaster" Inside Sources, July 30, 2015, https://insidesources. com/donald-trump-is-a-disaster/.
2. Alexander Burns and Maggie Haberman, "How Donald Trump Finally Settled on Mike Pence," *New York Times*, July 15, 2016, https://www.nytimes.com/2016/07/16/us/politics/mike-pence-donald -trump-vice-president.html.

Chapter 7

1. Alexandra Jaffe, "Melania Trump Republican Convention Speech Bears Striking Similarities to Michelle Obama Address," NBC News, July 19, 2016, https://www.nbcnews.com/politics/2016-election/melania-trump-appears-plagiarize-michelle-obama-convention-speech-n612141.
2. David E. Sanger and Nicole Perlroth, "As Democrats Gather, a Russian Subplot Raises Intrigue," *New York Times*, https://www.nytimes.com/2016/07/25/us/politics/donald-trump-russia-emails.html.
3. Eric Bradner, "Clinton's Campaign Manager: Russia Helping Trump," CNN, July 25, 2016, https://edition.cnn.com/2016/07/24/politics/robby-mook-russia-dnc-emails-trump/index.html.
4. Andrew E. Kramer, Mike McIntire, and Barry Meier, "Secret Ledger in Ukraine Lists Cash for Donald Trump's Campaign Chief," *New York Times*, https://www.nytimes.com/2016/08/15/us/politics/what-is-the-black-ledger.html.
5. Alan Rappeport, "Trump Campaign and Its Chief, Paul Manafort, Try to Move Past Ukraine Report," *New York Times*, August 15, 2016, https://www.nytimes.com/2016/08/16/us/politics/trump-campaign-paul-manafort-ukraine-cash-payments-russia.html.

Chapter 8

1. John Solomon, "FBI, Warned Early and Often That Manafort File Might Be Fake, Used It Anyway," *The Hill*, June 19, 2019, https://thehill.com/opinion/white-house/449206-fbi-warned-early-and-often-that-manafort-file-might-be-fake-used-it-anyway/.
2. Matt Palumbo, "Excerpt: How Soros's Secret Network Used Ukraine to Cover for Hillary, Hunter, and Target Donald Trump," *The National Pulse*, November 5, 2021, https://thenationalpulse.com/2021/11/05/excerpt-how-soross-secret-network-used-ukraine-to-cover-for-hillary-hunter-and-target-donald-trump/.
3. Evan Perez, Jim Sciutto, Jake Tapper, and Carl Bernstein, "Intel Chiefs Presented Trump with Claims of Russian Efforts to Compromise Him," CNN, January 12, 2017, https://edition.cnn.com/2017/01/10/politics/donald-trump-intelligence-report-russia/index.html.
4. Ken Bensinger, Miriam Elder, and Mark Schoofs, "These Reports Allege Trump Has Deep Ties To Russia," Buzzfeed, January 10, 2017, https://www.buzzfeednews.com/article/kenbensinger/these-reports-allege-trump-has-deep-ties-to-russia.
5. Marshall Cohen, "The Steele dossier: A reckoning," CNN, November 19, 2021, https://edition.cnn.com/2021/11/18/politics/steele-dossier-reckoning/index.html.
6. Cohen, "Reckoning," https://edition.cnn.com/2021/11/18/politics/steele-dossier-reckoning/index.html.
7. Byron York, "Why the Sussmann Jury Matters," *Washington Examiner, June 2, 2022, https://www.washingtonexaminer.com/opinion/why-the-sussmann-jury-matters.*)
8. Katelyn Polantz and Marshall Cohen, "7 New Things We Learned from the Horowitz Report," CNN, December 10, 2019, https://edition.cnn.com/2019/12/09/politics/horowitz-reports-new-things/index.html.
9. Meg Wagner and Veronica Rocha, "Inspector General Report on Russia Investigation Is Out," CNN, December 9, 2019, https://edition.cnn.com/politics/live-news/inspector-general-report-russia-investigation/h_d7312cd39caf14fb6f5afdd4fc87c5af.
10. Jeremy Herb, Marshall Cohen and Katelyn Polantz, "Bipartisan Senate Report Details Trump Campaign Contacts with Russia in 2016, Adding to Mueller Findings," CNN, August 20, 2020, https://edition.cnn.com/2020/08/18/politics/senate-intelligence-report-russia-election-interference-efforts/index.html.
11. Jeremy Herb and Evan Perez, "GOP Seizes on Newly Declassified Material to Raise Further Questions about Steele Dossier," CNN, April 16, 2020, https://edition.cnn.com/2020/04/16/politics/christopher-steele-footnotes-russian-disinformation/index.html.
12. Kenneth P. Vogel and David Stern, "Ukrainian Efforts to Sabotage Trump Backfire," *Politico*, January 11, 2017, https://www.politico.com/story/2017/01/ukraine-sabotage-trump-backfire-233446.
13. Paul Sperry, "Ukraine Worked with Democrats Against Trump in Election 2016 to Stop Putin. That Bet Backfired Badly," RealClearInvestigations, March 10, 2022, https://www.realclearinvestigations.com/articles/2022/03/10/how_ukraine_conspired_with_dems_against_trump_to_prevent_the_kind_of_war_happening_now_under_biden_820873.html.
14. John Solomon, "How the Obama White House Engaged Ukraine to Give Russia Collusion Narrative an Early Boost," *The Hill*, April 26, 2019, https://thehill.com/opinion/white-house/440730-how-the-obama-white-house-engaged-ukraine-to-give-russia-collusion/.
15. David Ignatius, "Why Did Obama Dawdle on Russia's Hacking?," *Washington Post*, January 12, 2017, https://www.washingtonpost.com/opinions/why-did-obama-dawdle-on-russias-hacking/2017/01/12/75f878a0-d90c-11e6-9a36-1d296534b31e_story.html?utm_term=.74ec7ce59d16.

Chapter 9

1. Andrew E. Kramer, "Paul Manafort, Former Trump Campaign Chief, Faces New Allegations in Ukraine," *New York Times,* March 20, 2017, https://www.nytimes.com/2017/03/20/world/europe /paul-manafort-ukraine-allegations-trump.html.

Chapter 10

1. The United States Department of Justice, FARA Index and Act, https://www.justice.gov/nsd-fara /fara-index-and-act#611e.
2. The United States Department of Justice, "Appointment of Special Counsel," May 17, 2017, https:// www.justice.gov/opa/pr/appointment-special-counsel.
3. Jo Becker, Matt Apuzzo and Adam Goldman, "Trump Team Met With Lawyer Linked to Kremlin During Campaign," *New York Times,* July 8, 2017, https://www.nytimes.com/2017/07/08/us/politics /trump-russia-kushner-manafort.html.
4. Margot Cleveland, "Papadopoulos Hints Conversation That Launched Trump-Russia Probe Was FBI Setup," *The Federalist,* April 1, 2019, https://thefederalist.com/2019/04/01/papadopoulos-hints -conversation-launched-trump-russia-probe-fbi-setup/.
5. George Papadopoulos, *Deep State Target: How I Got Caught in the Crosshairs of the Plot to Bring Down President Trump* (New York: Diversion Books, 2019).

Chapter 12

1. Oleg Voloshin, "Paul Manafort, European Integration's Unknown Soldier for Ukraine," *Kyiv Post,* December 7, 2017, https://www.kyivpost.com/article/opinion/op-ed/oleg-voloshin-paul-manafort -european-integrations-unknown-soldier-ukraine.html.
2. United States v. Paul J. Manafort, Jr, and Konstantin Kilimnik, Superseding Indictment, https:// www.justice.gov/file/1070306/download.

Chapter 14

1. United States v. Paul J. Manafort, Jr., Transcript of Jury Trial Before The Honorable T. S. Ellis, III, 23.
2. United States v. Paul J. Manafort, Jr., Transcript, 1105.
3. United States v. Paul J. Manafort, Jr., Transcript, 1107.
4. United States v. Paul J. Manafort, Jr., Transcript, 1110.
5. United States v. Paul J. Manafort, Jr., Transcript, 1364.
6. United States v. Paul J. Manafort, Jr., Transcript, 1370–73.
7. United States v. Paul J. Manafort, Jr., Transcript, 1416.
8. United States v. Paul J. Manafort, Jr., Transcript, 1419.
9. United States v. Paul J. Manafort, Jr., Transcript, 1429-30-31.
10. United States v. Paul J. Manafort, Jr., Transcript, 1433–4.
11. United States v. Paul J. Manafort, Jr., Transcript, 1436.
12. United States v. Paul J. Manafort, Jr., Transcript, 1438–9.
13. United States v. Paul J. Manafort, Jr., Transcript, 1439.
14. United States v. Paul J. Manafort, Jr., Transcript, 1443.
15. United States v. Paul J. Manafort, Jr., Transcript, 1444.
16. United States v. Paul J. Manafort, Jr., Transcript, 1455.
17. Marianne Levine and Burgess Everett, "Jackson's Hearings Are Over. Meet the 9 Potential Senate Swing Votes," *Politico,* March 24, 2022, https://www.politico.com/news/2022/03/24/kentanji-brown-jackson-confirmation-swing-votes-senate-00018883.

Chapter 16

1. Kenneth P. Vogel and David Stern, "Ukrainian Efforts to Sabotage Trump Backfire," *Politico,* January 11, 2017, https://www.politico.com/story/2017/01/ukraine-sabotage-trump-backfire-233446.
2. Michael S. Schmidt, Sharon LaFraniere, and Maggie Haberman, "Manafort's Lawyer Said to Brief Trump Attorneys on What He Told Mueller," *New York Times,* November 27, 2018, https://www .nytimes.com/2018/11/27/us/politics/manafort-lawyer-trump-cooperation.html.

Chapter 17

1. Sharon LaFraniere, "Paul Manafort Is Sentenced to Less Than 4 Years in 1 of 2 Cases Against Him," *New York Times,* March 7, 2019, https://www.nytimes.com/2019/03/07/us/politics/paul-manafort -sentencing.html.

Chapter 18
1. Josh Gerstein, "Manafort Hit with Mortgage Fraud Charges in New York," *Politico*, March 13, 2019, https://www.politico.com/story/2019/03/13/paul-manafort-charged-new-york-fraud-1220399.
2. U.S. Department of the Treasury, "Treasury Escalates Sanctions Against the Russian Government's Attempts to Influence U.S. Elections," April 15, 2021, https://home.treasury.gov/news/press-releases/jy0126.
3. Aaron Maté, "Five Trump-Russia 'Collusion' Corrections We Need From the Media Now—Just for Starters," November 24, 2021, https://www.realclearinvestigations.com/articles/2021/11/24/five_trump-russia_collusion_corrections_we_need_from_the_media_now_-_just_for_starters_804205.html.
4. Maté, "Five Trump-Russia 'Collusion' Corrections."
5. Aaron Maté, "Accused Russiagate 'Spy' Kilimnik Speaks—and Evidence Backs His 'No Collusion' Account," May 19, 2021, https://www.realclearinvestigations.com/articles/2021/05/19/accused_russiagate_spy_kilimnik_speaks_-_and_evidence_backs_his_no_collusion_account_777328.html.

Acknowledgments

Of course, a book is a collaboration of so many people. I apologize to those not included. To do so would have required another chapter.

First, to my daughters, Andrea and Jessica, and my incredible son-in-law, Chris, who inspired me with their love and gave me the strength to persevere.

To all of my incredible friends who believed in me and supported Kathy and my family with love and affection during the darkest moments, and especially:

Rosann and Michael, Courtney and Bruce, Wayne and Lily, Michael and Dorothy, Dennis, David and Ellen, Paul and Barbara, Starr and Matt, John and Donna, Dennis and Theresa, Bill Greener, Laury Gay, Michael Caputo, Michael Conforti, Doug Davenport, John and Janet, Bill Glavin, Rene and Kathy, Terry and Pam, Michael and Blair, Chuck and Paula, Fitz and Mo, Tony and Libby, Angela, Jon and Lisa, Jason, and all of my cousins.

To the thousands of strangers who wrote me letters of prayers that sustained me through this ordeal. You have no idea how powerful your prayers were in helping me get through the dark days of solitary confinement.

To my attorneys who were warriors and became my friends, especially Dick Hibey, Todd Blanche, Bruce Baldinger, Kevin Downing, Jay Nanavati, Rich Westling, Brian Ketcham, and Tom Zehnle. And to Jason Maloni, a PR wizard who handled all of the daily bombs thrown at me by the Twitter hate mongers and fake media.

To Tony Lyons, Jon Arlan, Hector Carosso, Mark Gompertz, and my Skyhorse team who guided me through this morass of details to help me tell my story. I cannot imagine that a more professional team exists in the publishing world.

And especially to David Limbaugh and Sean Hannity, who encouraged me to write this book.

Finally, to President Donald J. Trump, who had the courage to confront the mob and gave me my life back with his Presidential Pardon that undid the injustice of the corrupt political and judicial systems.